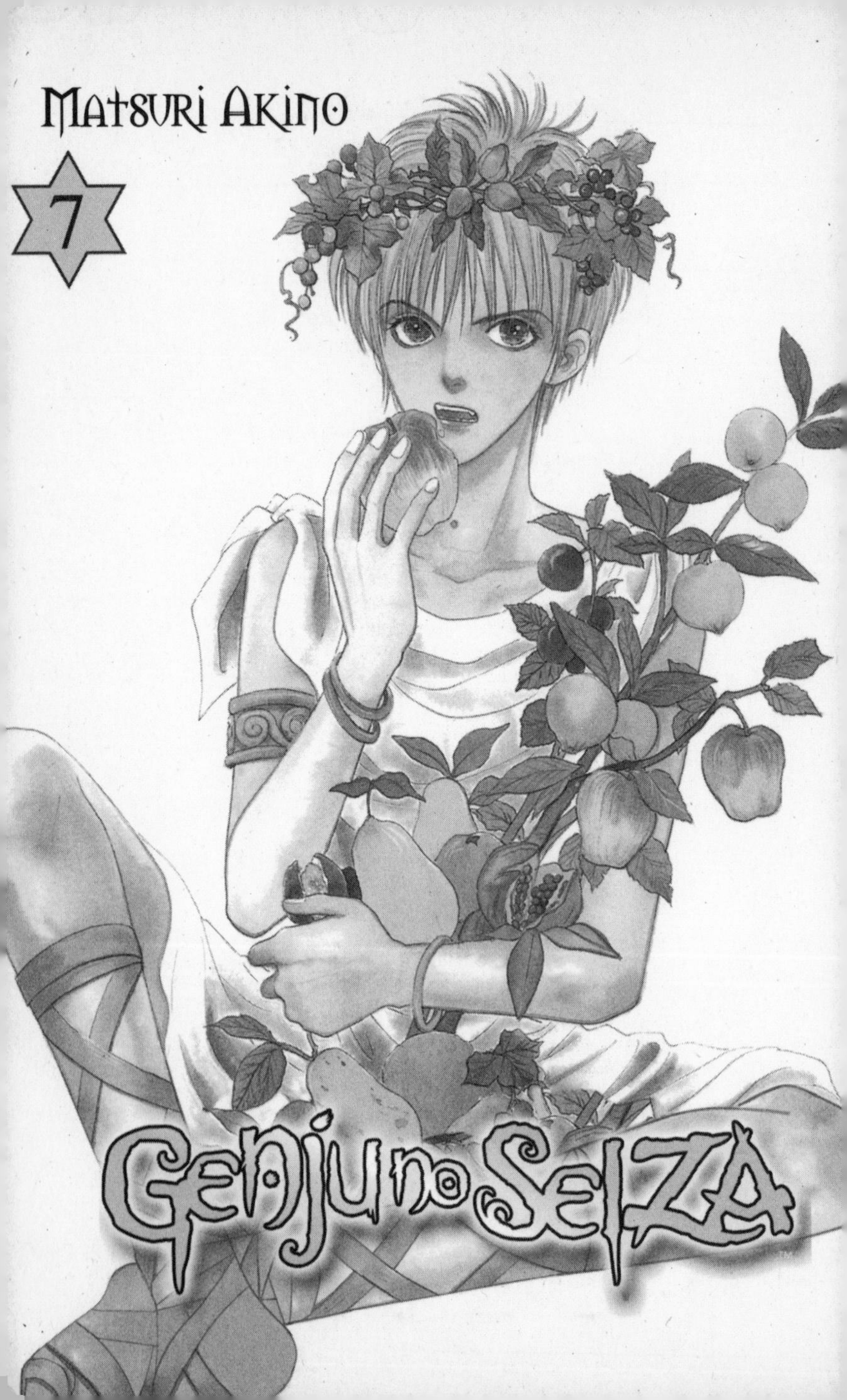
Matsuri Akino
7
Genju no Seiza™

Genju no Seiza Volume 7
Created by Matsuri Akino

Translation - Haruko Furukawa
English Adaption - Christine Boylan
Copy Editor - Shannon Watters
Retouch and Lettering - Star Print Brokers
Production Artist - Lauren O'Connell
Graphic Designer - John Lo

Editor - Nikhil Burman
Digital Imaging Manager - Chris Buford
Pre-Production Supervisor - Vicente Rivera Jr.
Production Specialist - Lucas Rivera
Managing Editor - Vy Nguyen
Creative Director - Anne Marie Horne
Editor-in-Chief - Rob Tokar
Publisher - Mike Kiley
President and C.O.O. - John Parker
C.E.O. and Chief Creative Officer - Stu Levy

A  **TOKYOPOP** Manga

TOKYOPOP and  are trademarks or registered trademarks of TOKYOPOP Inc.

TOKYOPOP Inc.
5900 Wilshire Blvd. Suite 2000
Los Angeles, CA 90036

E-mail: info@TOKYOPOP.com
Come visit us online at www.TOKYOPOP.com

ISBN: 978-1-59816-613-2
First TOKYOPOP printing: August 2008
10 9 8 7 6 5 4 3 2 1
Printed in the USA

Genju no Seiza™

Volume 7

Created by
Matsuri Akino

TOKYOPOP®

HAMBURG // LONDON // LOS ANGELES // TOKYO

Genju no Seiza

Table of Contents

STORY SO FAR

An empty throne...

Not in the literal sense (but I'll get to that in a moment), but for the past forty years, that is in truth what Dhalashar has had. For forty years, we've been without a king. But that has all changed now. We have found our heir to the throne. He is the half-Sherpa son of a world-famous photographer, and his name is Fuuto Kamishina. Currently living in Japan with his mother, young Fuuto has already begun to exhibit some of the powers of our king, and although he is unaware of this, his use of them has affirmed to me that he will be a good king. However, he is also a tad stubborn, and to this day, he refuses to accept his role as our new sovereign and religious leader.

There are further complications, as well. While the people of Dhalashar have been without their TRUE king for quite some time, they have not been without a king. The Snake-God, Naga, a treacherous and deceitful deity, recently sensed opportunity upon our vacant throne. He has instilled an impostor king—little more than a puppet to Naga's ambitions—to rule Dhalashar. And much to my chagrin, many people of my nation have accepted this false sovereign as our next heir to the throne. However, Naga knows his king is false and that the emergence of the true sovereign will prove that to the people of Dhalashar . He fears young Fuuto Kamishina and will do what he can to ensure Fuuto never ascends to the throne. He has already dispatched several assassins, and I fear more may be on the way.

—Garuda, Guardian Beast of the true King of Dhalashar

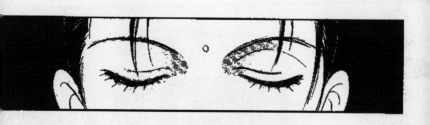

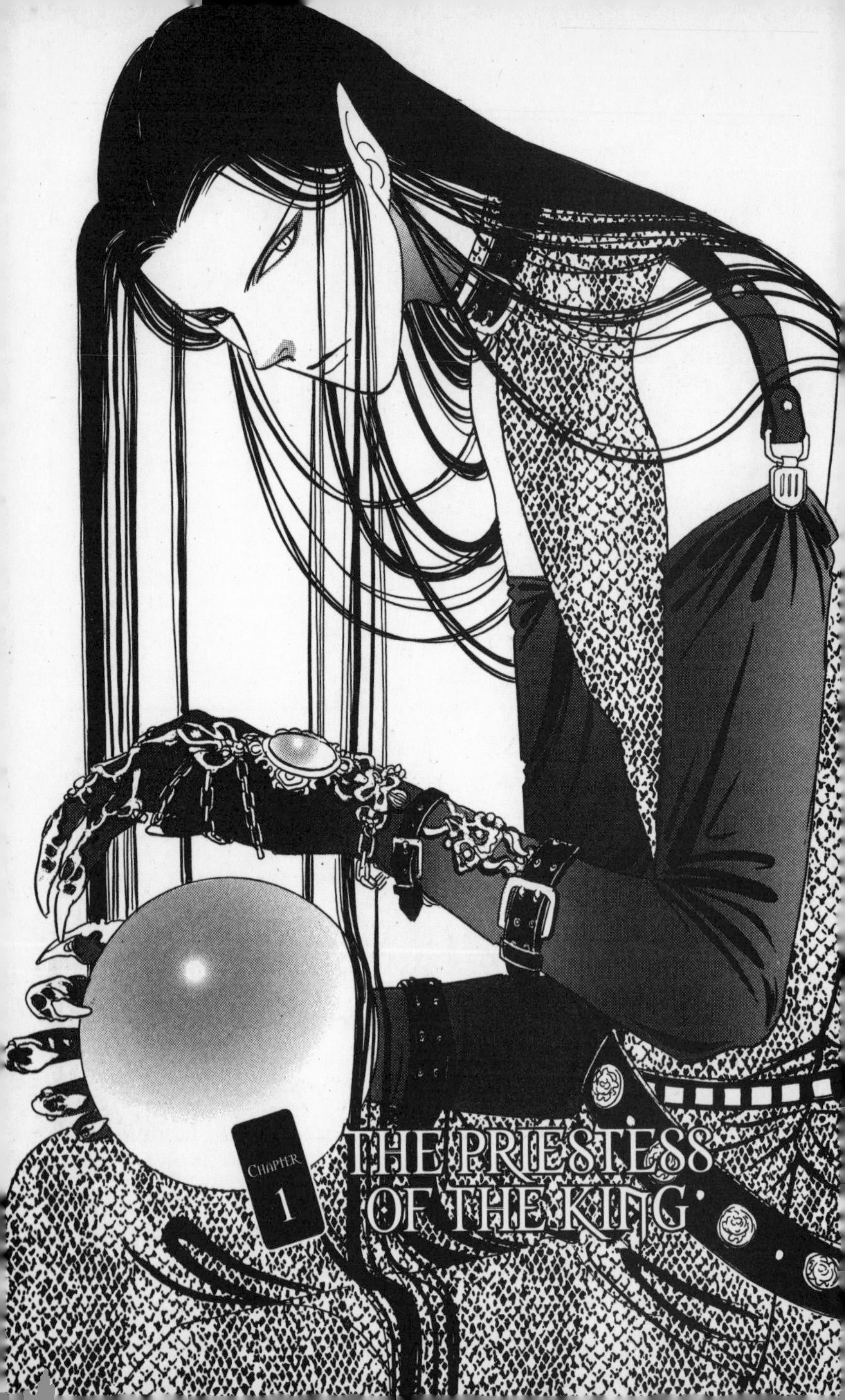
CHAPTER 1
THE PRIESTESS OF THE KING

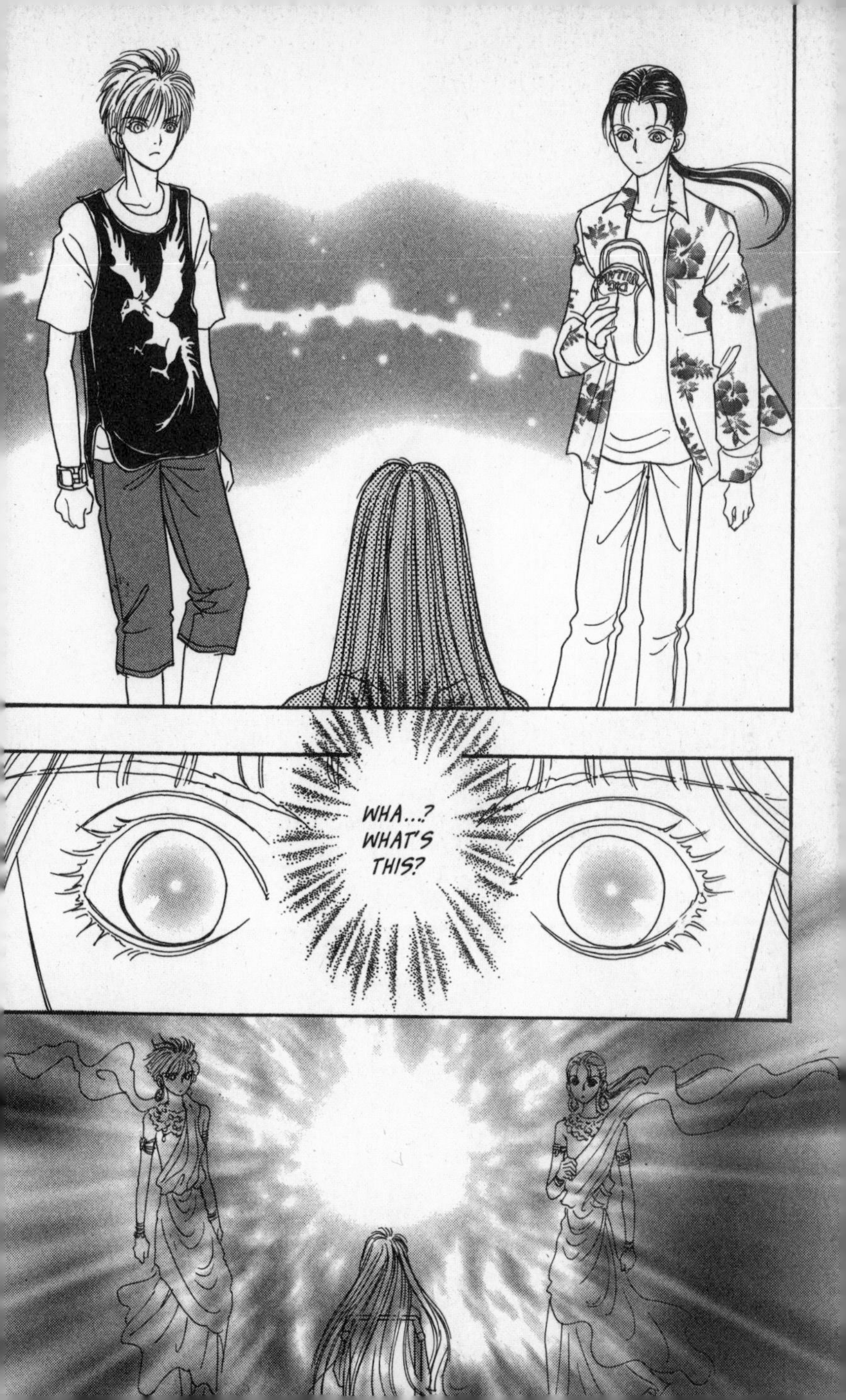
WHA...?
WHAT'S
THIS?

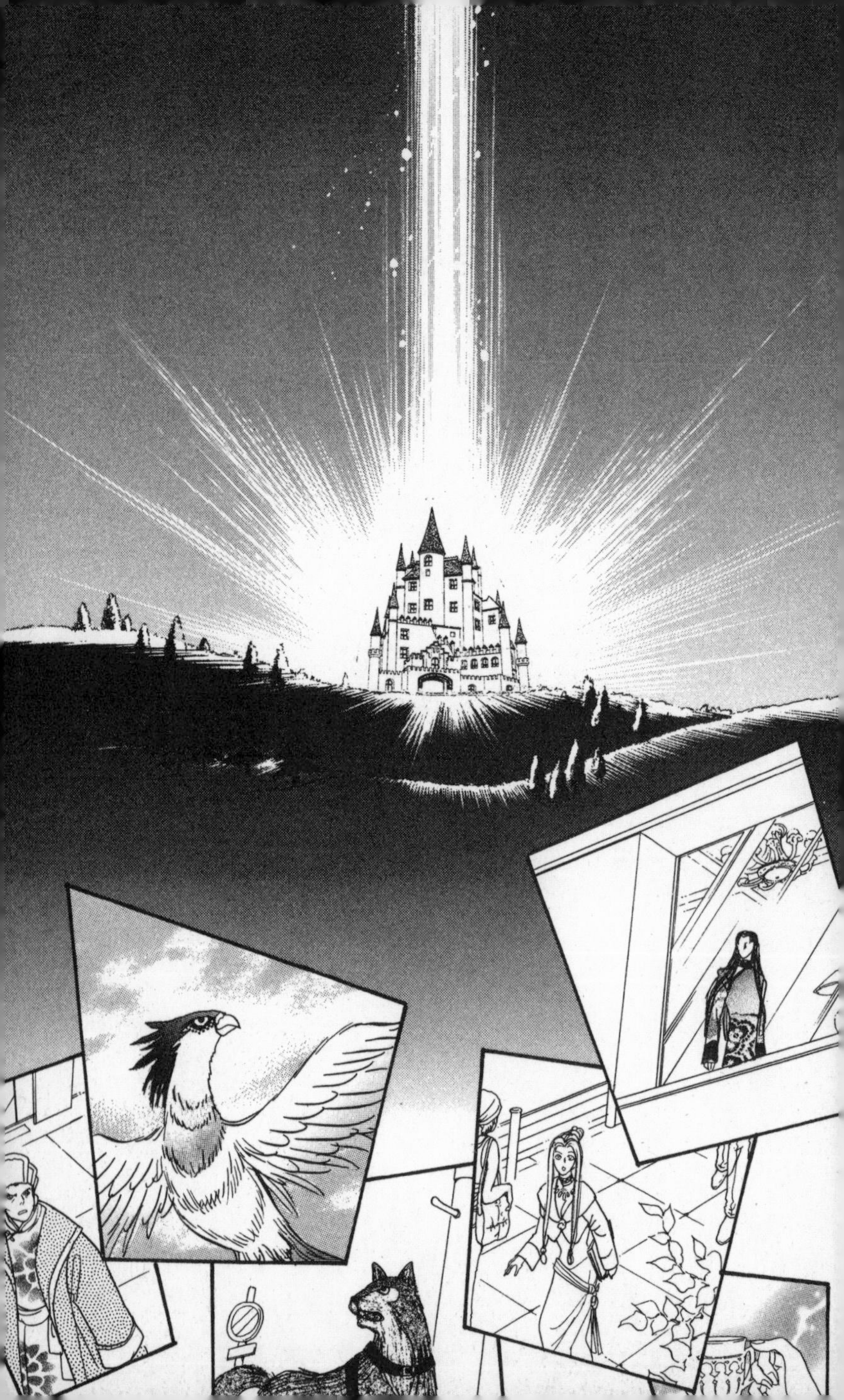

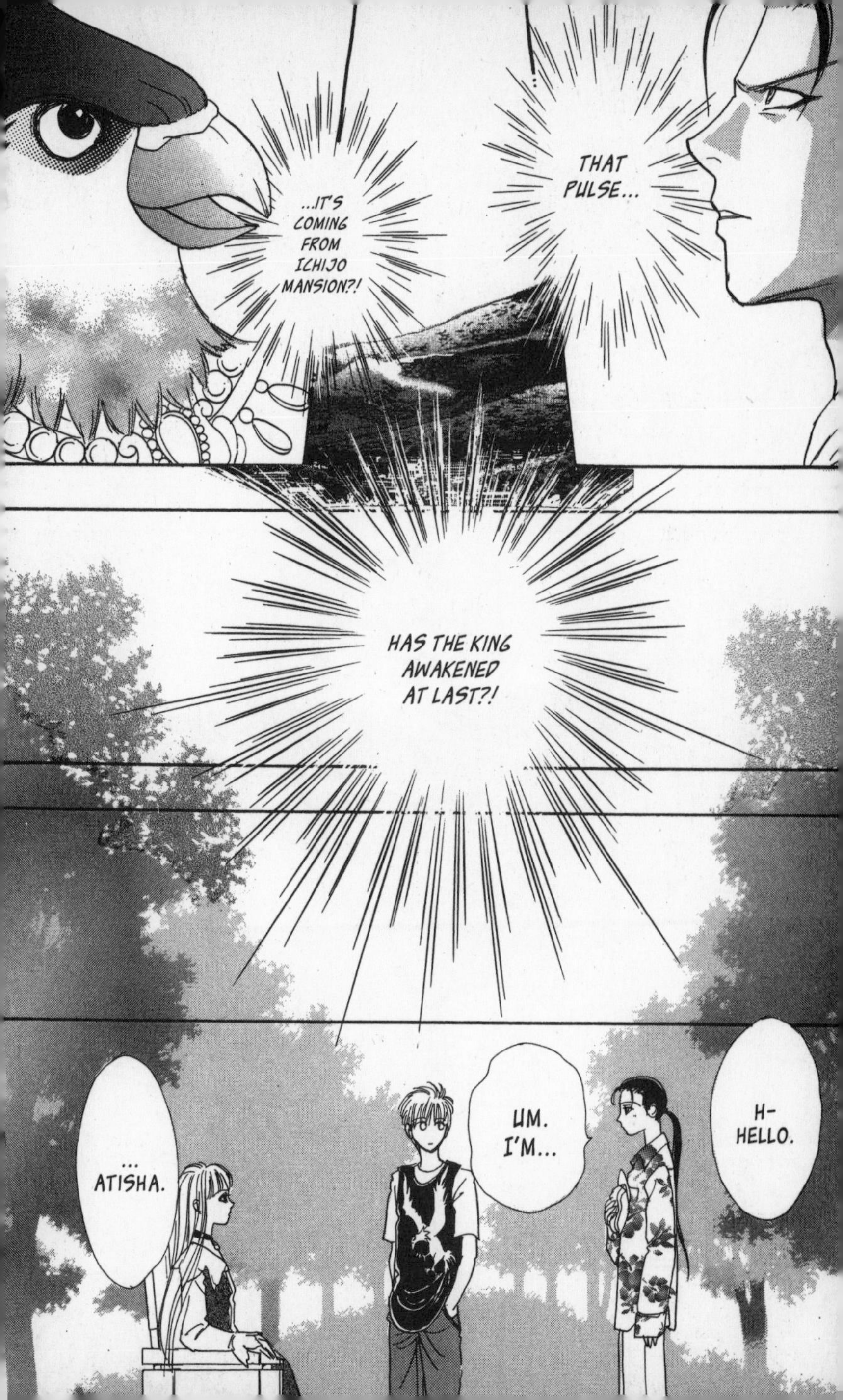
THAT PULSE...
...IT'S COMING FROM ICHIJO MANSION?!
HAS THE KING AWAKENED AT LAST?!
H- HELLO.
UM. I'M...
... ATISHA.

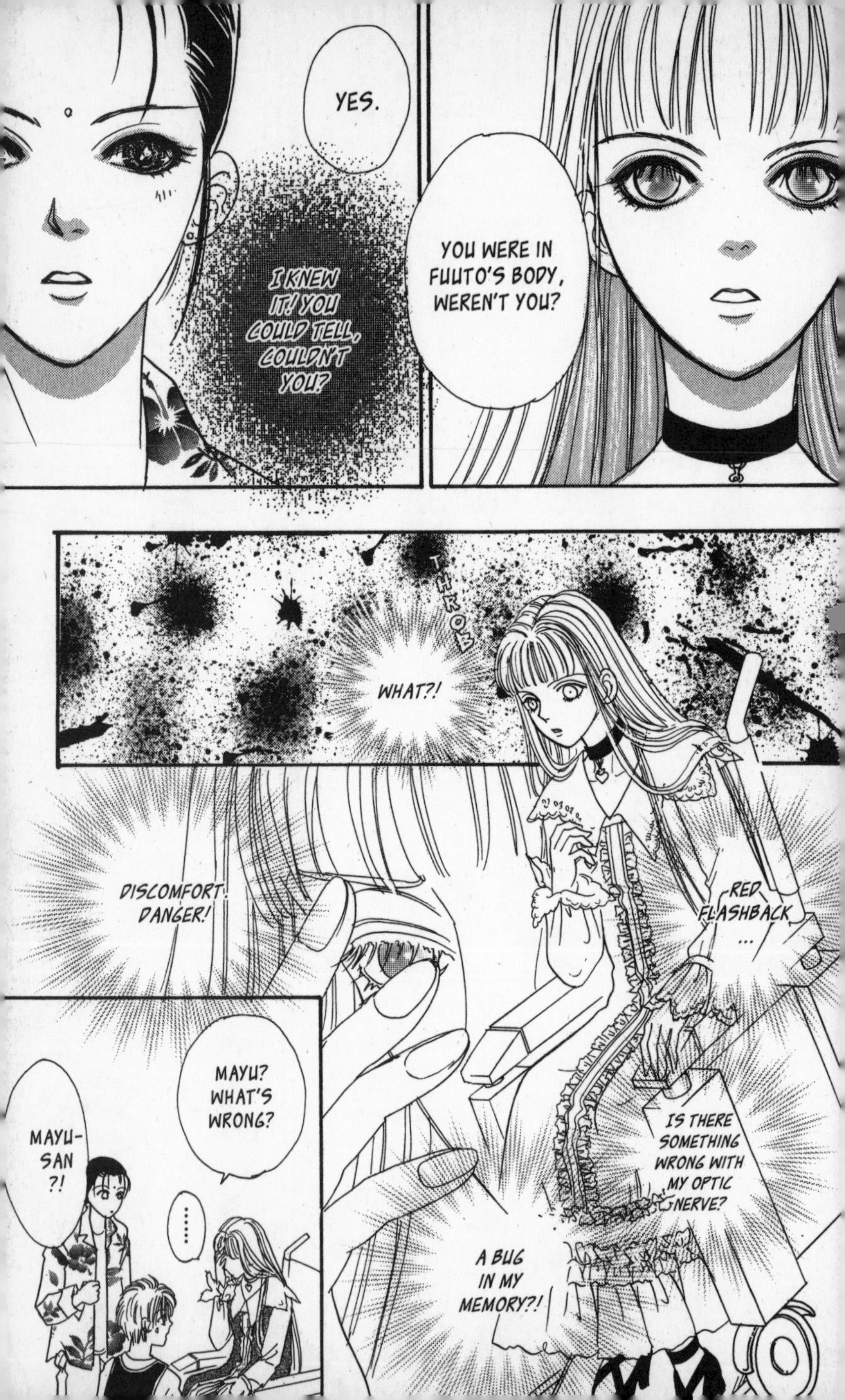
YOU WERE IN FUUTO'S BODY, WEREN'T YOU?
YES.
I KNEW IT! YOU COULD TELL, COULDN'T YOU?
THROB
WHAT?!
RED FLASHBACK...
DISCOMFORT! DANGER!
IS THERE SOMETHING WRONG WITH MY OPTIC NERVE?
A BUG IN MY MEMORY?!
MAYU? WHAT'S WRONG?
MAYU-SAN?!
......

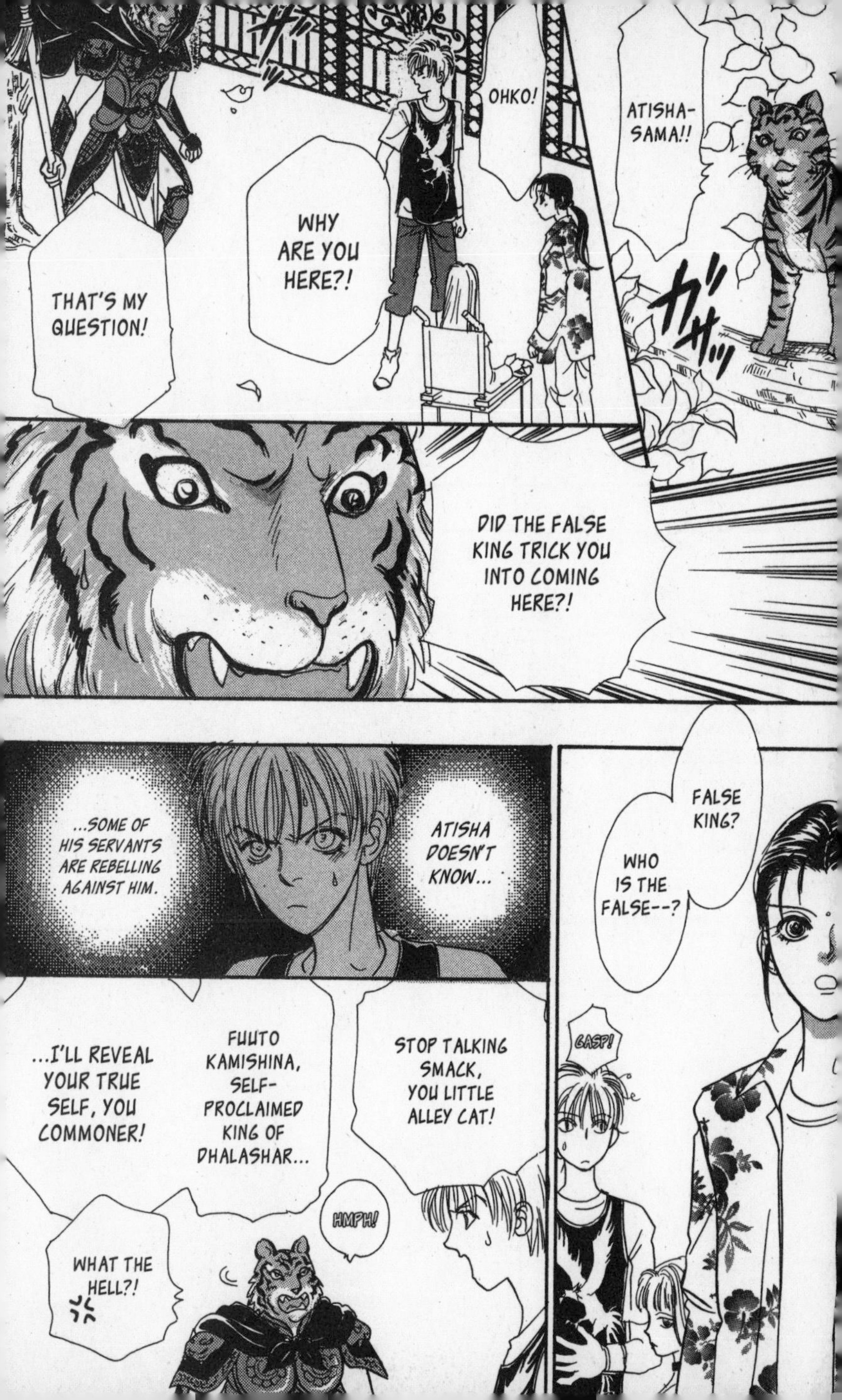
ATISHA-SAMA!!
OHKO!
WHY ARE YOU HERE?!
THAT'S MY QUESTION!
DID THE FALSE KING TRICK YOU INTO COMING HERE?!
FALSE KING?
WHO IS THE FALSE--?
GASP!
ATISHA DOESN'T KNOW...
...SOME OF HIS SERVANTS ARE REBELLING AGAINST HIM.
STOP TALKING SMACK, YOU LITTLE ALLEY CAT!
HMPH!
FUUTO KAMISHINA, SELF-PROCLAIMED KING OF DHALASHAR...
...I'LL REVEAL YOUR TRUE SELF, YOU COMMONER!
WHAT THE HELL?!

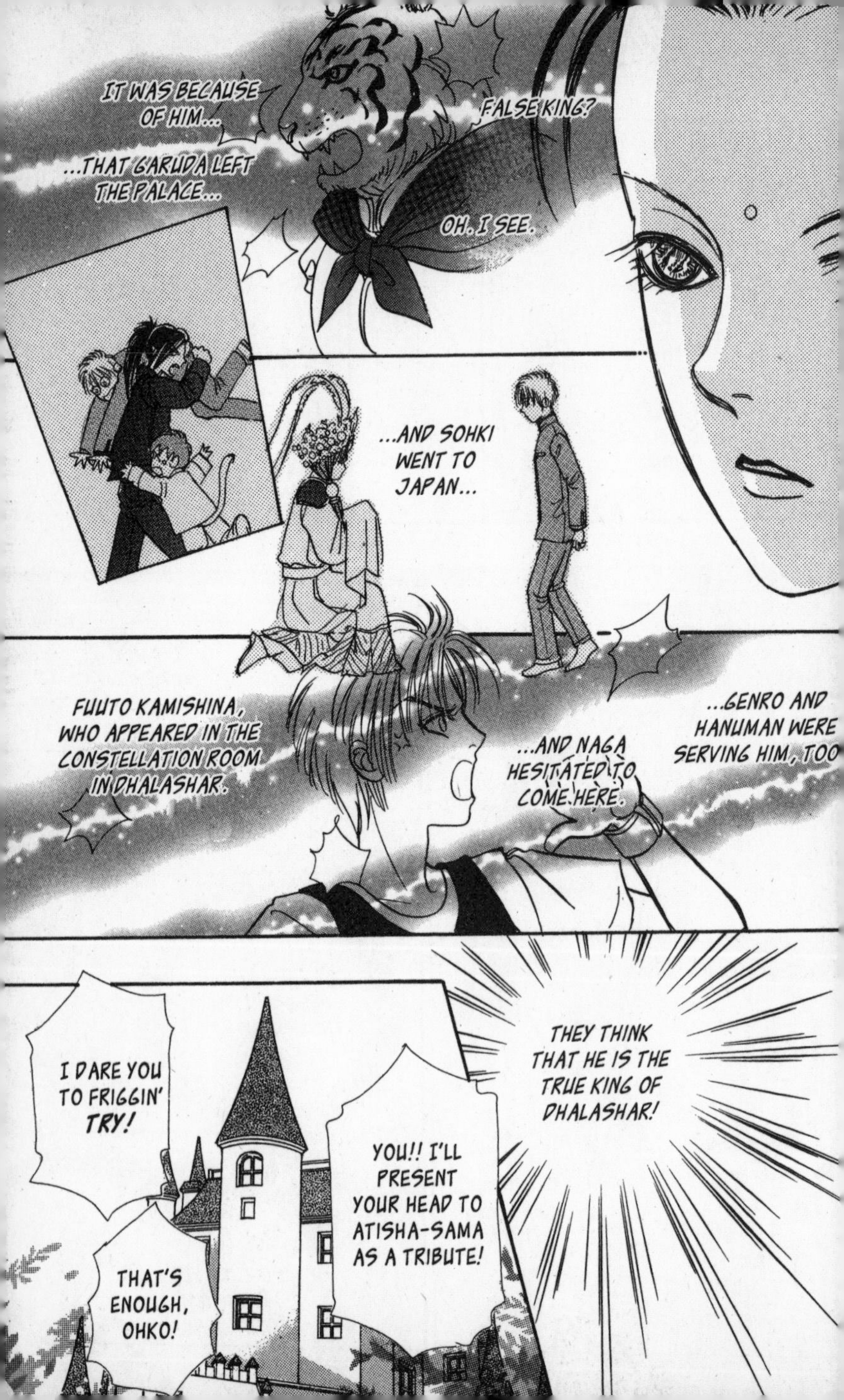
FALSE KING?
OH. I SEE.
IT WAS BECAUSE OF HIM...
...THAT GARUDA LEFT THE PALACE...
...AND SOHKI WENT TO JAPAN...
...GENRO AND HANUMAN WERE SERVING HIM, TOO
...AND NAGA HESITATED TO COME HERE.
FUUTO KAMISHINA, WHO APPEARED IN THE CONSTELLATION ROOM IN DHALASHAR.
THEY THINK THAT HE IS THE TRUE KING OF DHALASHAR!
YOU!! I'LL PRESENT YOUR HEAD TO ATISHA-SAMA AS A TRIBUTE!
I DARE YOU TO FRIGGIN' TRY!
THAT'S ENOUGH, OHKO!

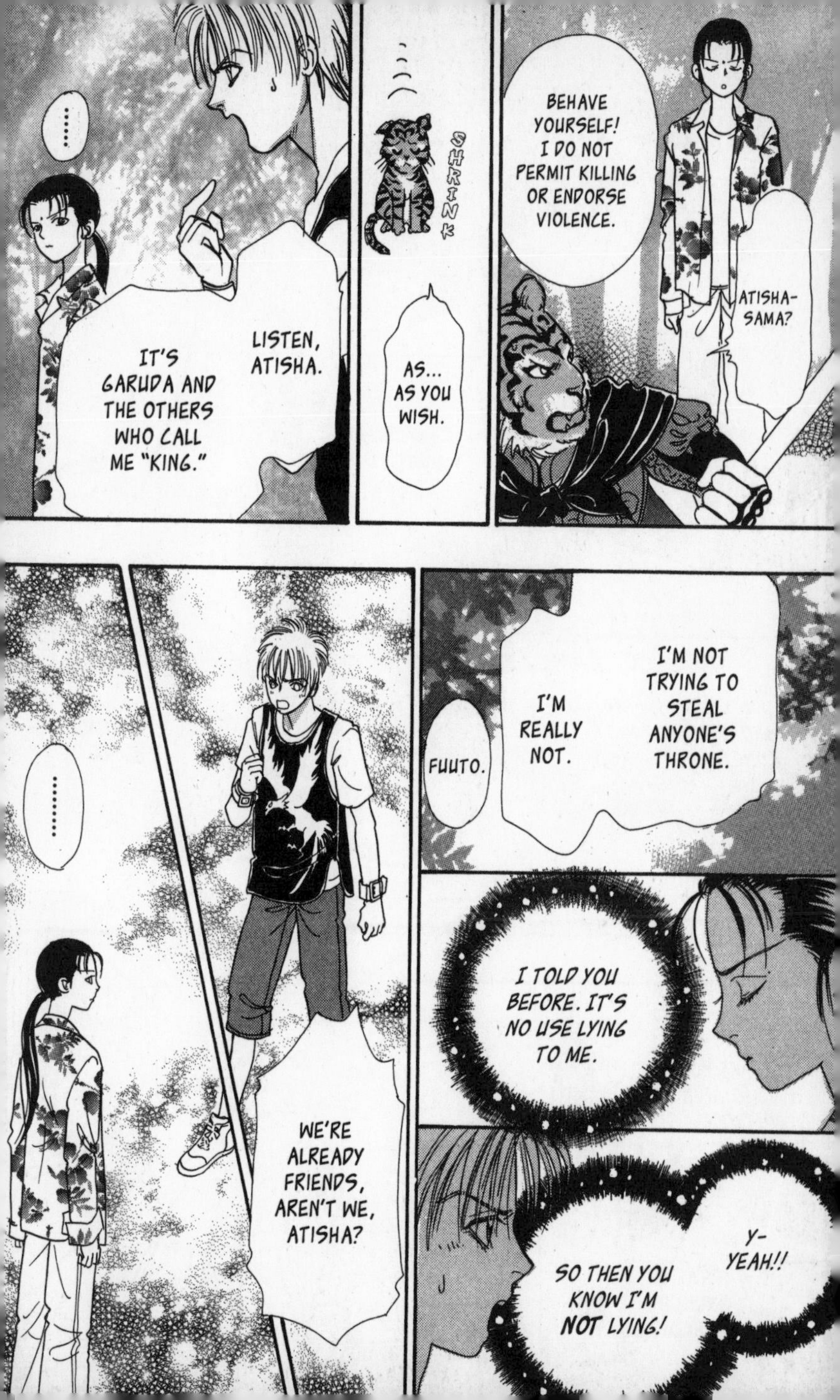

BEHAVE YOURSELF! I DO NOT PERMIT KILLING OR ENDORSE VIOLENCE.
ATISHA-SAMA?
SHRINK
AS... AS YOU WISH.
......
LISTEN, ATISHA.
IT'S GARUDA AND THE OTHERS WHO CALL ME "KING."
I'M NOT TRYING TO STEAL ANYONE'S THRONE.
I'M REALLY NOT.
FUUTO.
I TOLD YOU BEFORE. IT'S NO USE LYING TO ME.
Y-YEAH!!
SO THEN YOU KNOW I'M **NOT** LYING!
WE'RE ALREADY FRIENDS, AREN'T WE, ATISHA?
......

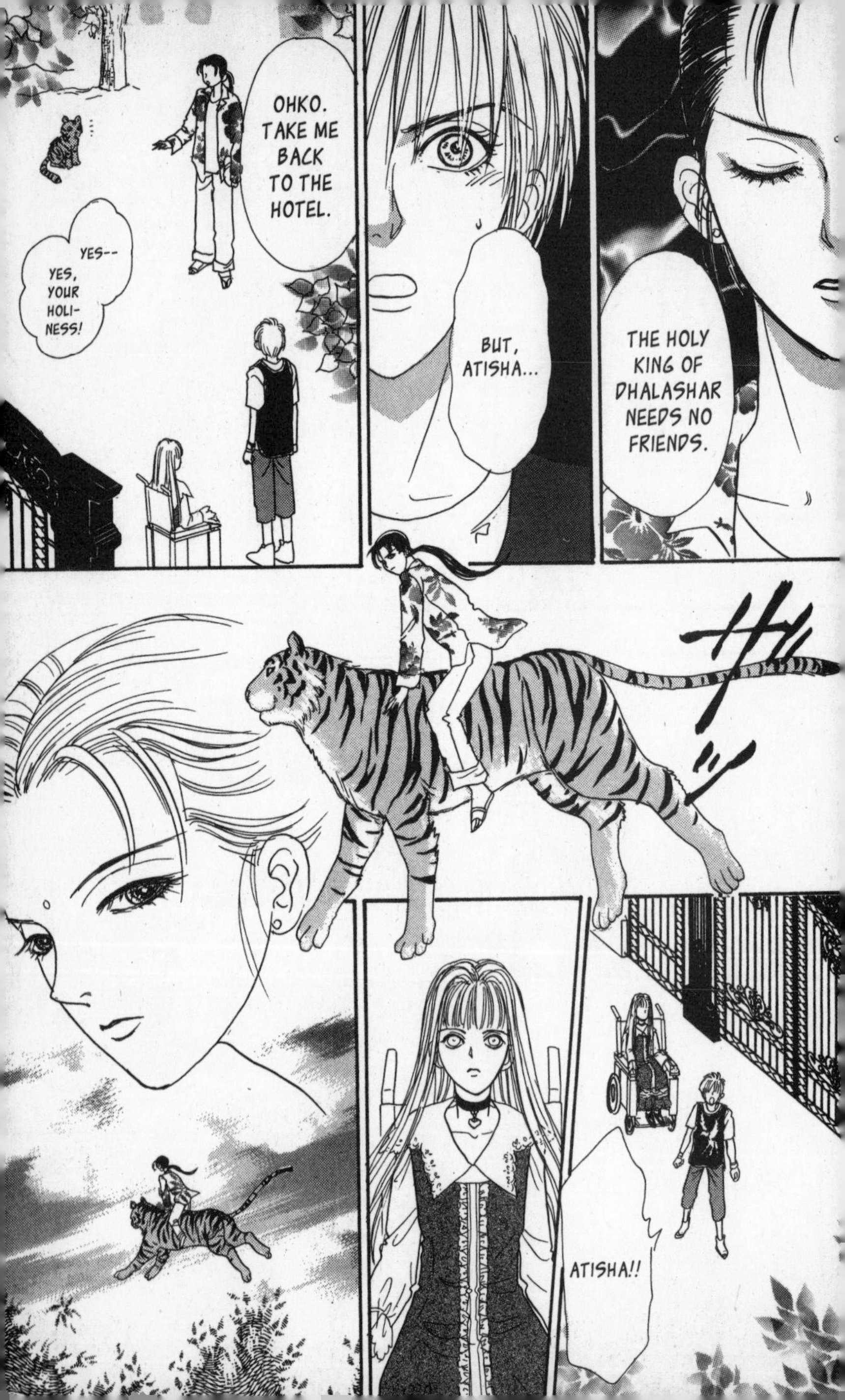
THE HOLY KING OF DHALASHAR NEEDS NO FRIENDS.
BUT, ATISHA...
OHKO. TAKE ME BACK TO THE HOTEL.
YES-- YES, YOUR HOLINESS!
ATISHA!!

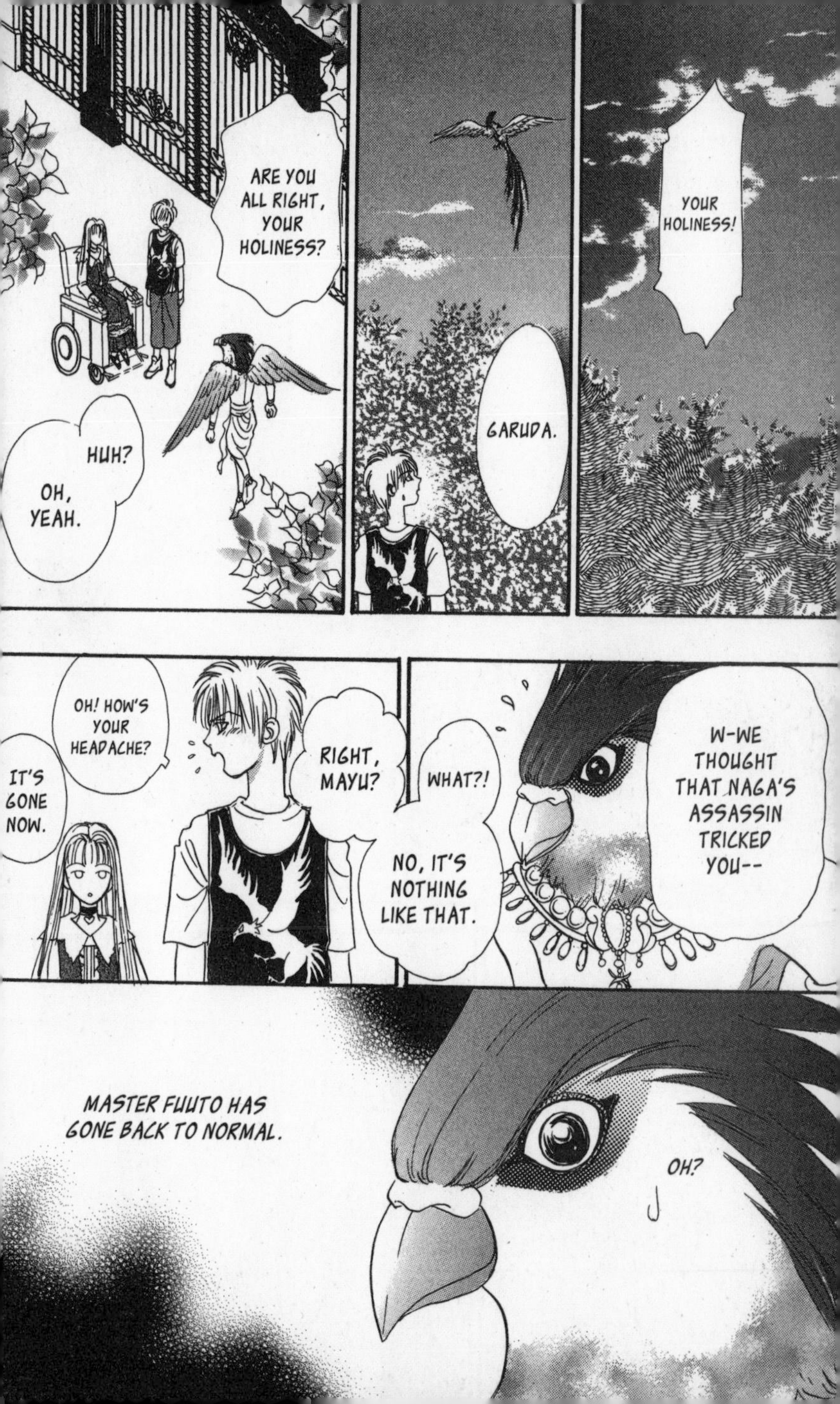

YOUR HOLINESS!
GARUDA.
ARE YOU ALL RIGHT, YOUR HOLINESS?
HUH?
OH, YEAH.
W-WE THOUGHT THAT NAGA'S ASSASSIN TRICKED YOU--
WHAT?!
NO, IT'S NOTHING LIKE THAT.
RIGHT, MAYU?
OH! HOW'S YOUR HEADACHE?
IT'S GONE NOW.
OH?
MASTER FUUTO HAS GONE BACK TO NORMAL.

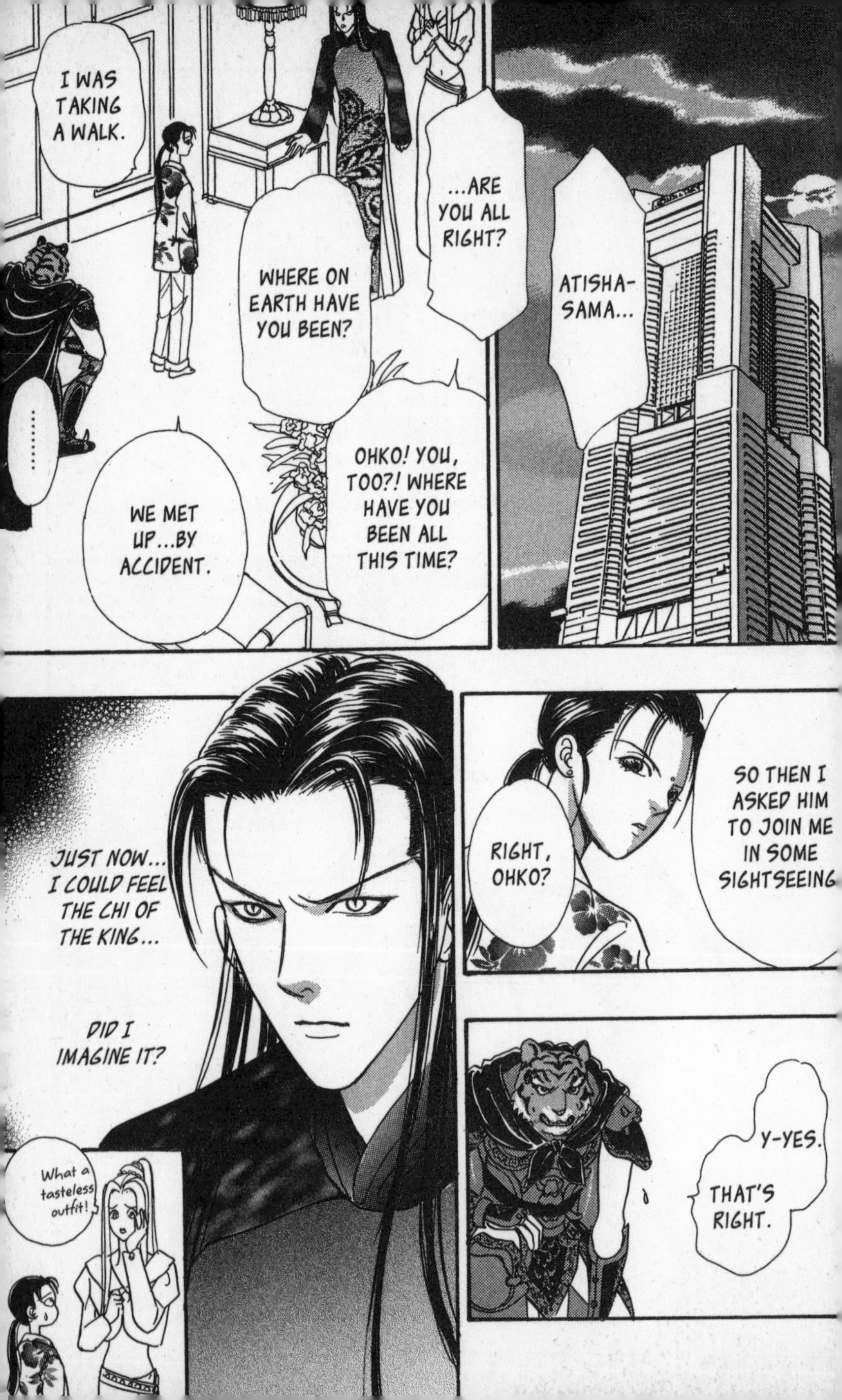
ATISHA-SAMA...
...ARE YOU ALL RIGHT?
WHERE ON EARTH HAVE YOU BEEN?
I WAS TAKING A WALK.
OHKO! YOU, TOO?! WHERE HAVE YOU BEEN ALL THIS TIME?
WE MET UP...BY ACCIDENT.
......
SO THEN I ASKED HIM TO JOIN ME IN SOME SIGHTSEEING
RIGHT, OHKO?
Y-YES.
THAT'S RIGHT.
JUST NOW... I COULD FEEL THE CHI OF THE KING...
DID I IMAGINE IT?
What a tasteless outfit!

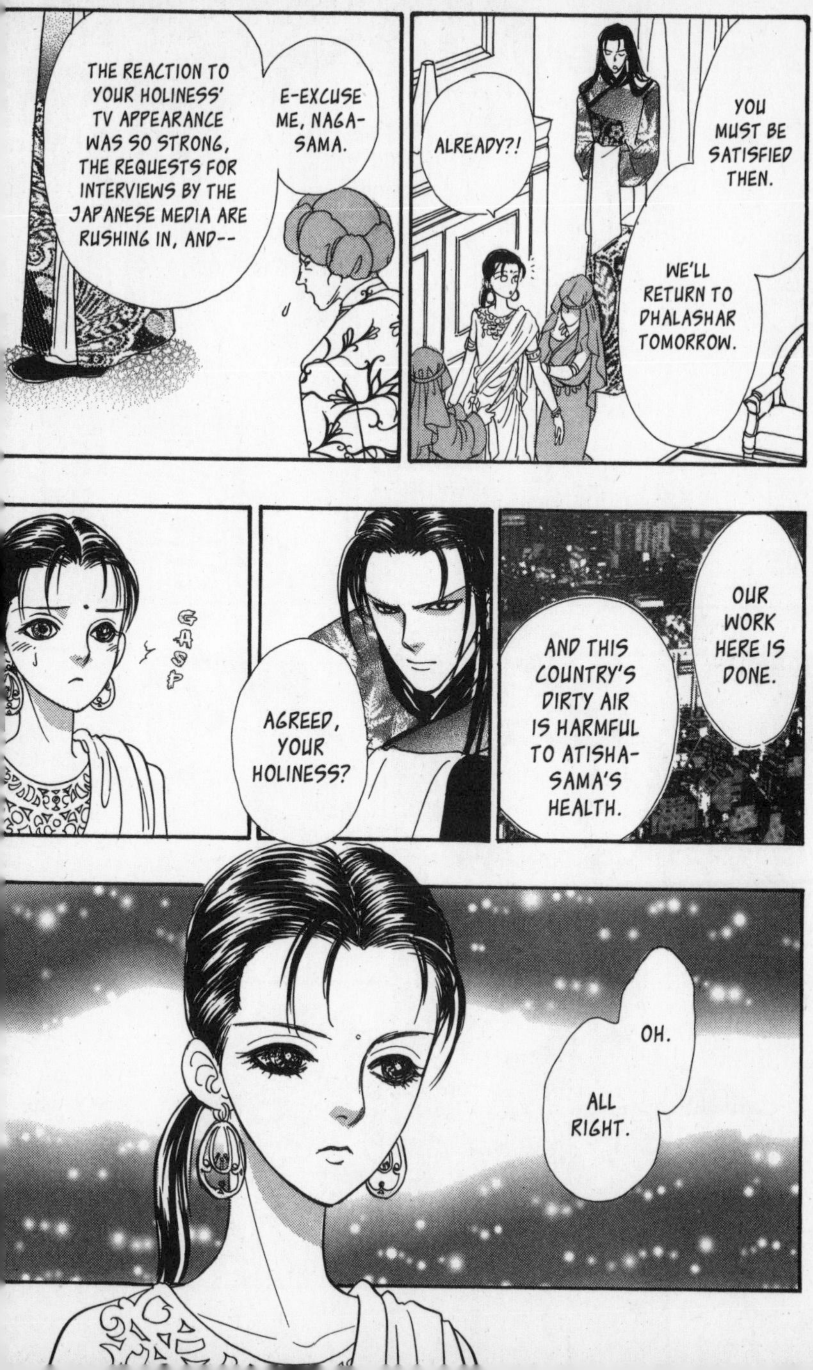
YOU MUST BE SATISFIED THEN.
WE'LL RETURN TO DHALASHAR TOMORROW.
ALREADY?!
E-EXCUSE ME, NAGA-SAMA.
THE REACTION TO YOUR HOLINESS' TV APPEARANCE WAS SO STRONG, THE REQUESTS FOR INTERVIEWS BY THE JAPANESE MEDIA ARE RUSHING IN, AND--
OUR WORK HERE IS DONE.
AND THIS COUNTRY'S DIRTY AIR IS HARMFUL TO ATISHA-SAMA'S HEALTH.
AGREED, YOUR HOLINESS?
GASP
OH.
ALL RIGHT.

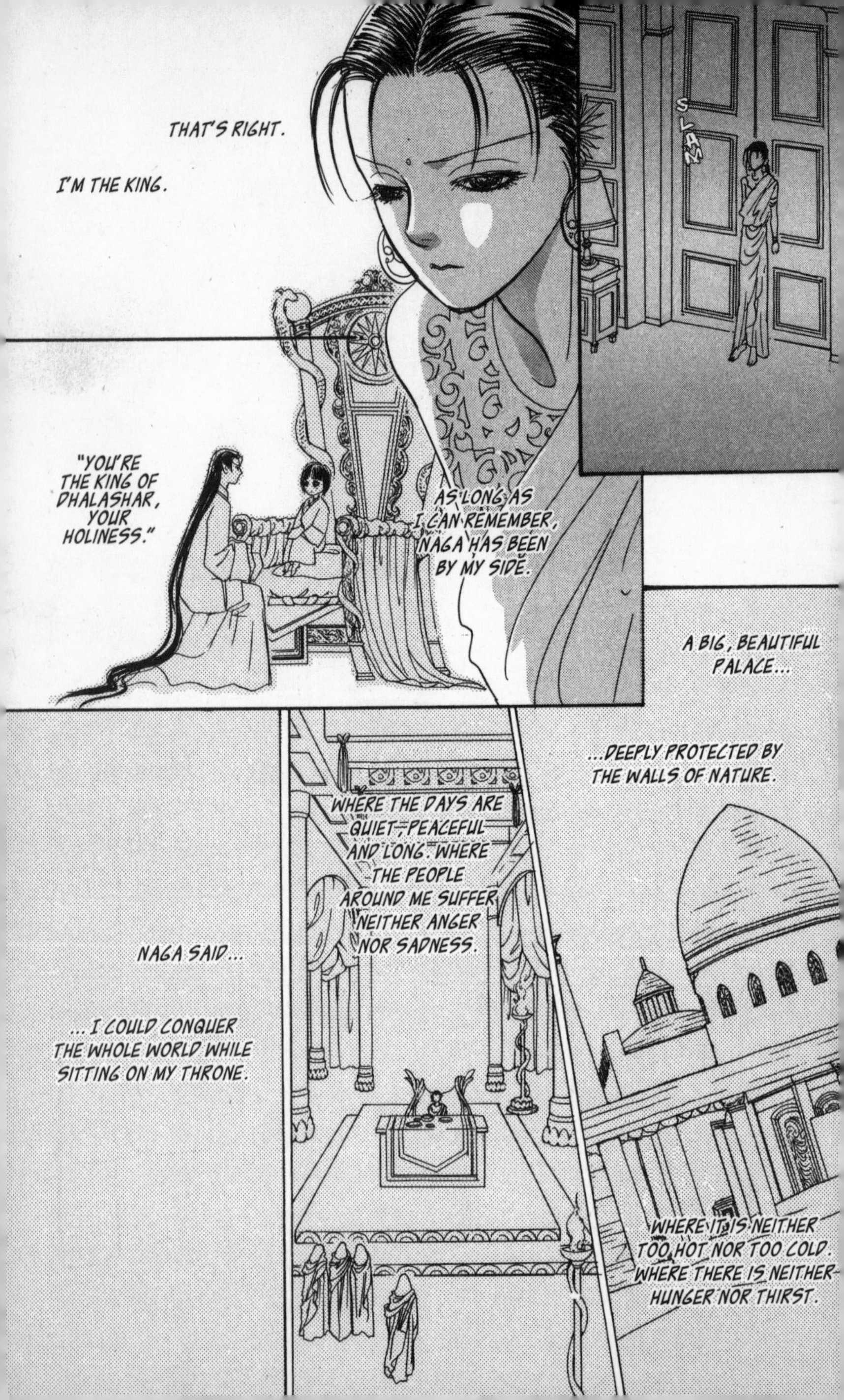
SLAM
THAT'S RIGHT.
I'M THE KING.
AS LONG AS I CAN REMEMBER, NAGA HAS BEEN BY MY SIDE.
"YOU'RE THE KING OF DHALASHAR, YOUR HOLINESS."
A BIG, BEAUTIFUL PALACE...
...DEEPLY PROTECTED BY THE WALLS OF NATURE.
WHERE IT IS NEITHER TOO HOT NOR TOO COLD. WHERE THERE IS NEITHER HUNGER NOR THIRST.
WHERE THE DAYS ARE QUIET, PEACEFUL AND LONG. WHERE THE PEOPLE AROUND ME SUFFER NEITHER ANGER NOR SADNESS.
NAGA SAID...
...I COULD CONQUER THE WHOLE WORLD WHILE SITTING ON MY THRONE.

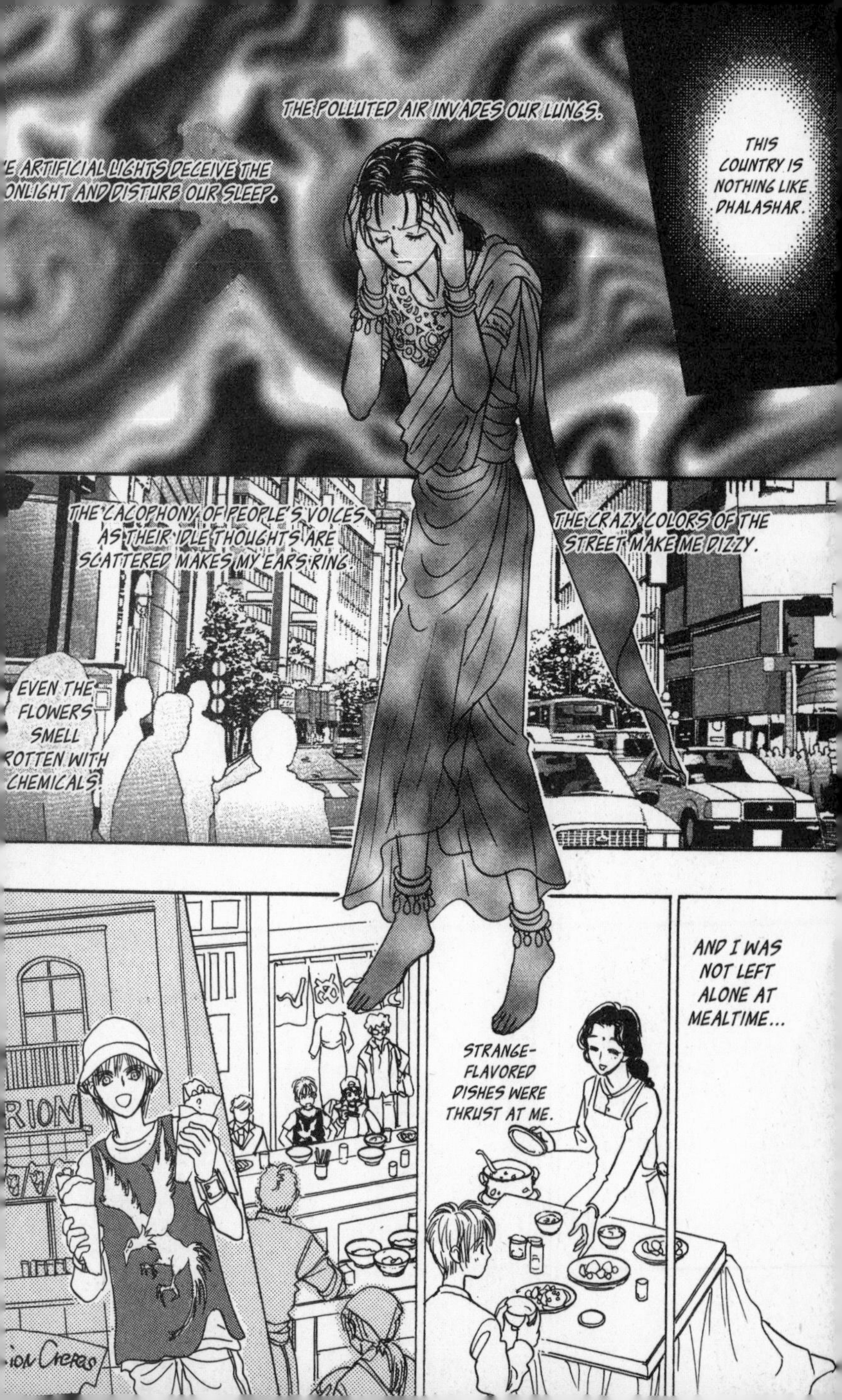
THIS COUNTRY IS NOTHING LIKE DHALASHAR.
THE POLLUTED AIR INVADES OUR LUNGS.
E ARTIFICIAL LIGHTS DECEIVE THE ONLIGHT AND DISTURB OUR SLEEP.
THE CRAZY COLORS OF THE STREET MAKE ME DIZZY.
THE CACOPHONY OF PEOPLE'S VOICES AS THEIR IDLE THOUGHTS ARE SCATTERED MAKES MY EARS RING.
EVEN THE FLOWERS SMELL ROTTEN WITH CHEMICALS.
AND I WAS NOT LEFT ALONE AT MEALTIME...
STRANGE-FLAVORED DISHES WERE THRUST AT ME.
RION
ion Crepes

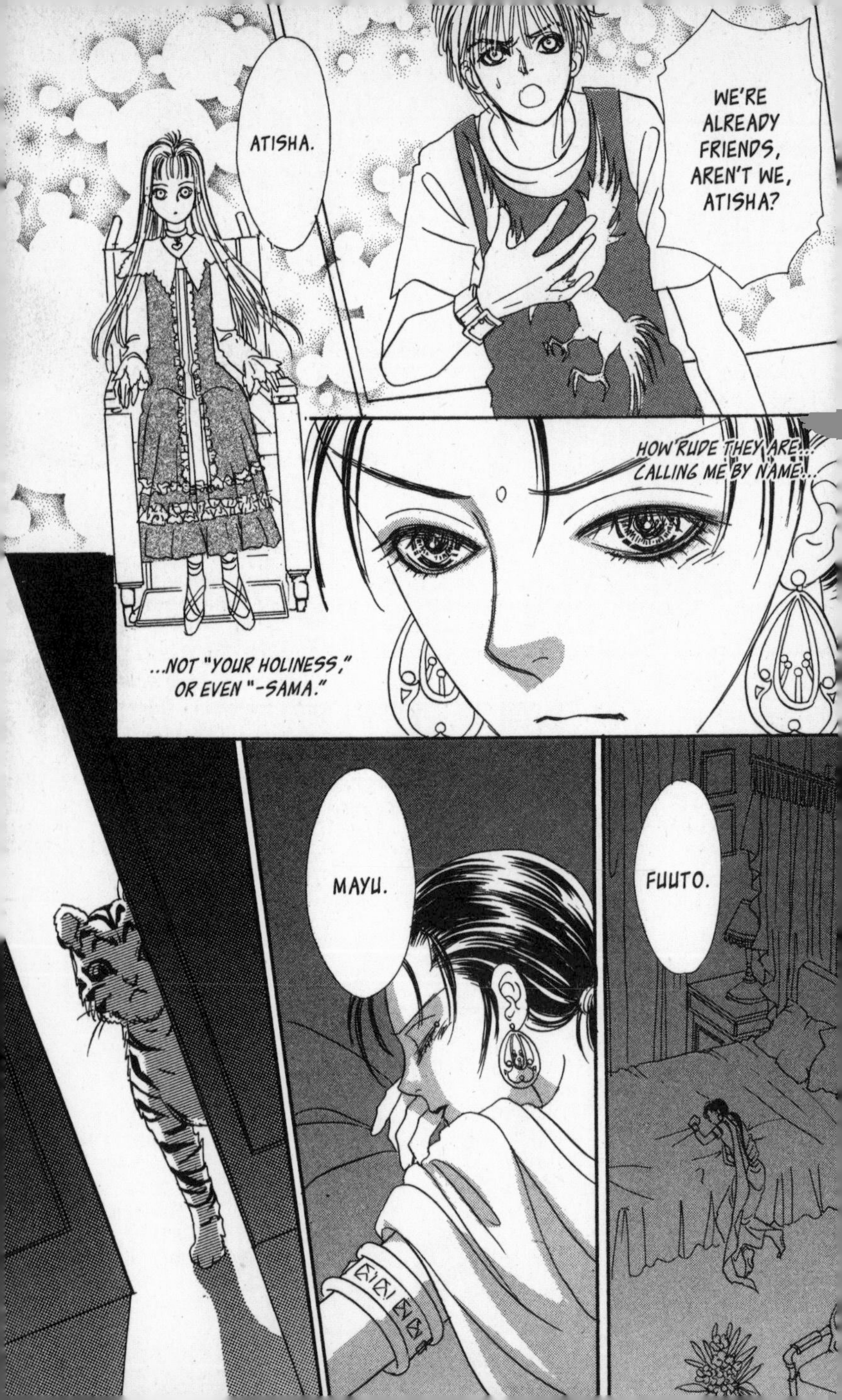
WE'RE ALREADY FRIENDS, AREN'T WE, ATISHA?
ATISHA.
HOW RUDE THEY ARE... CALLING ME BY NAME...
...NOT "YOUR HOLINESS," OR EVEN "-SAMA."
FUUTO.
MAYU.

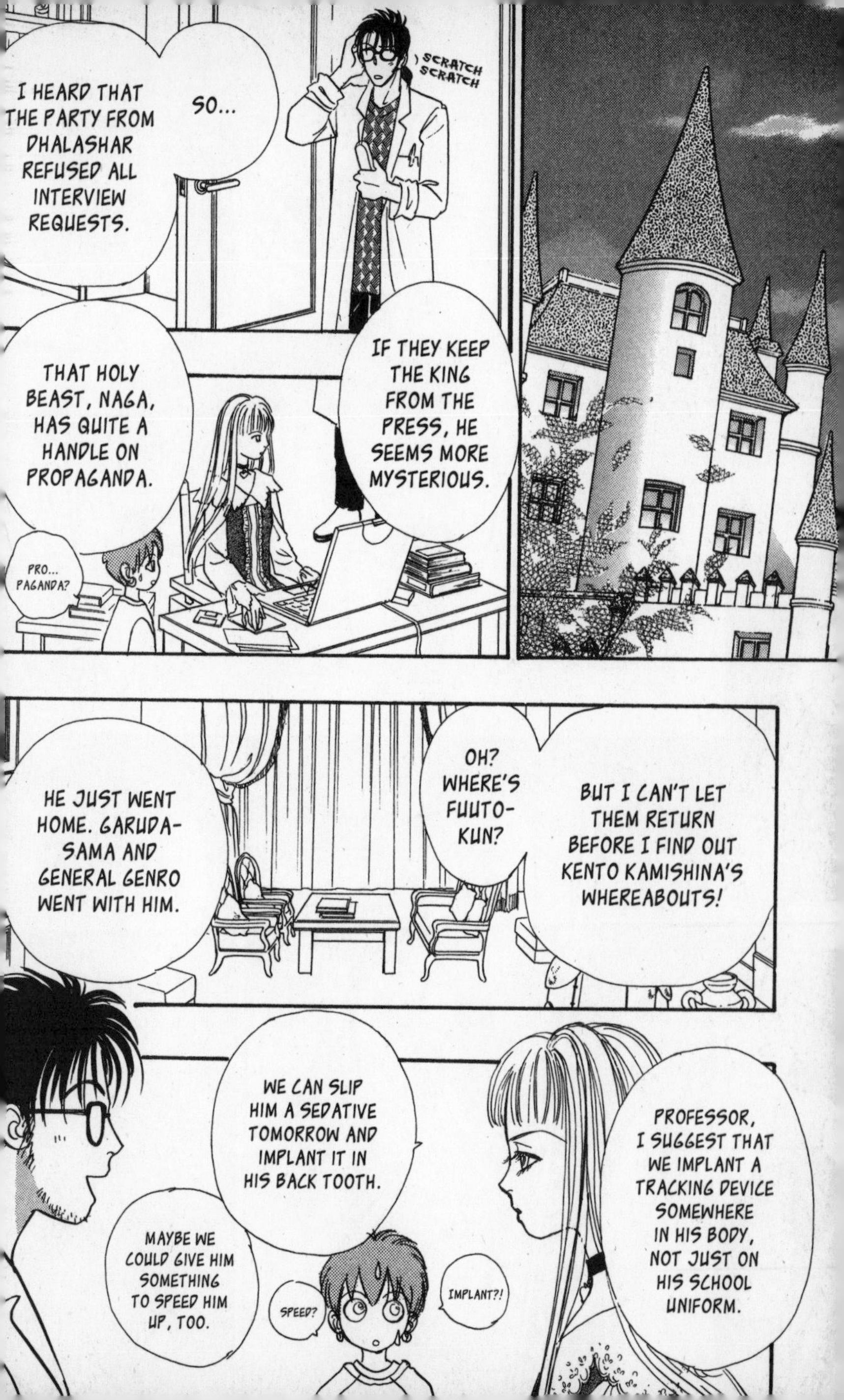
SCRATCH SCRATCH
SO...
I HEARD THAT THE PARTY FROM DHALASHAR REFUSED ALL INTERVIEW REQUESTS.
IF THEY KEEP THE KING FROM THE PRESS, HE SEEMS MORE MYSTERIOUS.
THAT HOLY BEAST, NAGA, HAS QUITE A HANDLE ON PROPAGANDA.
PRO... PAGANDA?
BUT I CAN'T LET THEM RETURN BEFORE I FIND OUT KENTO KAMISHINA'S WHEREABOUTS!
OH? WHERE'S FUUTO-KUN?
HE JUST WENT HOME. GARUDA-SAMA AND GENERAL GENRO WENT WITH HIM.
PROFESSOR, I SUGGEST THAT WE IMPLANT A TRACKING DEVICE SOMEWHERE IN HIS BODY, NOT JUST ON HIS SCHOOL UNIFORM.
IMPLANT?!
WE CAN SLIP HIM A SEDATIVE TOMORROW AND IMPLANT IT IN HIS BACK TOOTH.
MAYBE WE COULD GIVE HIM SOMETHING TO SPEED HIM UP, TOO.
SPEED?

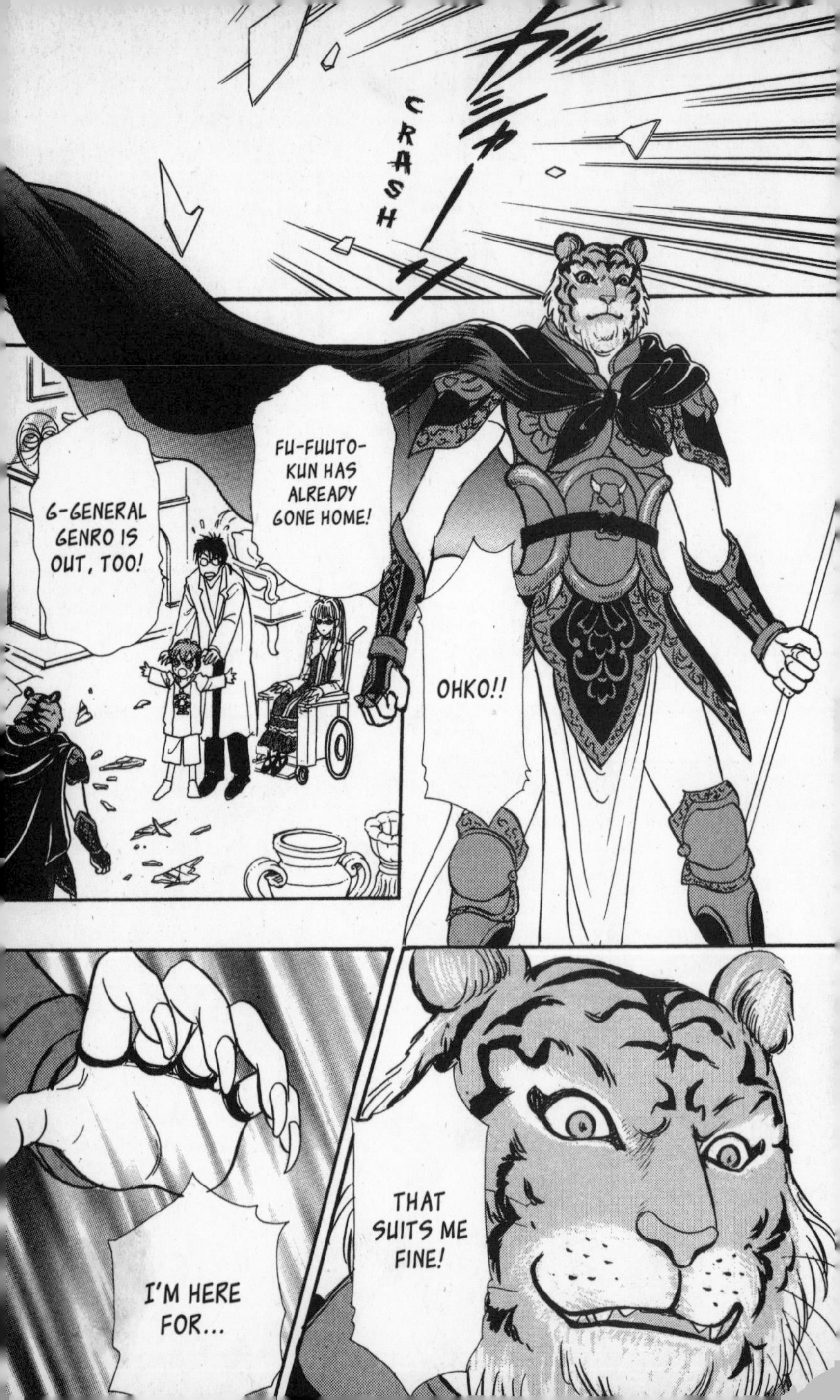
CRASH
OHKO!!
FU-FUUTO-KUN HAS ALREADY GONE HOME!
G-GENERAL GENRO IS OUT, TOO!
THAT SUITS ME FINE!
I'M HERE FOR...

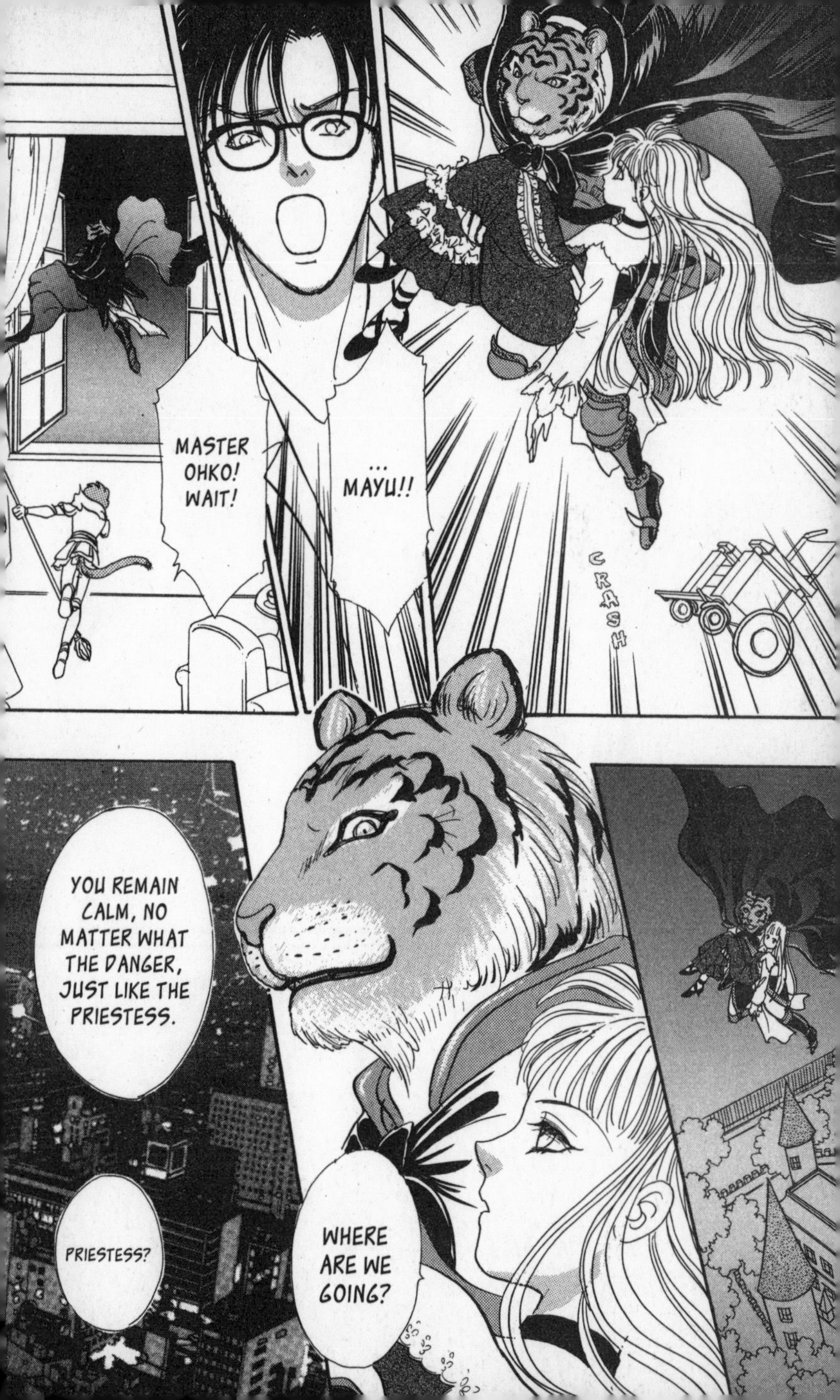

...MAYU!!
MASTER OHKO! WAIT!
CRASH
WHERE ARE WE GOING?
YOU REMAIN CALM, NO MATTER WHAT THE DANGER, JUST LIKE THE PRIESTESS.
PRIESTESS?

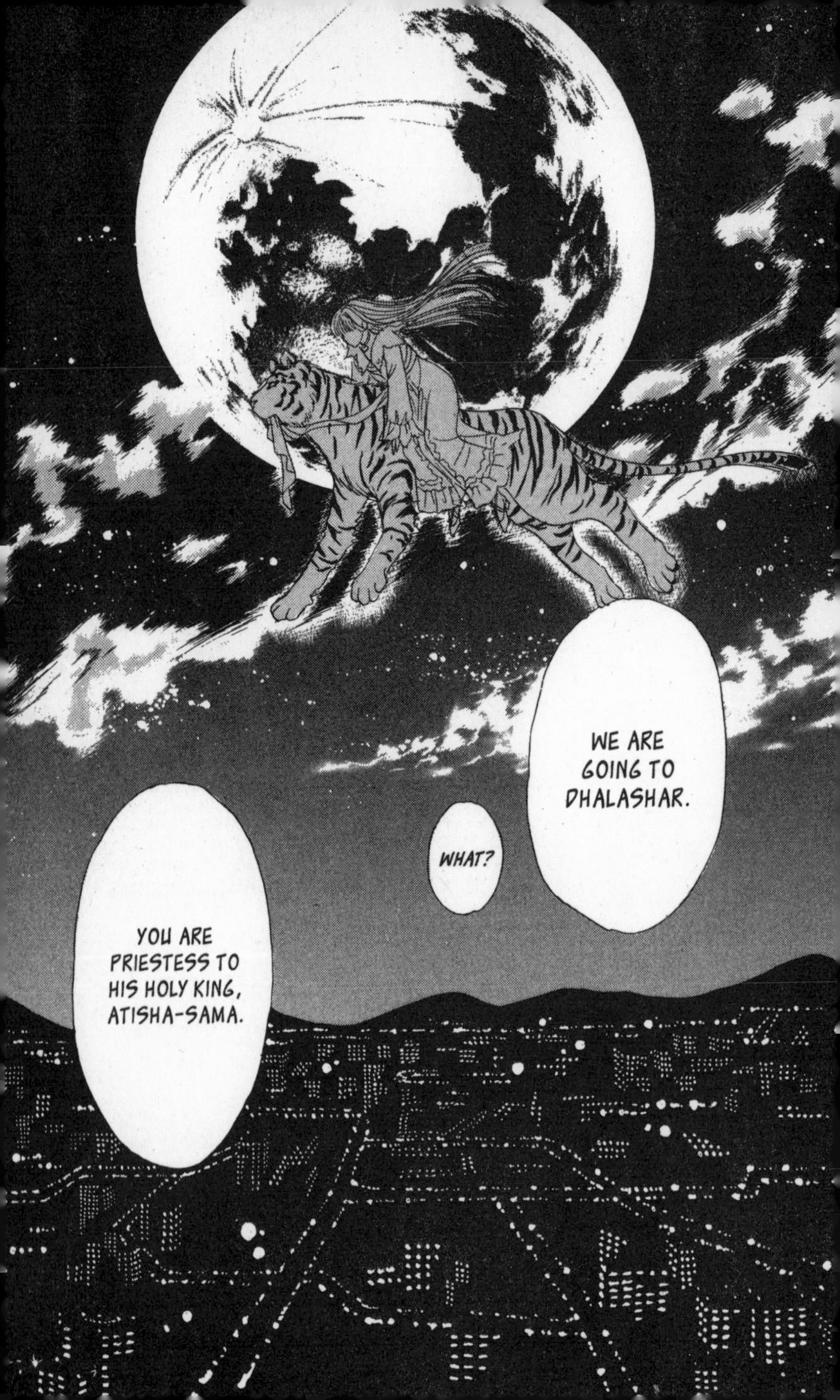
WE ARE GOING TO DHALASHAR.
WHAT?
YOU ARE PRIESTESS TO HIS HOLY KING, ATISHA-SAMA.

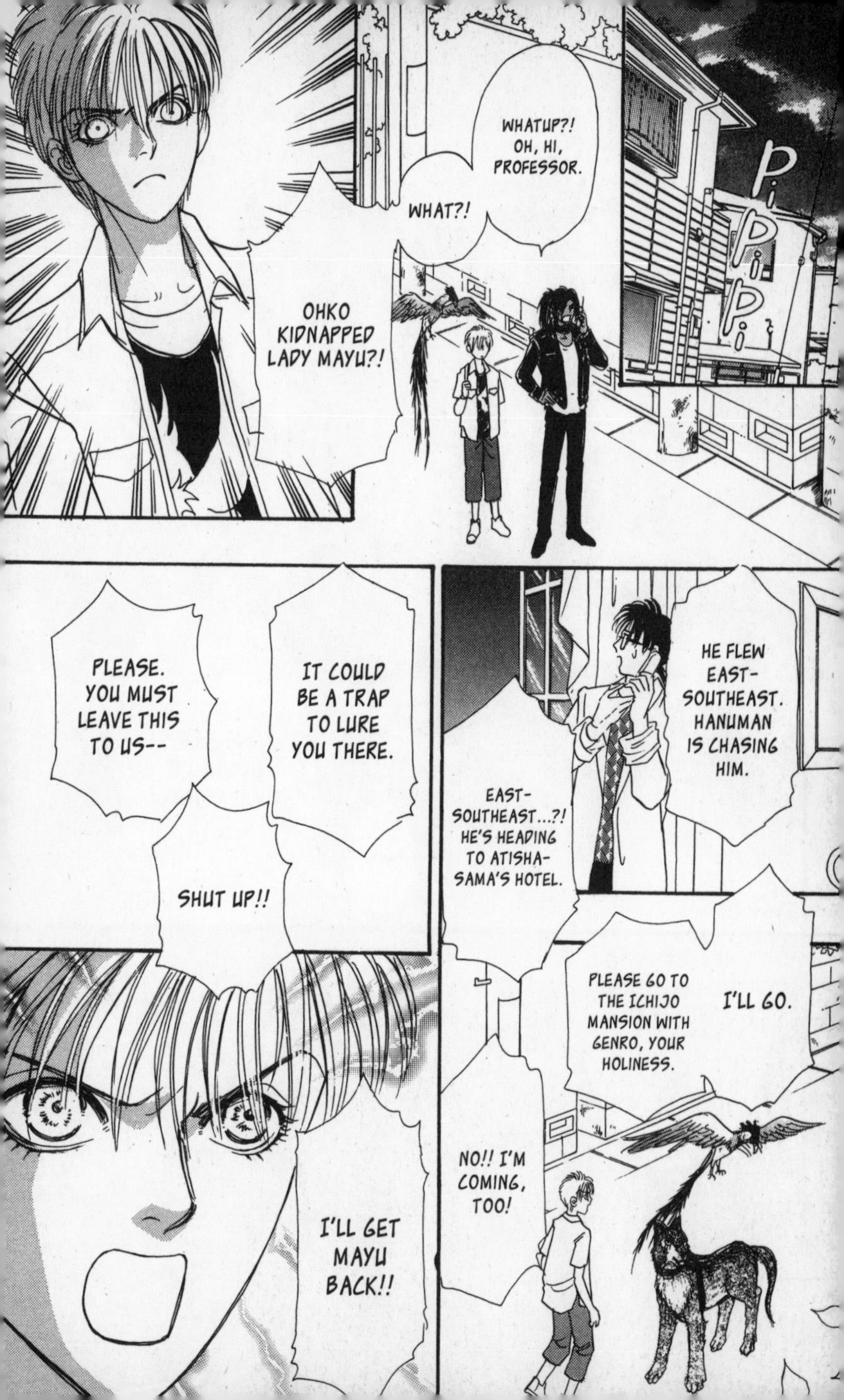
PiPiPiPi
WHATUP?! OH, HI, PROFESSOR.
WHAT?!
OHKO KIDNAPPED LADY MAYU?!
HE FLEW EAST-SOUTHEAST. HANUMAN IS CHASING HIM.
EAST-SOUTHEAST...?! HE'S HEADING TO ATISHA-SAMA'S HOTEL.
IT COULD BE A TRAP TO LURE YOU THERE.
PLEASE. YOU MUST LEAVE THIS TO US--
SHUT UP!!
I'LL GO.
PLEASE GO TO THE ICHIJO MANSION WITH GENRO, YOUR HOLINESS.
NO!! I'M COMING, TOO!
I'LL GET MAYU BACK!!

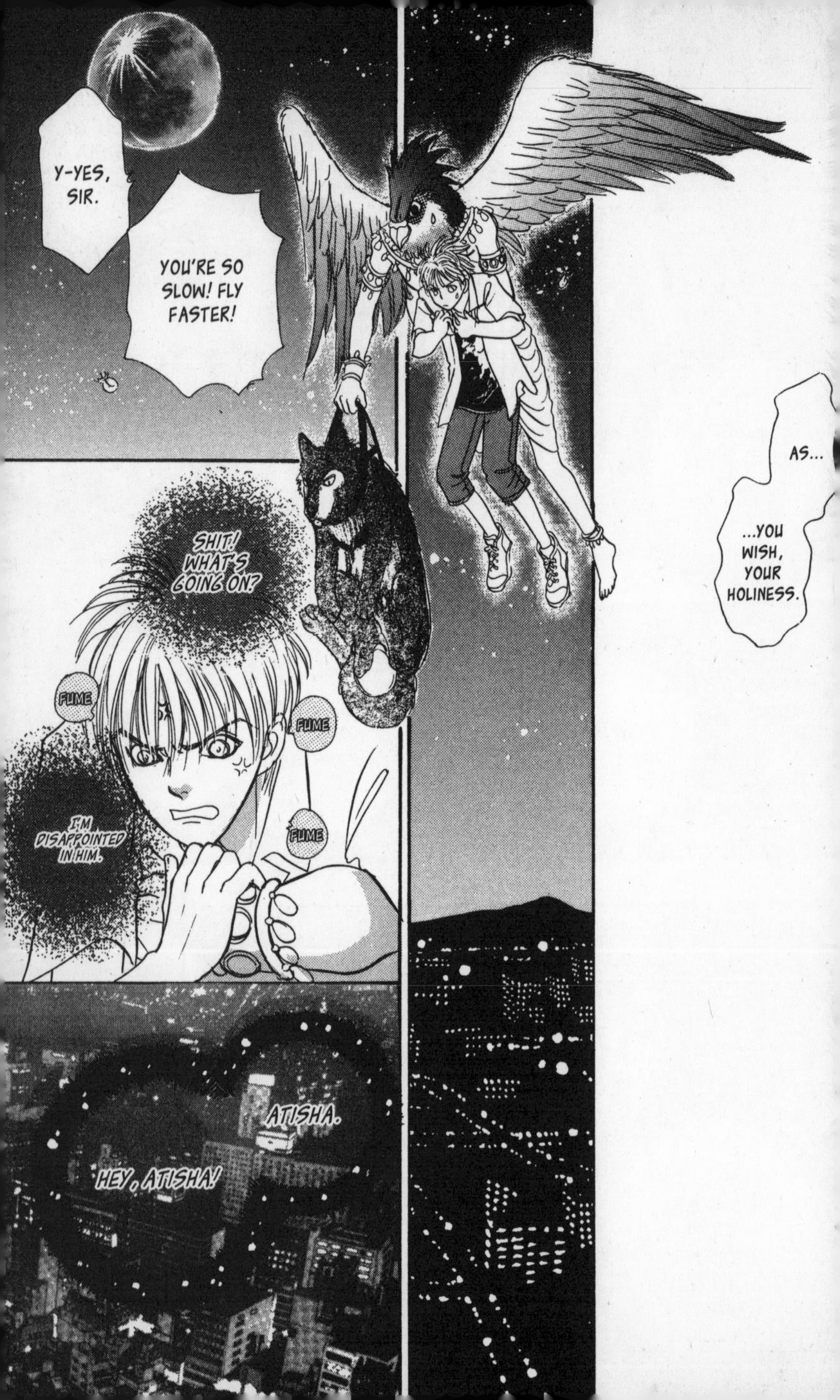
AS...
...YOU WISH, YOUR HOLINESS.
YOU'RE SO SLOW! FLY FASTER!
Y-YES, SIR.
SHIT! WHAT'S GOING ON?
FUME
FUME
FUME
I'M DISAPPOINTED IN HIM.
ATISHA.
HEY, ATISHA!

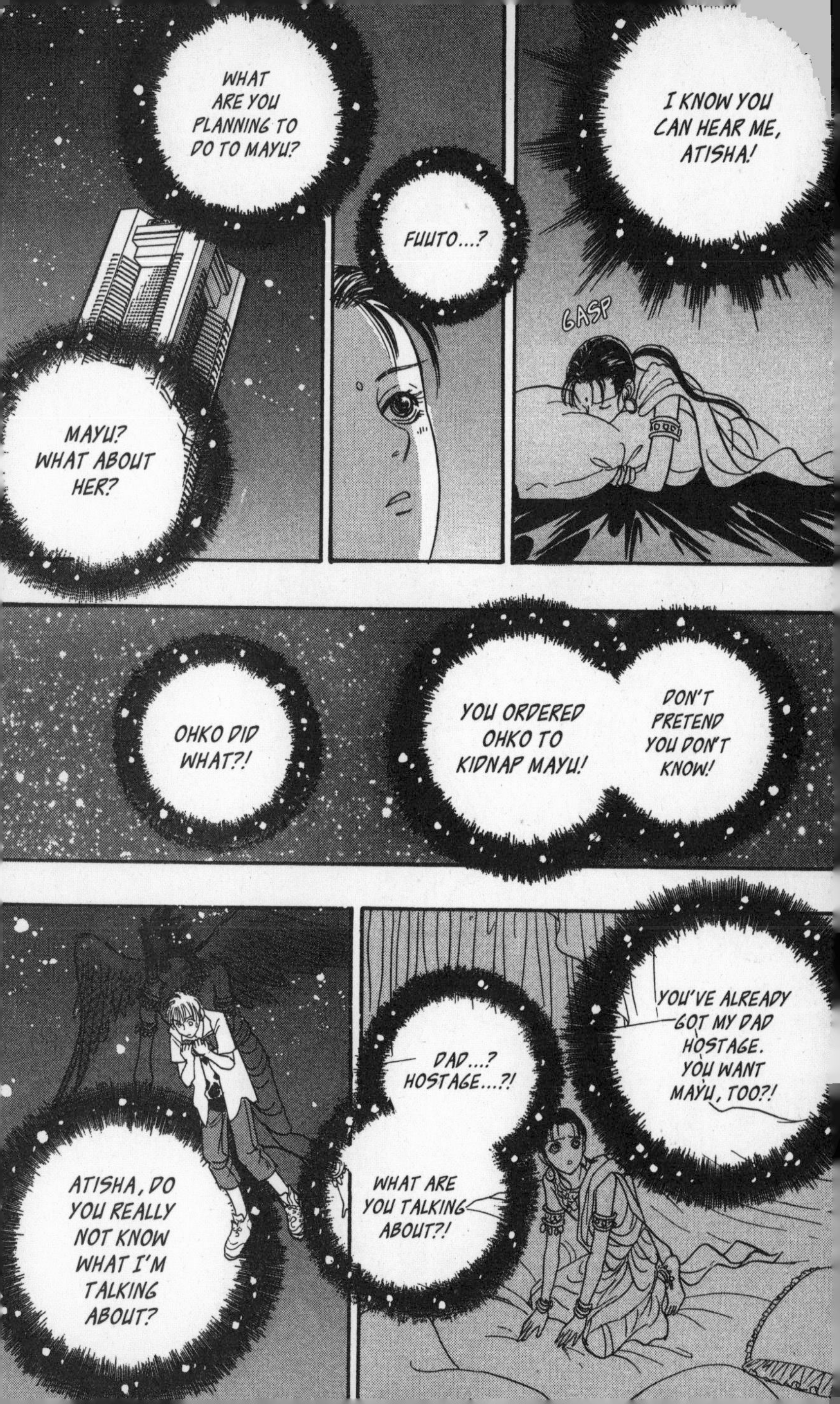
I KNOW YOU CAN HEAR ME, ATISHA!
GASP
FUUTO...?
WHAT ARE YOU PLANNING TO DO TO MAYU?
MAYU? WHAT ABOUT HER?
DON'T PRETEND YOU DON'T KNOW!
YOU ORDERED OHKO TO KIDNAP MAYU!
OHKO DID WHAT?!
YOU'VE ALREADY GOT MY DAD HOSTAGE. YOU WANT MAYU, TOO?!
DAD...? HOSTAGE...?!
WHAT ARE YOU TALKING ABOUT?!
ATISHA, DO YOU REALLY NOT KNOW WHAT I'M TALKING ABOUT?

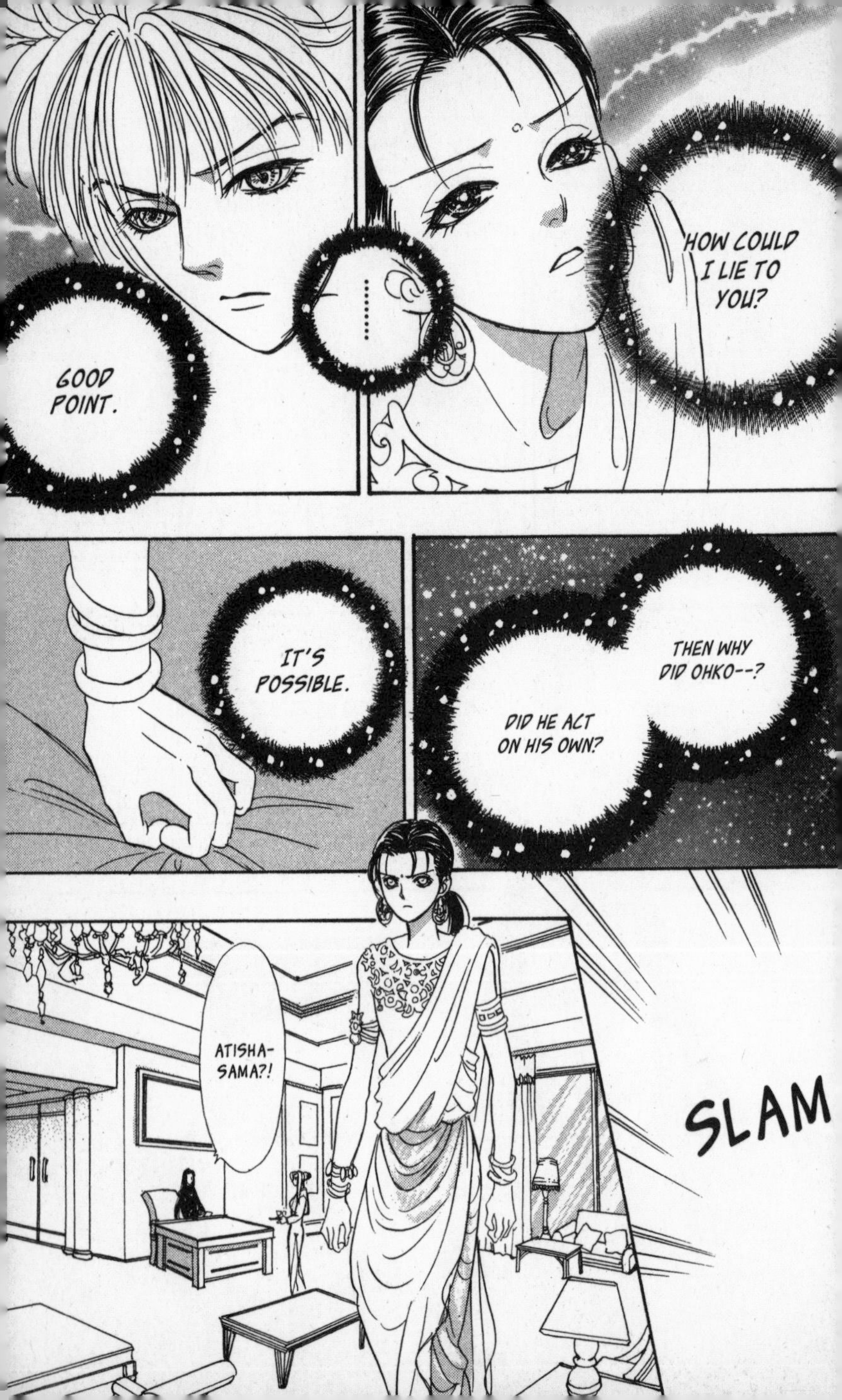
HOW COULD I LIE TO YOU?
......
GOOD POINT.
THEN WHY DID OHKO--?
DID HE ACT ON HIS OWN?
IT'S POSSIBLE.
SLAM
ATISHA-SAMA?!

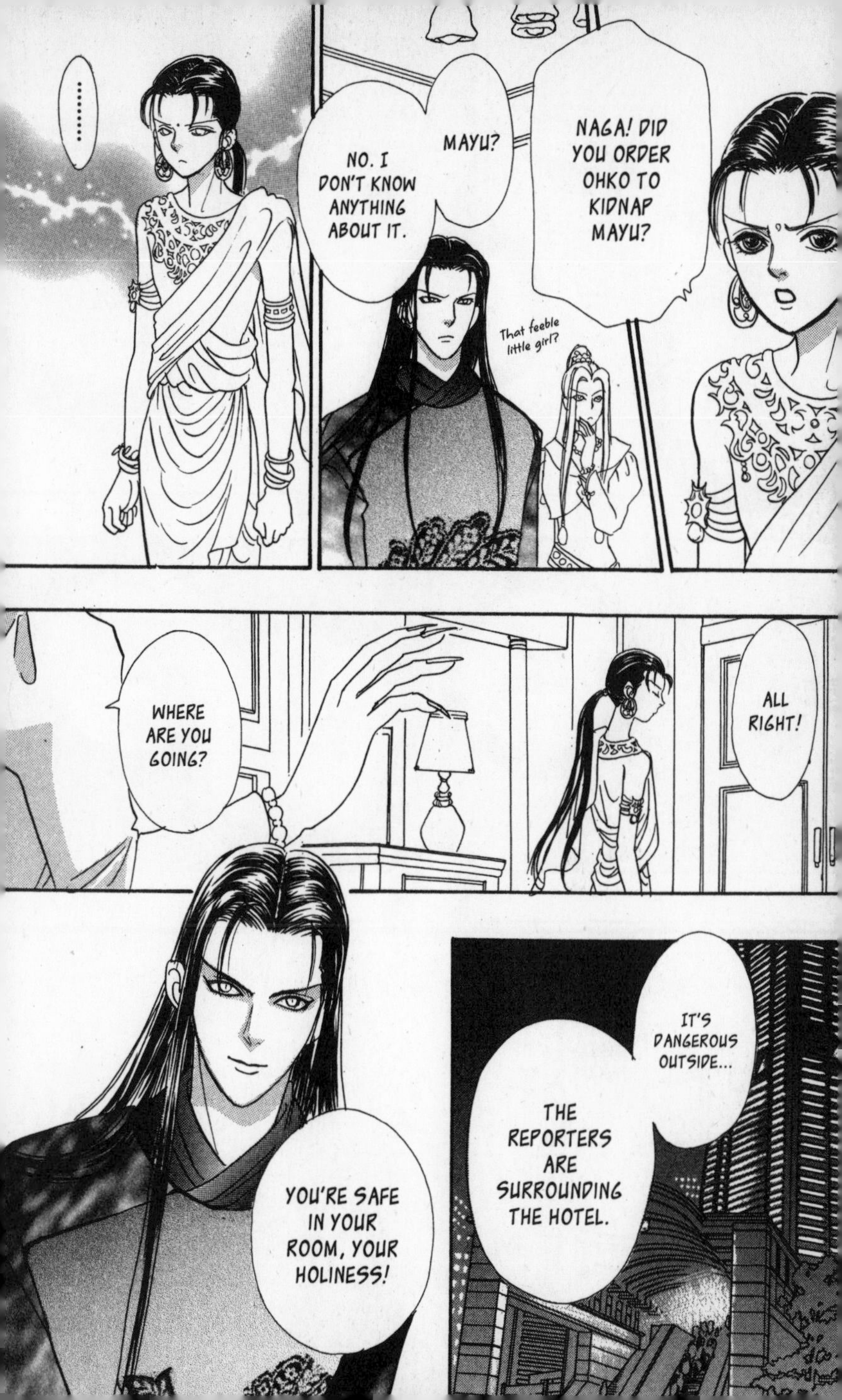
NAGA! DID YOU ORDER OHKO TO KIDNAP MAYU?
MAYU?
NO. I DON'T KNOW ANYTHING ABOUT IT.
That feeble little girl?
......
ALL RIGHT!
WHERE ARE YOU GOING?
IT'S DANGEROUS OUTSIDE...
THE REPORTERS ARE SURROUNDING THE HOTEL.
YOU'RE SAFE IN YOUR ROOM, YOUR HOLINESS!

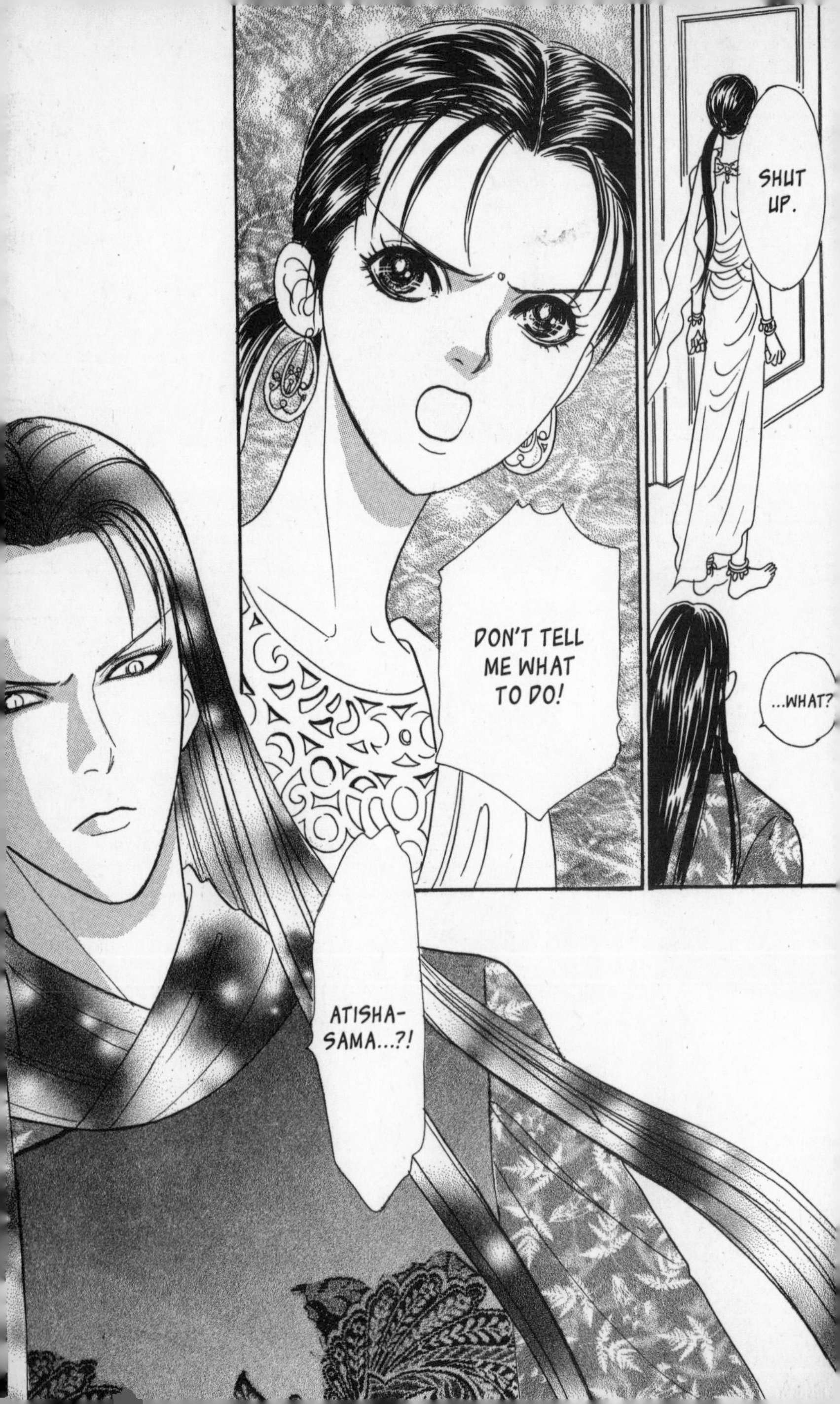
SHUT UP.
...WHAT?
DON'T TELL ME WHAT TO DO!
ATISHA-SAMA...?!

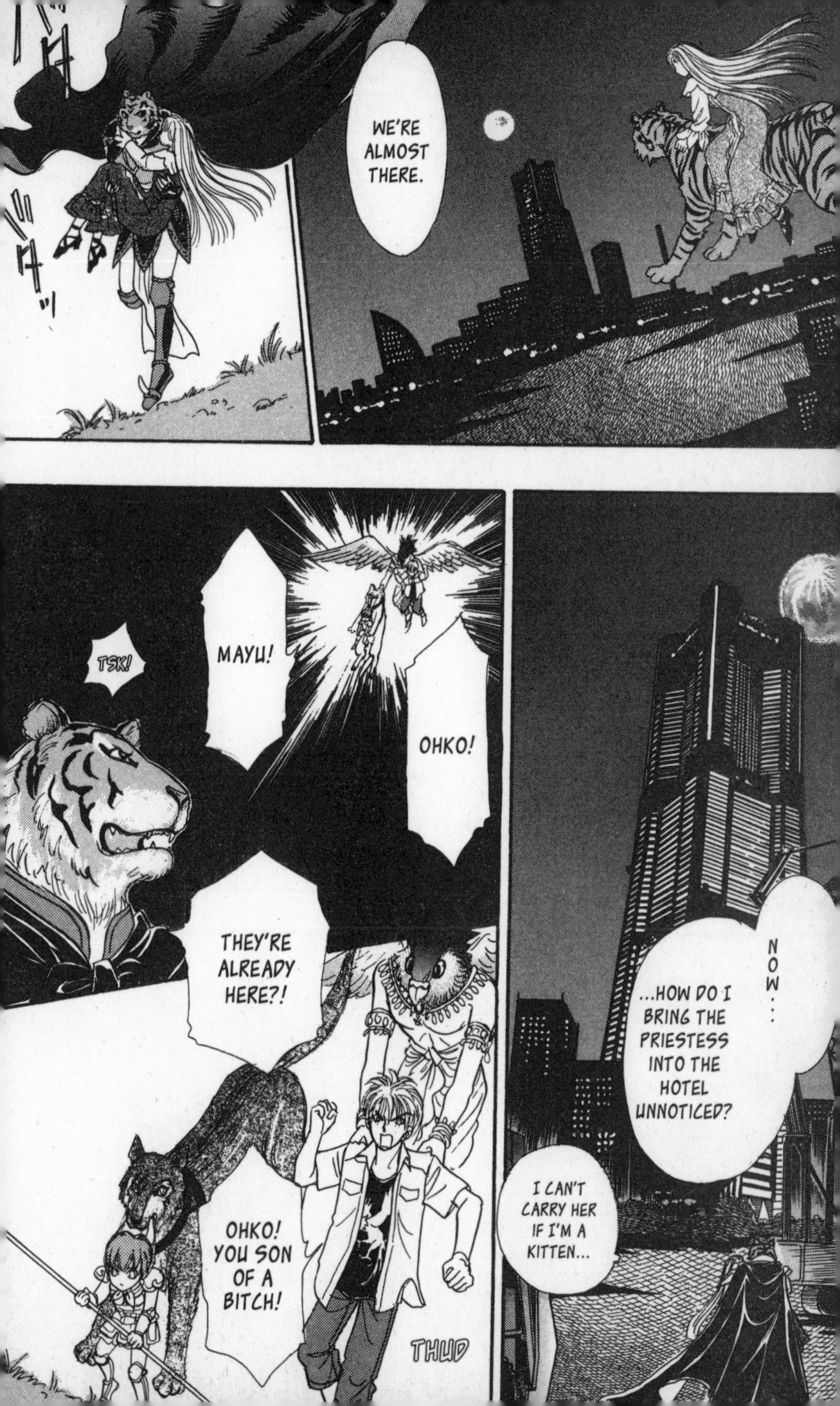
WE'RE ALMOST THERE.
NOW...
...HOW DO I BRING THE PRIESTESS INTO THE HOTEL UNNOTICED?
I CAN'T CARRY HER IF I'M A KITTEN...
MAYU!
OHKO!
TSK!
THEY'RE ALREADY HERE?!
OHKO! YOU SON OF A BITCH!
THUD

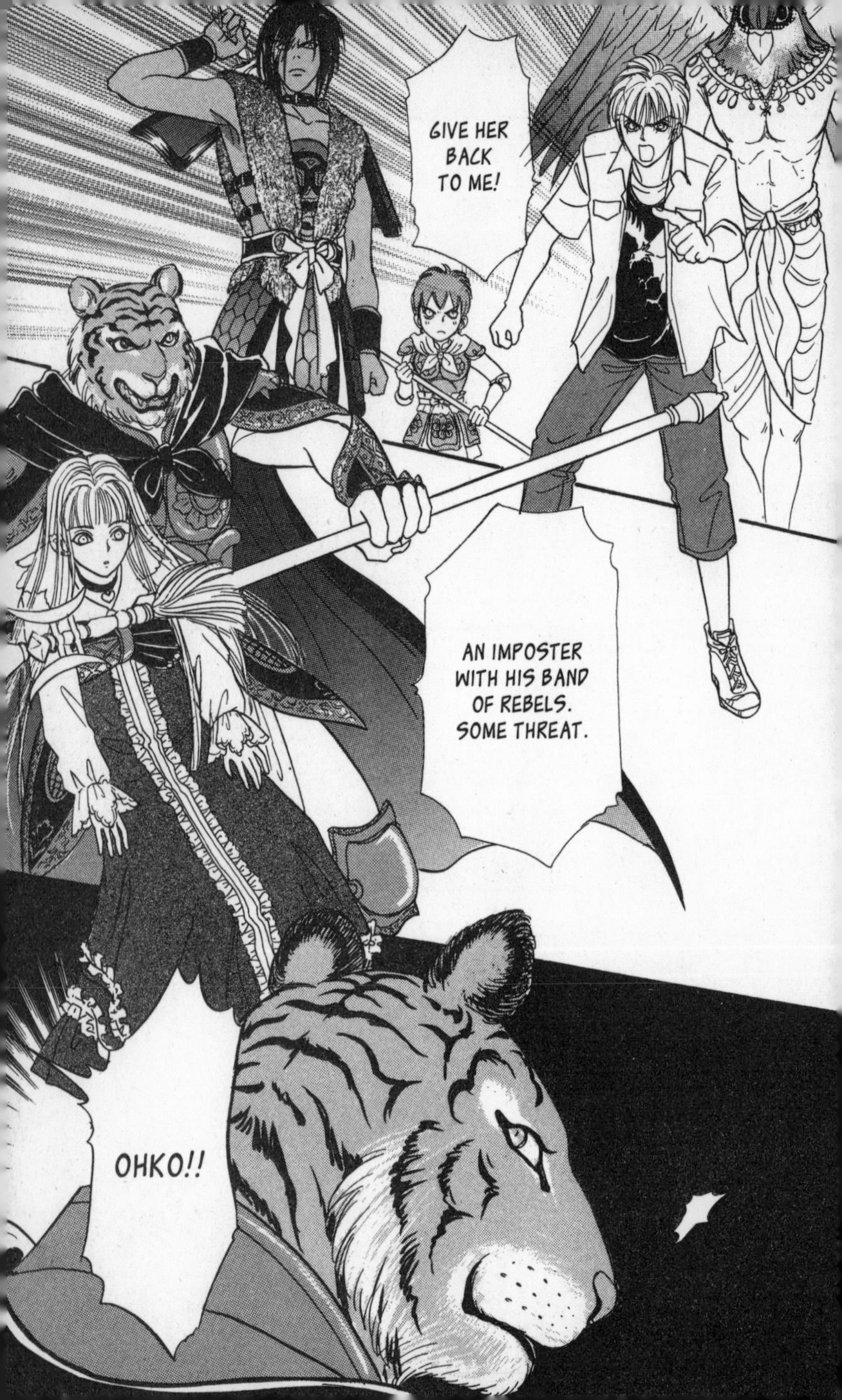
GIVE HER BACK TO ME!
AN IMPOSTER WITH HIS BAND OF REBELS. SOME THREAT.
OHKO!!

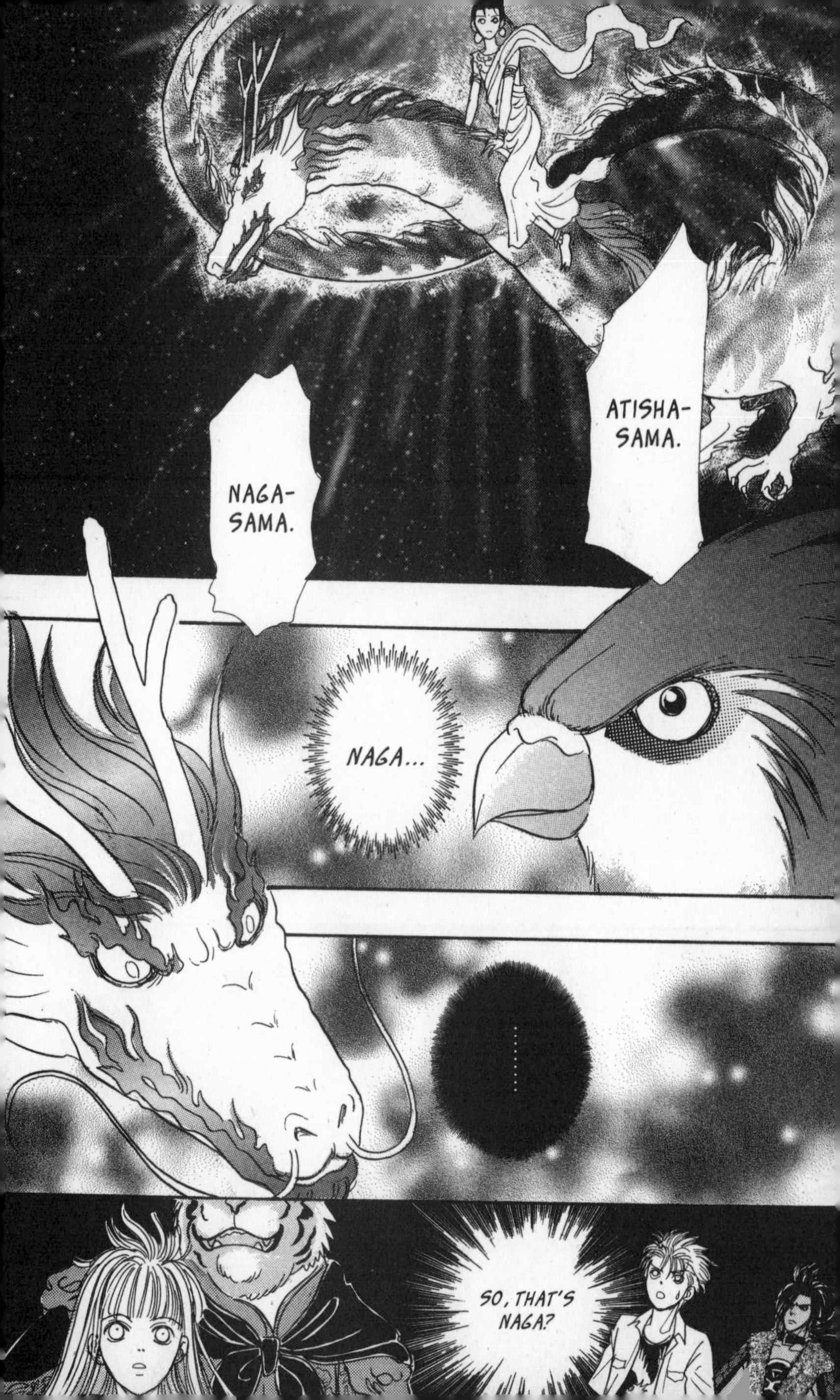
ATISHA-SAMA.
NAGA-SAMA.
NAGA...
......
SO, THAT'S NAGA?

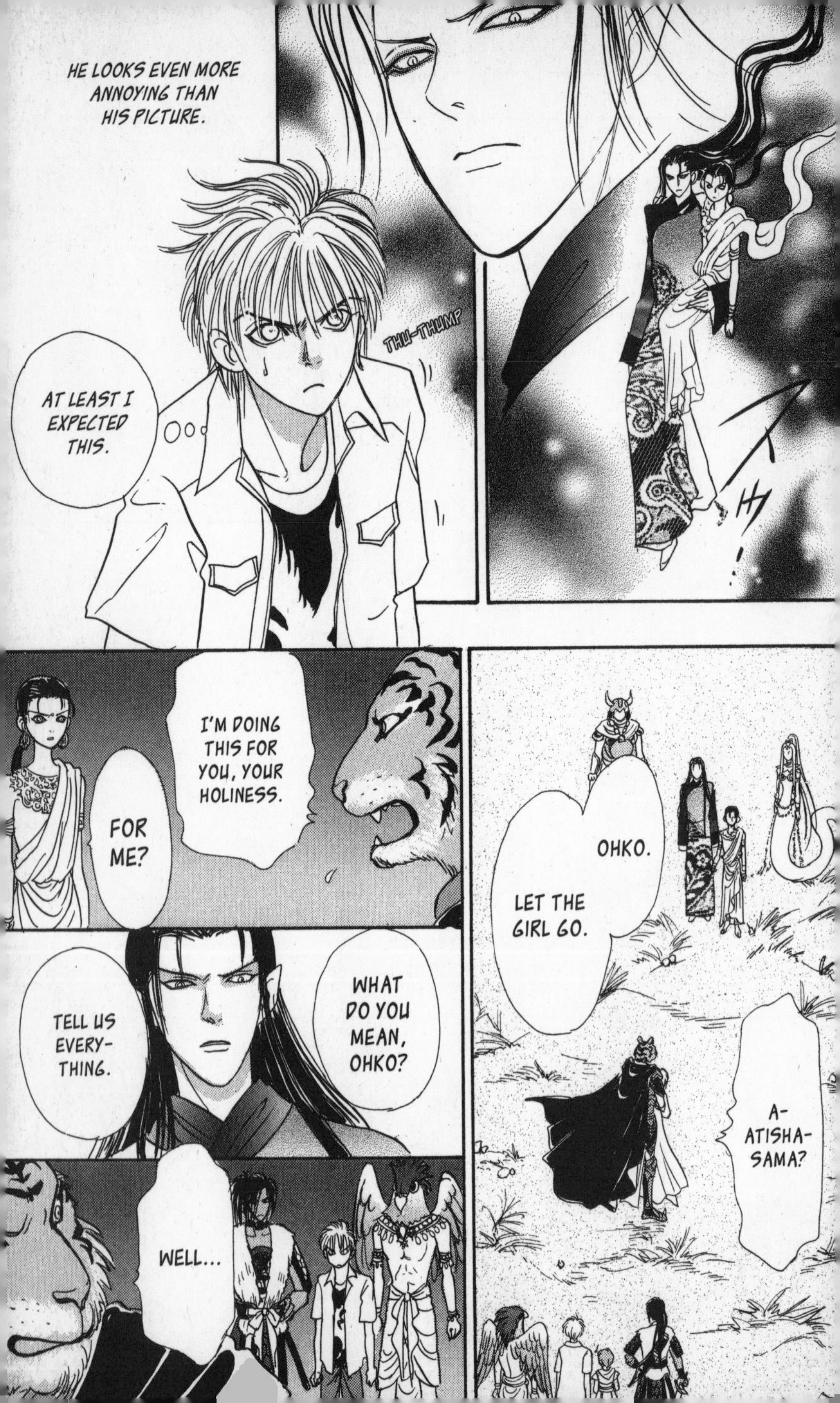
HE LOOKS EVEN MORE ANNOYING THAN HIS PICTURE.
THU-THUMP
AT LEAST I EXPECTED THIS.
OHKO.
LET THE GIRL GO.
A-ATISHA-SAMA?
I'M DOING THIS FOR YOU, YOUR HOLINESS.
FOR ME?
WHAT DO YOU MEAN, OHKO?
TELL US EVERYTHING.
WELL...

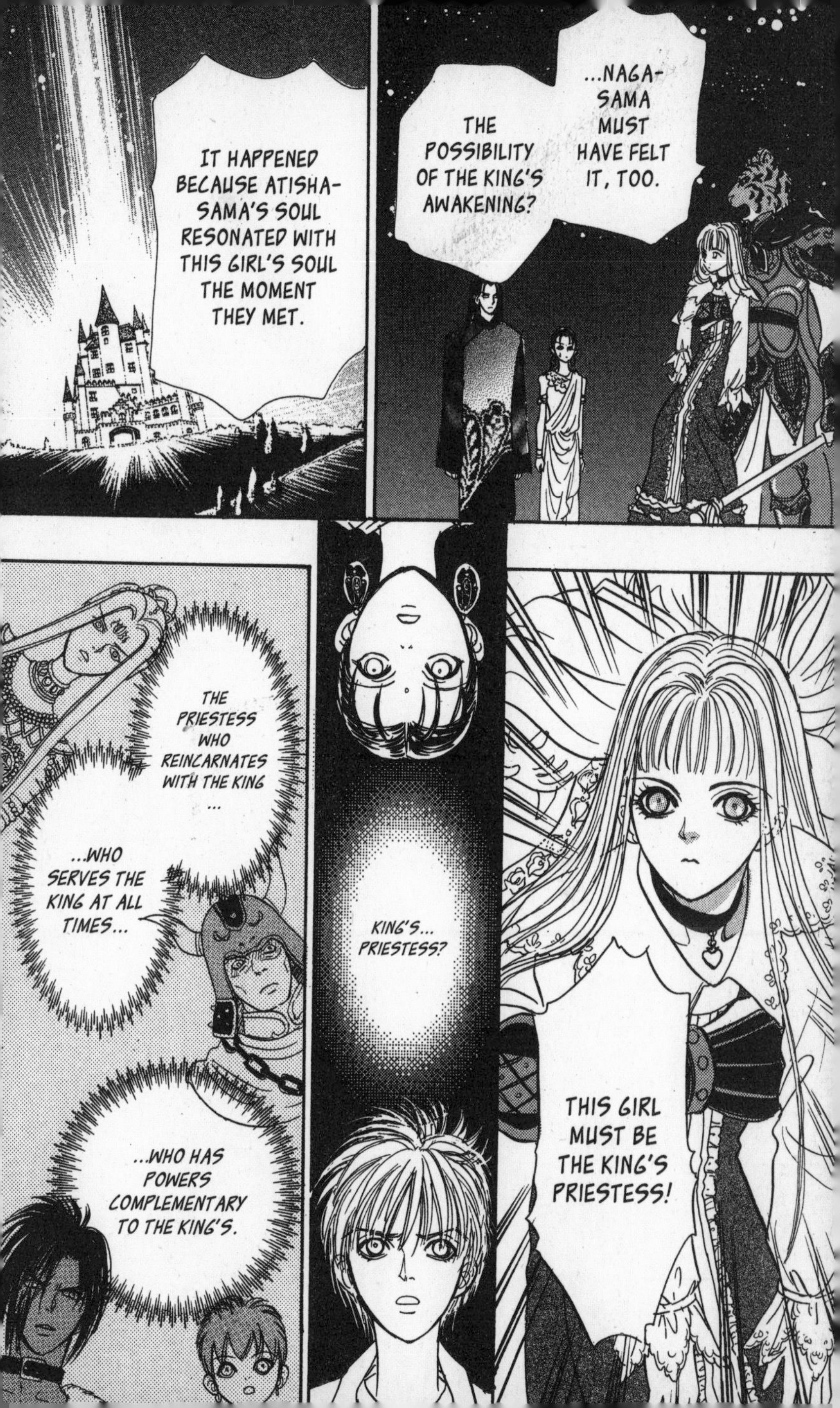
...NAGA-SAMA MUST HAVE FELT IT, TOO.
THE POSSIBILITY OF THE KING'S AWAKENING?
IT HAPPENED BECAUSE ATISHA-SAMA'S SOUL RESONATED WITH THIS GIRL'S SOUL THE MOMENT THEY MET.
THIS GIRL MUST BE THE KING'S PRIESTESS!
KING'S... PRIESTESS?
THE PRIESTESS WHO REINCARNATES WITH THE KING ...
...WHO SERVES THE KING AT ALL TIMES...
...WHO HAS POWERS COMPLEMENTARY TO THE KING'S.

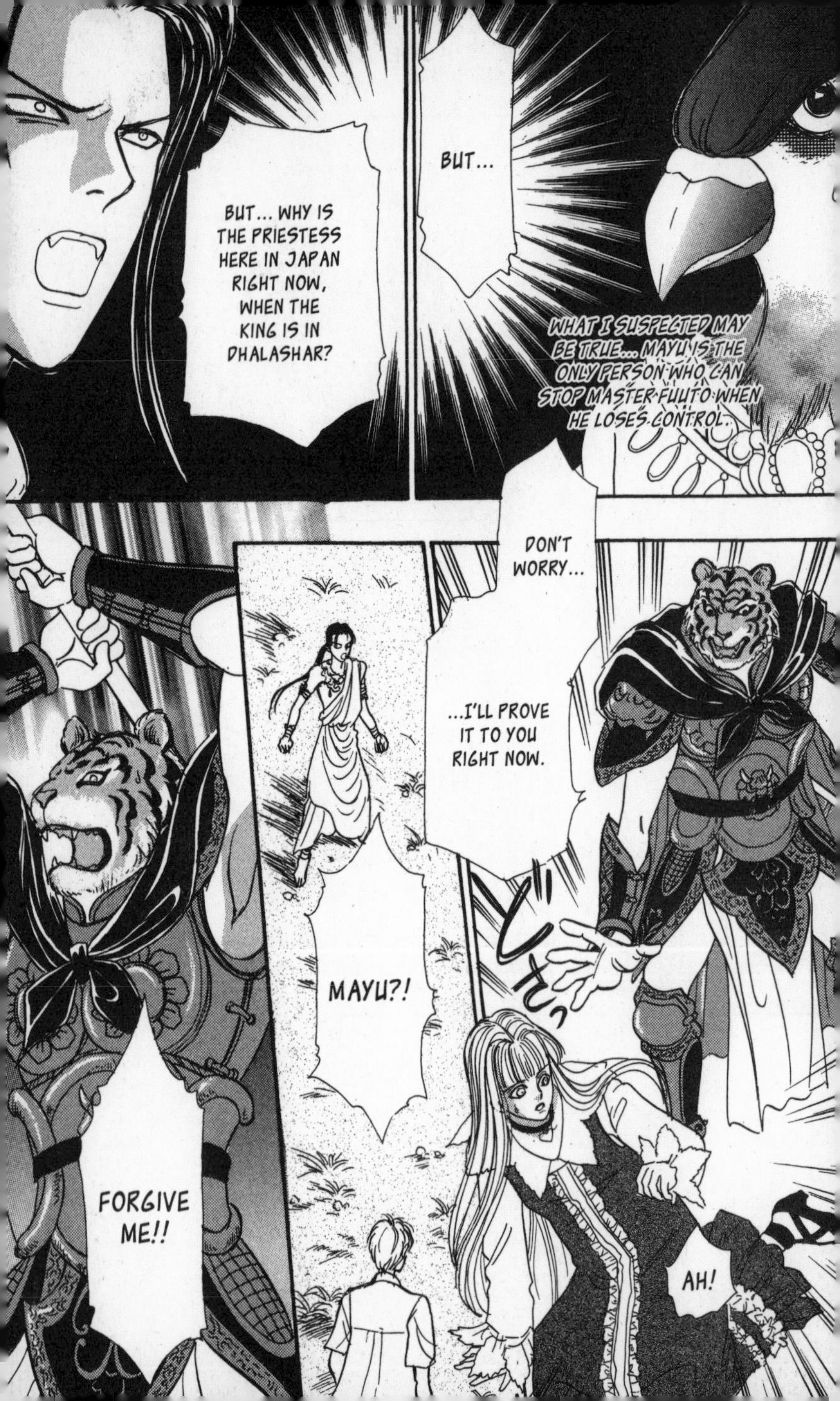
BUT...
WHAT I SUSPECTED MAY BE TRUE... MAYU IS THE ONLY PERSON WHO CAN STOP MASTER FUUTO WHEN HE LOSES CONTROL.
BUT... WHY IS THE PRIESTESS HERE IN JAPAN RIGHT NOW, WHEN THE KING IS IN DHALASHAR?
DON'T WORRY...
...I'LL PROVE IT TO YOU RIGHT NOW.
AH!
MAYU?!
FORGIVE ME!!

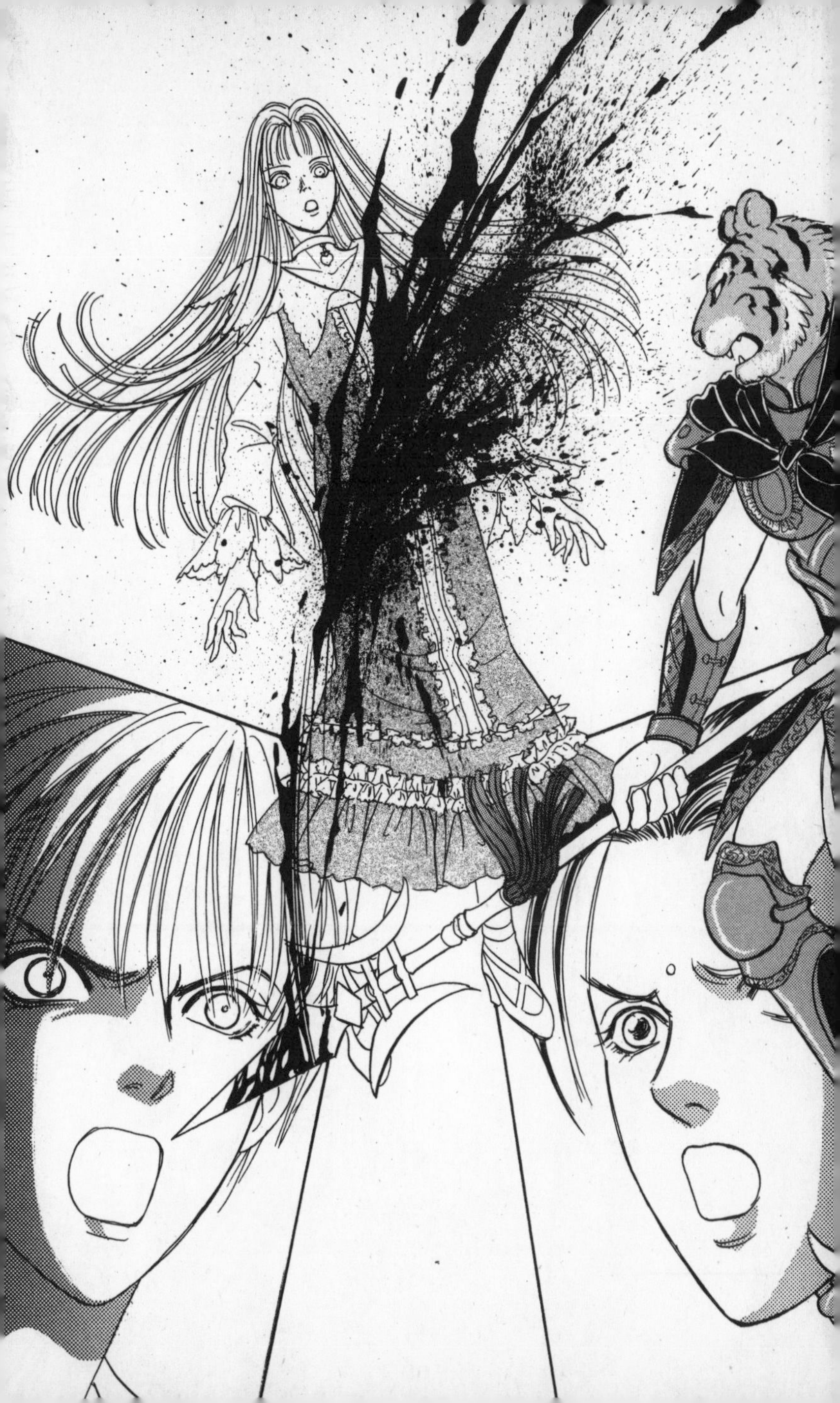

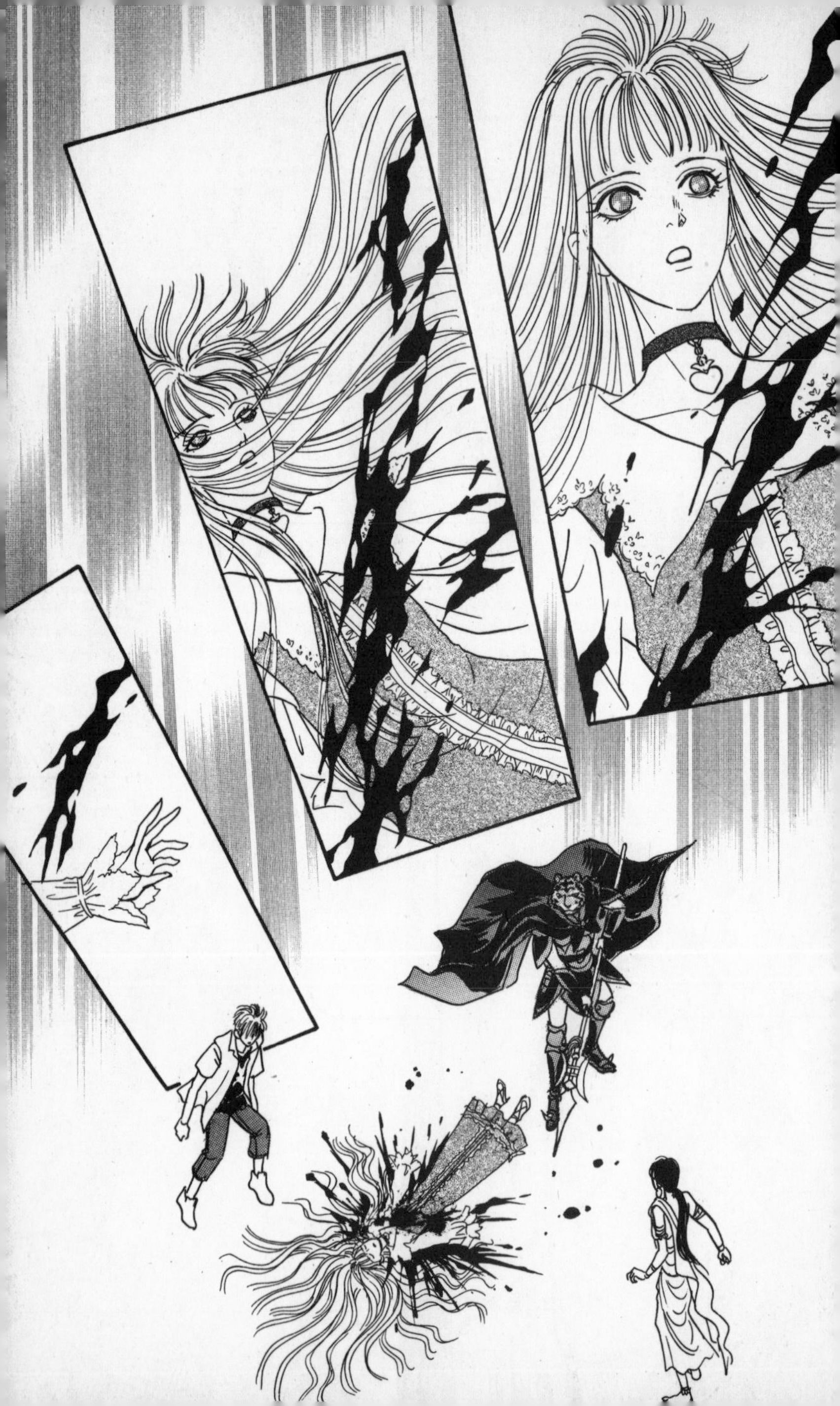

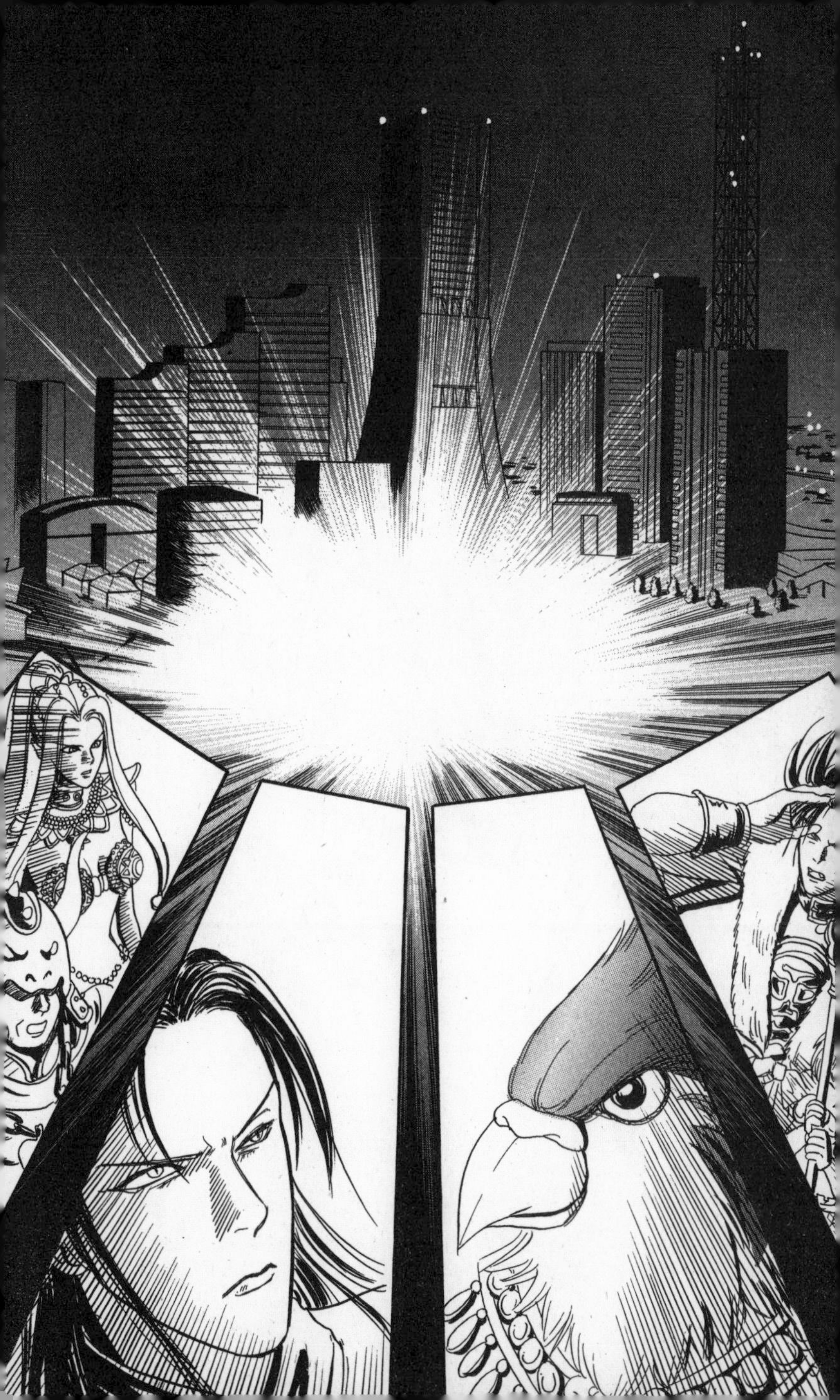

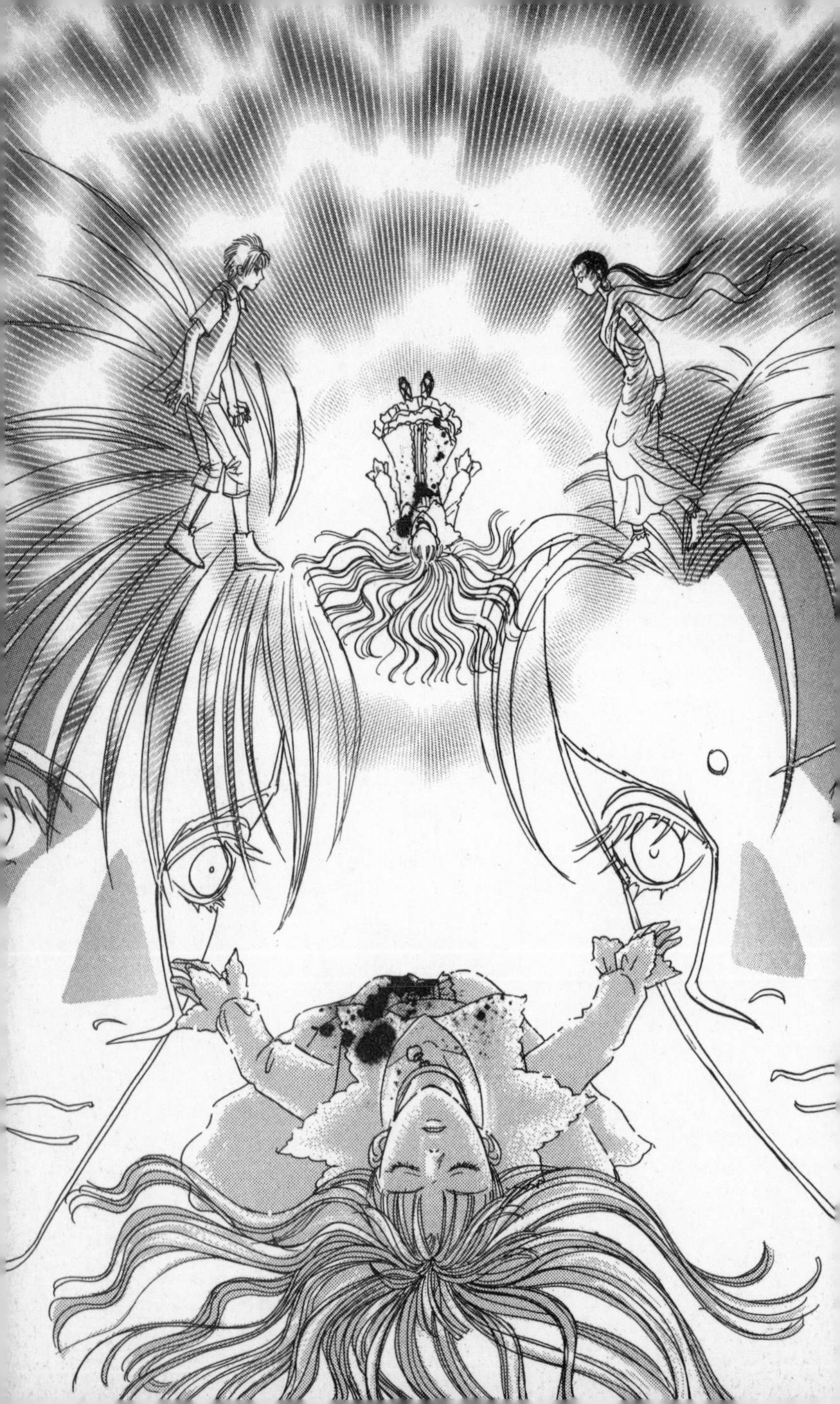

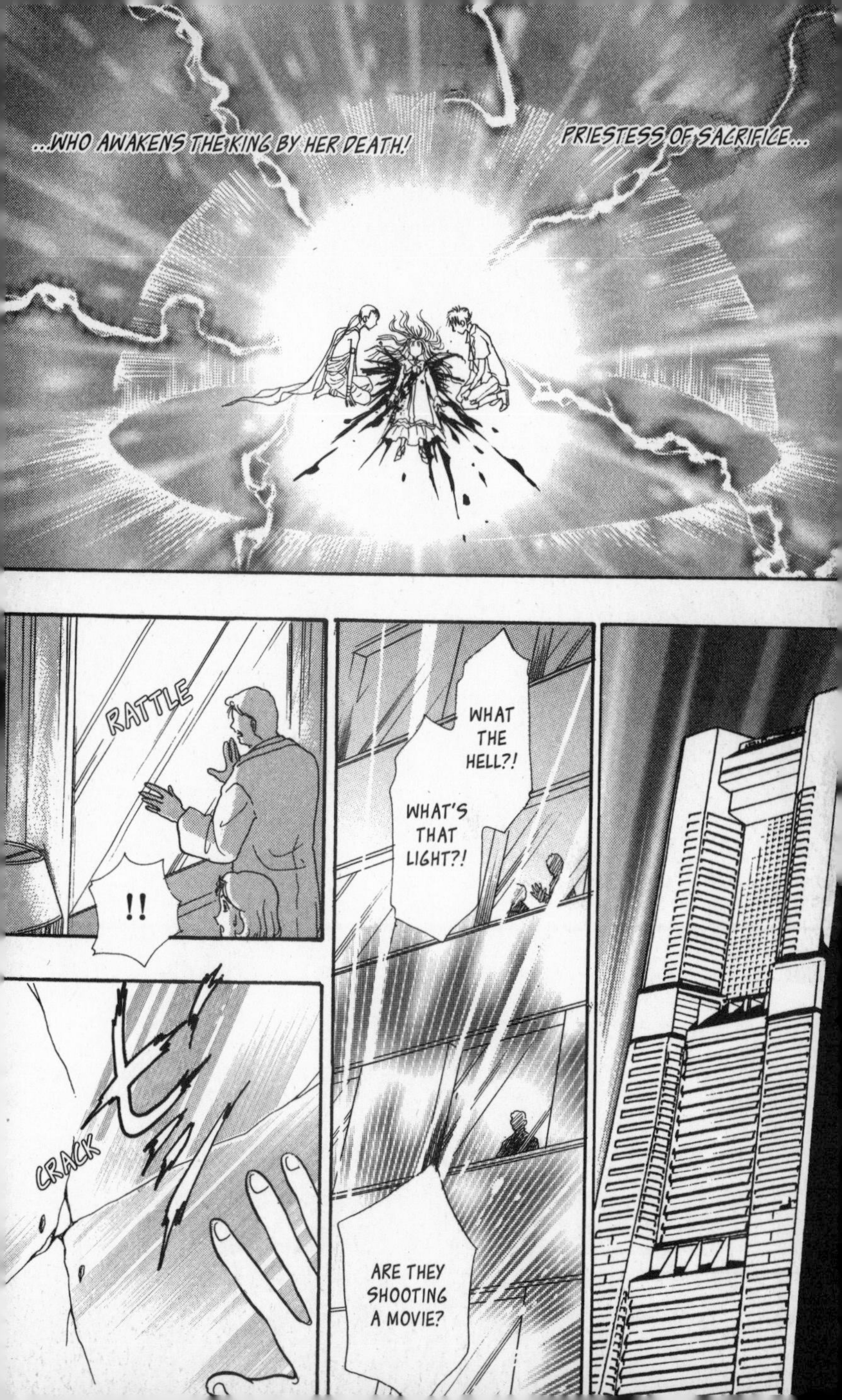
PRIESTESS OF SACRIFICE...
...WHO AWAKENS THE KING BY HER DEATH!
WHAT THE HELL?!
WHAT'S THAT LIGHT?!
ARE THEY SHOOTING A MOVIE?
RATTLE
!!
CRACK

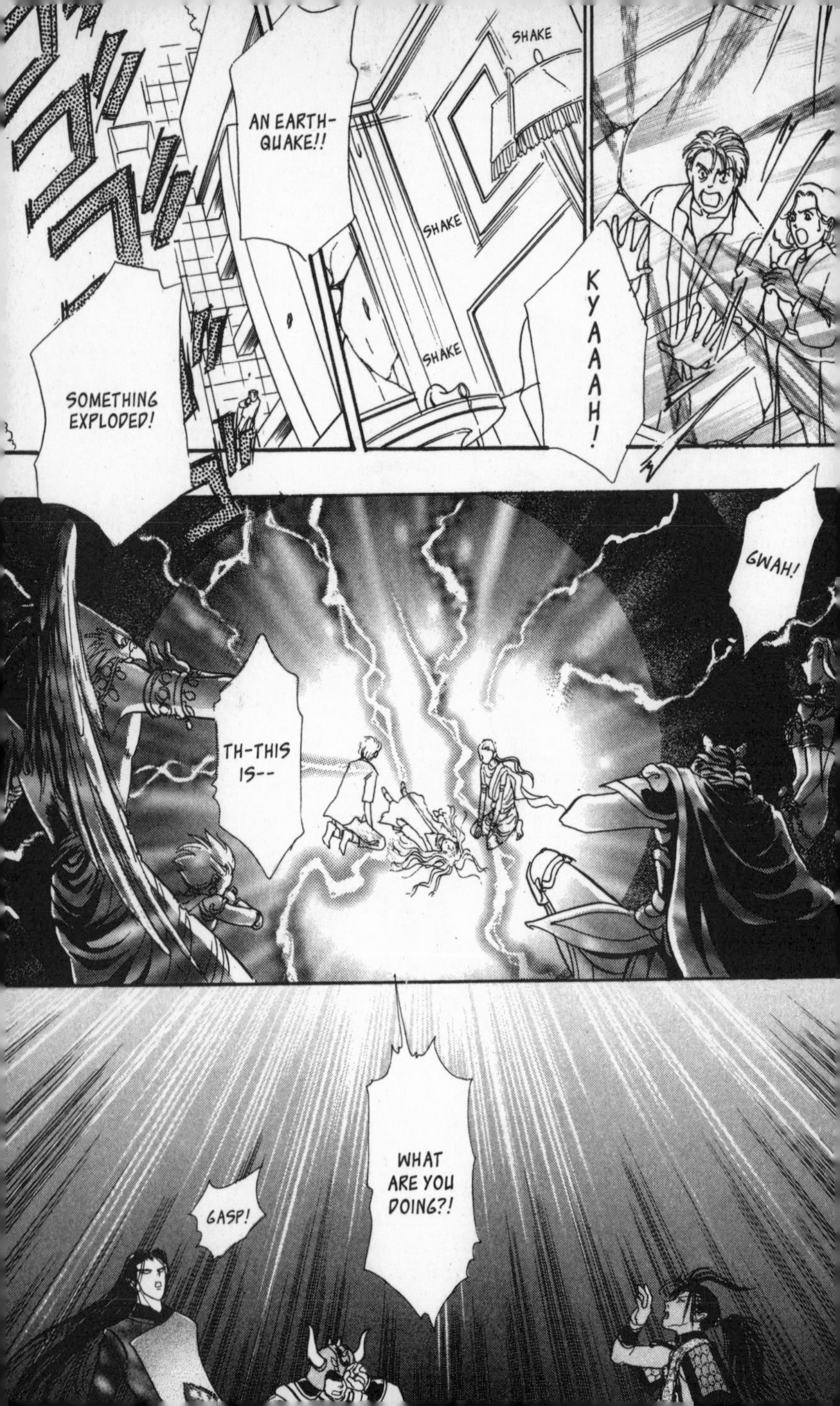
KYAAAAH!
SHAKE
SHAKE
SHAKE
AN EARTH-QUAKE!!
SOMETHING EXPLODED!
GWAH!
TH-THIS IS--
WHAT ARE YOU DOING?!
GASP!

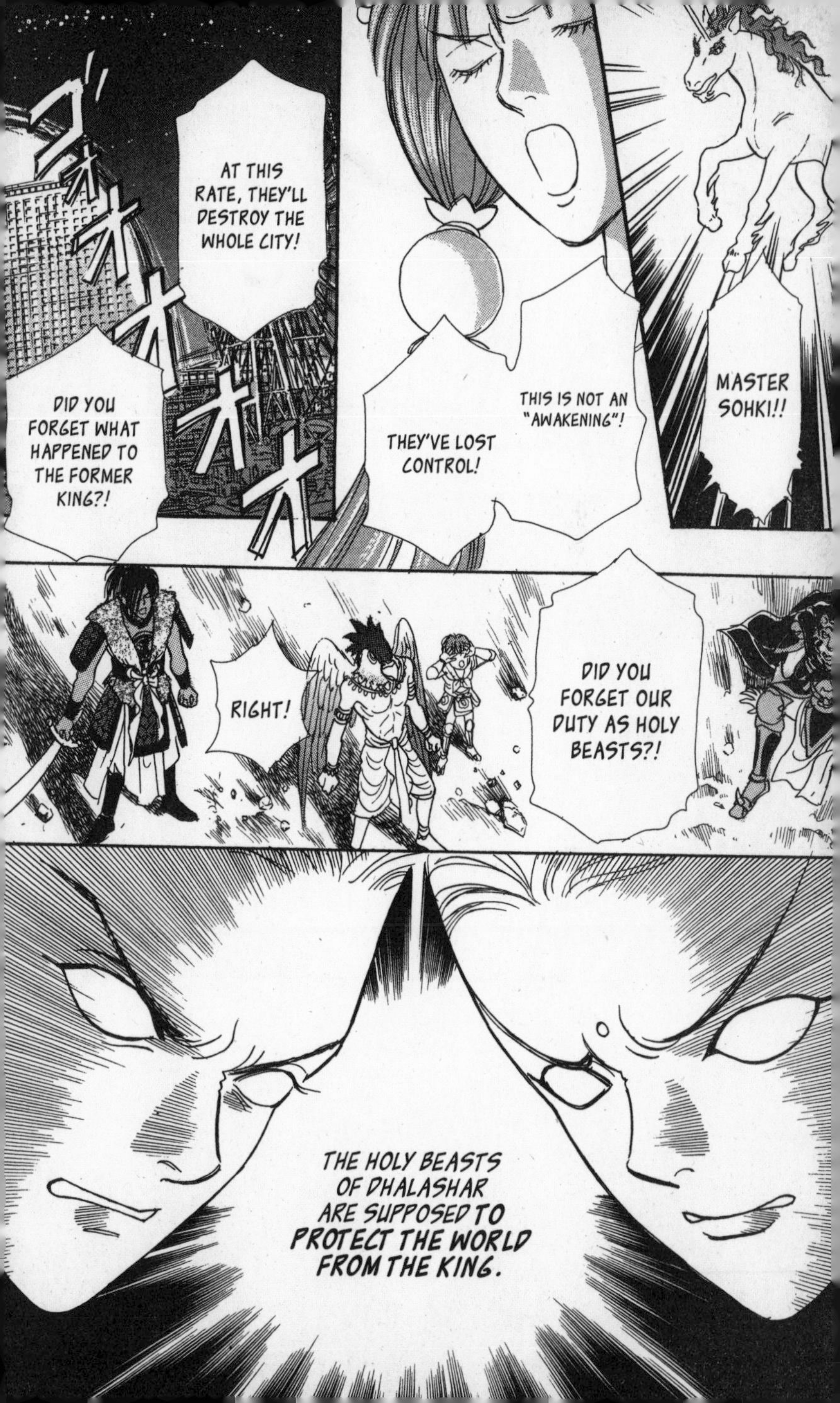
MASTER SOHKI!!
THIS IS NOT AN "AWAKENING"!
THEY'VE LOST CONTROL!
AT THIS RATE, THEY'LL DESTROY THE WHOLE CITY!
DID YOU FORGET WHAT HAPPENED TO THE FORMER KING?!
DID YOU FORGET OUR DUTY AS HOLY BEASTS?!
RIGHT!
THE HOLY BEASTS OF DHALASHAR ARE SUPPOSED TO PROTECT THE WORLD FROM THE KING.

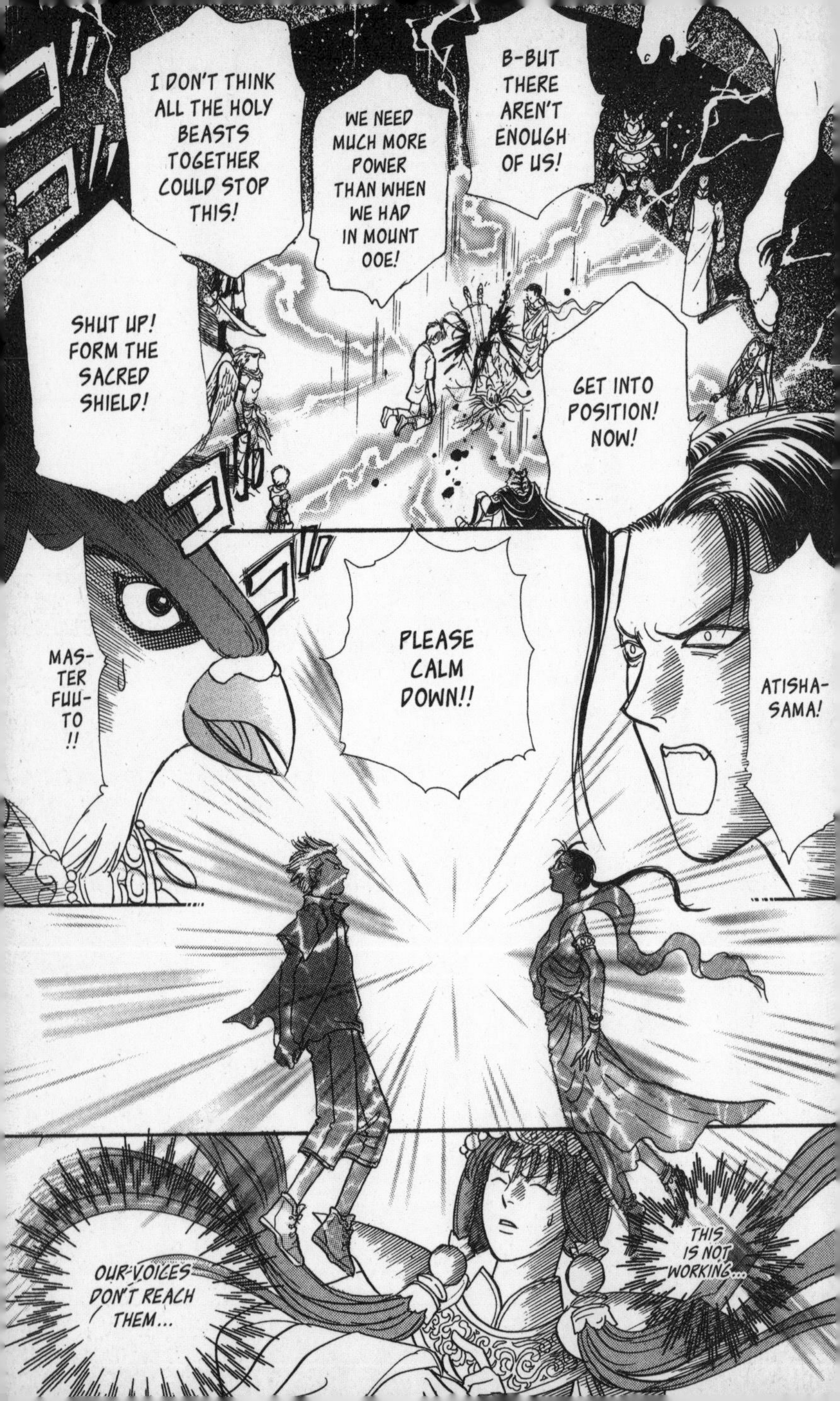
B-BUT THERE AREN'T ENOUGH OF US!
WE NEED MUCH MORE POWER THAN WHEN WE HAD IN MOUNT OOE!
I DON'T THINK ALL THE HOLY BEASTS TOGETHER COULD STOP THIS!
GET INTO POSITION! NOW!
SHUT UP! FORM THE SACRED SHIELD!
ATISHA-SAMA!
PLEASE CALM DOWN!!
MAS-TER FUU-TO !!
THIS IS NOT WORKING...
OUR VOICES DON'T REACH THEM...

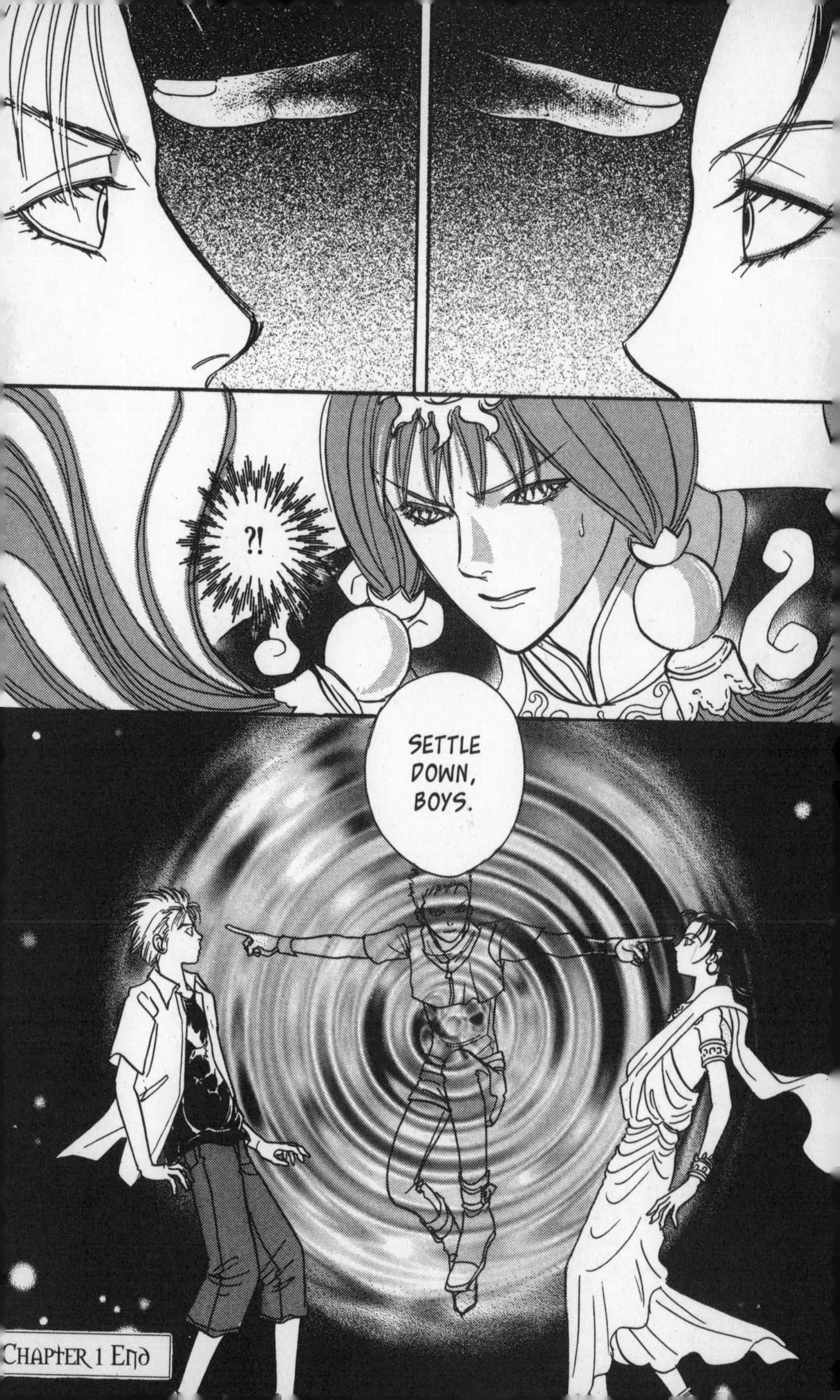
?!
SETTLE DOWN, BOYS.
CHAPTER 1 END

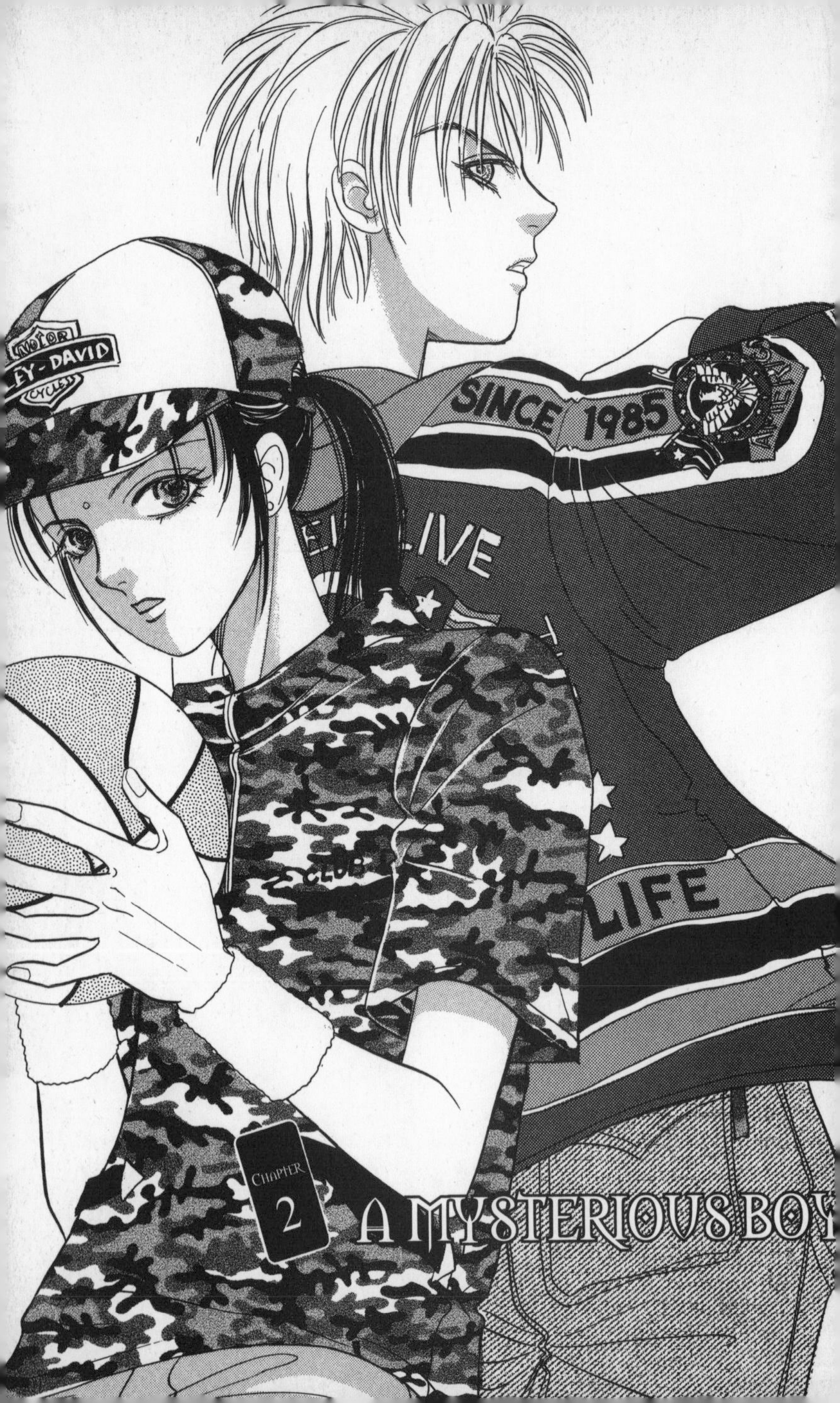
CHAPTER 2
A MYSTERIOUS BOY
SINCE 1985
LIFE

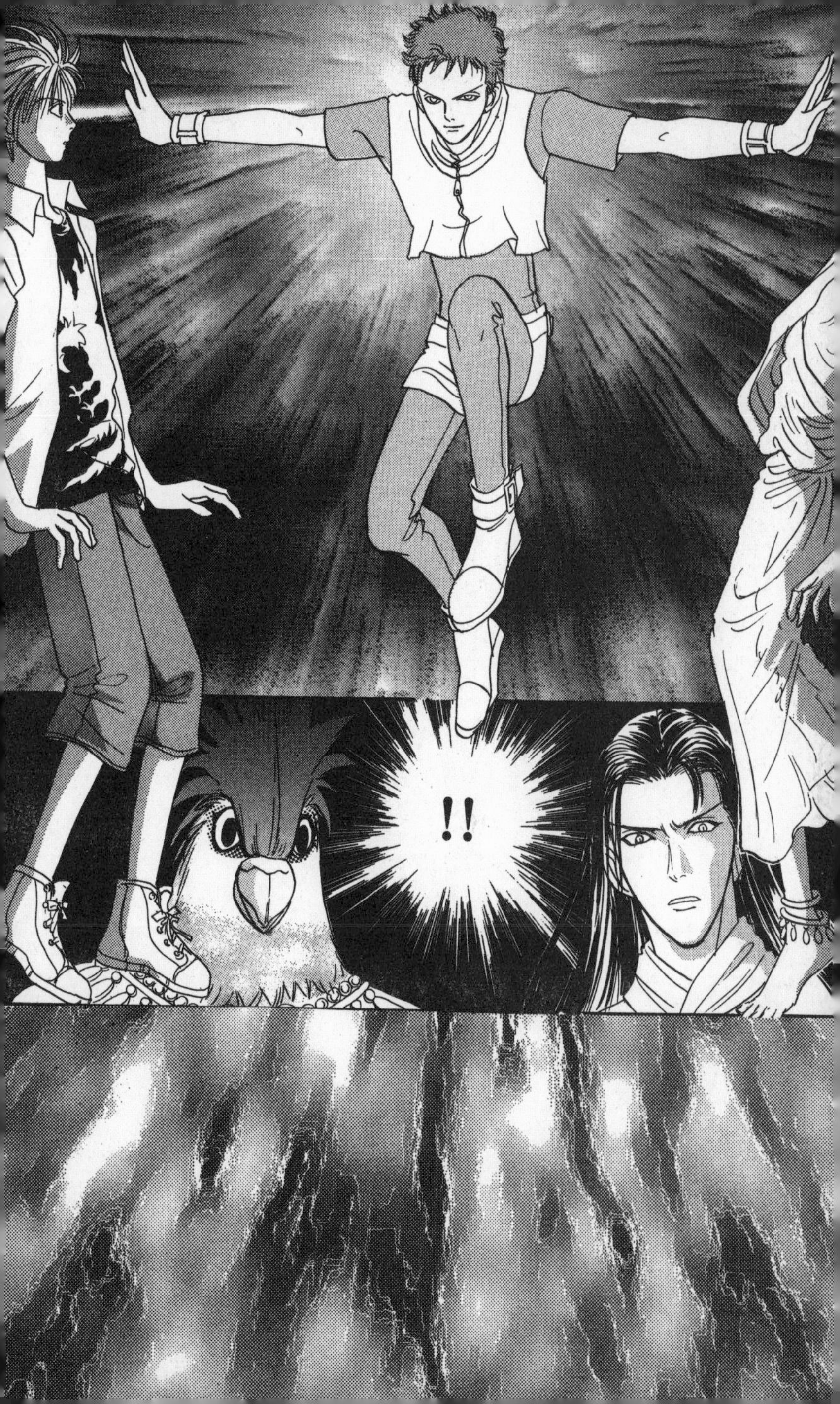
!!

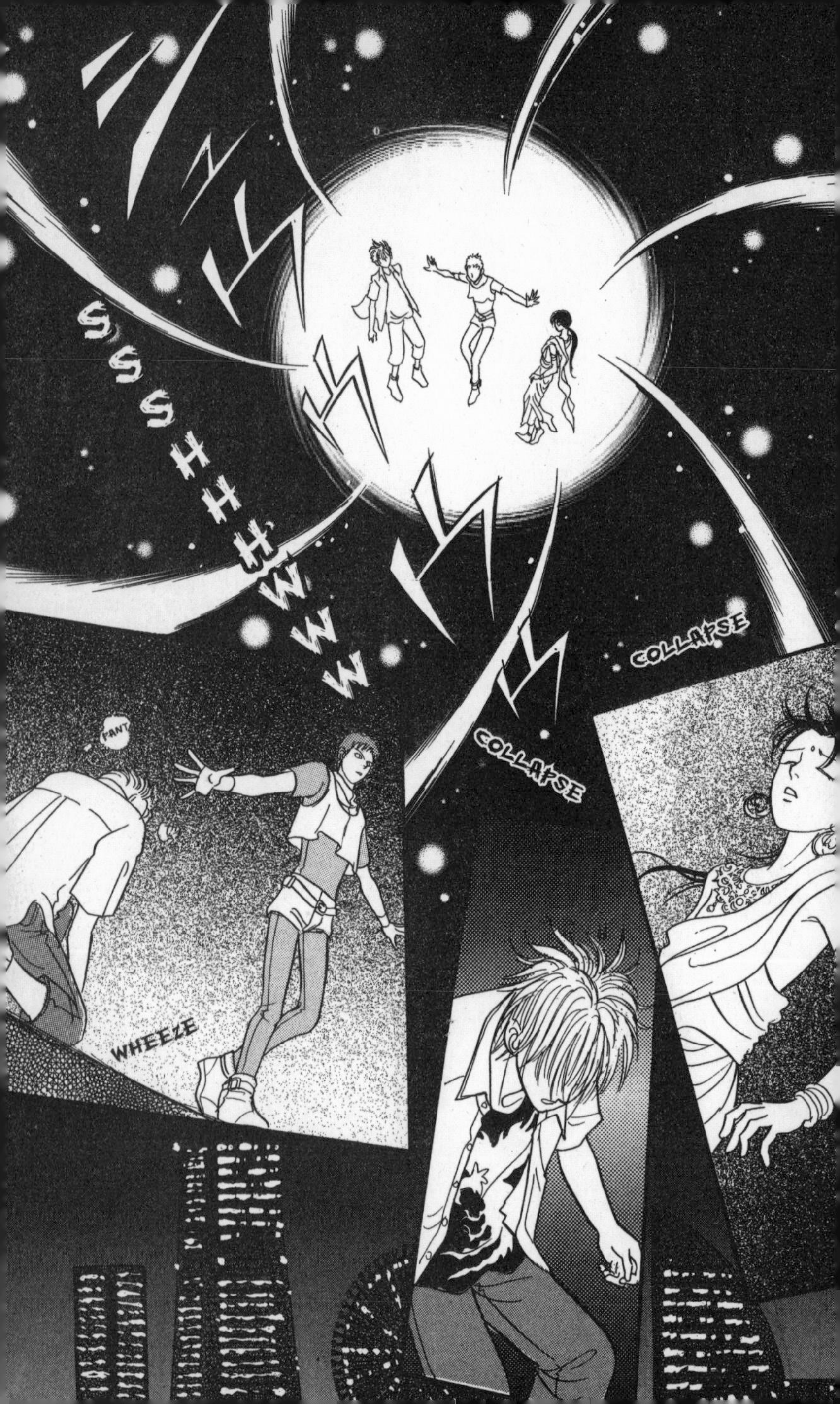
SSSHHHWWWW
COLLAPSE
COLLAPSE
PANT
WHEEZE

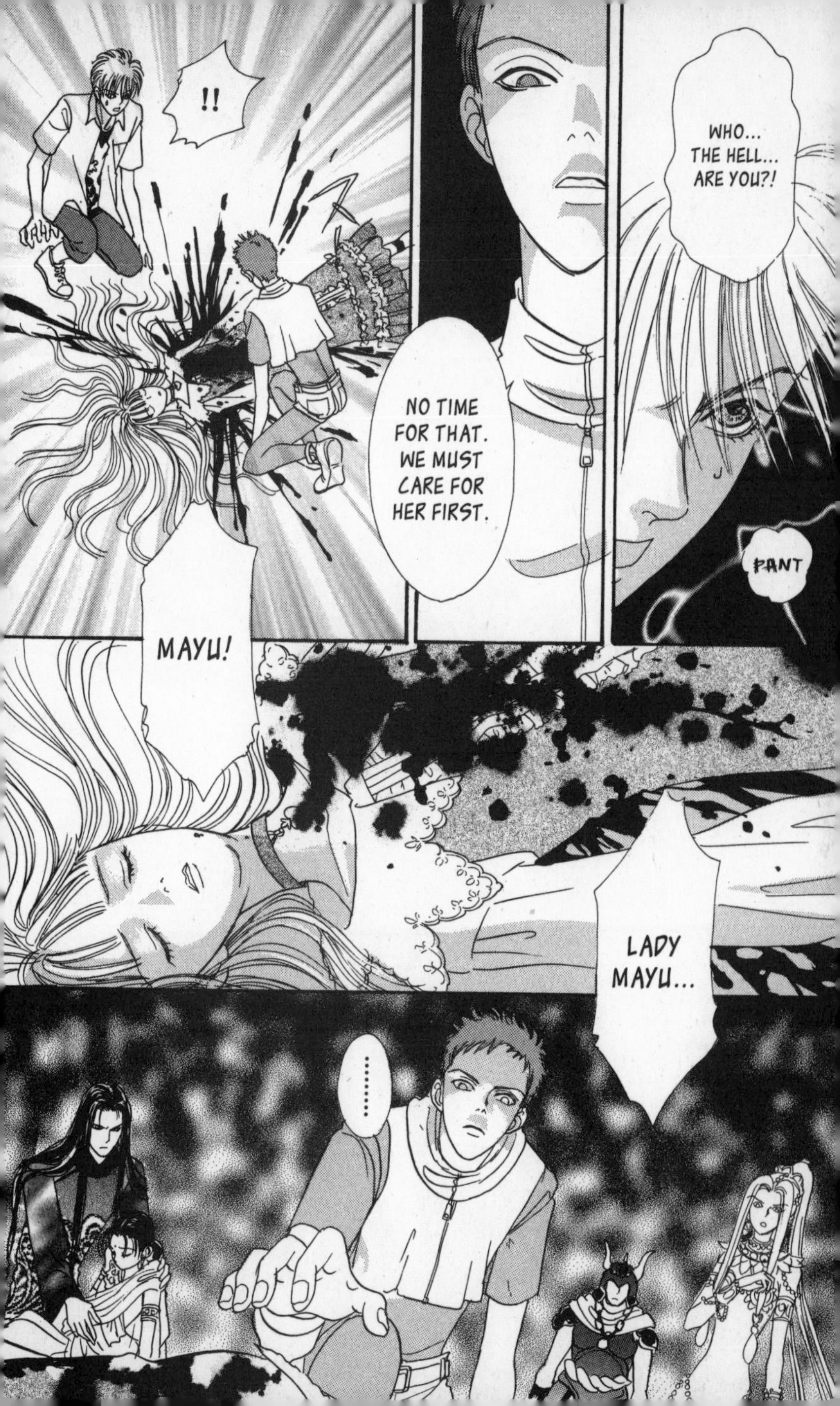
WHO... THE HELL... ARE YOU?!
PANT
NO TIME FOR THAT. WE MUST CARE FOR HER FIRST.
!!
LADY MAYU...
MAYU!
....

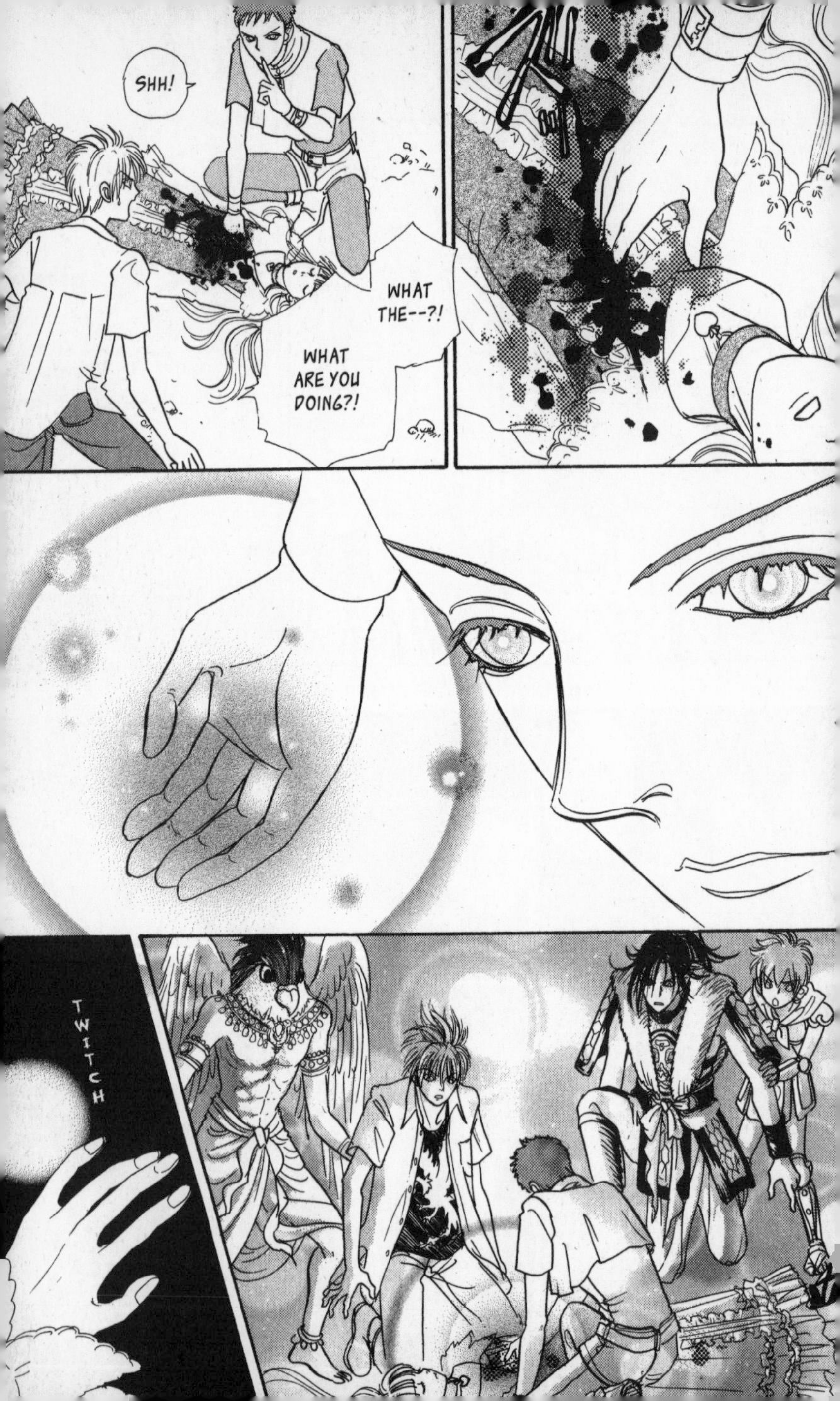
SHH!
WHAT THE--?!
WHAT ARE YOU DOING?!
TWITCH

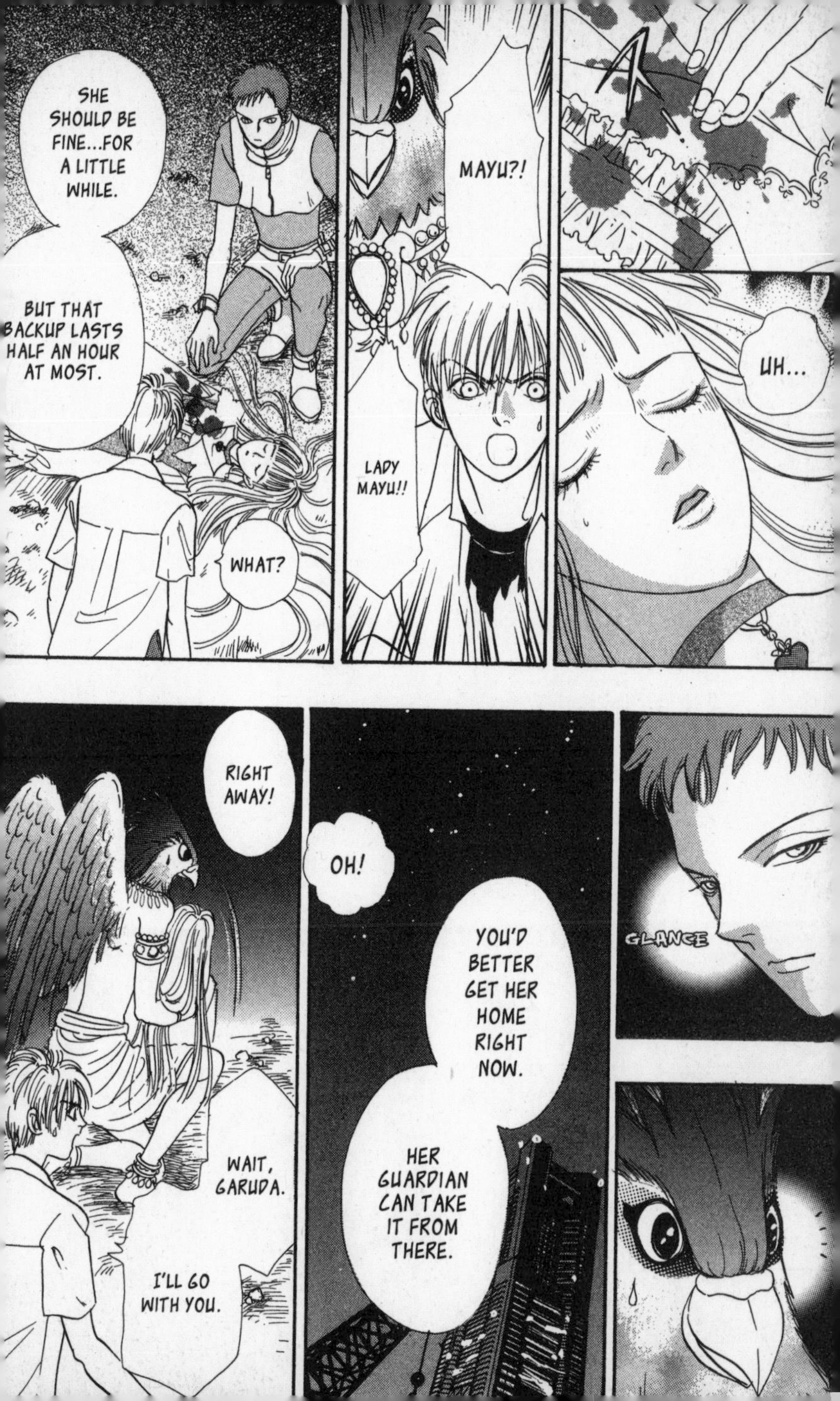
UH...
MAYU?!
LADY MAYU!!
SHE SHOULD BE FINE...FOR A LITTLE WHILE.
BUT THAT BACKUP LASTS HALF AN HOUR AT MOST.
WHAT?
GLANCE
OH!
YOU'D BETTER GET HER HOME RIGHT NOW.
HER GUARDIAN CAN TAKE IT FROM THERE.
RIGHT AWAY!
WAIT, GARUDA.
I'LL GO WITH YOU.

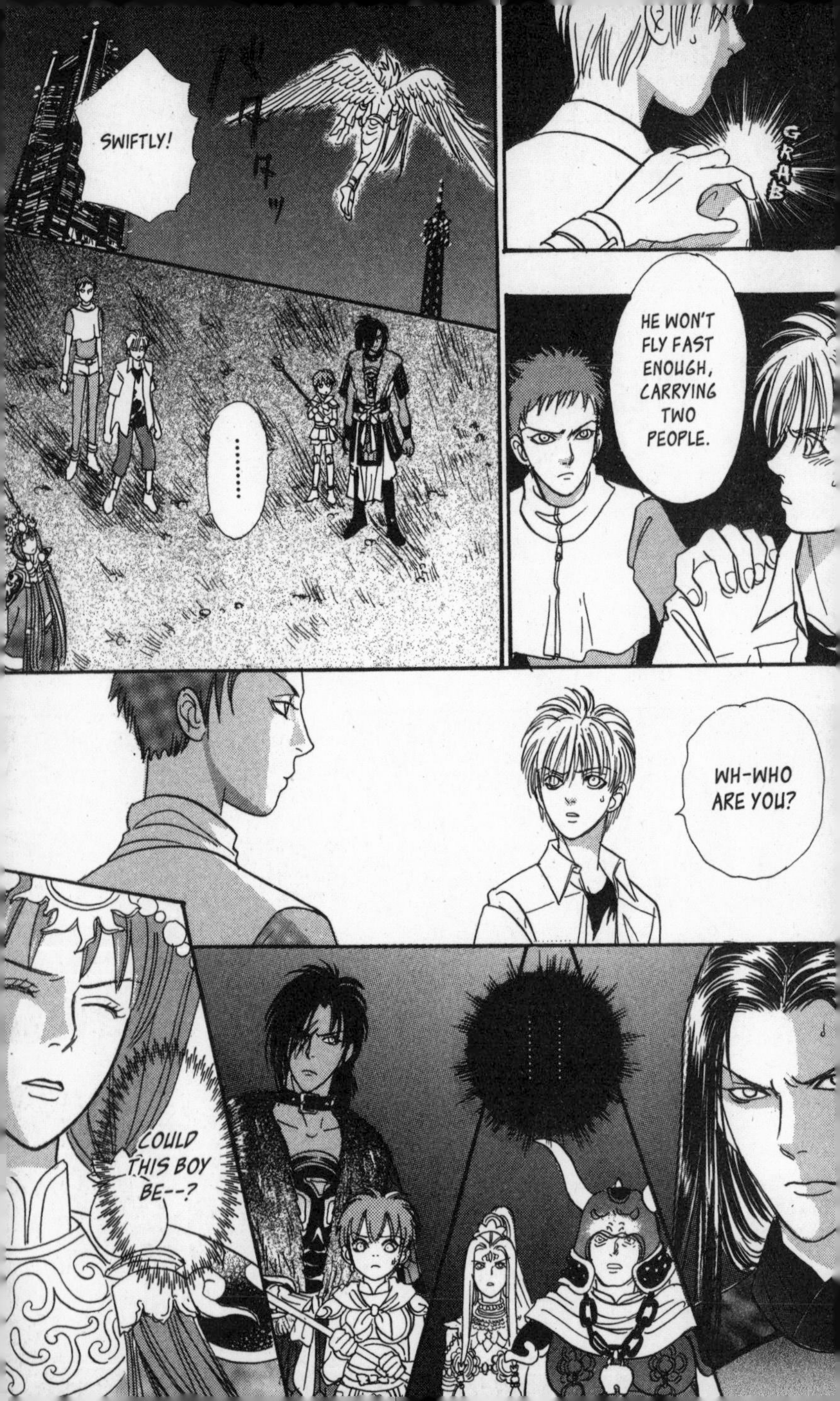
GRAB
SWIFTLY!
HE WON'T FLY FAST ENOUGH, CARRYING TWO PEOPLE.
......
WH-WHO ARE YOU?
......
COULD THIS BOY BE--?

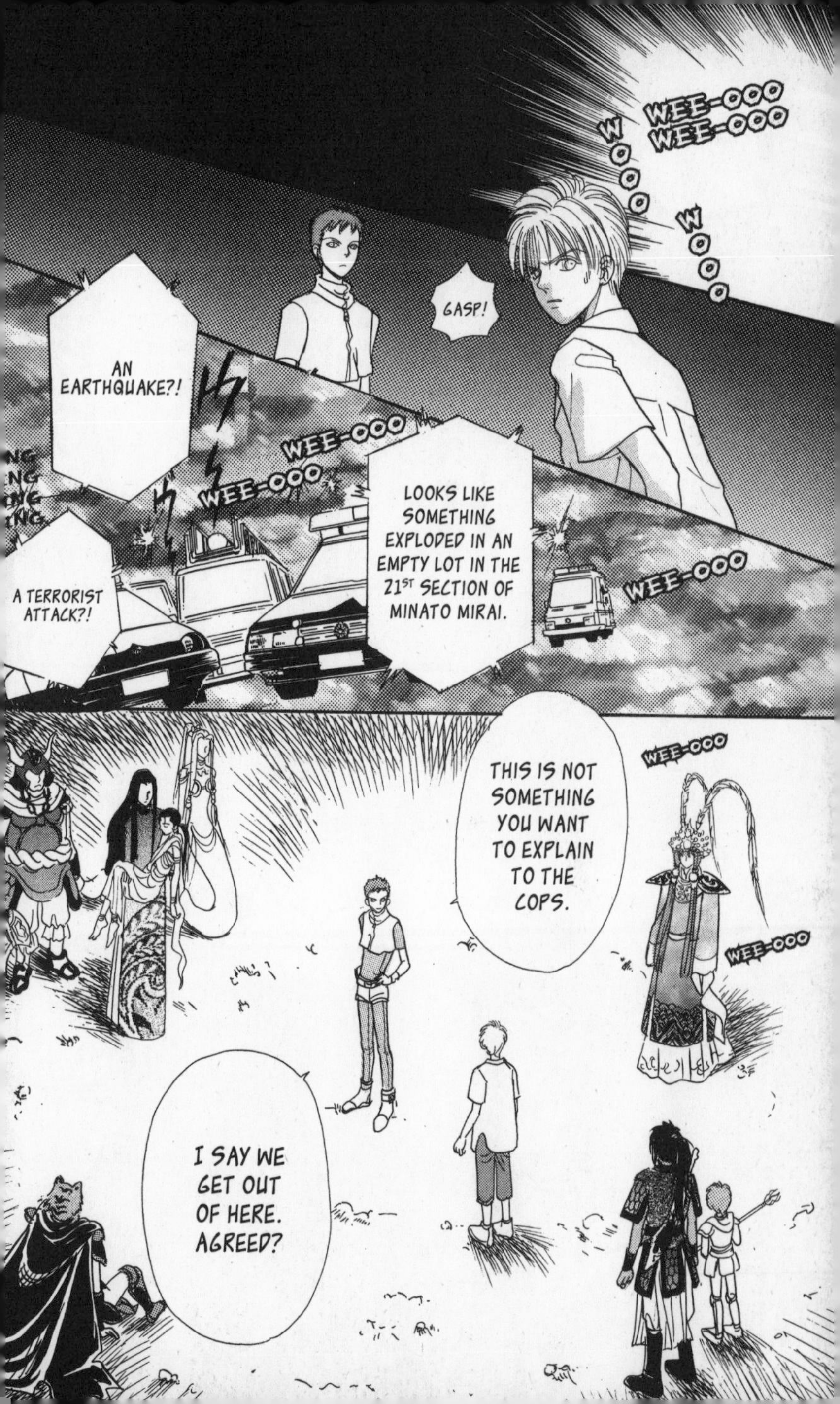
WEE-OOO
WEE-OOO
WOOOO
WOOOO
GASP!
WEE-OOO
LOOKS LIKE SOMETHING EXPLODED IN AN EMPTY LOT IN THE 21ST SECTION OF MINATO MIRAI.
WEE-OOO
WEE-OOO
AN EARTHQUAKE?!
A TERRORIST ATTACK?!
WEE-OOO
WEE-OOO
THIS IS NOT SOMETHING YOU WANT TO EXPLAIN TO THE COPS.
I SAY WE GET OUT OF HERE. AGREED?

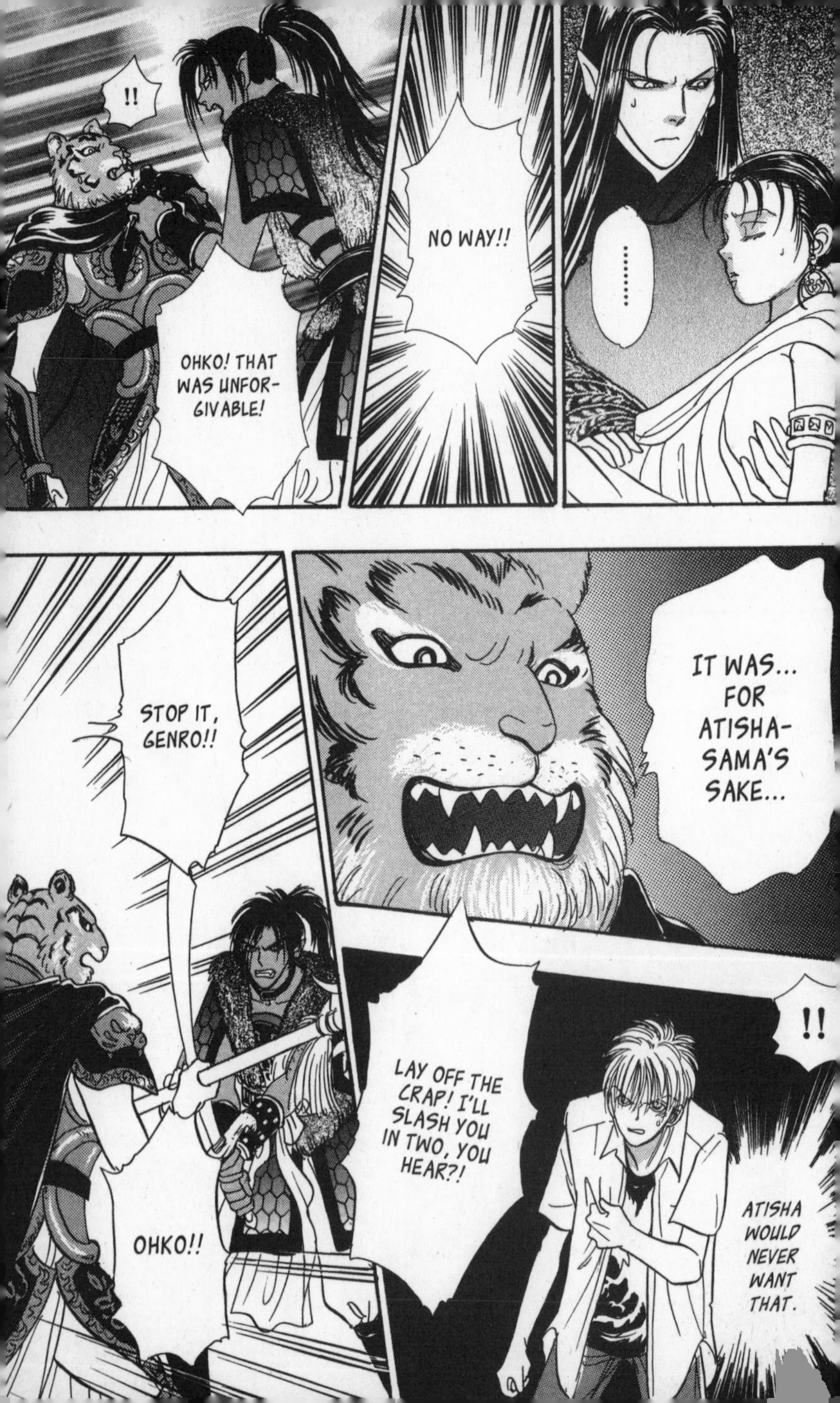

......
NO WAY!!
!!
OHKO! THAT WAS UNFORGIVABLE!
IT WAS... FOR ATISHA-SAMA'S SAKE...
!!
LAY OFF THE CRAP! I'LL SLASH YOU IN TWO, YOU HEAR?!
ATISHA WOULD NEVER WANT THAT.
STOP IT, GENRO!!
OHKO!!

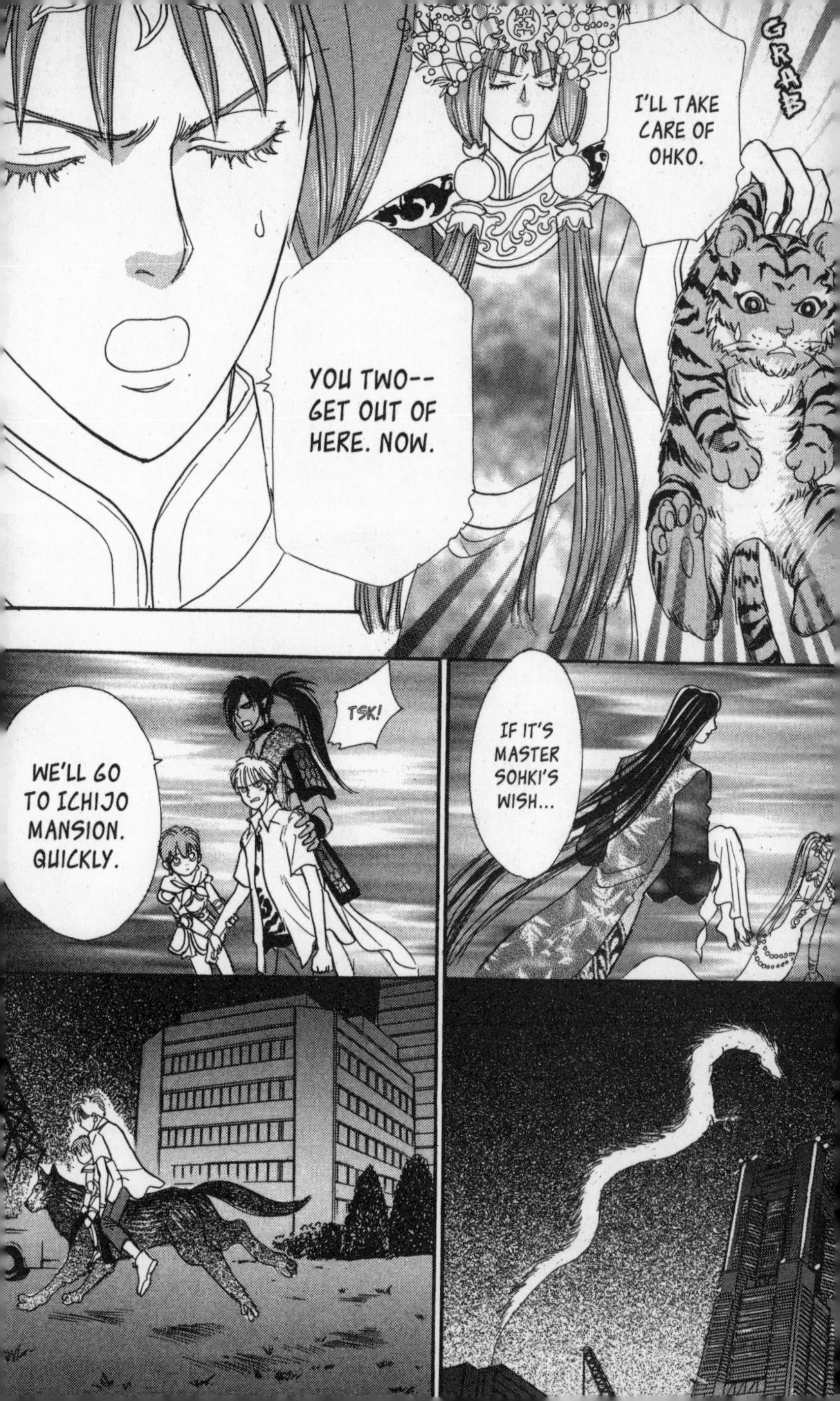
GRAB
I'LL TAKE CARE OF OHKO.
YOU TWO-- GET OUT OF HERE. NOW.
IF IT'S MASTER SOHKI'S WISH...
TSK!
WE'LL GO TO ICHIJO MANSION. QUICKLY.

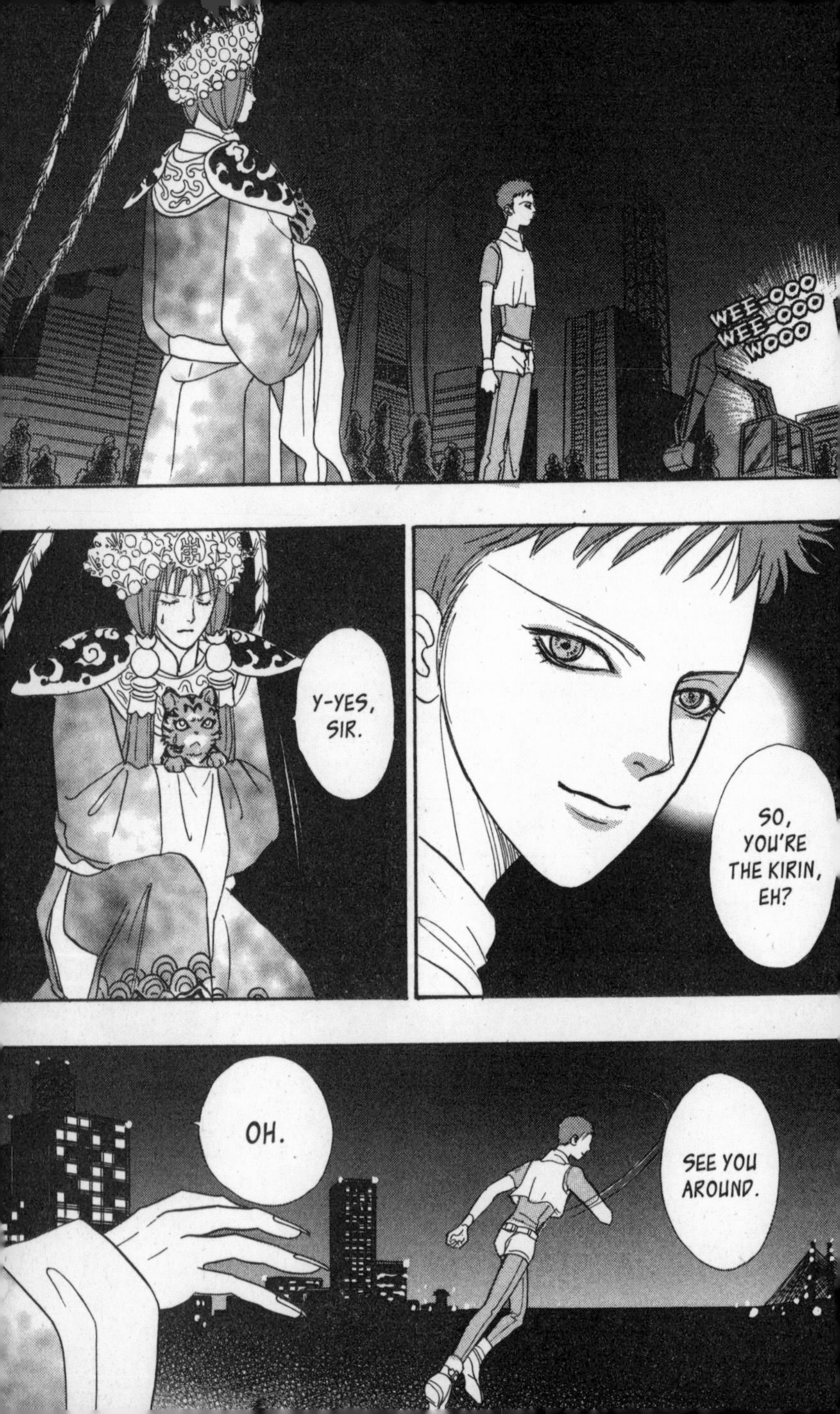
WEE-OOO WEE-OOO WOOO
SO, YOU'RE THE KIRIN, EH?
Y-YES, SIR.
SEE YOU AROUND.
OH.

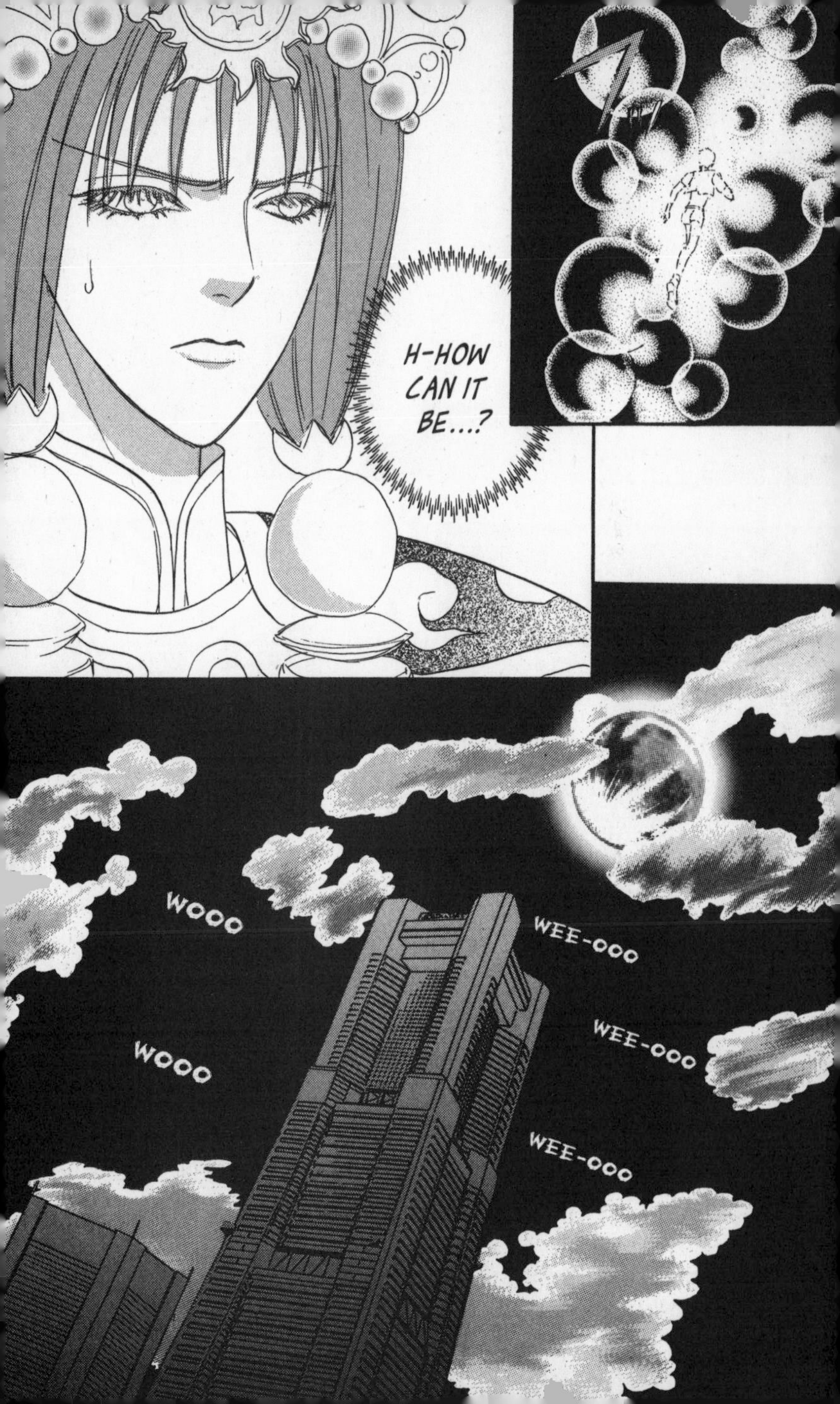
H-HOW CAN IT BE...?
WEE-OOO
WEE-OOO
WEE-OOO
WOOO
WOOO

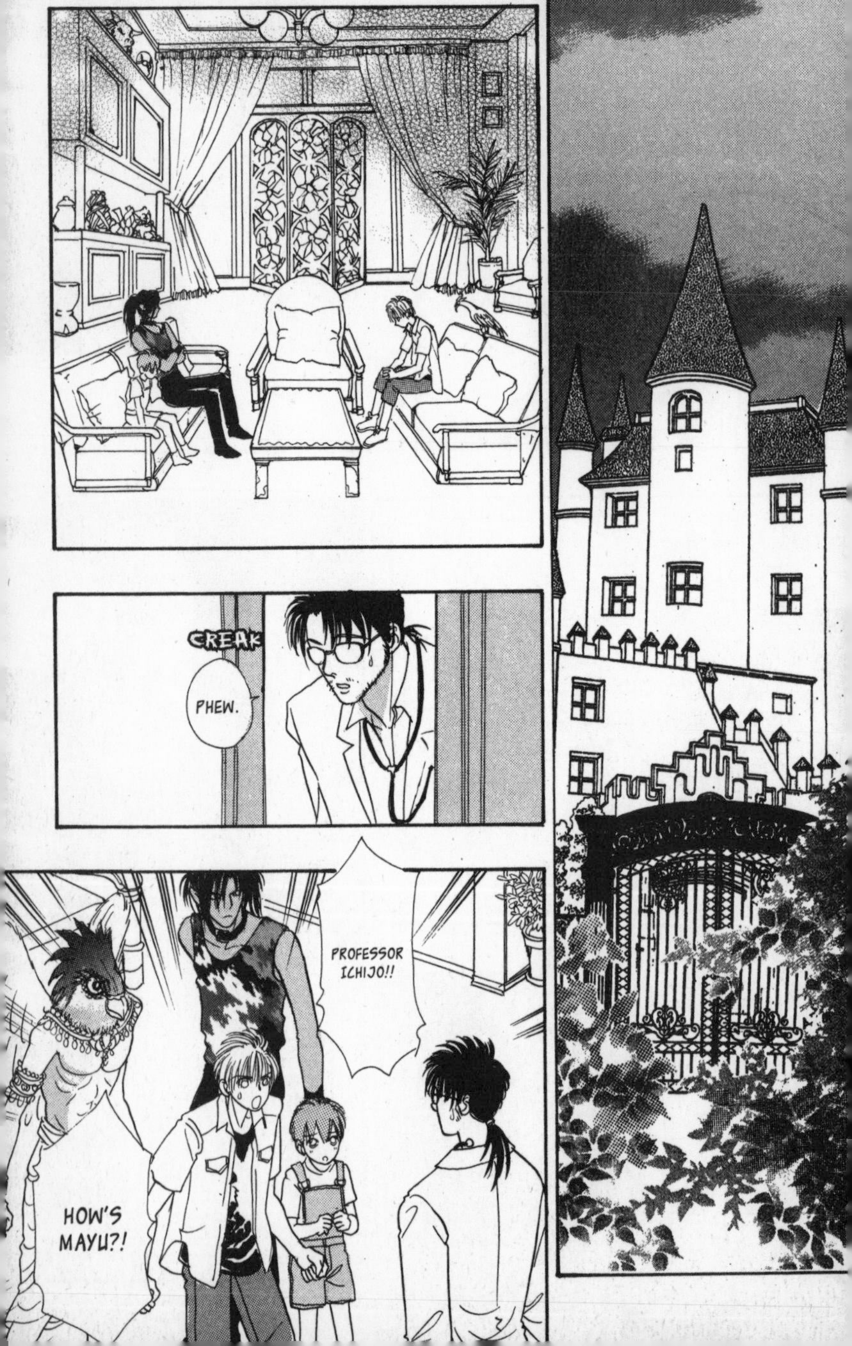
CREAK
PHEW.
PROFESSOR ICHIJO!!
HOW'S MAYU?!

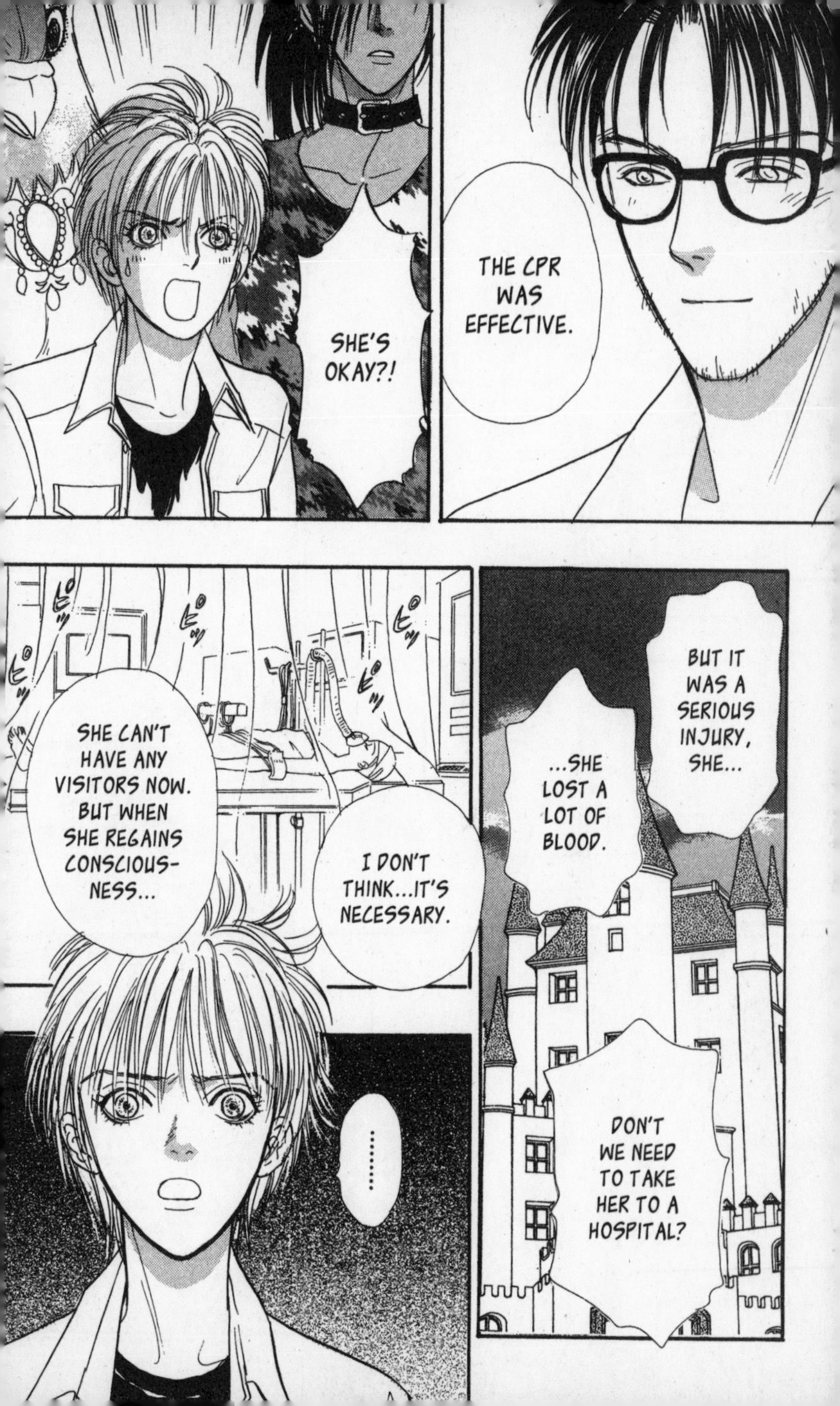
THE CPR WAS EFFECTIVE.
SHE'S OKAY?!
BUT IT WAS A SERIOUS INJURY, SHE...
...SHE LOST A LOT OF BLOOD.
DON'T WE NEED TO TAKE HER TO A HOSPITAL?
ピッ
ピッ
ピッ
ピッ
ピッ
I DON'T THINK...IT'S NECESSARY.
SHE CAN'T HAVE ANY VISITORS NOW. BUT WHEN SHE REGAINS CONSCIOUS-NESS...
......

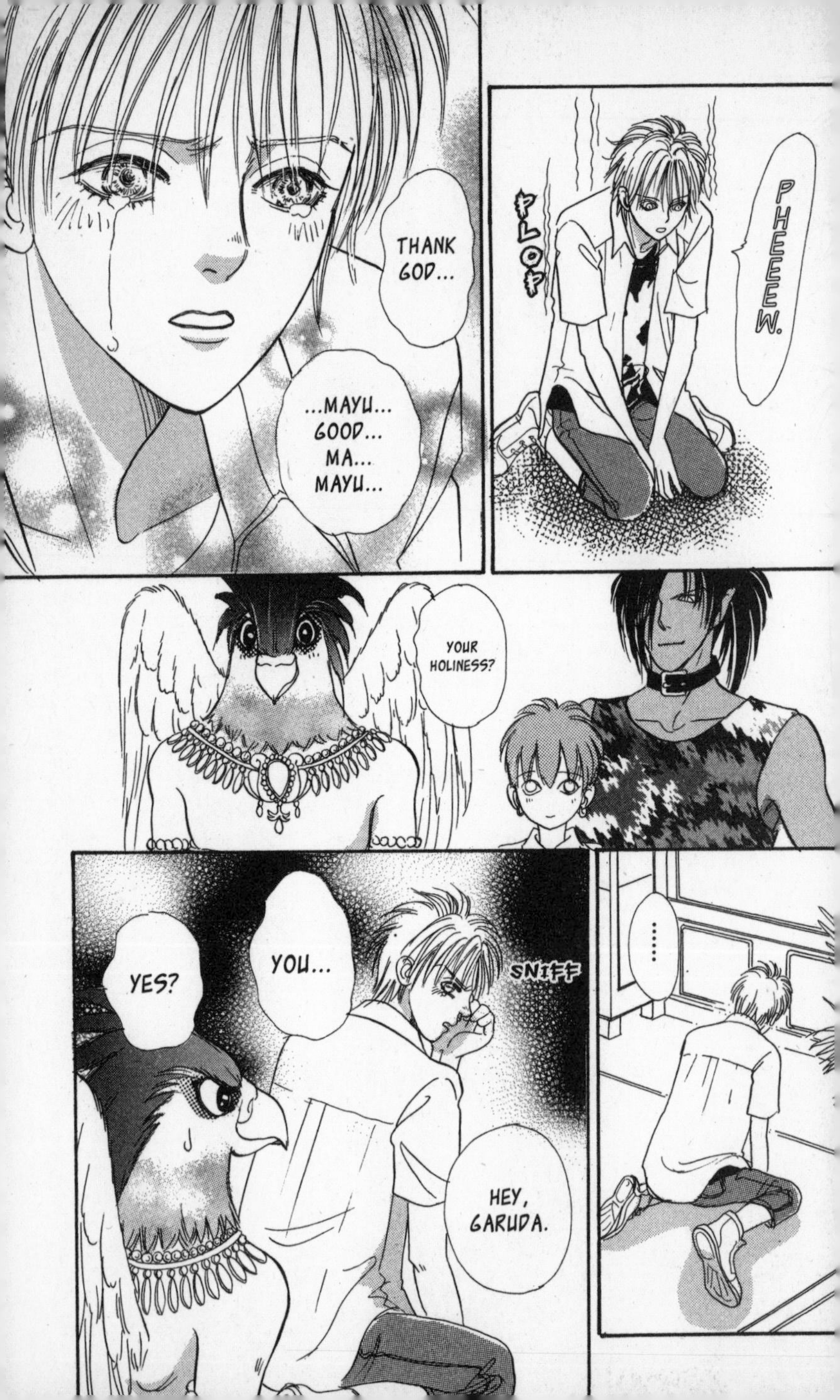
PHEEEW.
PLOP
THANK GOD...
...MAYU... GOOD... MA... MAYU...
YOUR HOLINESS?
......
SNIFF
YOU...
YES?
HEY, GARUDA.

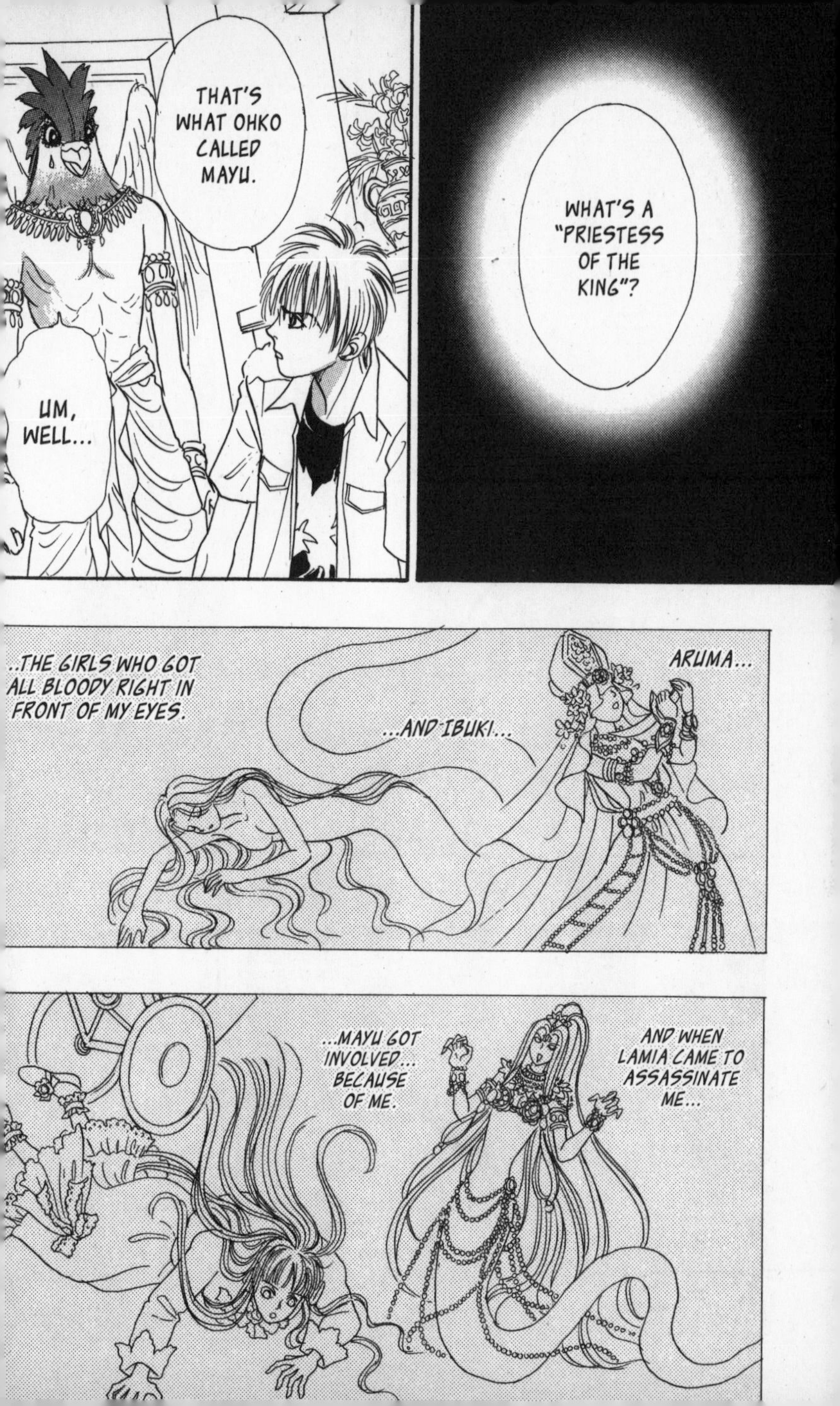
WHAT'S A "PRIESTESS OF THE KING"?
THAT'S WHAT OHKO CALLED MAYU.
UM, WELL...
ARUMA...
...AND IBUKI...
..THE GIRLS WHO GOT ALL BLOODY RIGHT IN FRONT OF MY EYES.
AND WHEN LAMIA CAME TO ASSASSINATE ME...
...MAYU GOT INVOLVED... BECAUSE OF ME.

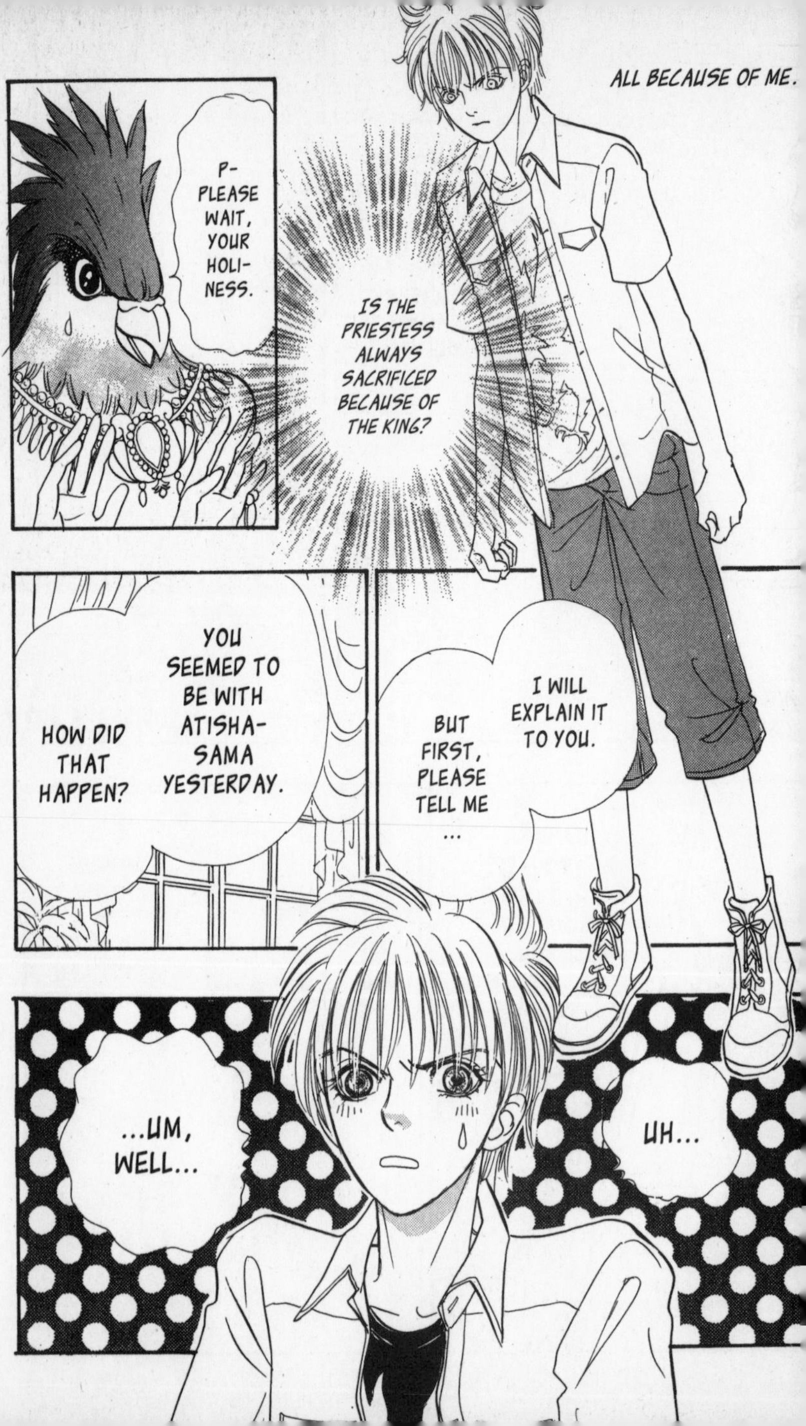
ALL BECAUSE OF ME.
IS THE PRIESTESS ALWAYS SACRIFICED BECAUSE OF THE KING?
P-PLEASE WAIT, YOUR HOLINESS.
I WILL EXPLAIN IT TO YOU.
BUT FIRST, PLEASE TELL ME ...
YOU SEEMED TO BE WITH ATISHA-SAMA YESTERDAY.
HOW DID THAT HAPPEN?
UH...
...UM, WELL...

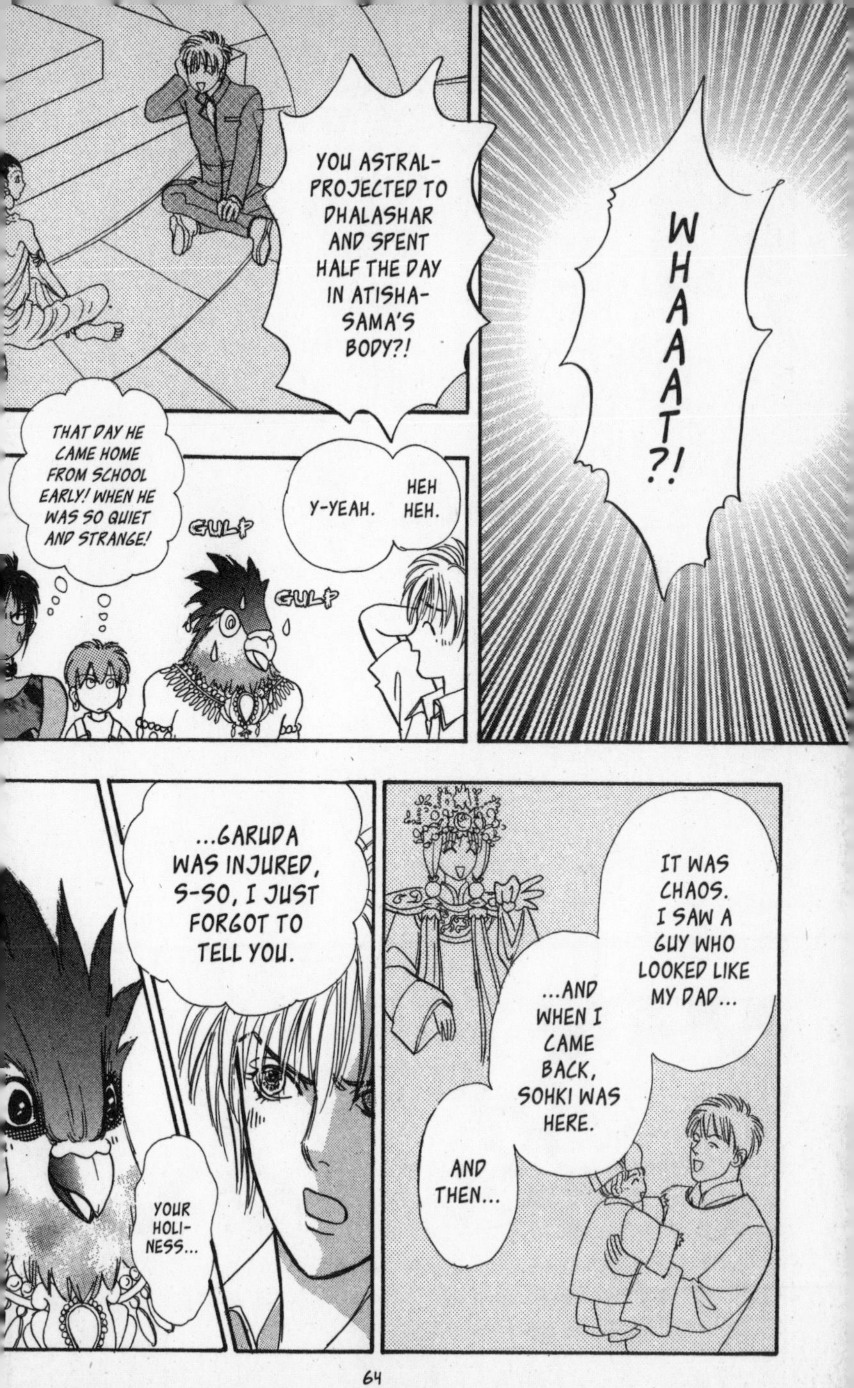
WHAAAAT?!
YOU ASTRAL-PROJECTED TO DHALASHAR AND SPENT HALF THE DAY IN ATISHA-SAMA'S BODY?!
HEH HEH.
Y-YEAH.
GULP
GULP
THAT DAY HE CAME HOME FROM SCHOOL EARLY! WHEN HE WAS SO QUIET AND STRANGE!
IT WAS CHAOS. I SAW A GUY WHO LOOKED LIKE MY DAD...
...AND WHEN I CAME BACK, SOHKI WAS HERE.
AND THEN...
...GARUDA WAS INJURED, S-SO, I JUST FORGOT TO TELL YOU.
YOUR HOLINESS...

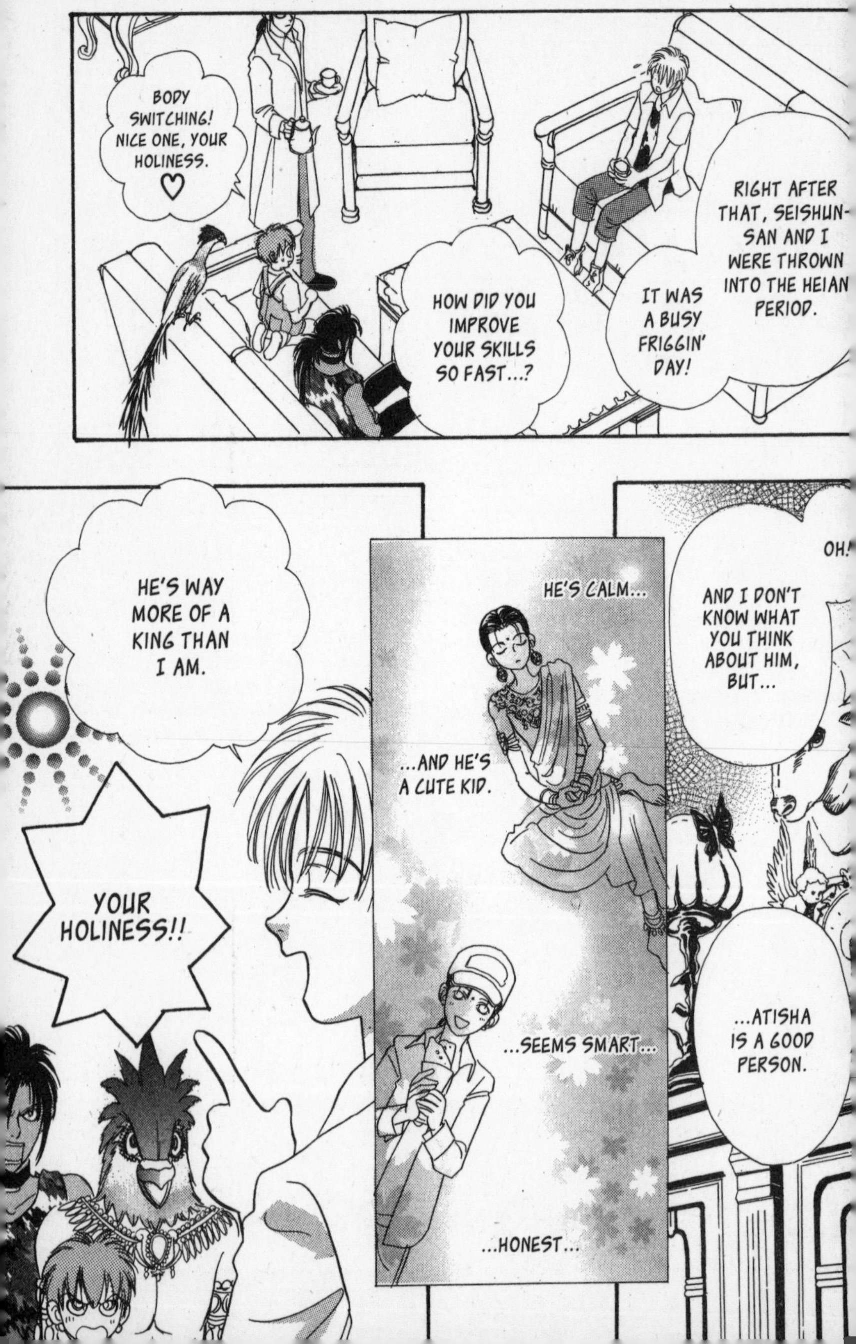
RIGHT AFTER THAT, SEISHUN-SAN AND I WERE THROWN INTO THE HEIAN PERIOD.
IT WAS A BUSY FRIGGIN' DAY!
HOW DID YOU IMPROVE YOUR SKILLS SO FAST...?
BODY SWITCHING! NICE ONE, YOUR HOLINESS. ♡
OH!
AND I DON'T KNOW WHAT YOU THINK ABOUT HIM, BUT...
...ATISHA IS A GOOD PERSON.
HE'S CALM...
...AND HE'S A CUTE KID.
...SEEMS SMART...
...HONEST...
HE'S WAY MORE OF A KING THAN I AM.
YOUR HOLINESS!!

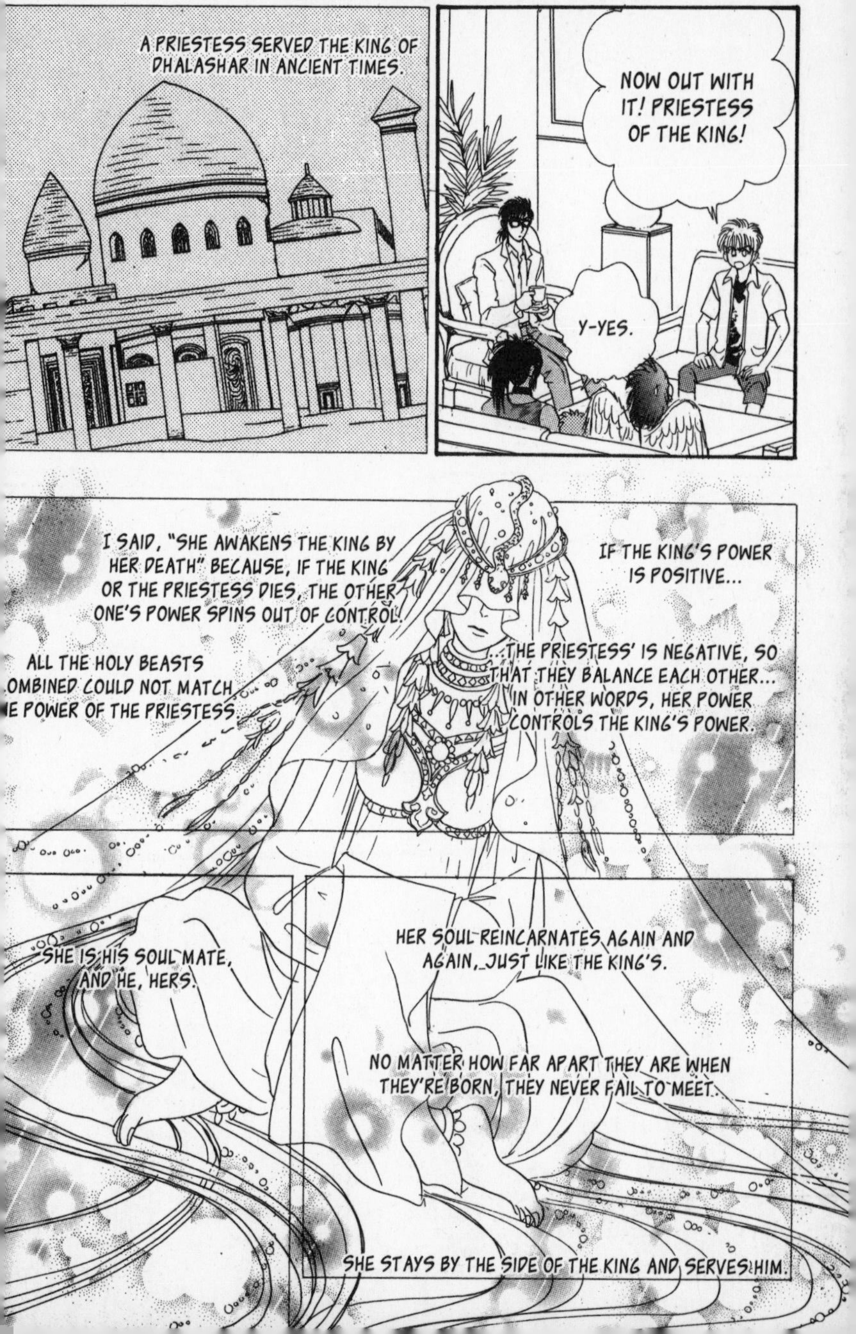

NOW OUT WITH IT! PRIESTESS OF THE KING!
Y-YES.
A PRIESTESS SERVED THE KING OF DHALASHAR IN ANCIENT TIMES.
IF THE KING'S POWER IS POSITIVE...
...THE PRIESTESS' IS NEGATIVE, SO THAT THEY BALANCE EACH OTHER... IN OTHER WORDS, HER POWER CONTROLS THE KING'S POWER.
I SAID, "SHE AWAKENS THE KING BY HER DEATH" BECAUSE, IF THE KING OR THE PRIESTESS DIES, THE OTHER ONE'S POWER SPINS OUT OF CONTROL.
ALL THE HOLY BEASTS OMBINED COULD NOT MATCH E POWER OF THE PRIESTESS.
HER SOUL REINCARNATES AGAIN AND AGAIN, JUST LIKE THE KING'S.
NO MATTER HOW FAR APART THEY ARE WHEN THEY'RE BORN, THEY NEVER FAIL TO MEET.
SHE STAYS BY THE SIDE OF THE KING AND SERVES HIM.
SHE IS HIS SOUL MATE, AND HE, HERS.

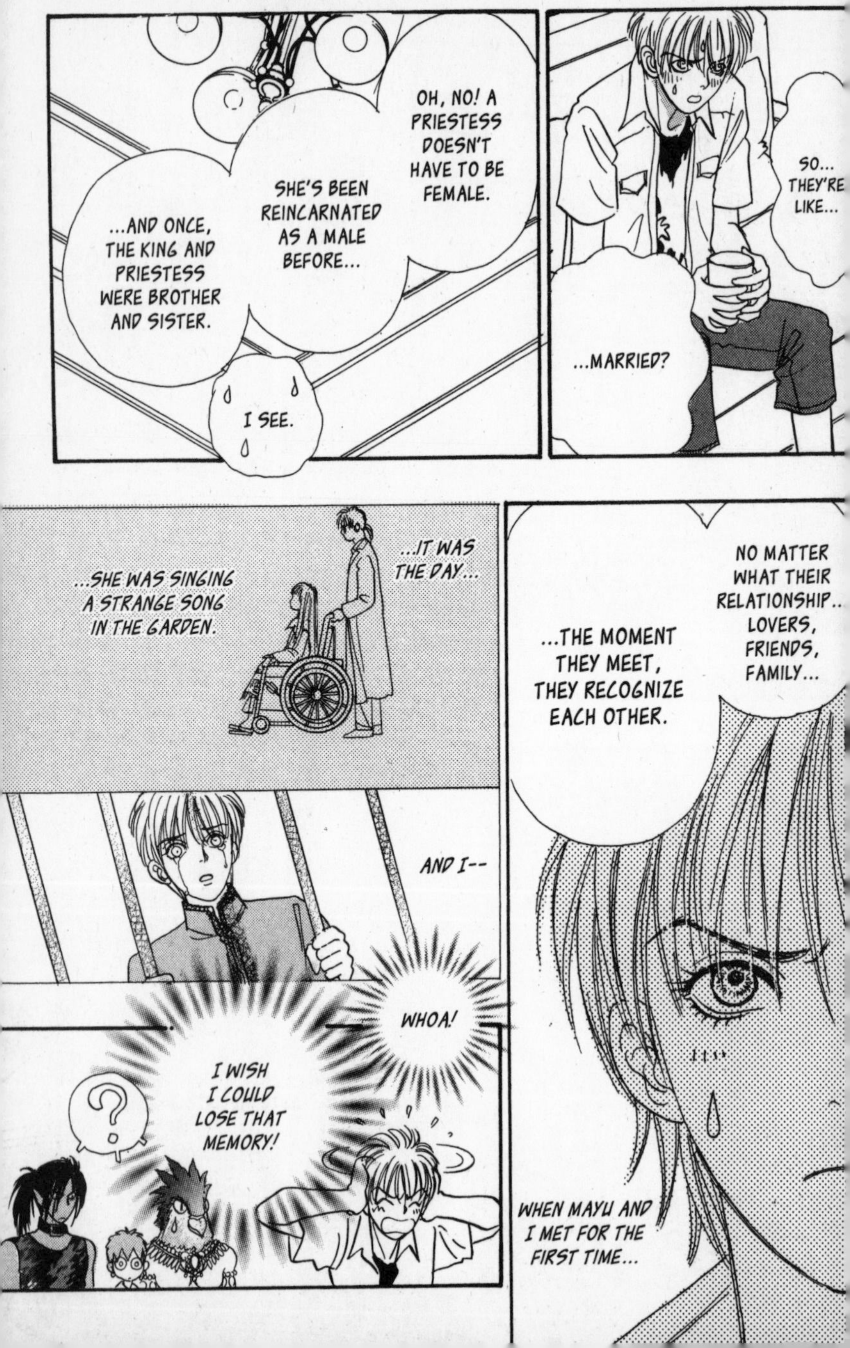
SO... THEY'RE LIKE...
...MARRIED?
OH, NO! A PRIESTESS DOESN'T HAVE TO BE FEMALE.
SHE'S BEEN REINCARNATED AS A MALE BEFORE...
...AND ONCE, THE KING AND PRIESTESS WERE BROTHER AND SISTER.
I SEE.
NO MATTER WHAT THEIR RELATIONSHIP... LOVERS, FRIENDS, FAMILY...
...THE MOMENT THEY MEET, THEY RECOGNIZE EACH OTHER.
WHEN MAYU AND I MET FOR THE FIRST TIME...
...IT WAS THE DAY...
...SHE WAS SINGING A STRANGE SONG IN THE GARDEN.
AND I--
WHOA!
I WISH I COULD LOSE THAT MEMORY!
?

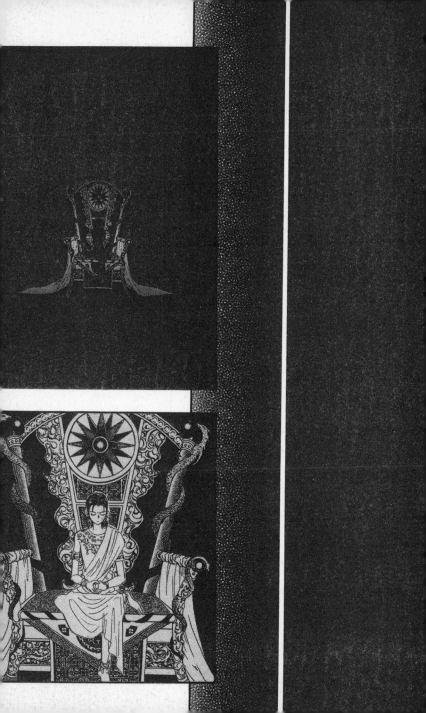

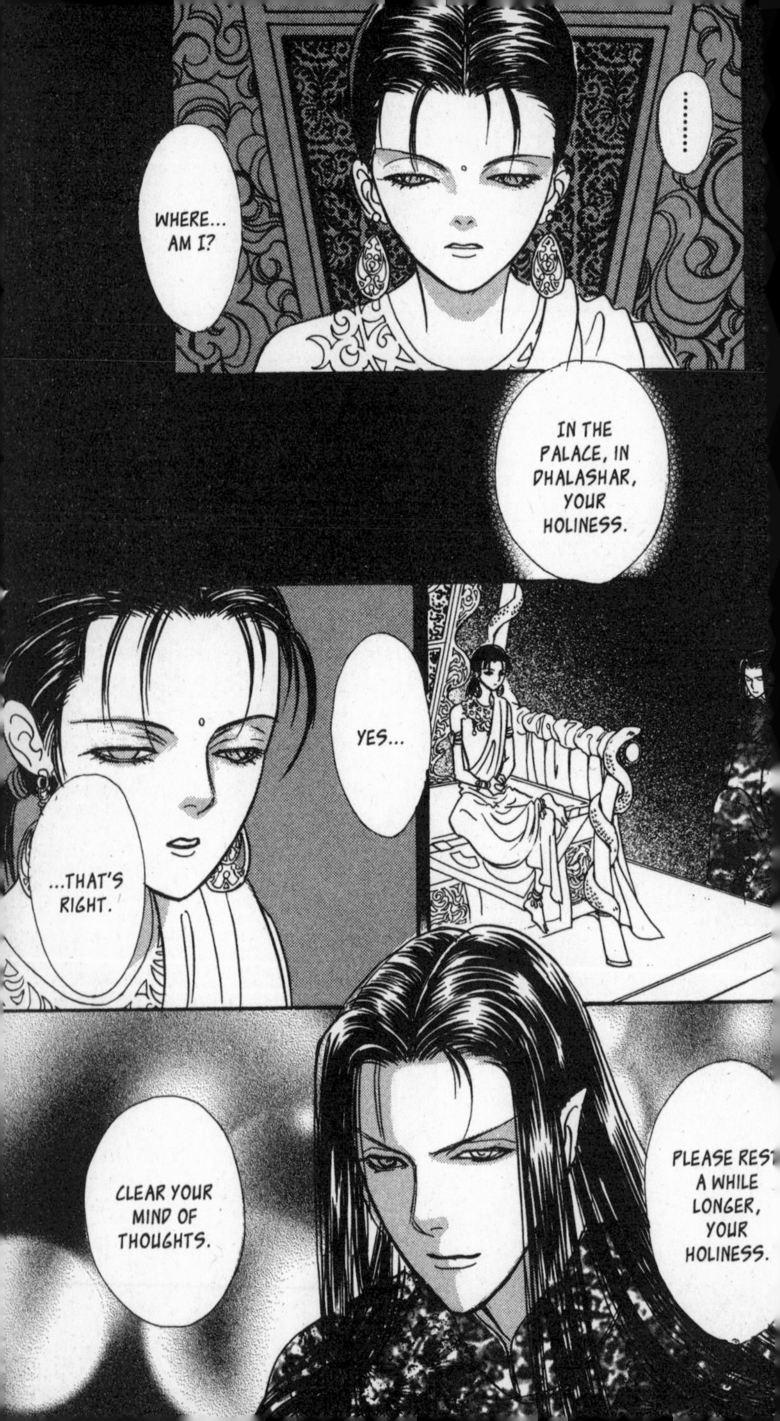
......
WHERE... AM I?
IN THE PALACE, IN DHALASHAR, YOUR HOLINESS.
YES...
...THAT'S RIGHT.
PLEASE REST A WHILE LONGER, YOUR HOLINESS.
CLEAR YOUR MIND OF THOUGHTS.

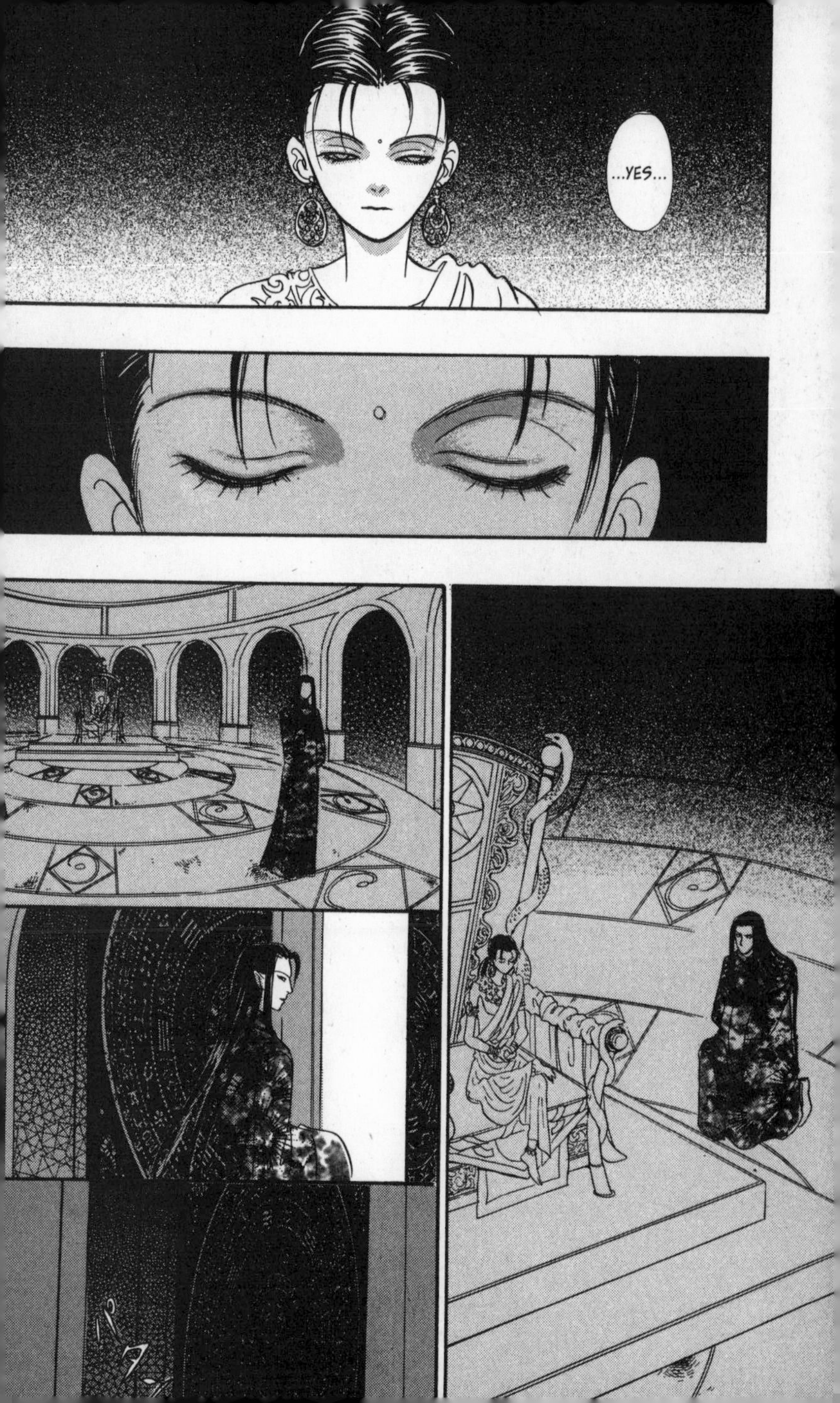
...YES...
パタ

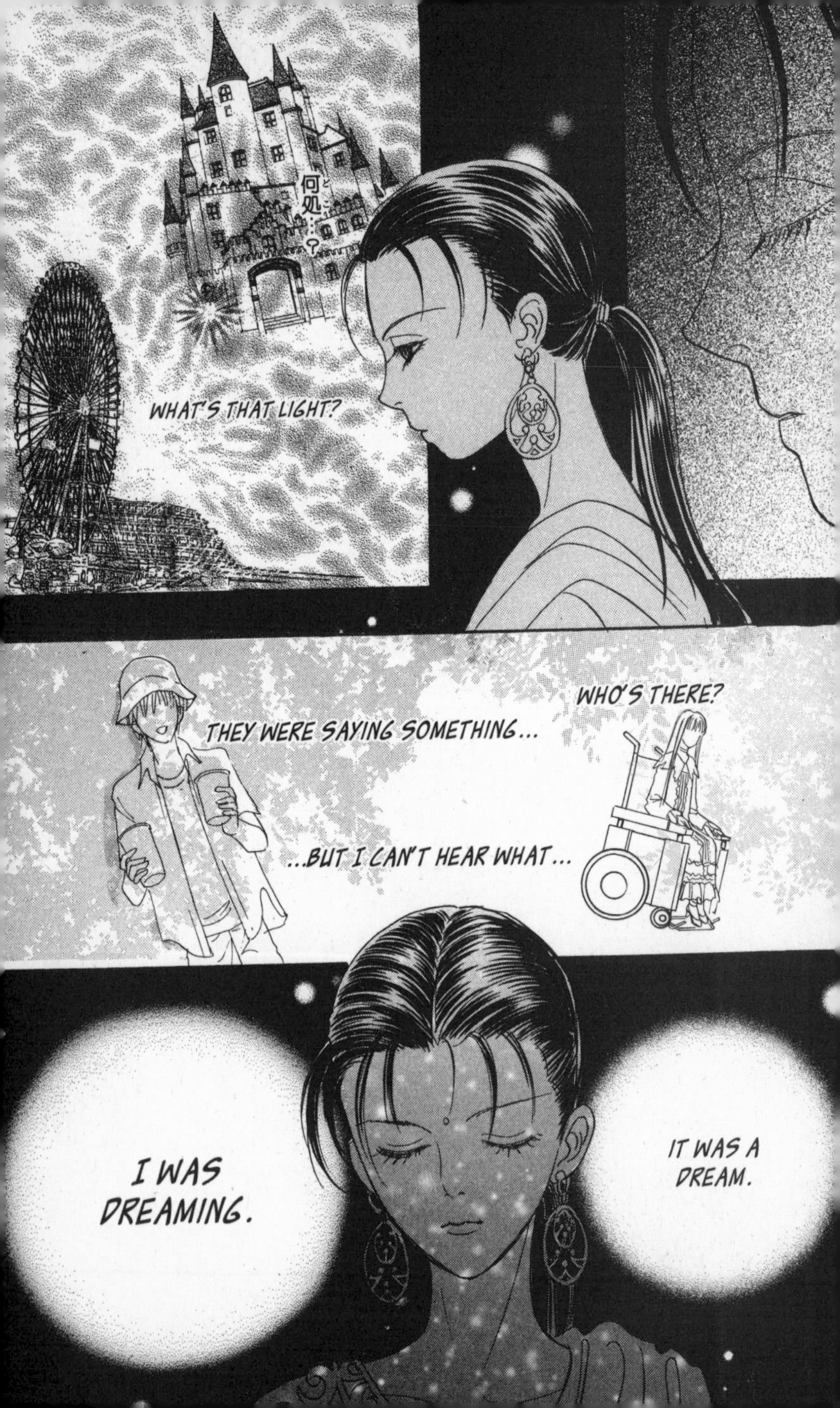
何処…?
WHAT'S THAT LIGHT?
WHO'S THERE?
THEY WERE SAYING SOMETHING...
...BUT I CAN'T HEAR WHAT...
IT WAS A DREAM.
I WAS DREAMING.

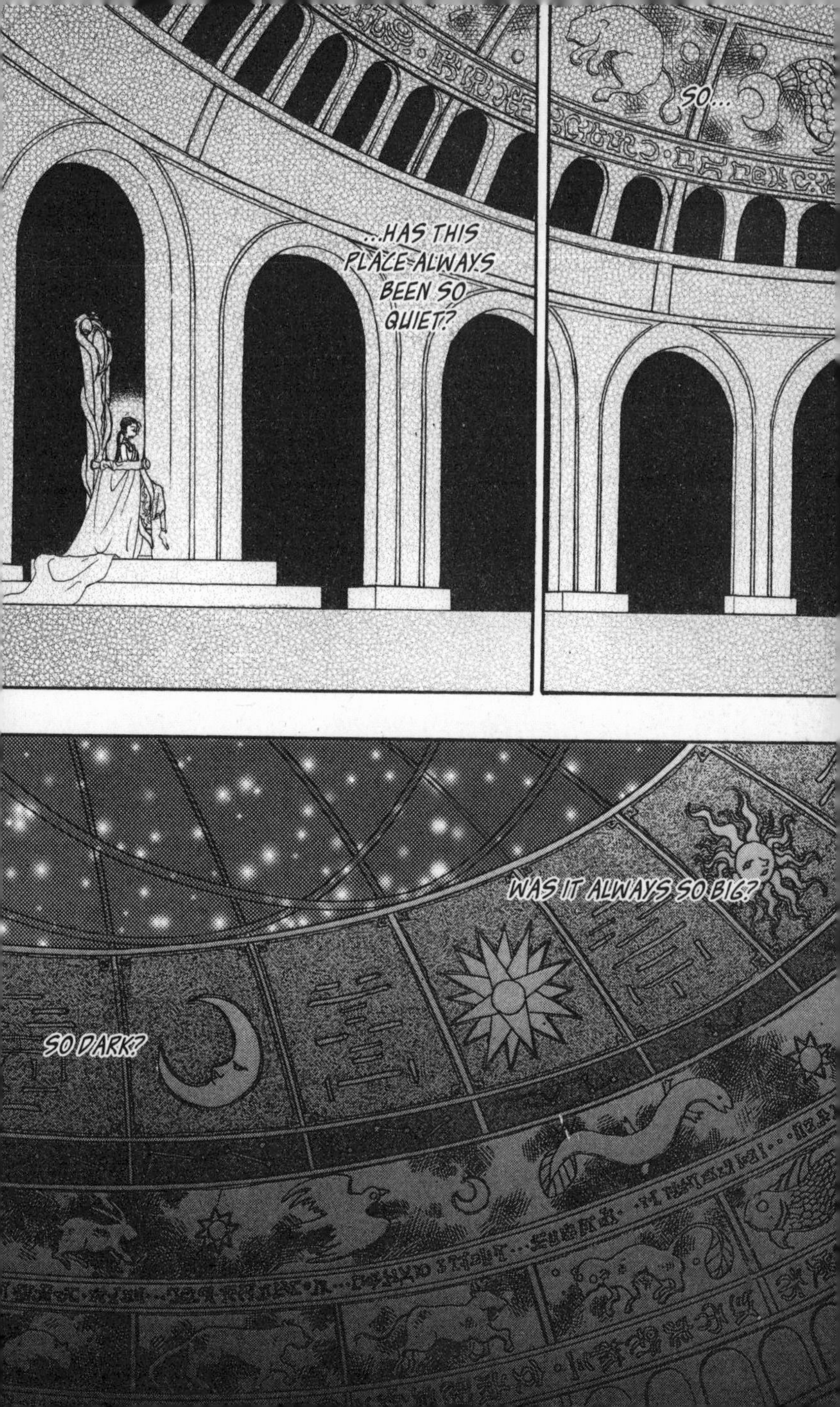
SO...
...HAS THIS PLACE ALWAYS BEEN SO QUIET?
WAS IT ALWAYS SO BIG?
SO DARK?

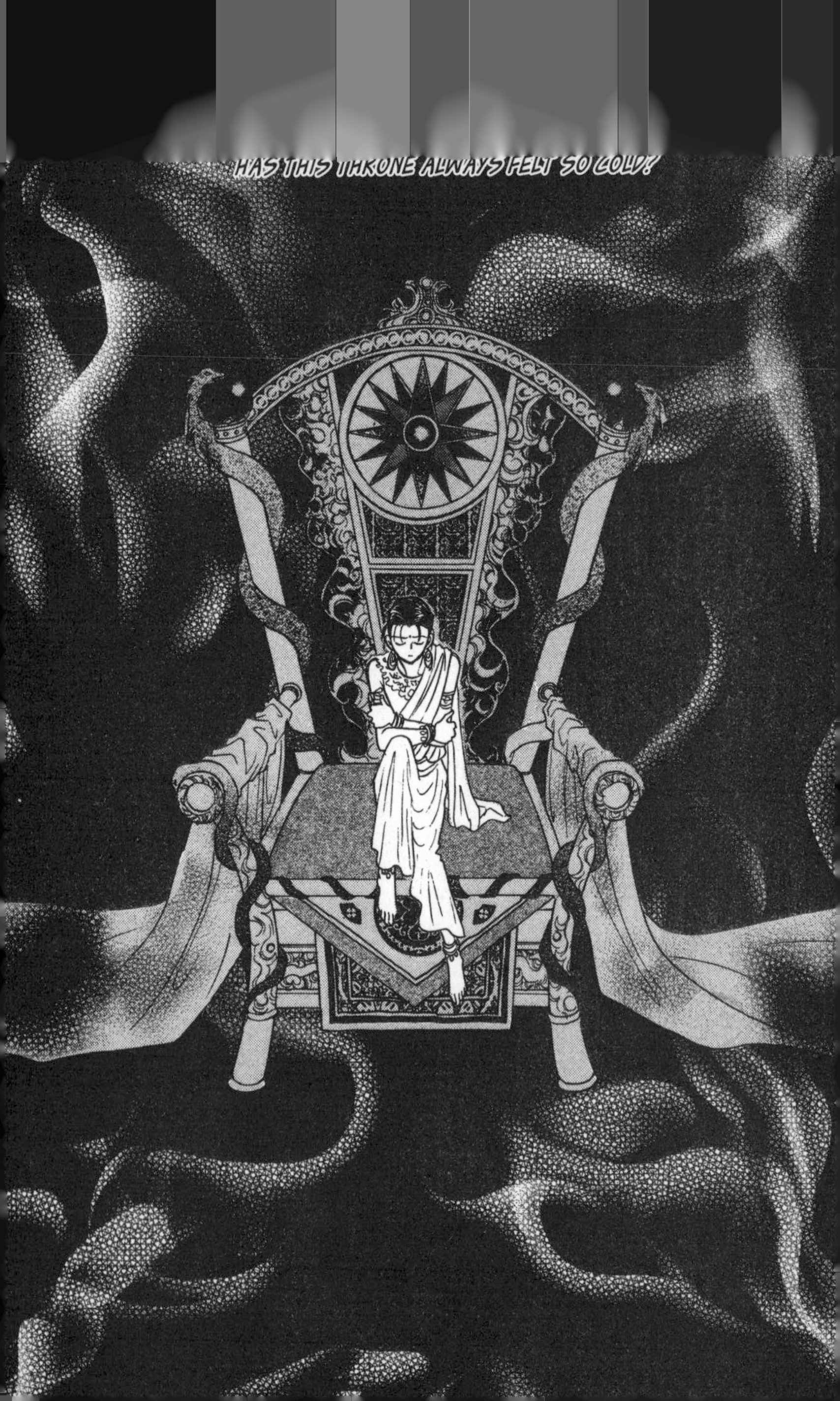
HAS THIS THRONE ALWAYS FELT SO COLD?

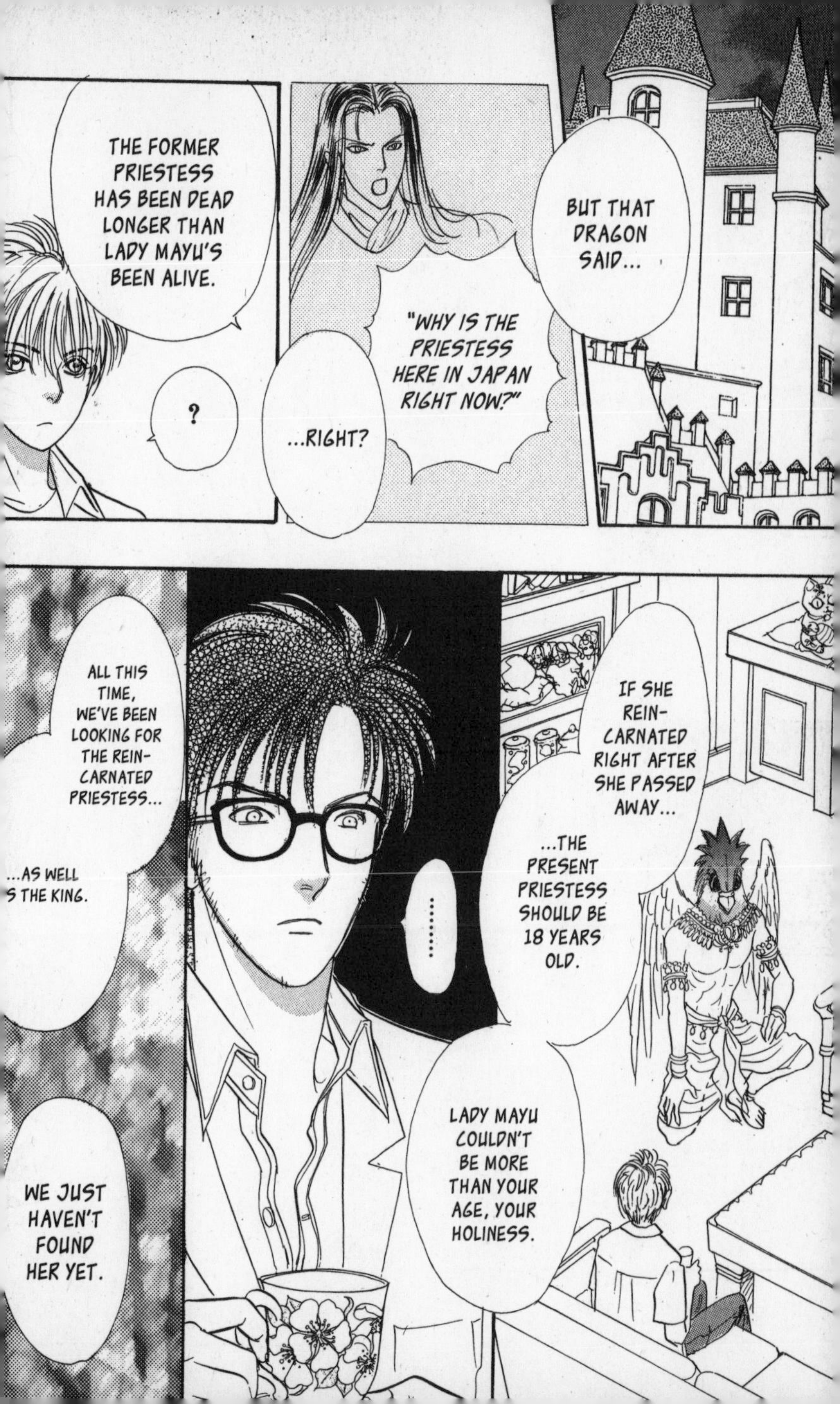
BUT THAT DRAGON SAID...
"WHY IS THE PRIESTESS HERE IN JAPAN RIGHT NOW?"
...RIGHT?
THE FORMER PRIESTESS HAS BEEN DEAD LONGER THAN LADY MAYU'S BEEN ALIVE.
?
IF SHE REIN-CARNATED RIGHT AFTER SHE PASSED AWAY...
...THE PRESENT PRIESTESS SHOULD BE 18 YEARS OLD.
LADY MAYU COULDN'T BE MORE THAN YOUR AGE, YOUR HOLINESS.
......
ALL THIS TIME, WE'VE BEEN LOOKING FOR THE REIN-CARNATED PRIESTESS...
...AS WELL S THE KING.
WE JUST HAVEN'T FOUND HER YET.

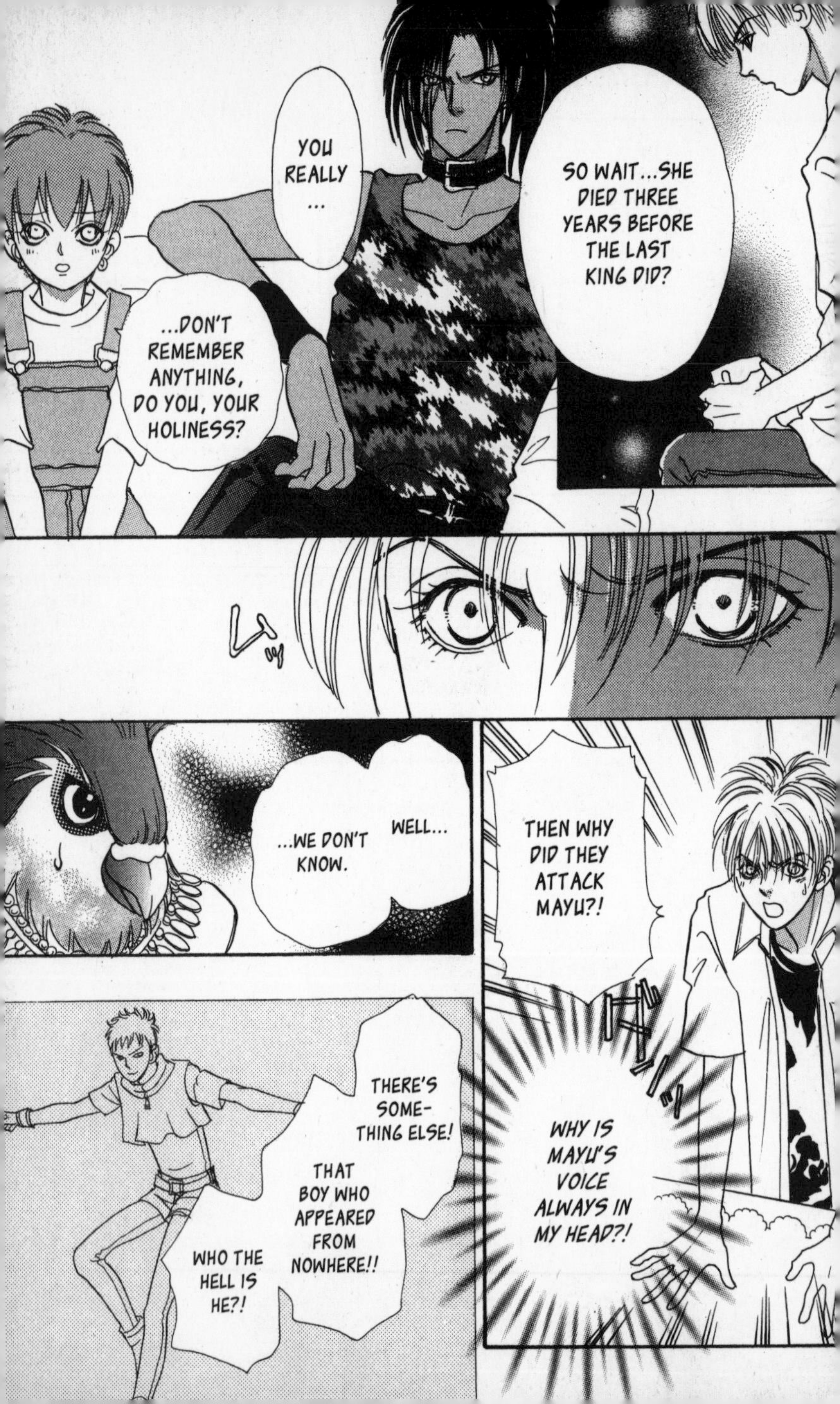
SO WAIT...SHE DIED THREE YEARS BEFORE THE LAST KING DID?
YOU REALLY ...
...DON'T REMEMBER ANYTHING, DO YOU, YOUR HOLINESS?
THEN WHY DID THEY ATTACK MAYU?!
WHY IS MAYU'S VOICE ALWAYS IN MY HEAD?!
WELL...
...WE DON'T KNOW.
THERE'S SOME-THING ELSE!
THAT BOY WHO APPEARED FROM NOWHERE!!
WHO THE HELL IS HE?!

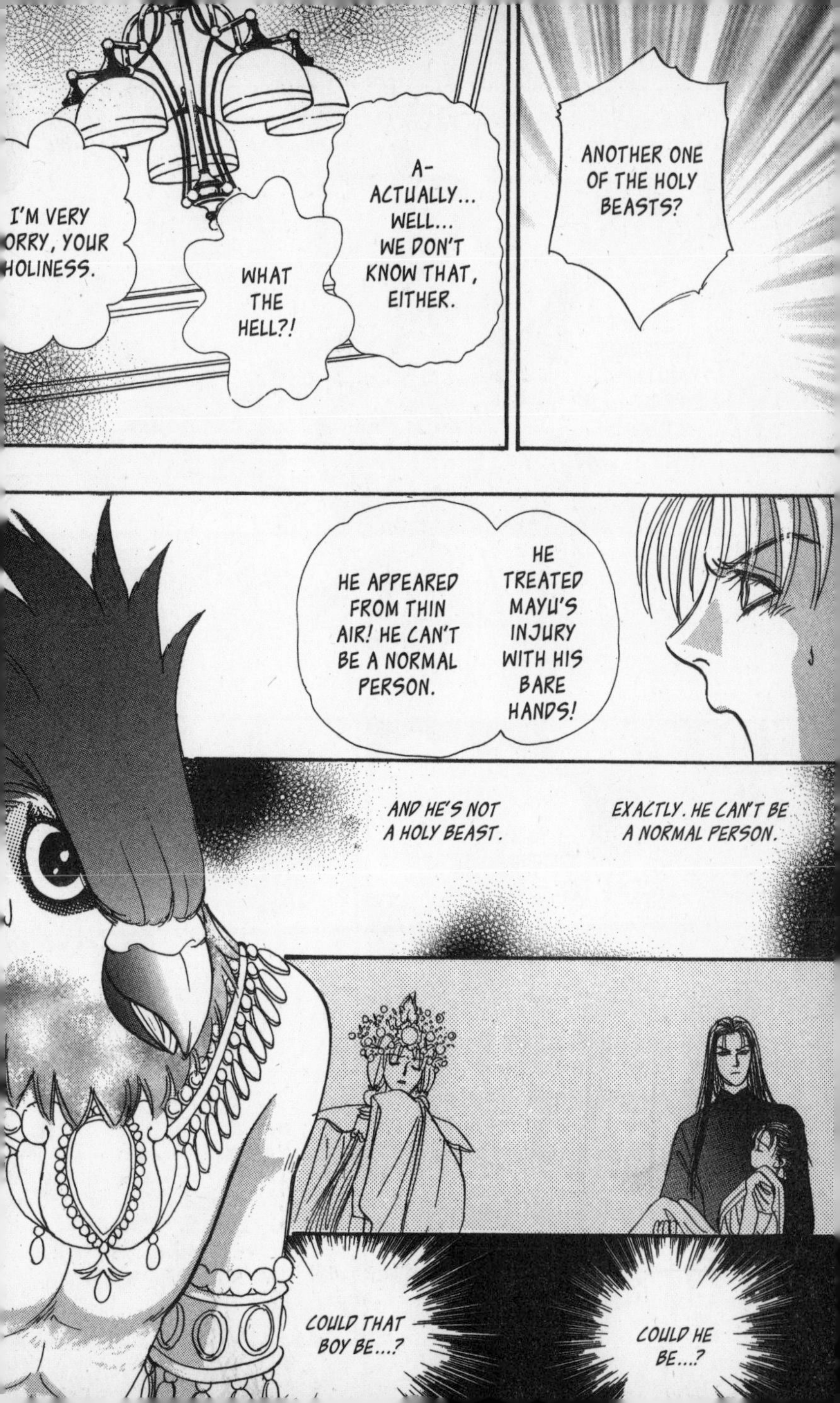
ANOTHER ONE OF THE HOLY BEASTS?
A- ACTUALLY... WELL... WE DON'T KNOW THAT, EITHER.
WHAT THE HELL?!
I'M VERY ORRY, YOUR HOLINESS.
HE TREATED MAYU'S INJURY WITH HIS BARE HANDS!
HE APPEARED FROM THIN AIR! HE CAN'T BE A NORMAL PERSON.
EXACTLY. HE CAN'T BE A NORMAL PERSON.
AND HE'S NOT A HOLY BEAST.
COULD HE BE...?
COULD THAT BOY BE...?

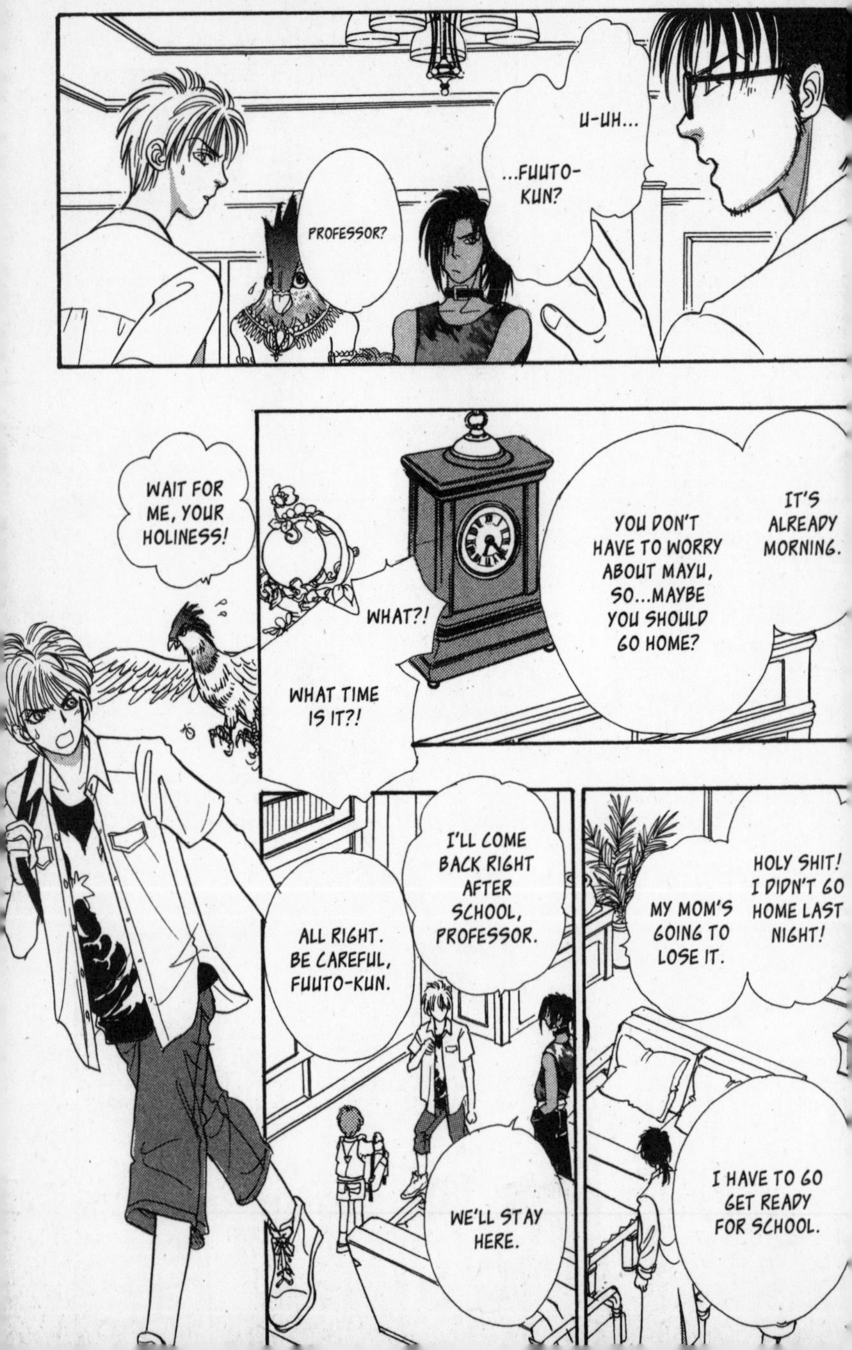
U-UH...
...FUUTO-KUN?
PROFESSOR?
IT'S ALREADY MORNING.
YOU DON'T HAVE TO WORRY ABOUT MAYU, SO...MAYBE YOU SHOULD GO HOME?
WHAT?!
WHAT TIME IS IT?!
HOLY SHIT! I DIDN'T GO HOME LAST NIGHT!
MY MOM'S GOING TO LOSE IT.
I HAVE TO GO GET READY FOR SCHOOL.
I'LL COME BACK RIGHT AFTER SCHOOL, PROFESSOR.
ALL RIGHT. BE CAREFUL, FUUTO-KUN.
WE'LL STAY HERE.
WAIT FOR ME, YOUR HOLINESS!

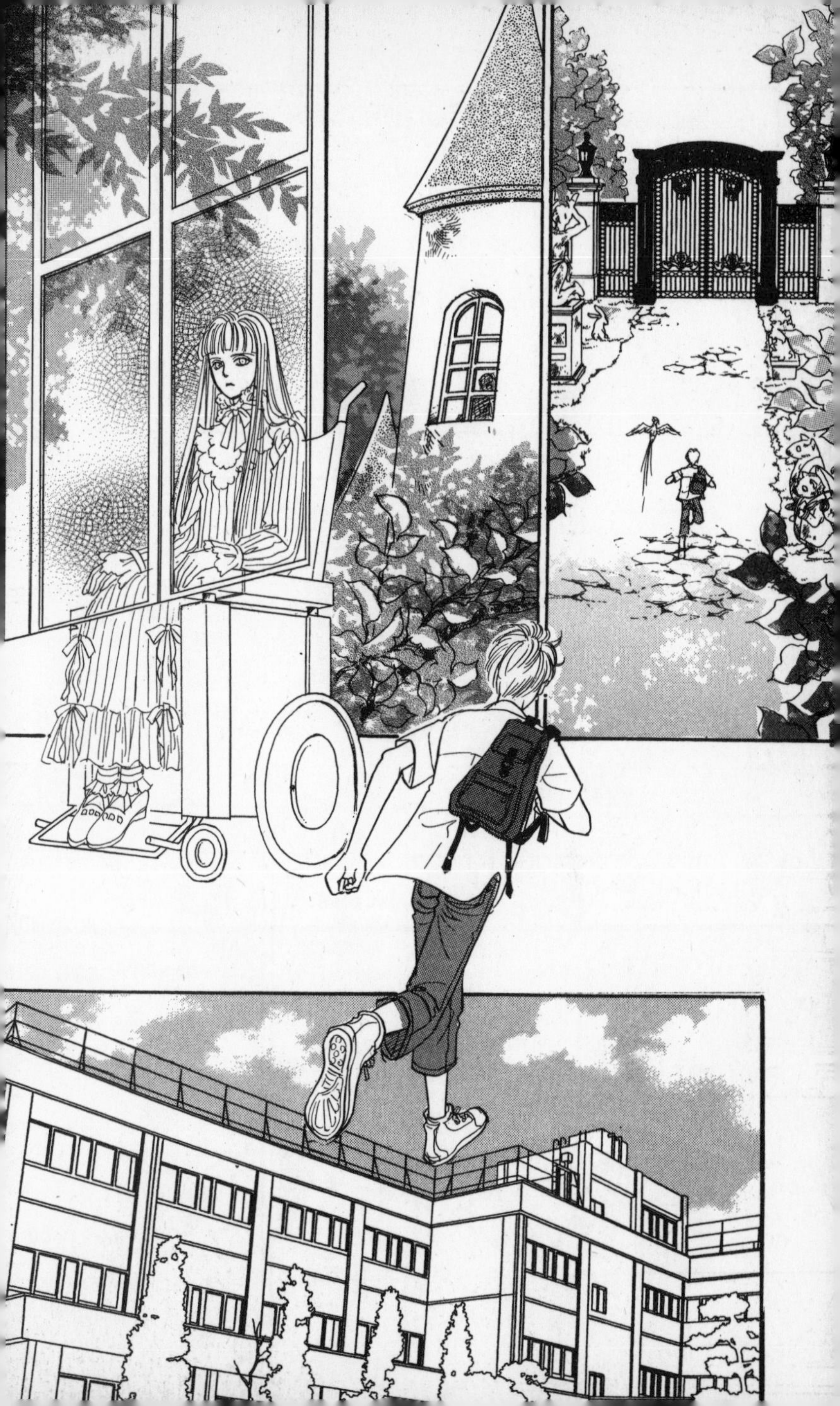

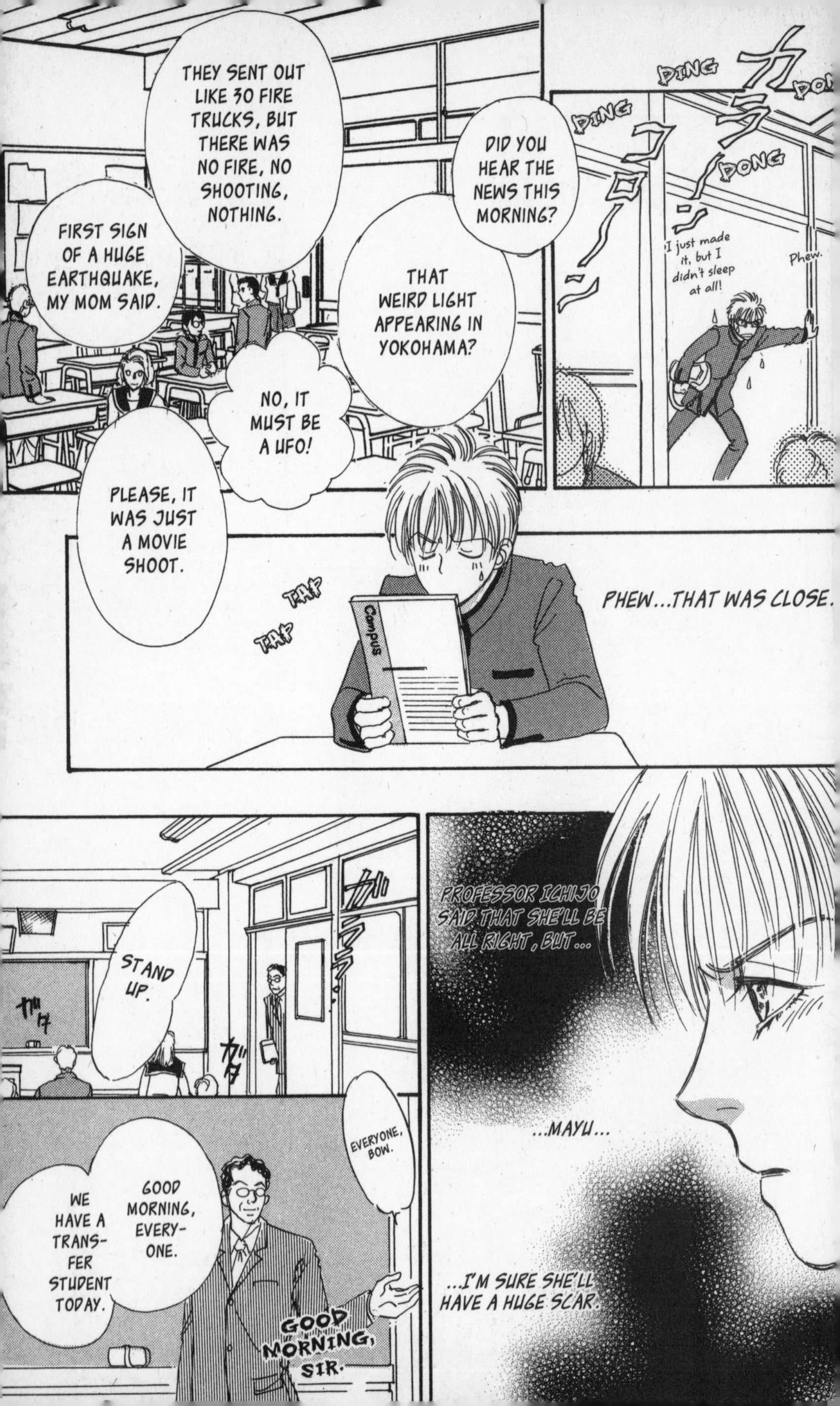

DING
DING
DONG
I just made it, but I didn't sleep at all!
Phew.
DID YOU HEAR THE NEWS THIS MORNING?
THAT WEIRD LIGHT APPEARING IN YOKOHAMA?
THEY SENT OUT LIKE 30 FIRE TRUCKS, BUT THERE WAS NO FIRE, NO SHOOTING, NOTHING.
FIRST SIGN OF A HUGE EARTHQUAKE, MY MOM SAID.
NO, IT MUST BE A UFO!
PLEASE, IT WAS JUST A MOVIE SHOOT.
PHEW...THAT WAS CLOSE.
TAP
TAP
Campus
PROFESSOR ICHIJO SAID THAT SHE'LL BE ALL RIGHT, BUT...
...MAYU...
...I'M SURE SHE'LL HAVE A HUGE SCAR.
STAND UP.
EVERYONE, BOW.
GOOD MORNING, SIR.
GOOD MORNING, EVERYONE.
WE HAVE A TRANSFER STUDENT TODAY.

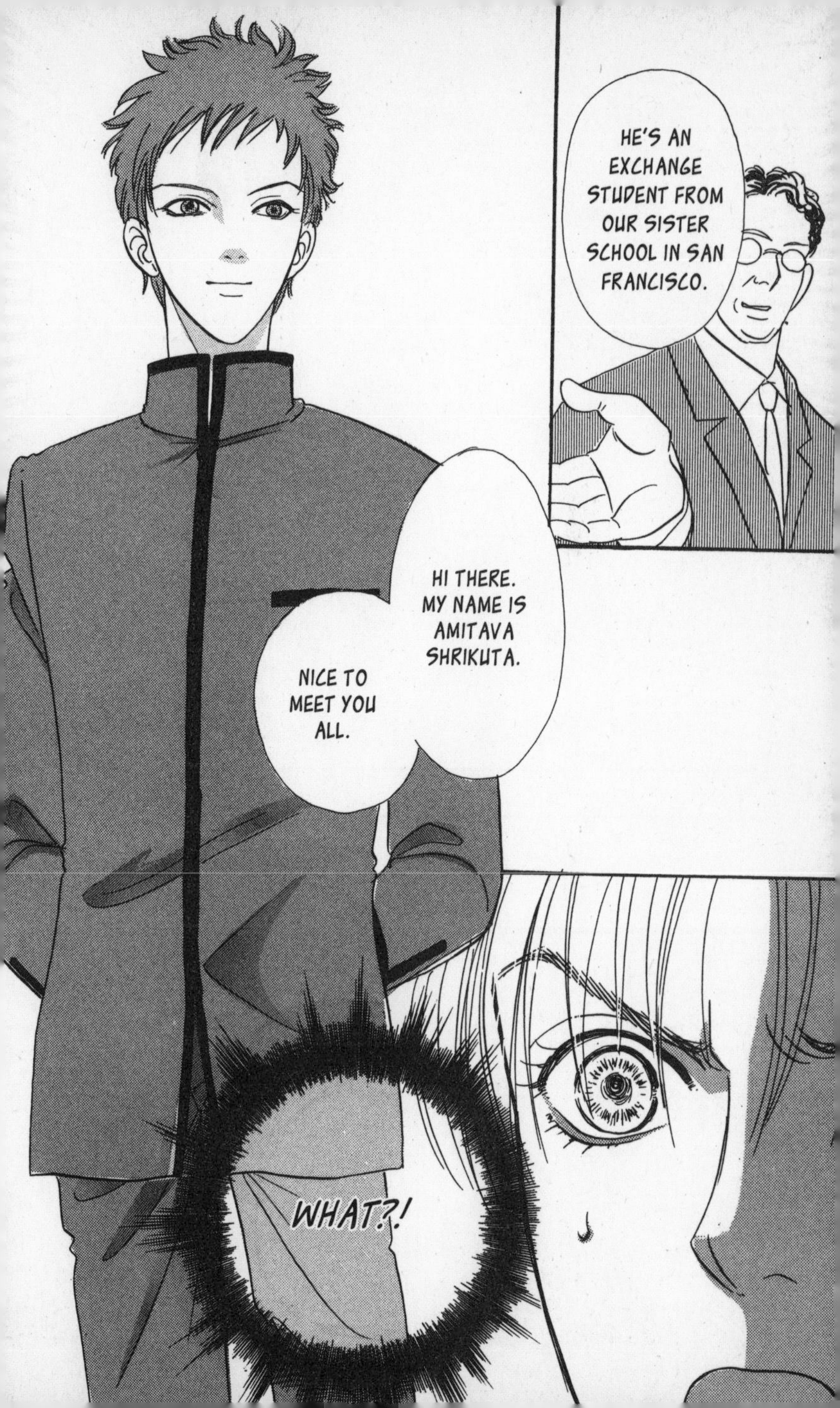
HE'S AN EXCHANGE STUDENT FROM OUR SISTER SCHOOL IN SAN FRANCISCO.
HI THERE. MY NAME IS AMITAVA SHRIKUTA.
NICE TO MEET YOU ALL.
WHAT?!

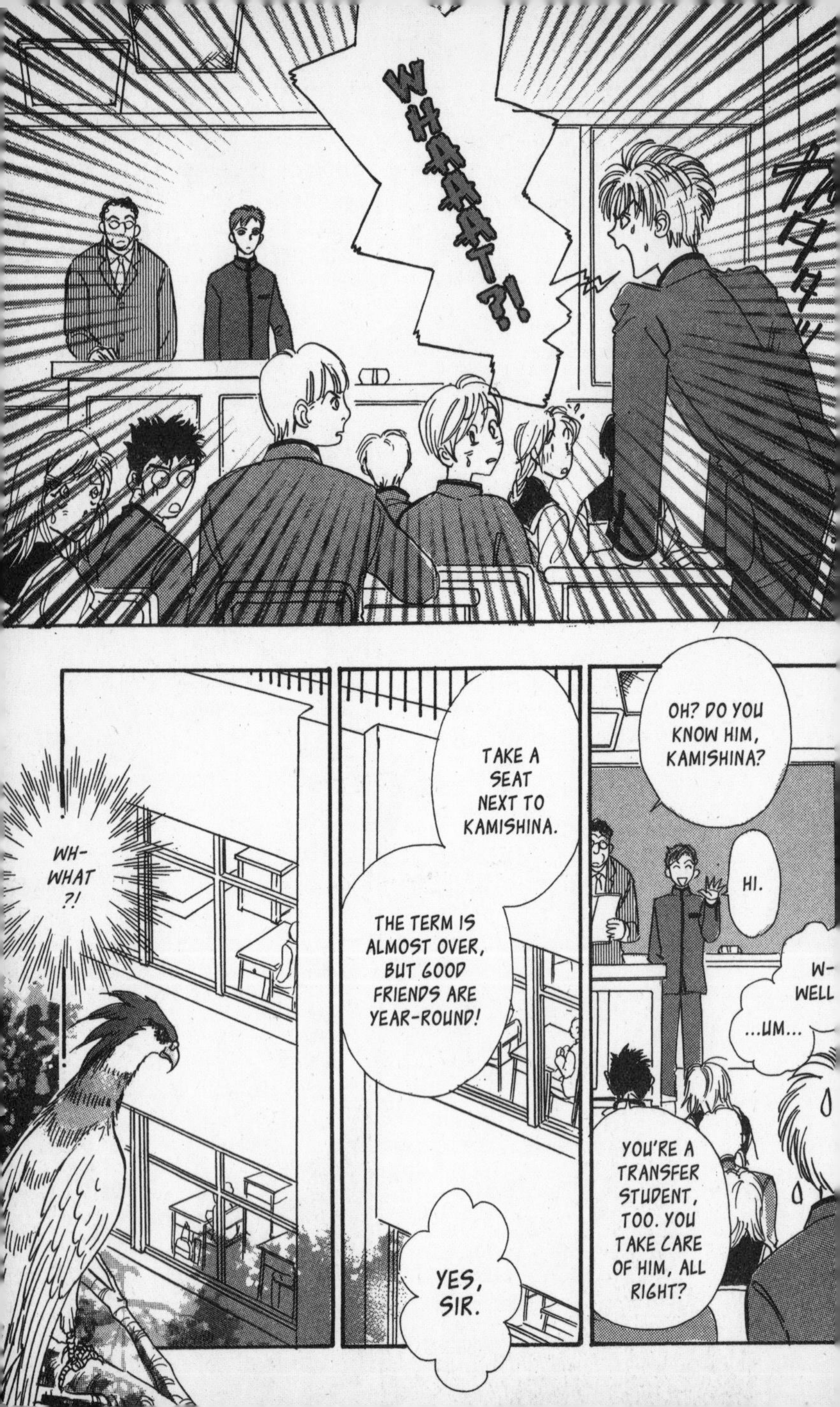
ガタタッ
WHAAAT?!
OH? DO YOU KNOW HIM, KAMISHINA?
HI.
W-WELL
...UM...
YOU'RE A TRANSFER STUDENT, TOO. YOU TAKE CARE OF HIM, ALL RIGHT?
TAKE A SEAT NEXT TO KAMISHINA.
THE TERM IS ALMOST OVER, BUT GOOD FRIENDS ARE YEAR-ROUND!
YES, SIR.
WH-WHAT?!

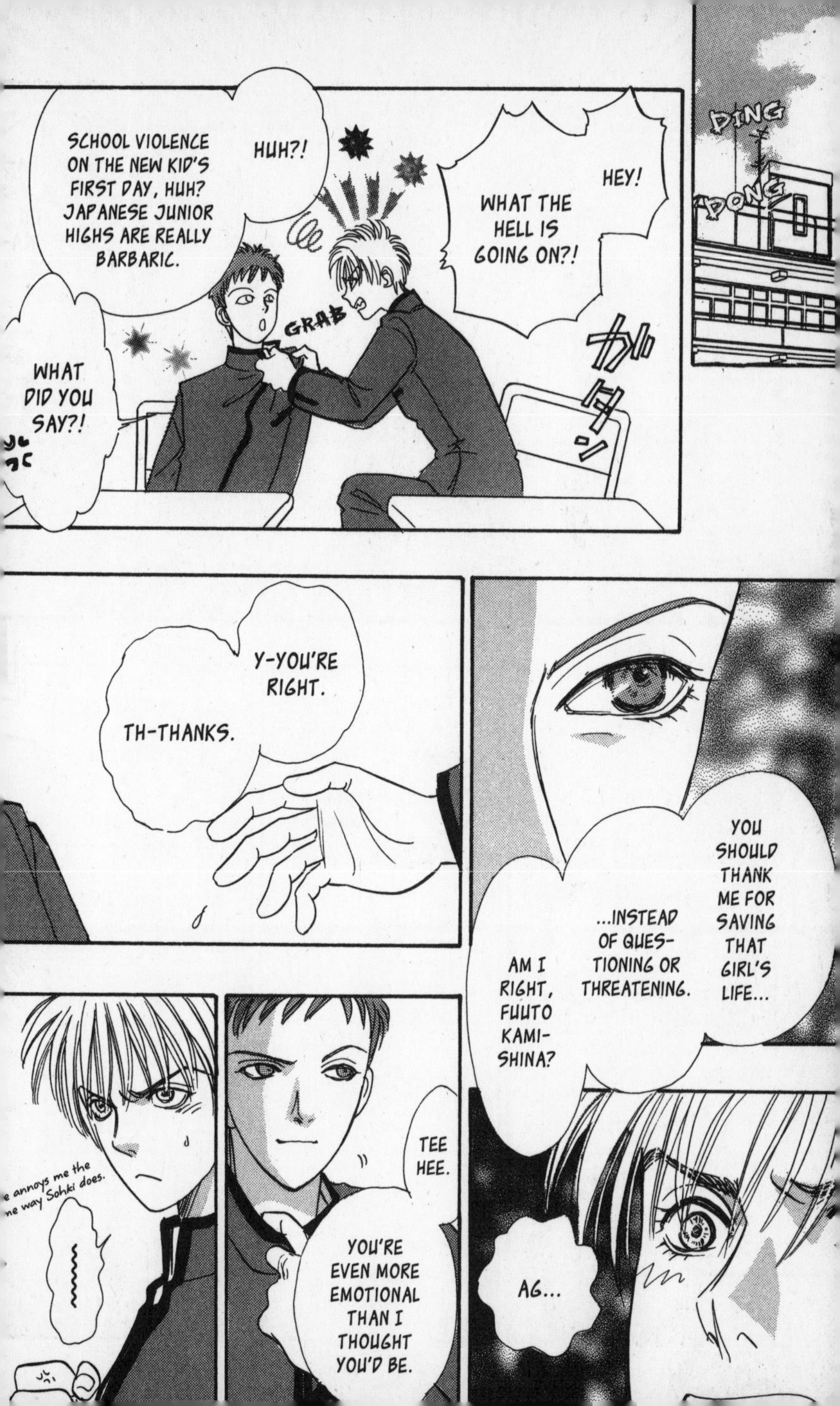
DING
DONG
HEY!
WHAT THE HELL IS GOING ON?!
GRAB
HUH?!
SCHOOL VIOLENCE ON THE NEW KID'S FIRST DAY, HUH? JAPANESE JUNIOR HIGHS ARE REALLY BARBARIC.
WHAT DID YOU SAY?!
YOU SHOULD THANK ME FOR SAVING THAT GIRL'S LIFE...
...INSTEAD OF QUES-TIONING OR THREATENING.
AM I RIGHT, FUUTO KAMI-SHINA?
Y-YOU'RE RIGHT.
TH-THANKS.
AG...
TEE HEE.
YOU'RE EVEN MORE EMOTIONAL THAN I THOUGHT YOU'D BE.
e annoys me the
ne way Sohki does.

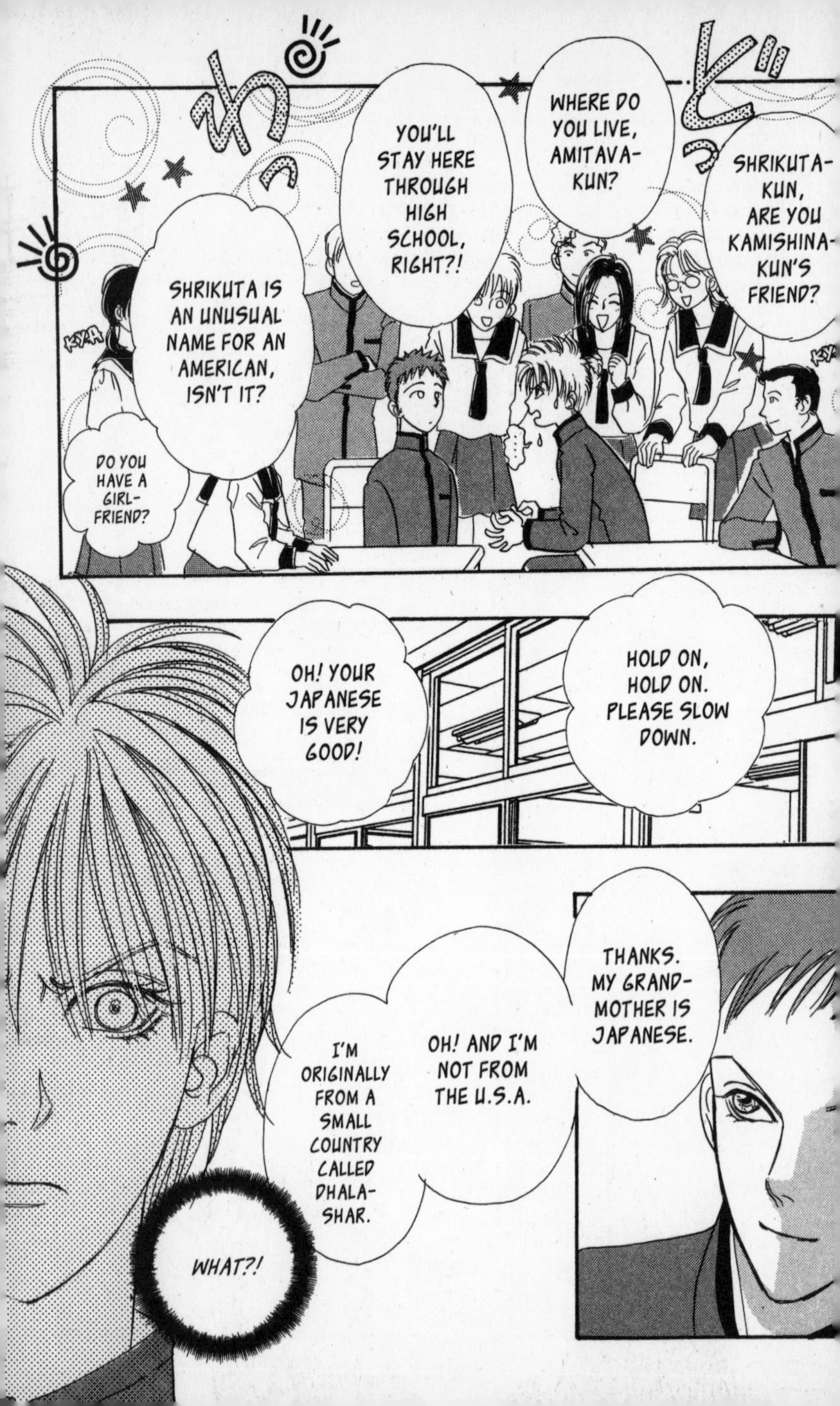
KYA
SHRIKUTA-KUN, ARE YOU KAMISHINA-KUN'S FRIEND?
WHERE DO YOU LIVE, AMITAVA-KUN?
YOU'LL STAY HERE THROUGH HIGH SCHOOL, RIGHT?!
SHRIKUTA IS AN UNUSUAL NAME FOR AN AMERICAN, ISN'T IT?
KYA
DO YOU HAVE A GIRLFRIEND?
HOLD ON, HOLD ON. PLEASE SLOW DOWN.
OH! YOUR JAPANESE IS VERY GOOD!
THANKS. MY GRANDMOTHER IS JAPANESE.
OH! AND I'M NOT FROM THE U.S.A.
I'M ORIGINALLY FROM A SMALL COUNTRY CALLED DHALASHAR.
WHAT?!

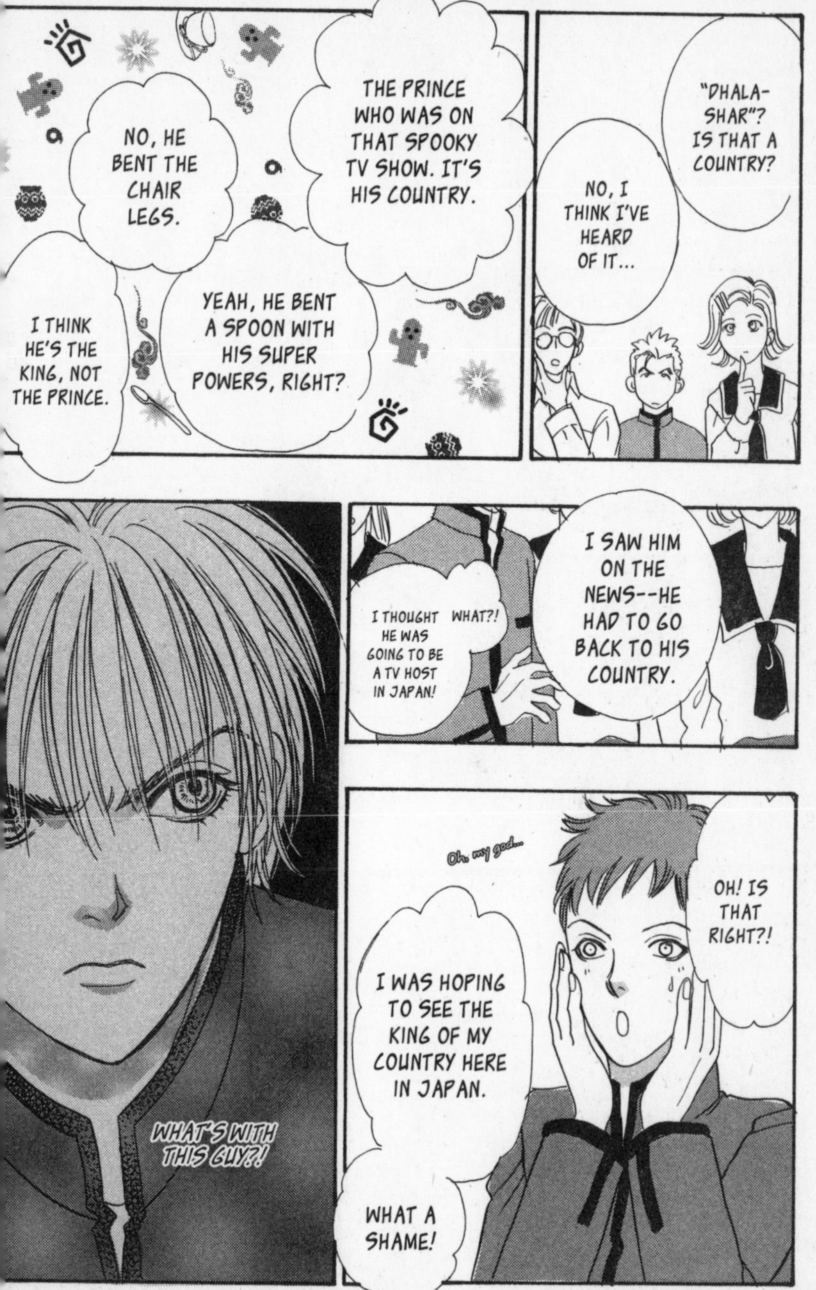
"DHALA-SHAR"? IS THAT A COUNTRY?
NO, I THINK I'VE HEARD OF IT...
THE PRINCE WHO WAS ON THAT SPOOKY TV SHOW. IT'S HIS COUNTRY.
NO, HE BENT THE CHAIR LEGS.
YEAH, HE BENT A SPOON WITH HIS SUPER POWERS, RIGHT?
I THINK HE'S THE KING, NOT THE PRINCE.
I SAW HIM ON THE NEWS--HE HAD TO GO BACK TO HIS COUNTRY.
WHAT?!
I THOUGHT HE WAS GOING TO BE A TV HOST IN JAPAN!
OH! IS THAT RIGHT?!
Oh, my god...
I WAS HOPING TO SEE THE KING OF MY COUNTRY HERE IN JAPAN.
WHAT A SHAME!
WHAT'S WITH THIS GUY?!

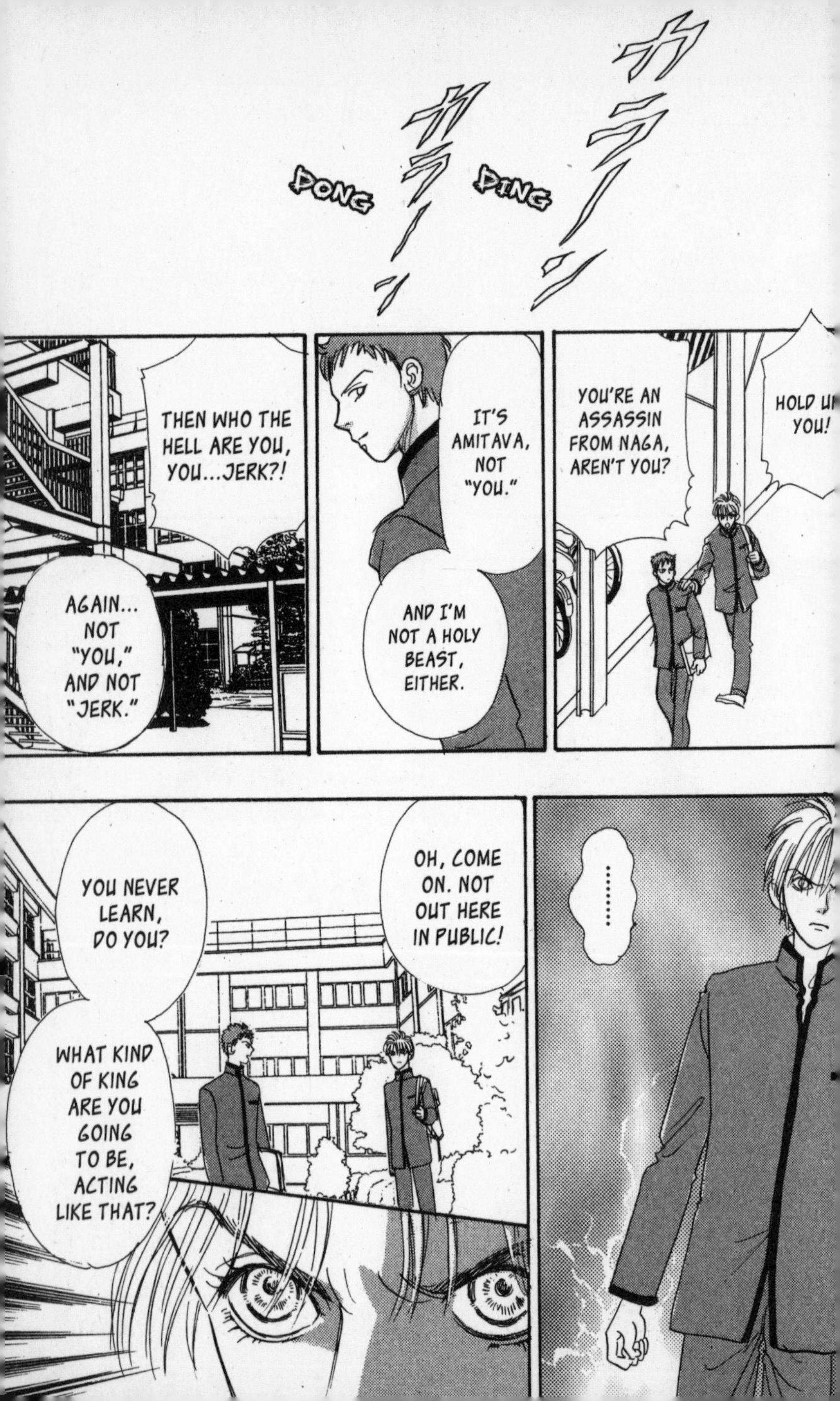

カラーン
DING
カラーン
DONG
HOLD U
YOU!
YOU'RE AN ASSASSIN FROM NAGA, AREN'T YOU?
IT'S AMITAVA, NOT "YOU."
AND I'M NOT A HOLY BEAST, EITHER.
THEN WHO THE HELL ARE YOU, YOU...JERK?!
AGAIN... NOT "YOU," AND NOT "JERK."
……
OH, COME ON. NOT OUT HERE IN PUBLIC!
YOU NEVER LEARN, DO YOU?
WHAT KIND OF KING ARE YOU GOING TO BE, ACTING LIKE THAT?

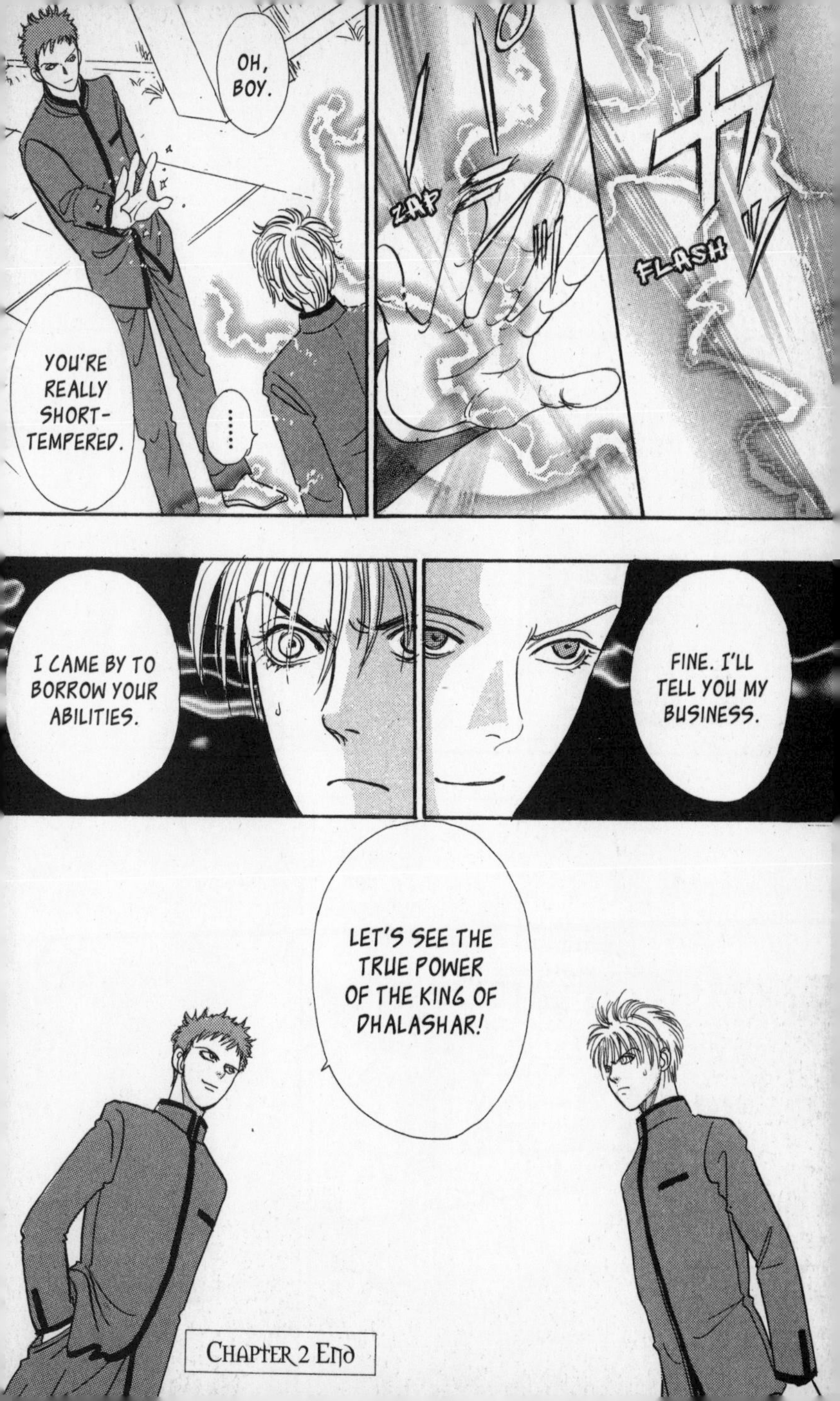
FLASH
ZAP
OH, BOY.
YOU'RE REALLY SHORT-TEMPERED.
......
FINE. I'LL TELL YOU MY BUSINESS.
I CAME BY TO BORROW YOUR ABILITIES.
LET'S SEE THE TRUE POWER OF THE KING OF DHALASHAR!
Chapter 2 End

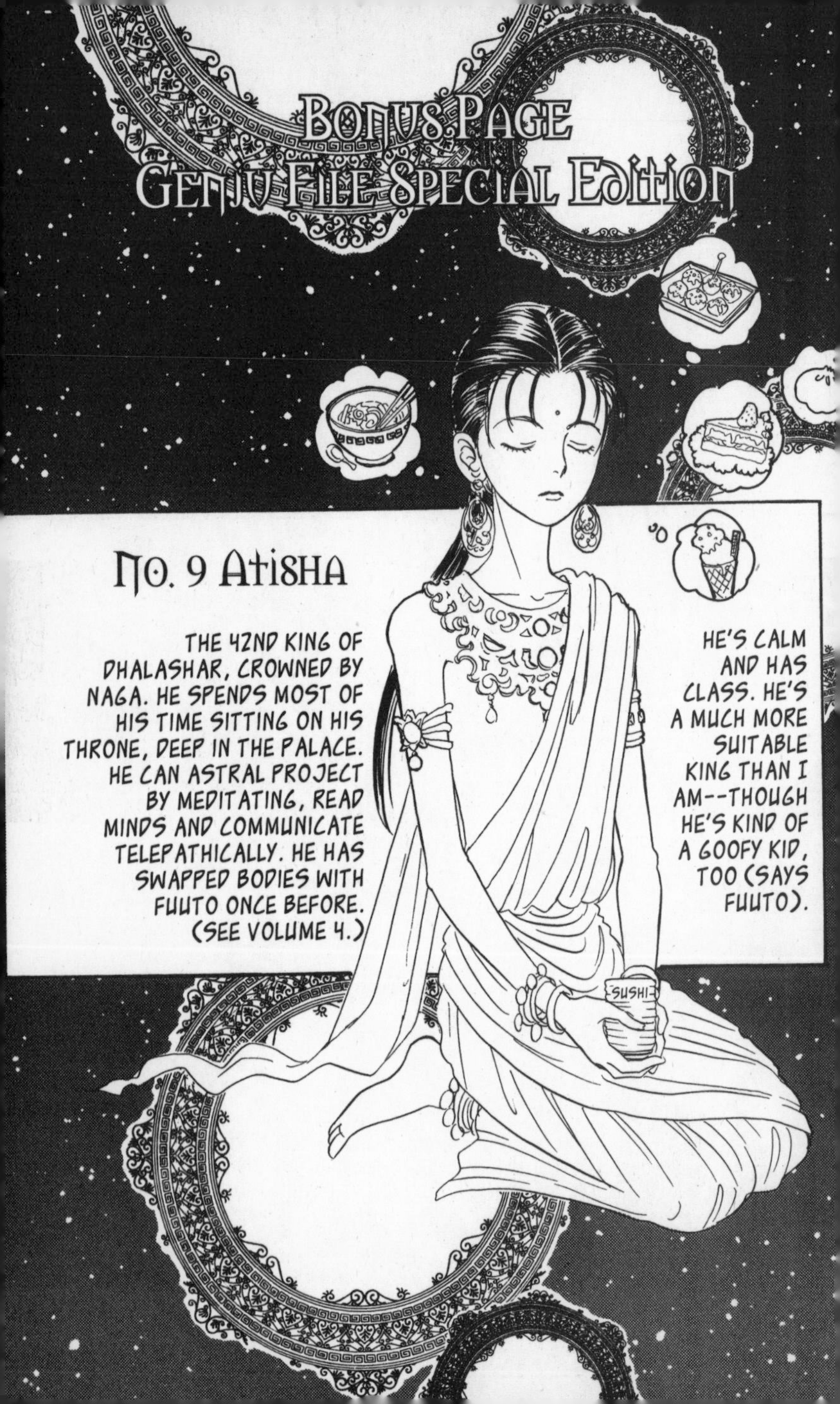
BONUS PAGE
GENJU FILE SPECIAL EDITION
NO. 9 ATISHA
THE 42ND KING OF DHALASHAR, CROWNED BY NAGA. HE SPENDS MOST OF HIS TIME SITTING ON HIS THRONE, DEEP IN THE PALACE. HE CAN ASTRAL PROJECT BY MEDITATING, READ MINDS AND COMMUNICATE TELEPATHICALLY. HE HAS SWAPPED BODIES WITH FUUTO ONCE BEFORE. (SEE VOLUME 4.)
HE'S CALM AND HAS CLASS. HE'S A MUCH MORE SUITABLE KING THAN I AM--THOUGH HE'S KIND OF A GOOFY KID, TOO (SAYS FUUTO).
SUSHI

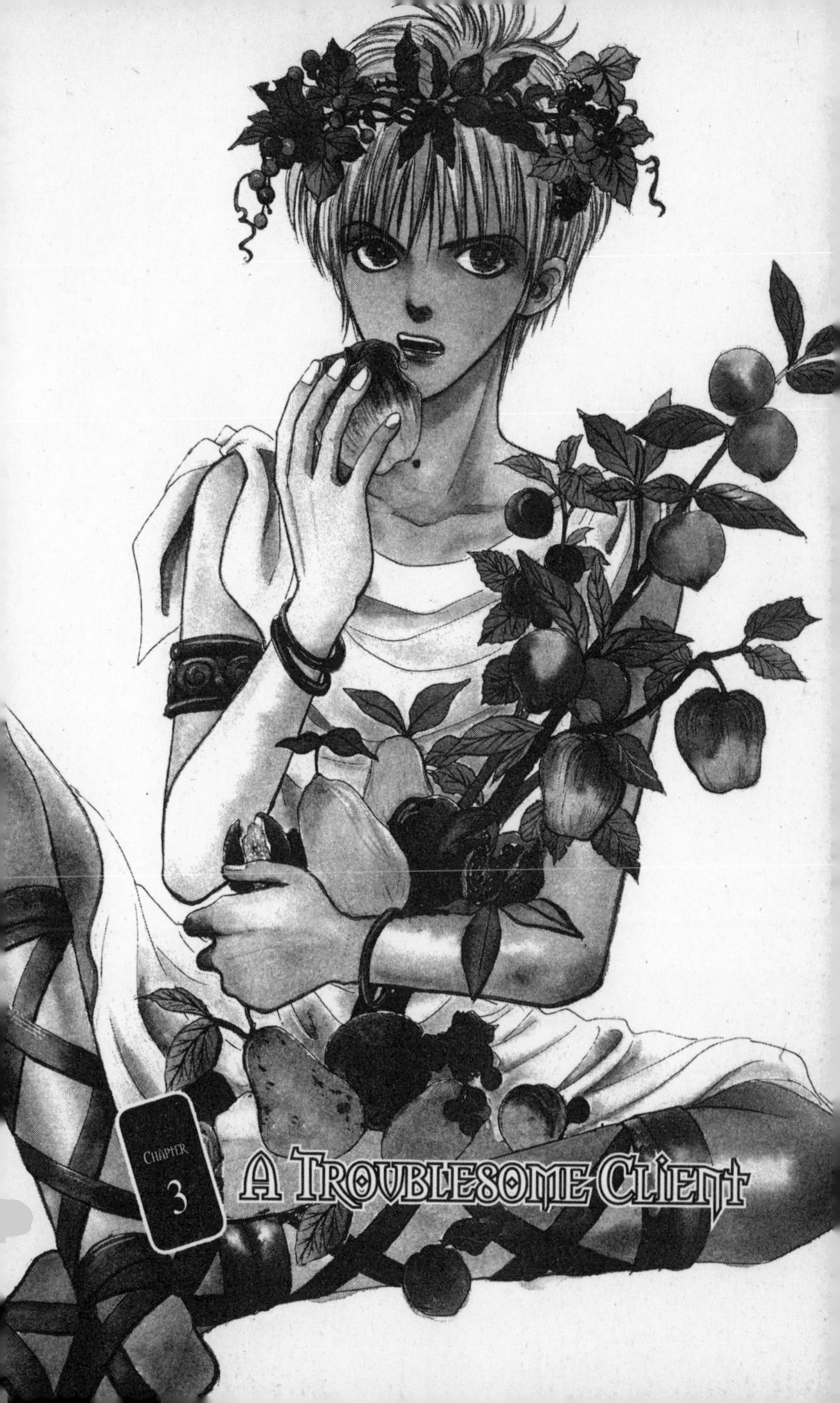
CHAPTER
3
A TROUBLESOME CLIENT

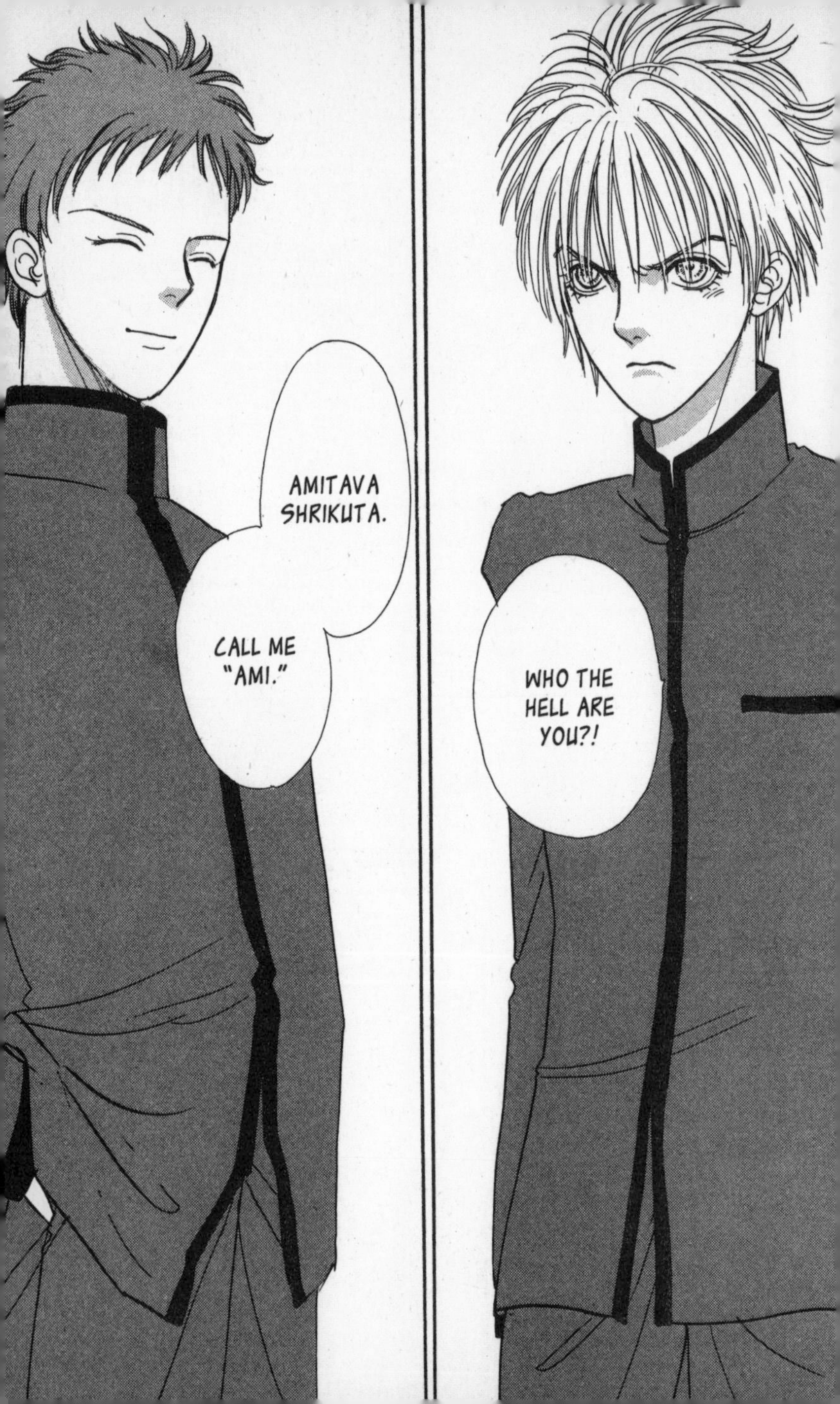
WHO THE HELL ARE YOU?!
AMITAVA SHRIKUTA.
CALL ME "AMI."

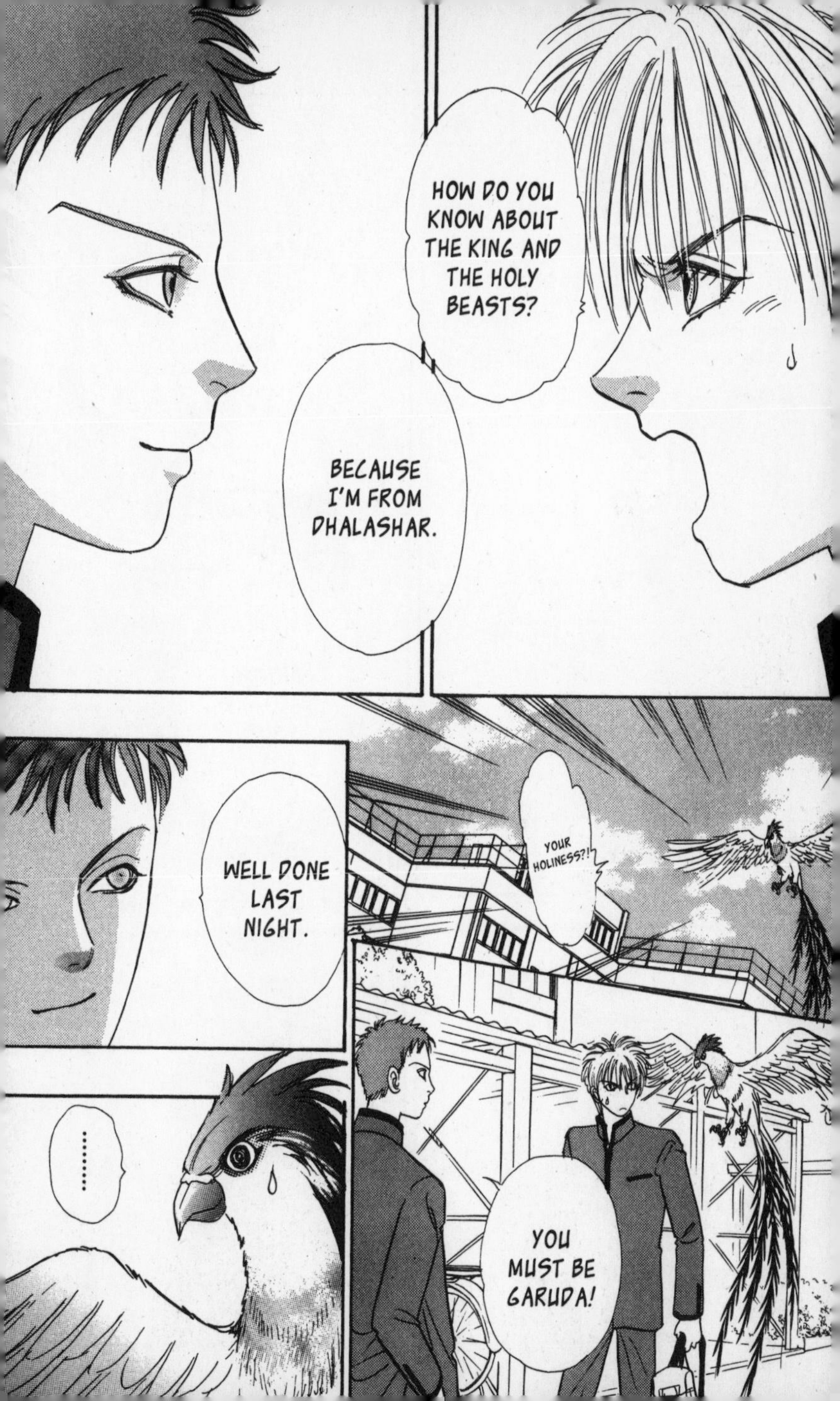
HOW DO YOU KNOW ABOUT THE KING AND THE HOLY BEASTS?
BECAUSE I'M FROM DHALASHAR.
YOUR HOLINESS?!
YOU MUST BE GARUDA!
WELL DONE LAST NIGHT.
......

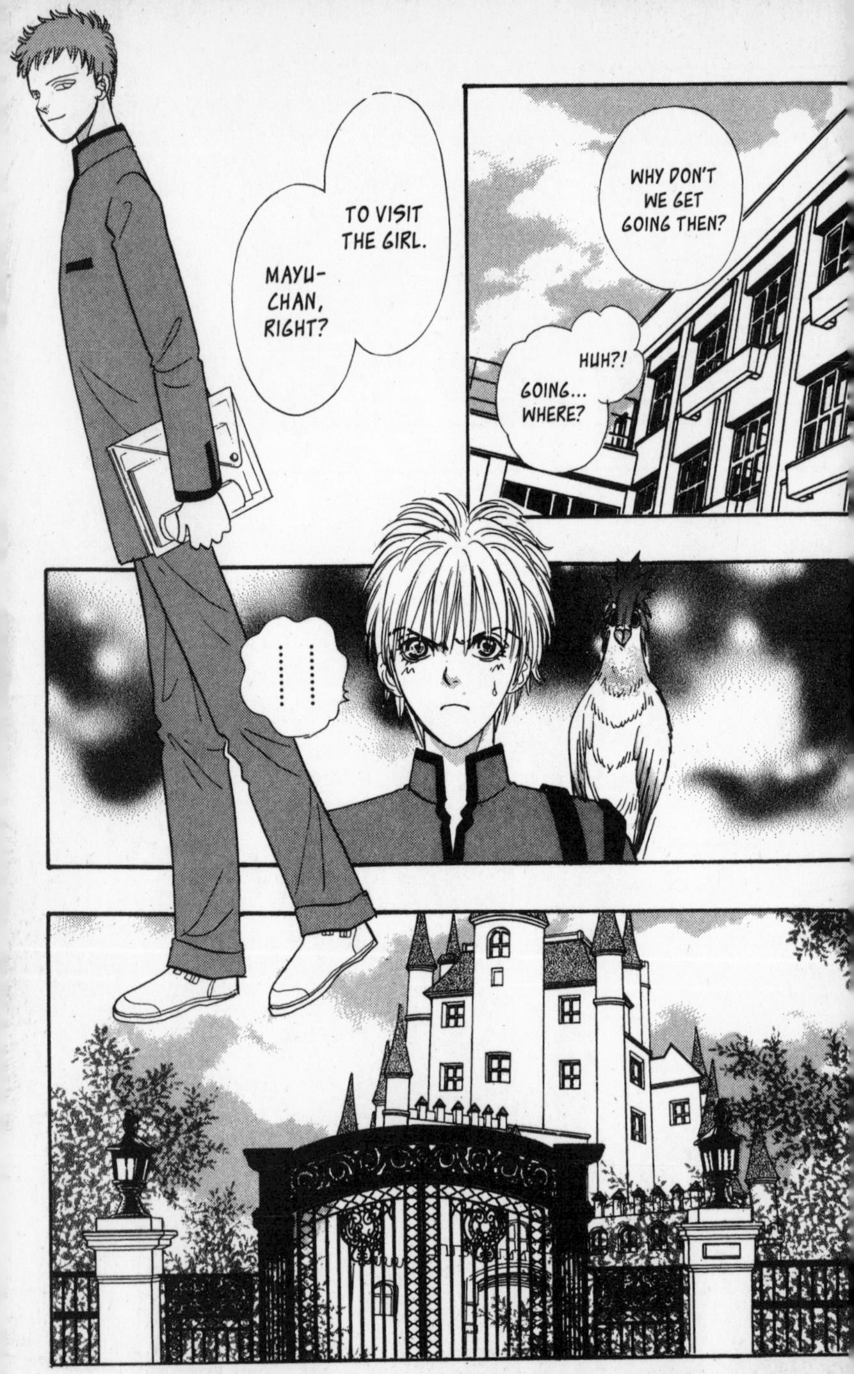
WHY DON'T WE GET GOING THEN?
HUH?! GOING... WHERE?
TO VISIT THE GIRL.
MAYU-CHAN, RIGHT?
......

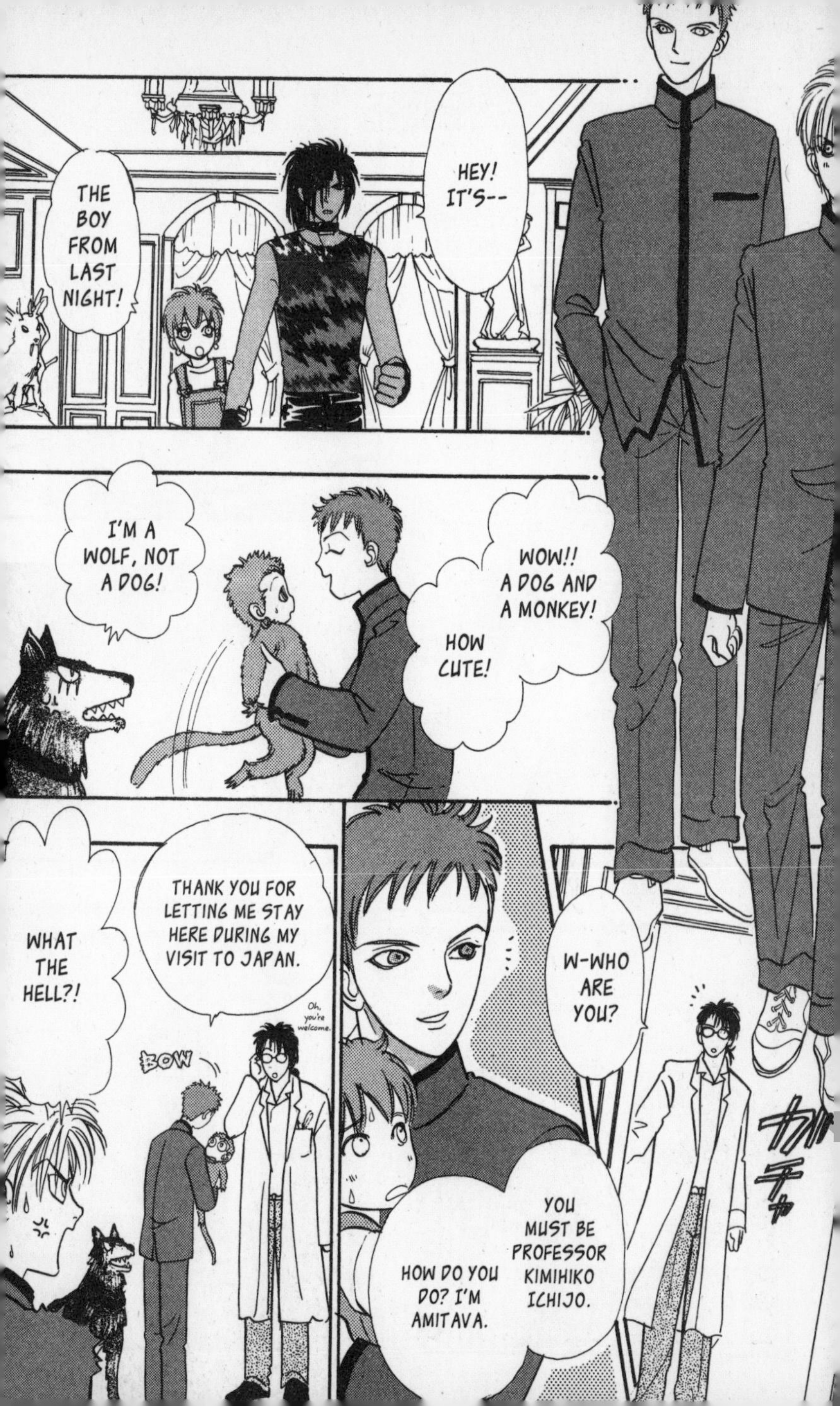
HEY! IT'S--
THE BOY FROM LAST NIGHT!
WOW!! A DOG AND A MONKEY!
HOW CUTE!
I'M A WOLF, NOT A DOG!
ガチャ
W-WHO ARE YOU?
YOU MUST BE PROFESSOR KIMIHIKO ICHIJO.
HOW DO YOU DO? I'M AMITAVA.
THANK YOU FOR LETTING ME STAY HERE DURING MY VISIT TO JAPAN.
Oh, you're welcome.
BOW
WHAT THE HELL?!

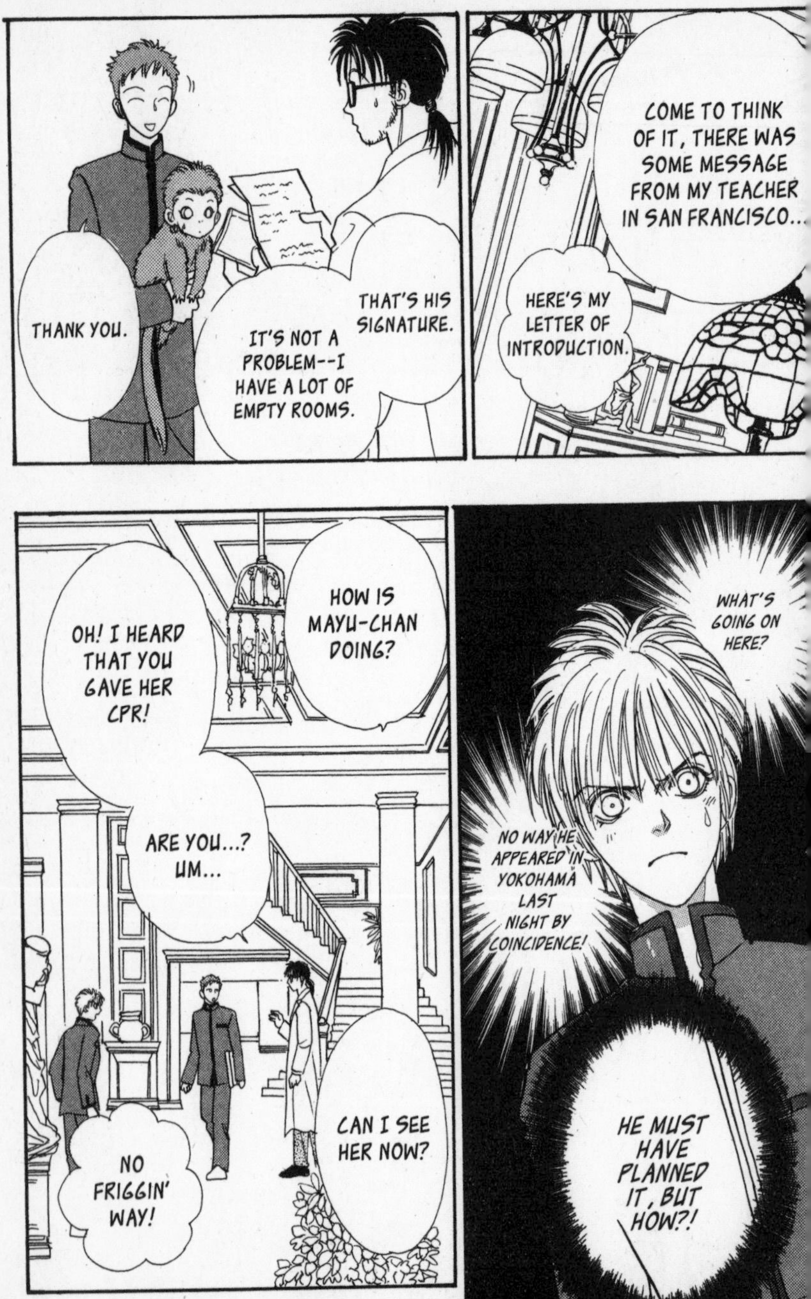
COME TO THINK OF IT, THERE WAS SOME MESSAGE FROM MY TEACHER IN SAN FRANCISCO...
HERE'S MY LETTER OF INTRODUCTION.
THAT'S HIS SIGNATURE.
IT'S NOT A PROBLEM--I HAVE A LOT OF EMPTY ROOMS.
THANK YOU.
WHAT'S GOING ON HERE?
NO WAY HE APPEARED IN YOKOHAMA LAST NIGHT BY COINCIDENCE!
HE MUST HAVE PLANNED IT, BUT HOW?!
HOW IS MAYU-CHAN DOING?
OH! I HEARD THAT YOU GAVE HER CPR!
ARE YOU...? UM...
CAN I SEE HER NOW?
NO FRIGGIN' WAY!

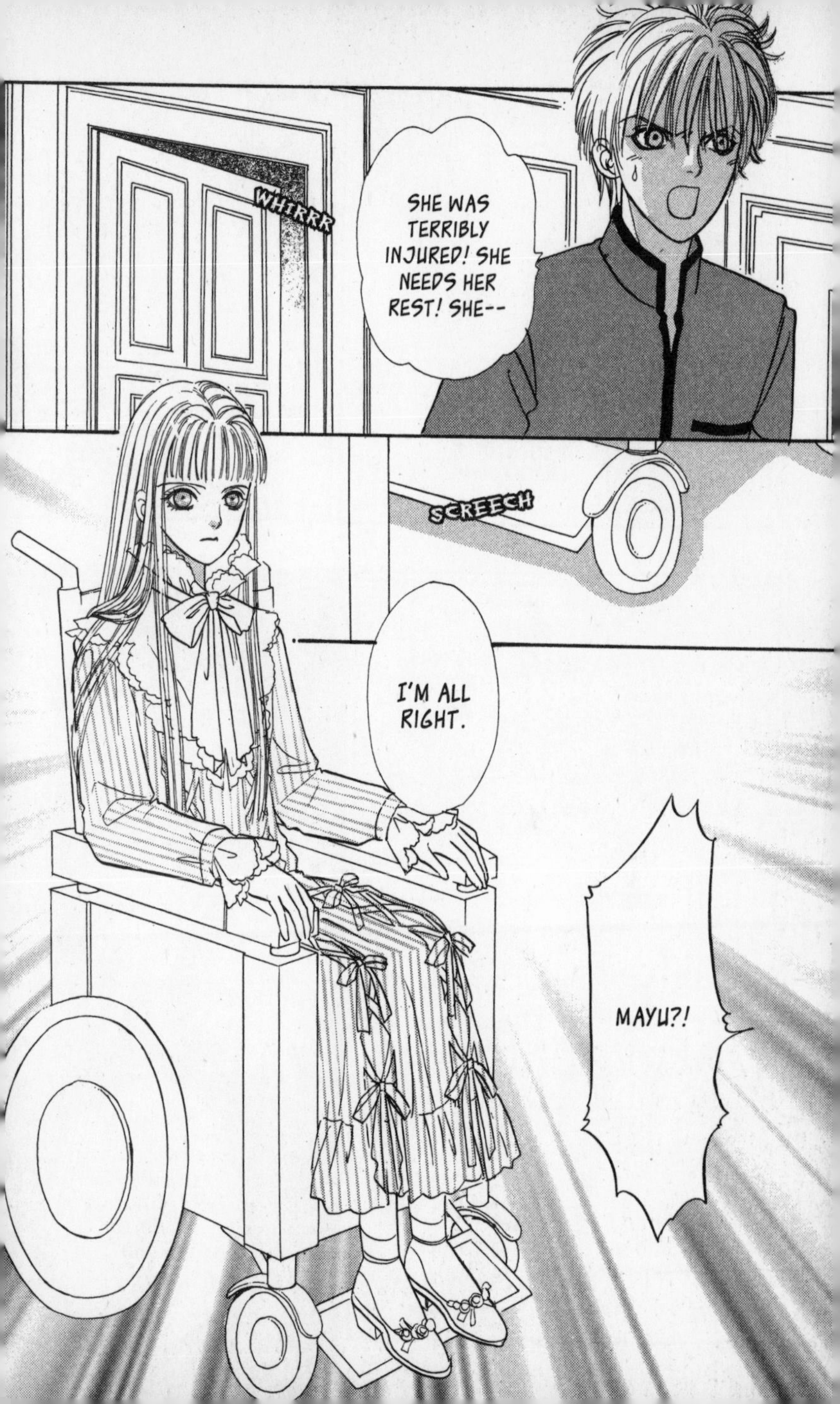
SHE WAS TERRIBLY INJURED! SHE NEEDS HER REST! SHE--
WHIRRR
SCREECH
I'M ALL RIGHT.
MAYU?!

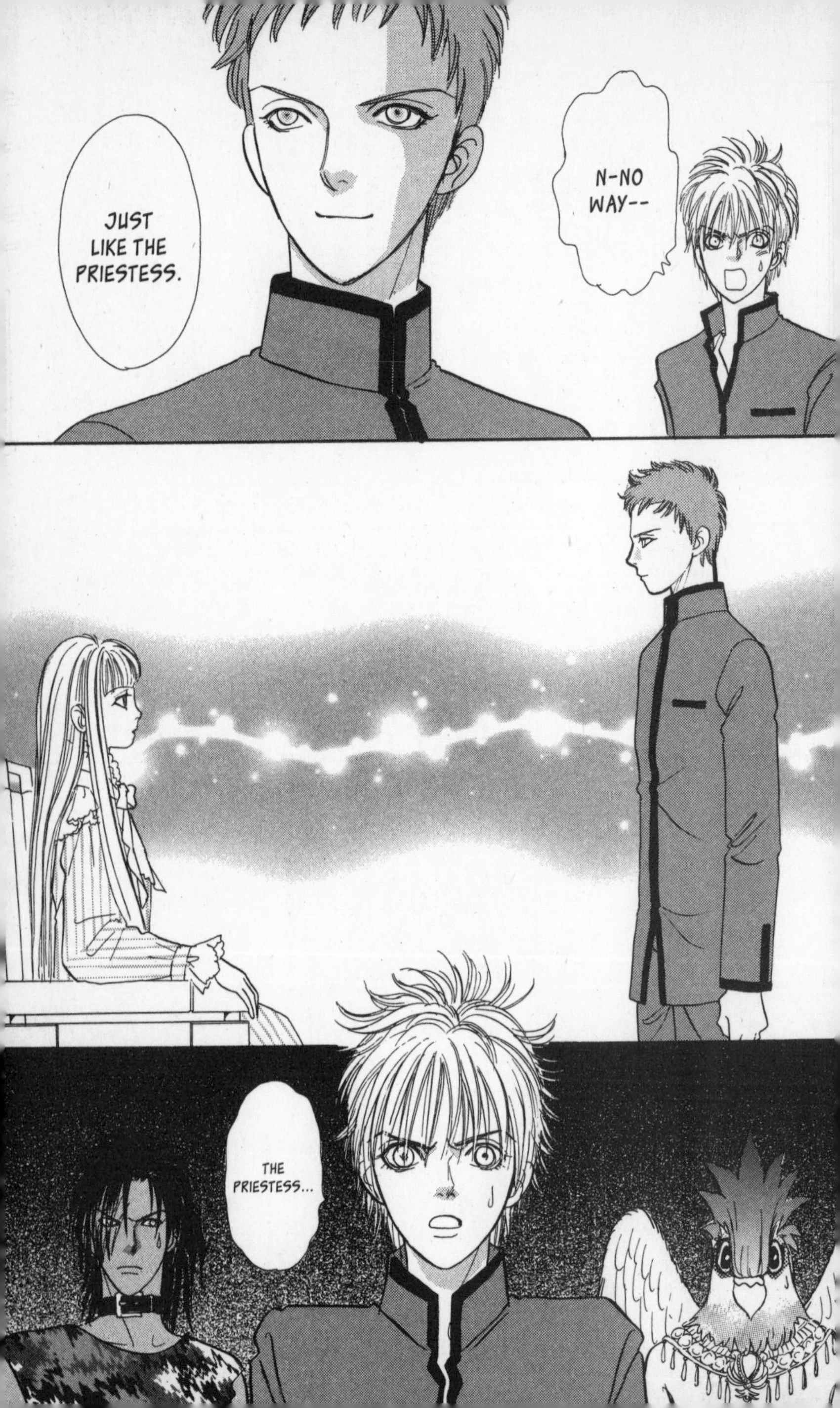
N-NO WAY--
JUST LIKE THE PRIESTESS.
THE PRIESTESS...

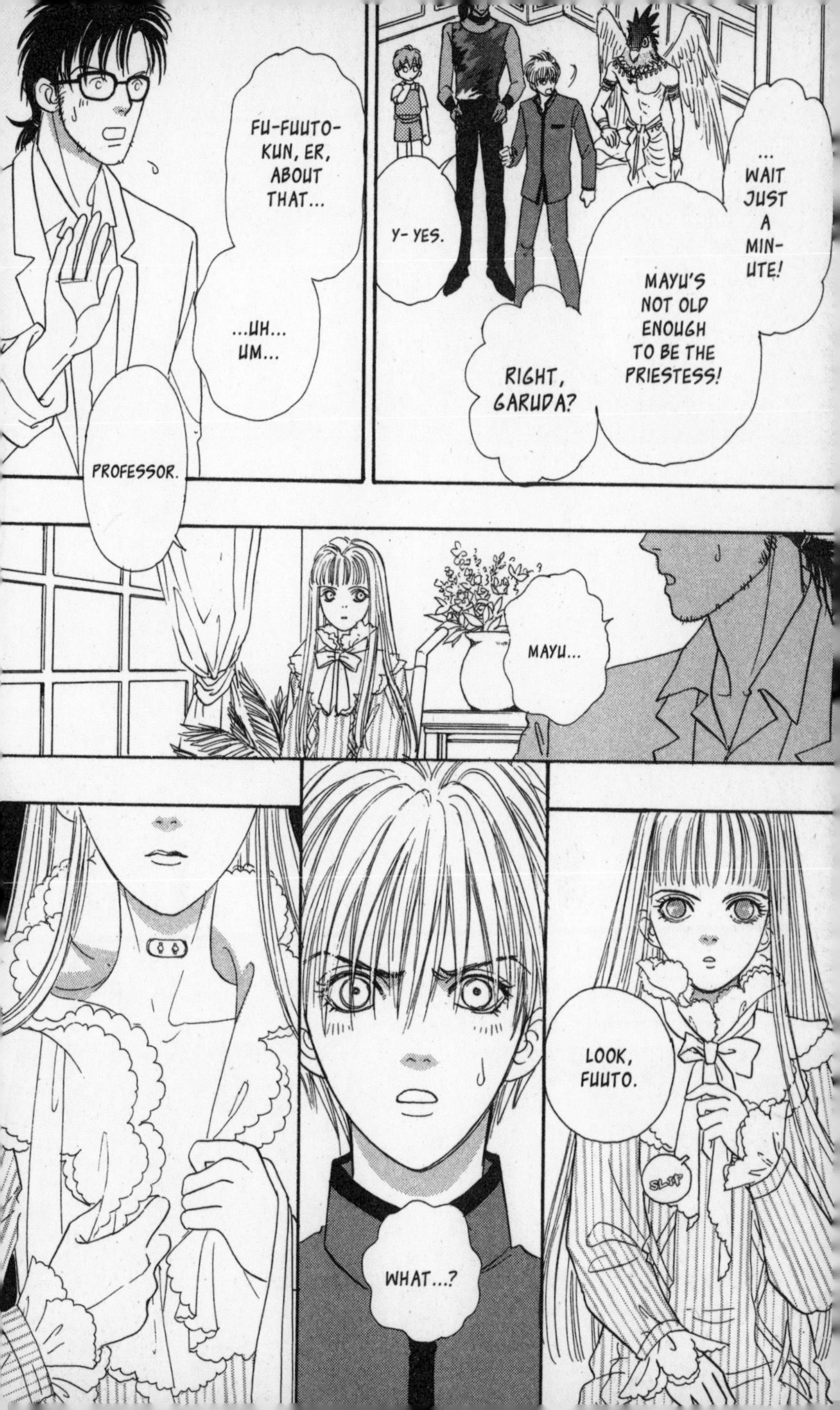
...WAIT JUST A MIN-UTE!
MAYU'S NOT OLD ENOUGH TO BE THE PRIESTESS!
RIGHT, GARUDA?
Y-YES.
FU-FUUTO-KUN, ER, ABOUT THAT...
...UH... UM...
PROFESSOR.
MAYU...
LOOK, FUUTO.
SLIP
WHAT...?

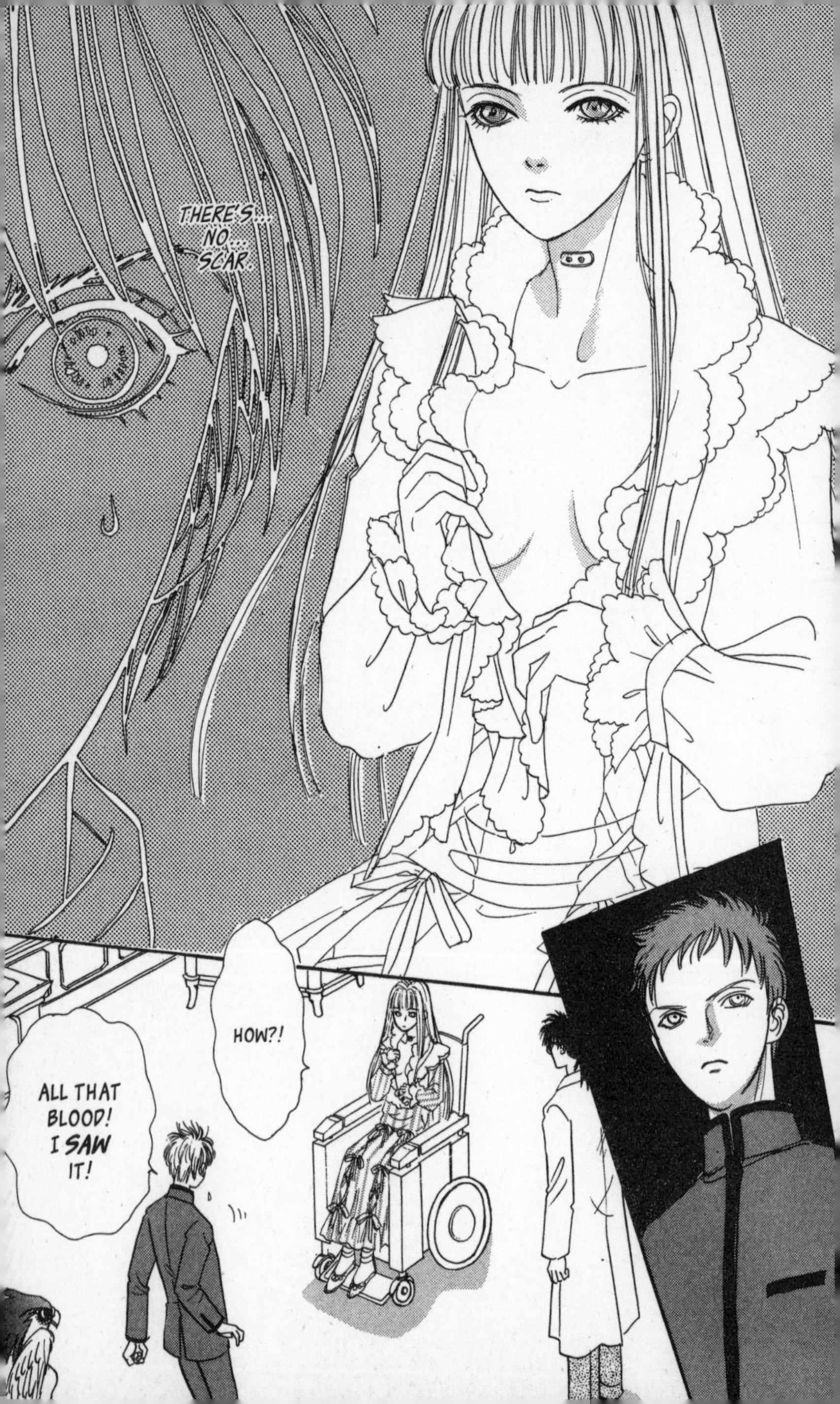
THERE'S... NO... SCAR.
HOW?!
ALL THAT BLOOD! I SAW IT!

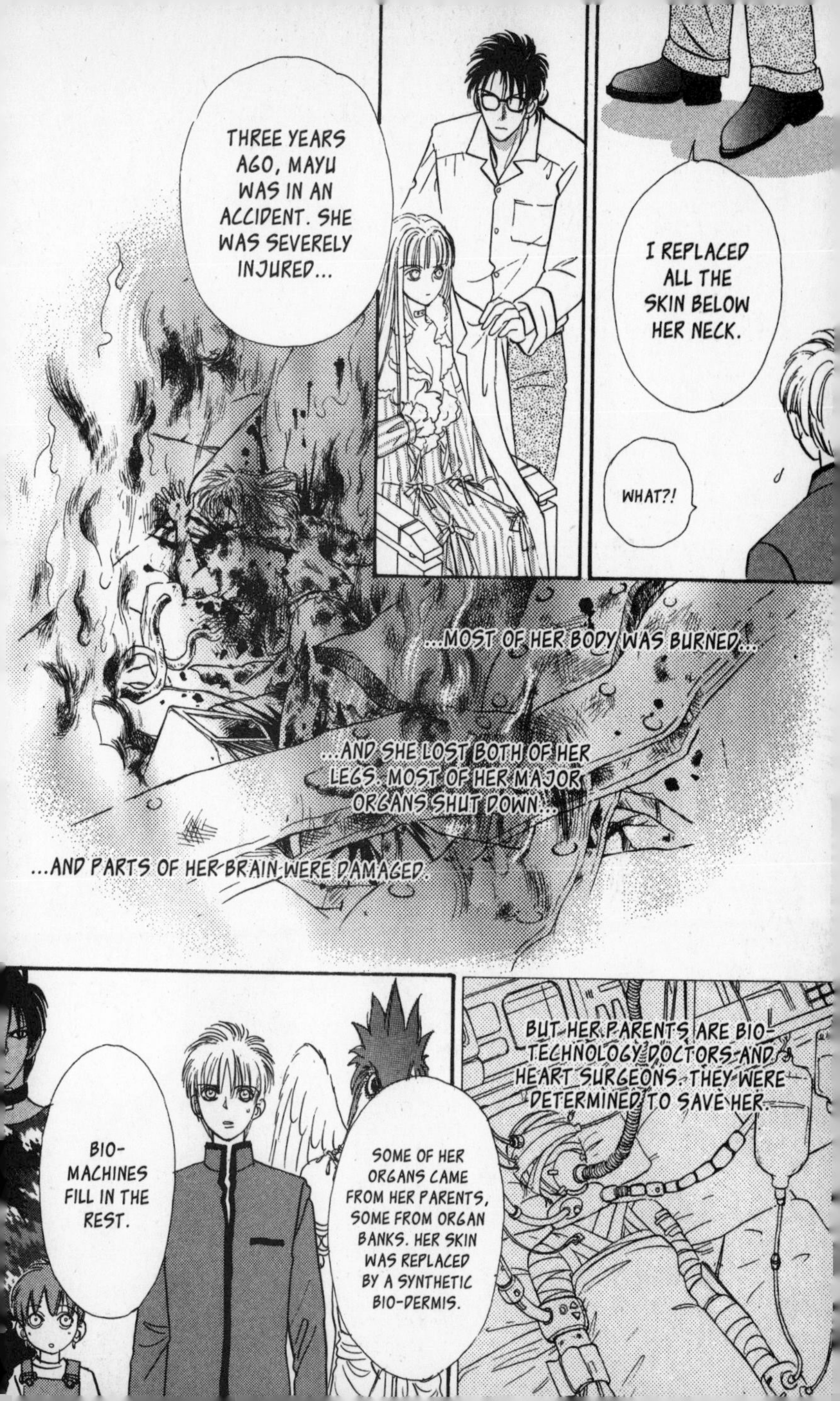
I REPLACED ALL THE SKIN BELOW HER NECK.
WHAT?!
THREE YEARS AGO, MAYU WAS IN AN ACCIDENT. SHE WAS SEVERELY INJURED...
...MOST OF HER BODY WAS BURNED...
...AND SHE LOST BOTH OF HER LEGS. MOST OF HER MAJOR ORGANS SHUT DOWN...
...AND PARTS OF HER BRAIN WERE DAMAGED.
BUT HER PARENTS ARE BIO-TECHNOLOGY DOCTORS AND HEART SURGEONS. THEY WERE DETERMINED TO SAVE HER.
SOME OF HER ORGANS CAME FROM HER PARENTS, SOME FROM ORGAN BANKS. HER SKIN WAS REPLACED BY A SYNTHETIC BIO-DERMIS.
BIO-MACHINES FILL IN THE REST.

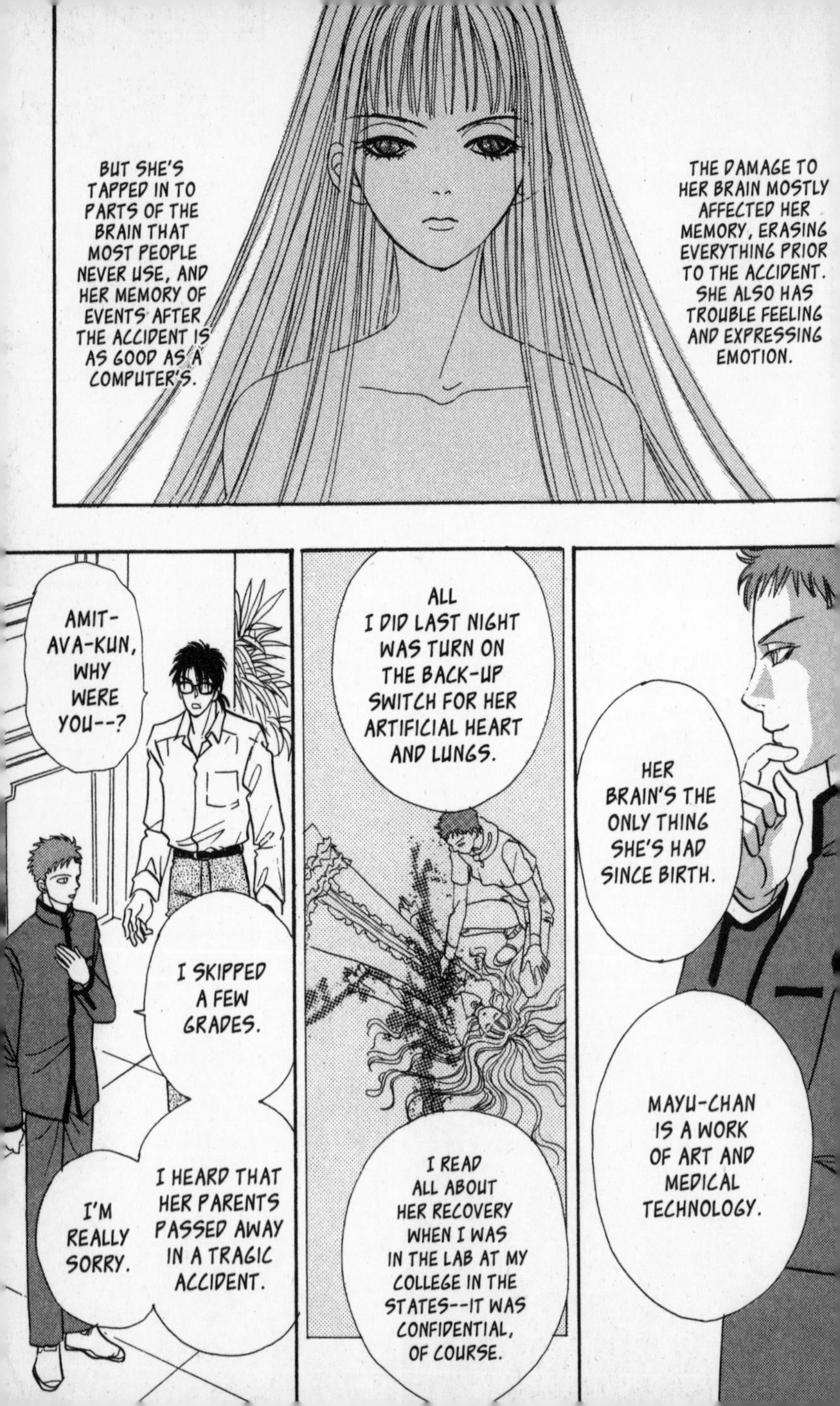
THE DAMAGE TO HER BRAIN MOSTLY AFFECTED HER MEMORY, ERASING EVERYTHING PRIOR TO THE ACCIDENT. SHE ALSO HAS TROUBLE FEELING AND EXPRESSING EMOTION.
BUT SHE'S TAPPED IN TO PARTS OF THE BRAIN THAT MOST PEOPLE NEVER USE, AND HER MEMORY OF EVENTS AFTER THE ACCIDENT IS AS GOOD AS A COMPUTER'S.
HER BRAIN'S THE ONLY THING SHE'S HAD SINCE BIRTH.
MAYU-CHAN IS A WORK OF ART AND MEDICAL TECHNOLOGY.
ALL I DID LAST NIGHT WAS TURN ON THE BACK-UP SWITCH FOR HER ARTIFICIAL HEART AND LUNGS.
I READ ALL ABOUT HER RECOVERY WHEN I WAS IN THE LAB AT MY COLLEGE IN THE STATES--IT WAS CONFIDENTIAL, OF COURSE.
AMIT-AVA-KUN, WHY WERE YOU--?
I SKIPPED A FEW GRADES.
I HEARD THAT HER PARENTS PASSED AWAY IN A TRAGIC ACCIDENT.
I'M REALLY SORRY.

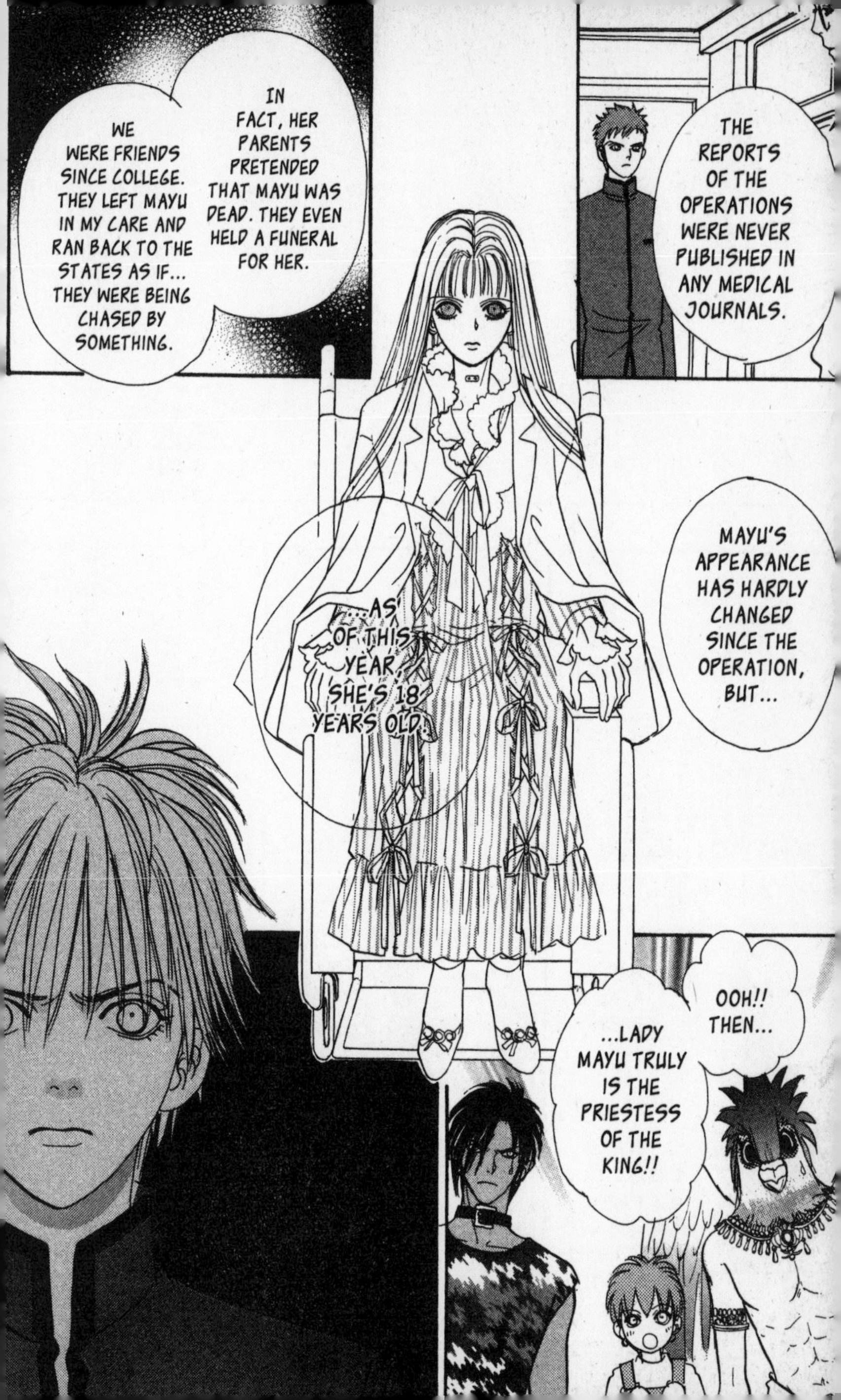
THE REPORTS OF THE OPERATIONS WERE NEVER PUBLISHED IN ANY MEDICAL JOURNALS.
IN FACT, HER PARENTS PRETENDED THAT MAYU WAS DEAD. THEY EVEN HELD A FUNERAL FOR HER.
WE WERE FRIENDS SINCE COLLEGE. THEY LEFT MAYU IN MY CARE AND RAN BACK TO THE STATES AS IF... THEY WERE BEING CHASED BY SOMETHING.
MAYU'S APPEARANCE HAS HARDLY CHANGED SINCE THE OPERATION, BUT...
...AS OF THIS YEAR, SHE'S 18 YEARS OLD.
OOH!! THEN...
...LADY MAYU TRULY IS THE PRIESTESS OF THE KING!!

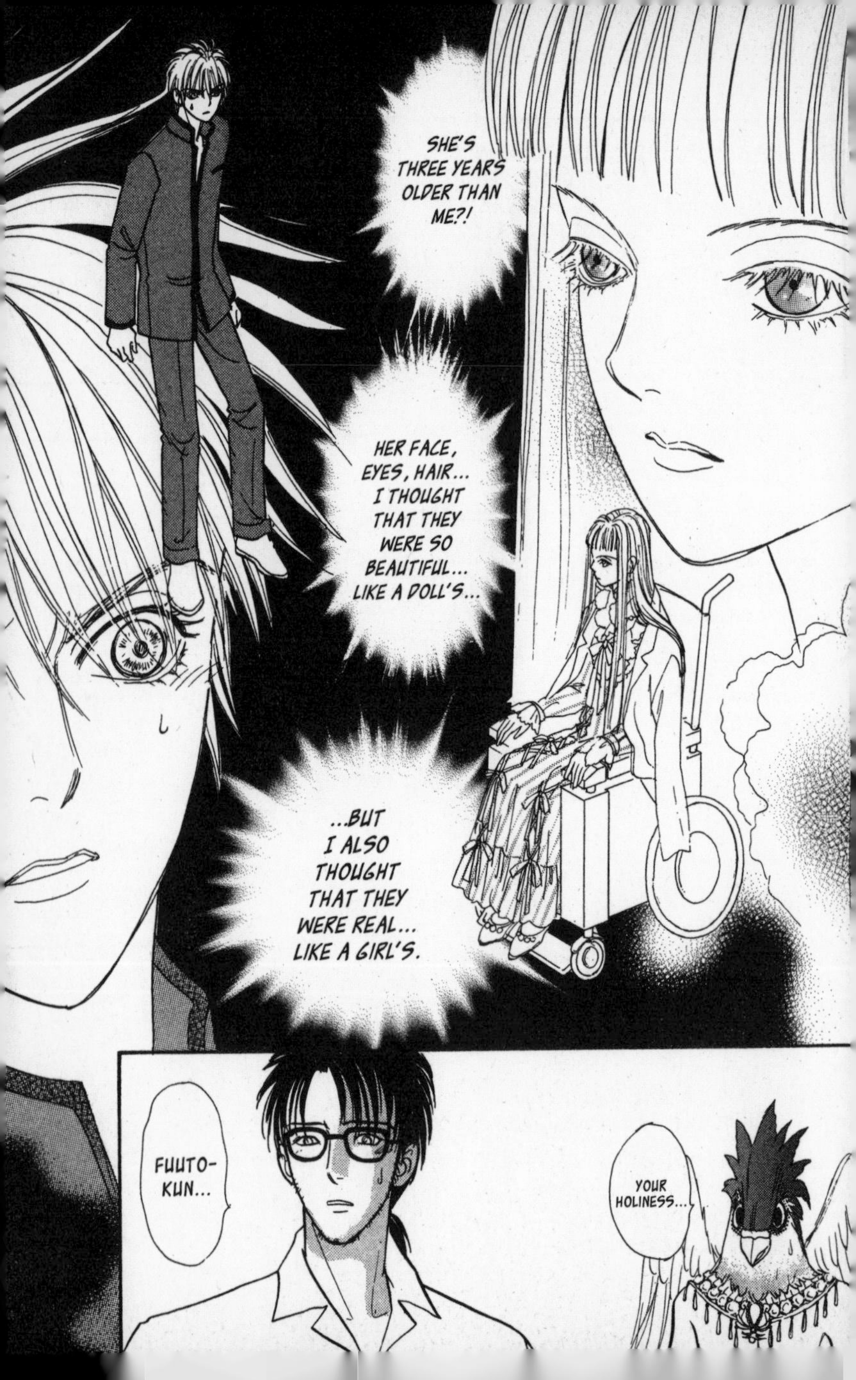
SHE'S THREE YEARS OLDER THAN ME?!
HER FACE, EYES, HAIR... I THOUGHT THAT THEY WERE SO BEAUTIFUL... LIKE A DOLL'S...
...BUT I ALSO THOUGHT THAT THEY WERE REAL... LIKE A GIRL'S.
YOUR HOLINESS...
FUUTO-KUN...

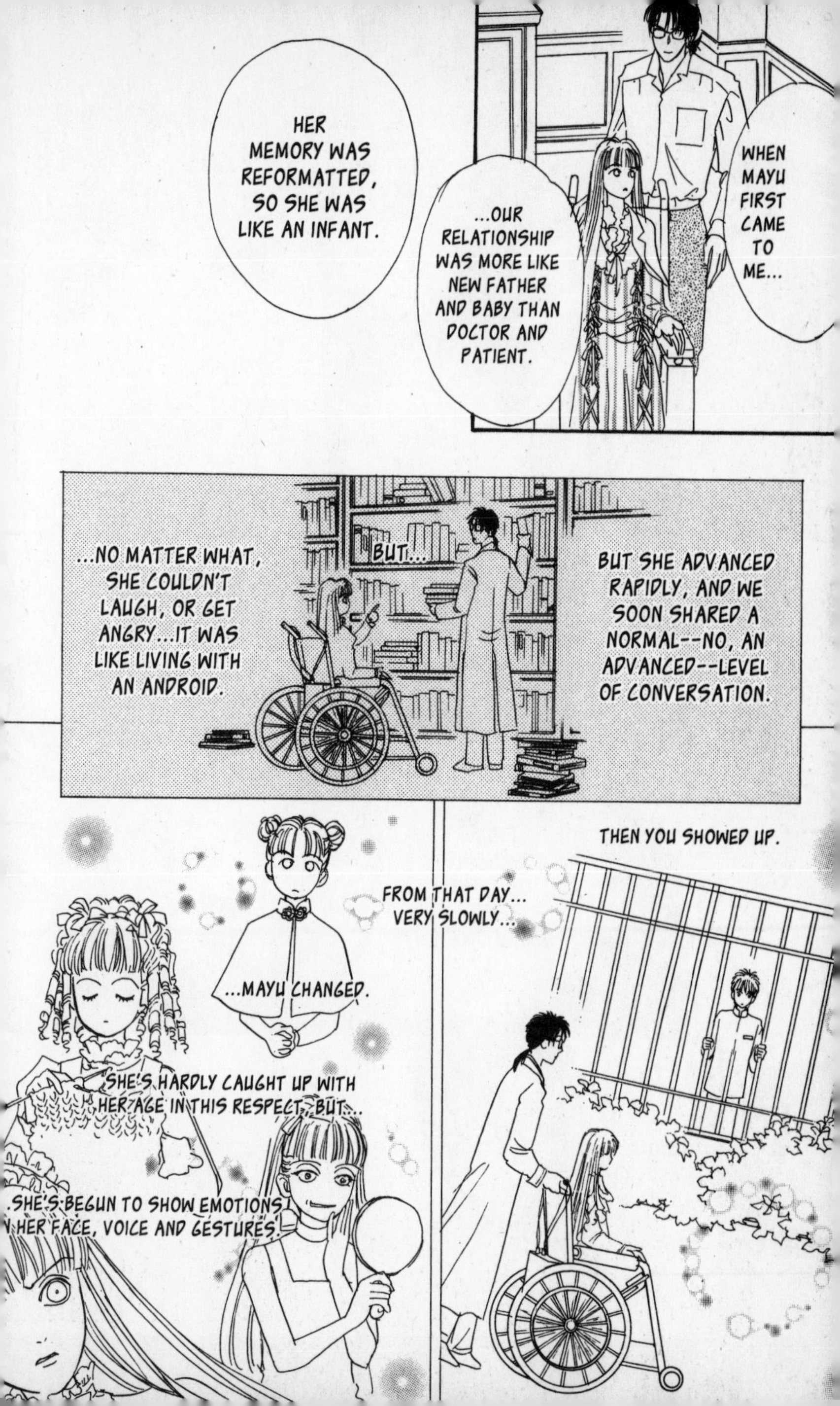
WHEN MAYU FIRST CAME TO ME...
...OUR RELATIONSHIP WAS MORE LIKE NEW FATHER AND BABY THAN DOCTOR AND PATIENT.
HER MEMORY WAS REFORMATTED, SO SHE WAS LIKE AN INFANT.
BUT SHE ADVANCED RAPIDLY, AND WE SOON SHARED A NORMAL--NO, AN ADVANCED--LEVEL OF CONVERSATION.
BUT...
...NO MATTER WHAT, SHE COULDN'T LAUGH, OR GET ANGRY...IT WAS LIKE LIVING WITH AN ANDROID.
THEN YOU SHOWED UP.
FROM THAT DAY... VERY SLOWLY...
...MAYU CHANGED.
SHE'S HARDLY CAUGHT UP WITH HER AGE IN THIS RESPECT, BUT...
SHE'S BEGUN TO SHOW EMOTIONS
HER FACE, VOICE AND GESTURES.

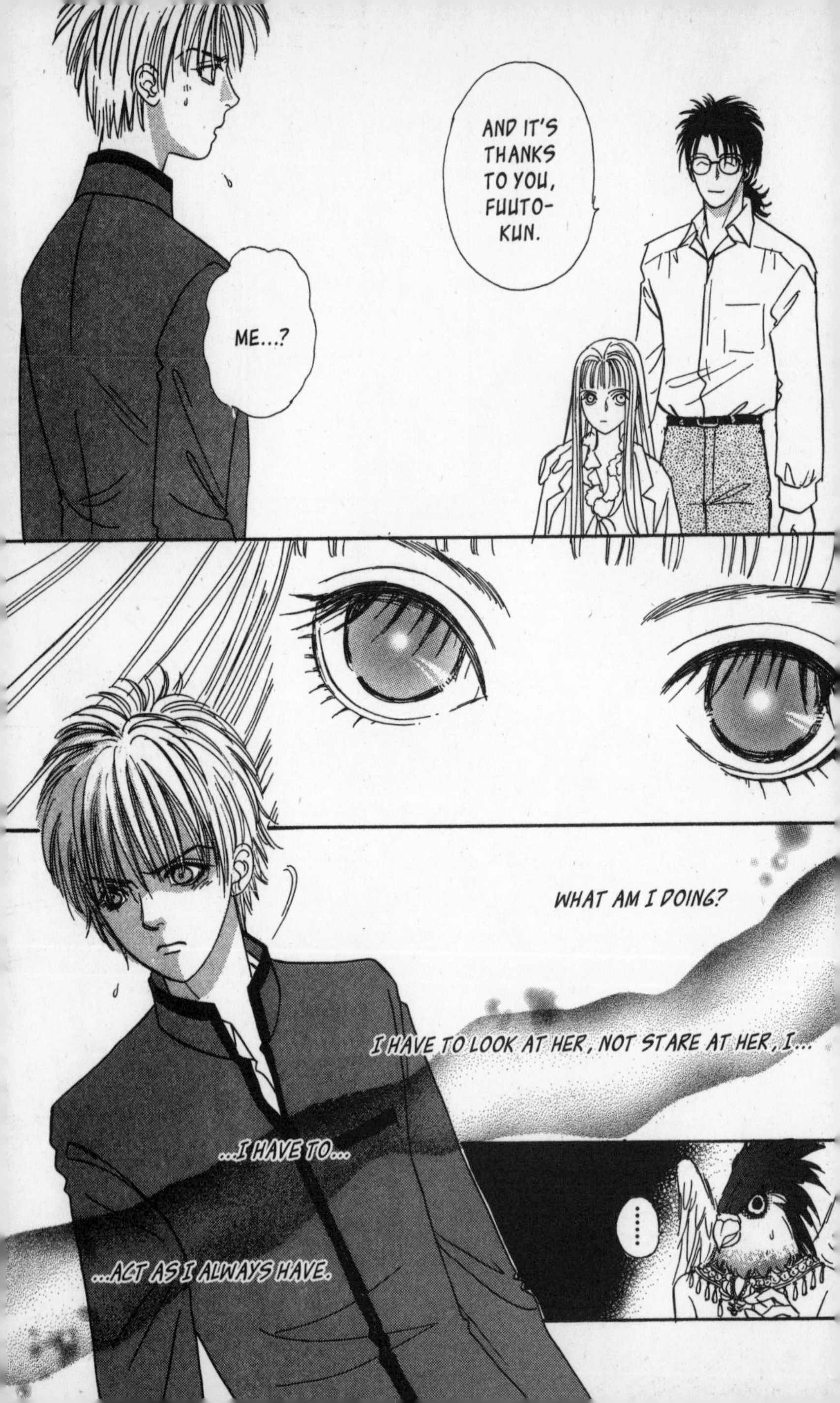
AND IT'S THANKS TO YOU, FUUTO-KUN.
ME...?
WHAT AM I DOING?
I HAVE TO LOOK AT HER, NOT STARE AT HER, I...
......
...I HAVE TO...
...ACT AS I ALWAYS HAVE.

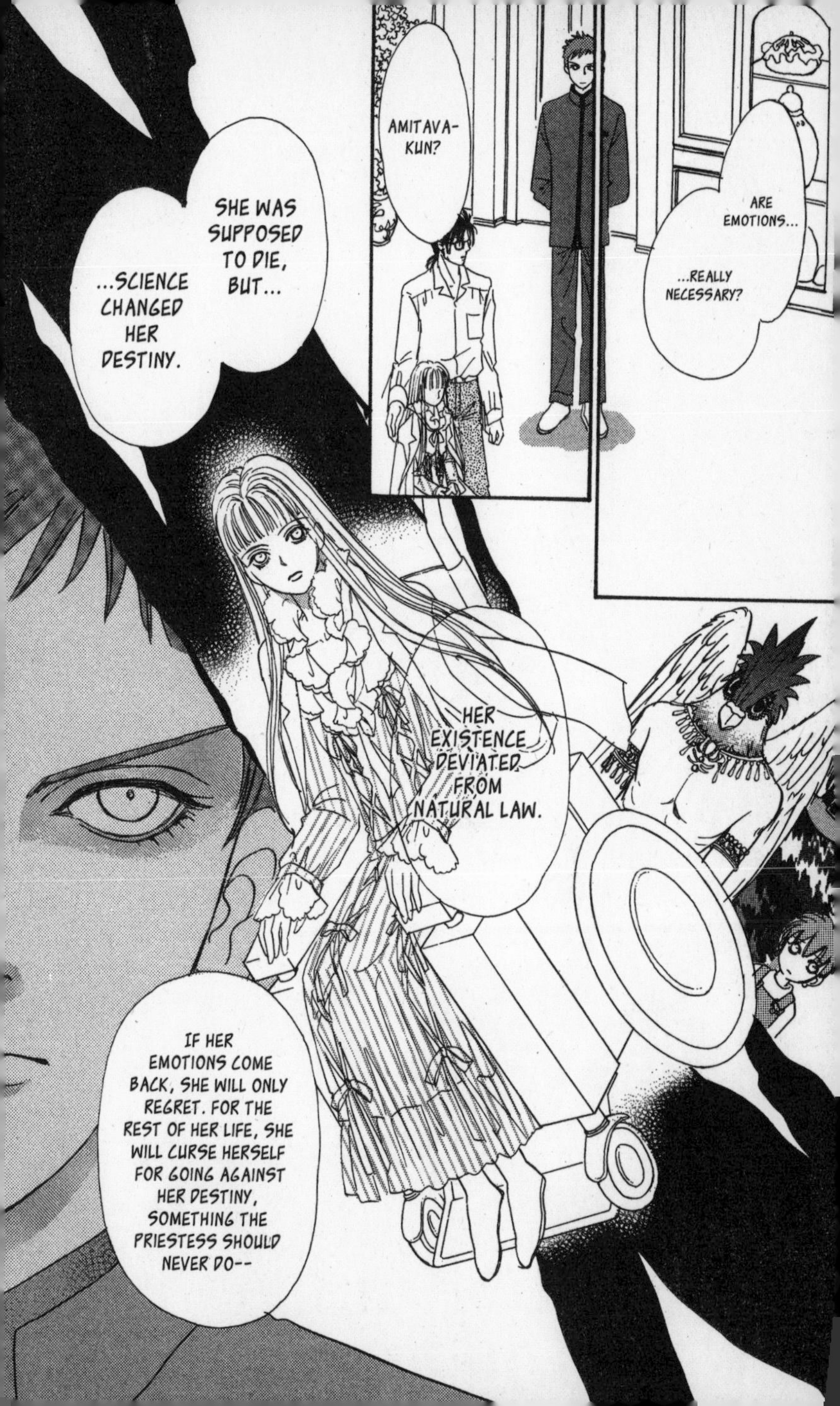
ARE EMOTIONS...
...REALLY NECESSARY?
AMITAVA-KUN?
SHE WAS SUPPOSED TO DIE, BUT...
...SCIENCE CHANGED HER DESTINY.
HER EXISTENCE DEVIATED FROM NATURAL LAW.
IF HER EMOTIONS COME BACK, SHE WILL ONLY REGRET. FOR THE REST OF HER LIFE, SHE WILL CURSE HERSELF FOR GOING AGAINST HER DESTINY, SOMETHING THE PRIESTESS SHOULD NEVER DO--

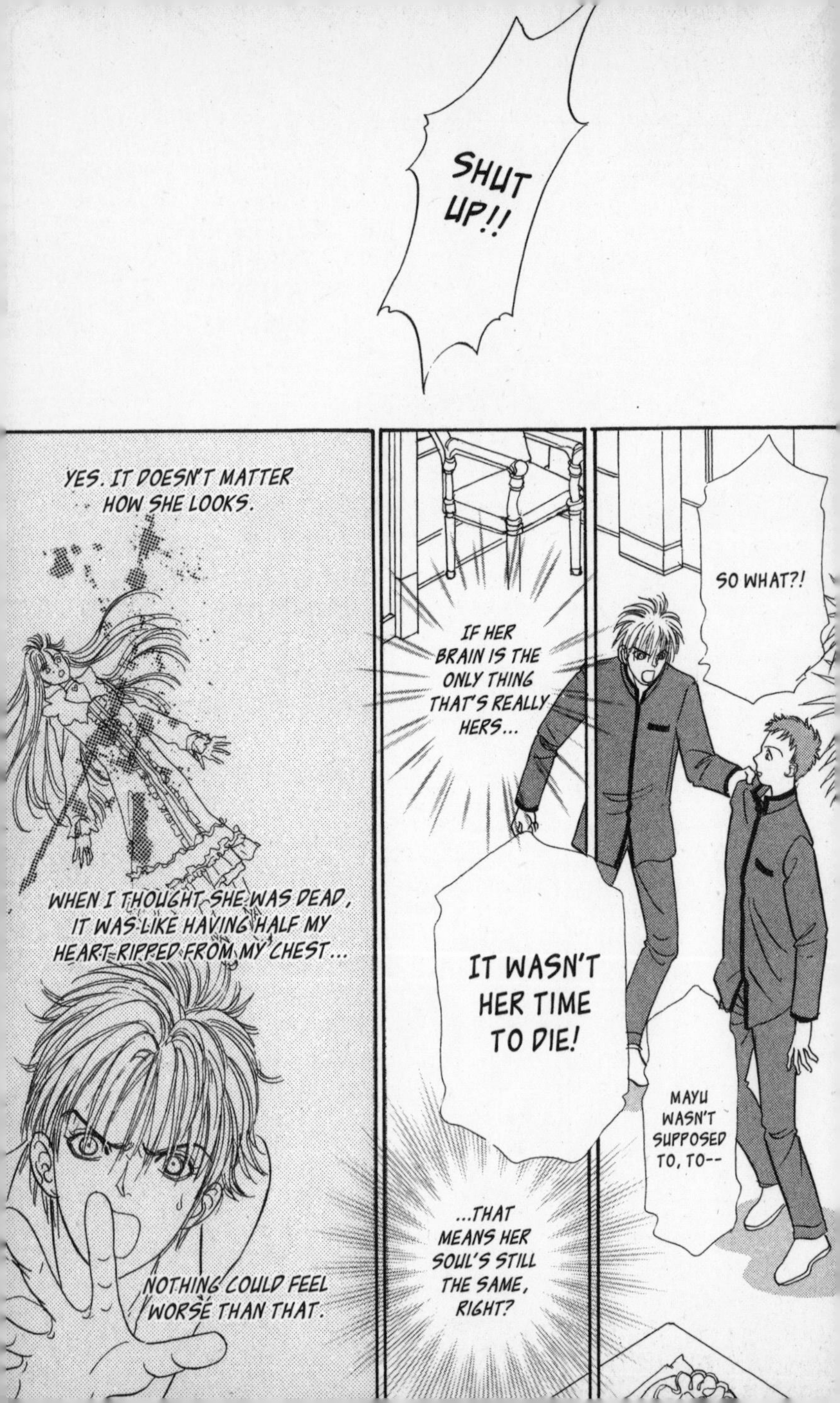

SHUT UP!!
SO WHAT?!
MAYU WASN'T SUPPOSED TO, TO--
IT WASN'T HER TIME TO DIE!
IF HER BRAIN IS THE ONLY THING THAT'S REALLY HERS...
...THAT MEANS HER SOUL'S STILL THE SAME, RIGHT?
YES. IT DOESN'T MATTER HOW SHE LOOKS.
WHEN I THOUGHT SHE WAS DEAD, IT WAS LIKE HAVING HALF MY HEART RIPPED FROM MY CHEST...
NOTHING COULD FEEL WORSE THAN THAT.

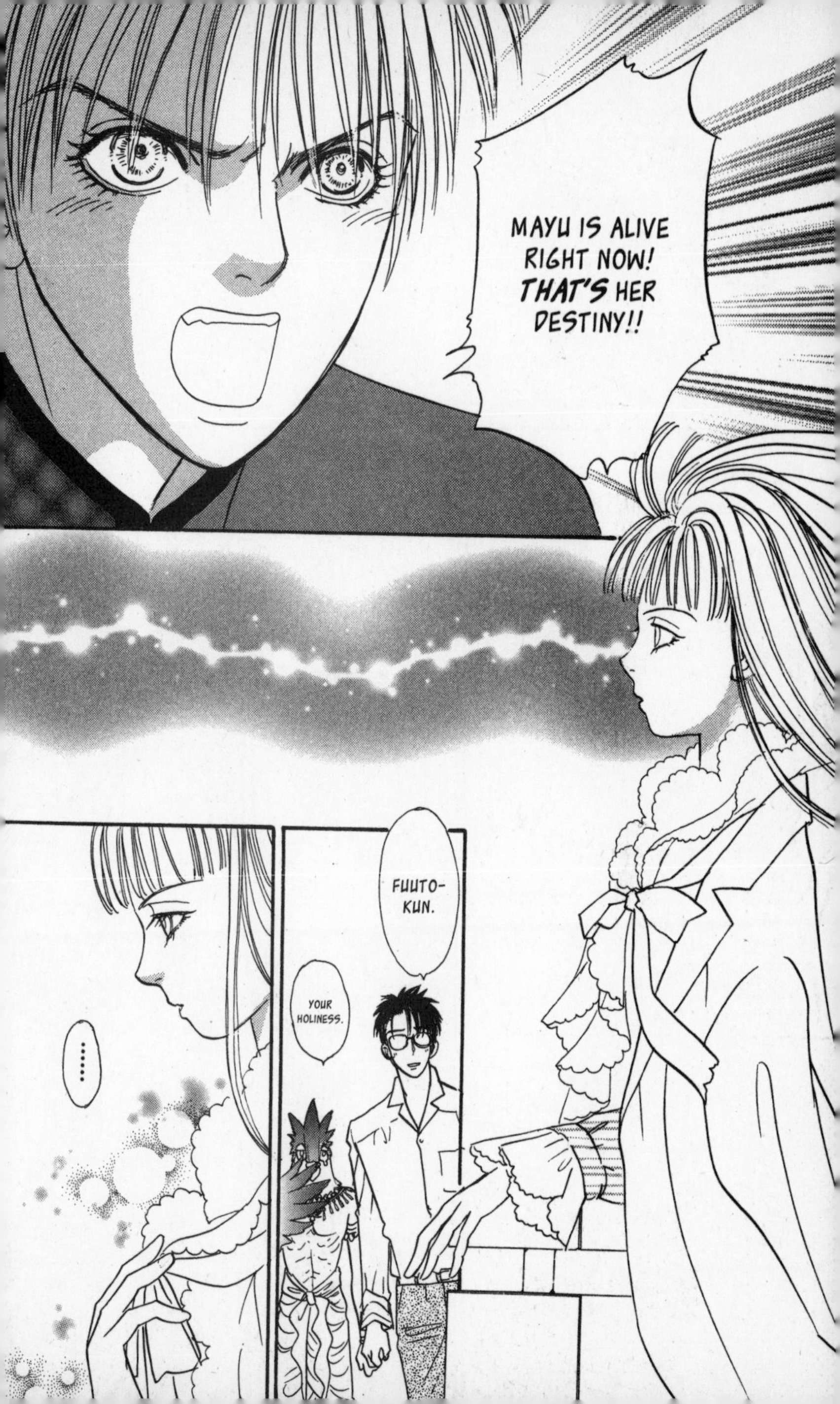
MAYU IS ALIVE RIGHT NOW! THAT'S HER DESTINY!!
FUUTO-KUN.
YOUR HOLINESS.
......

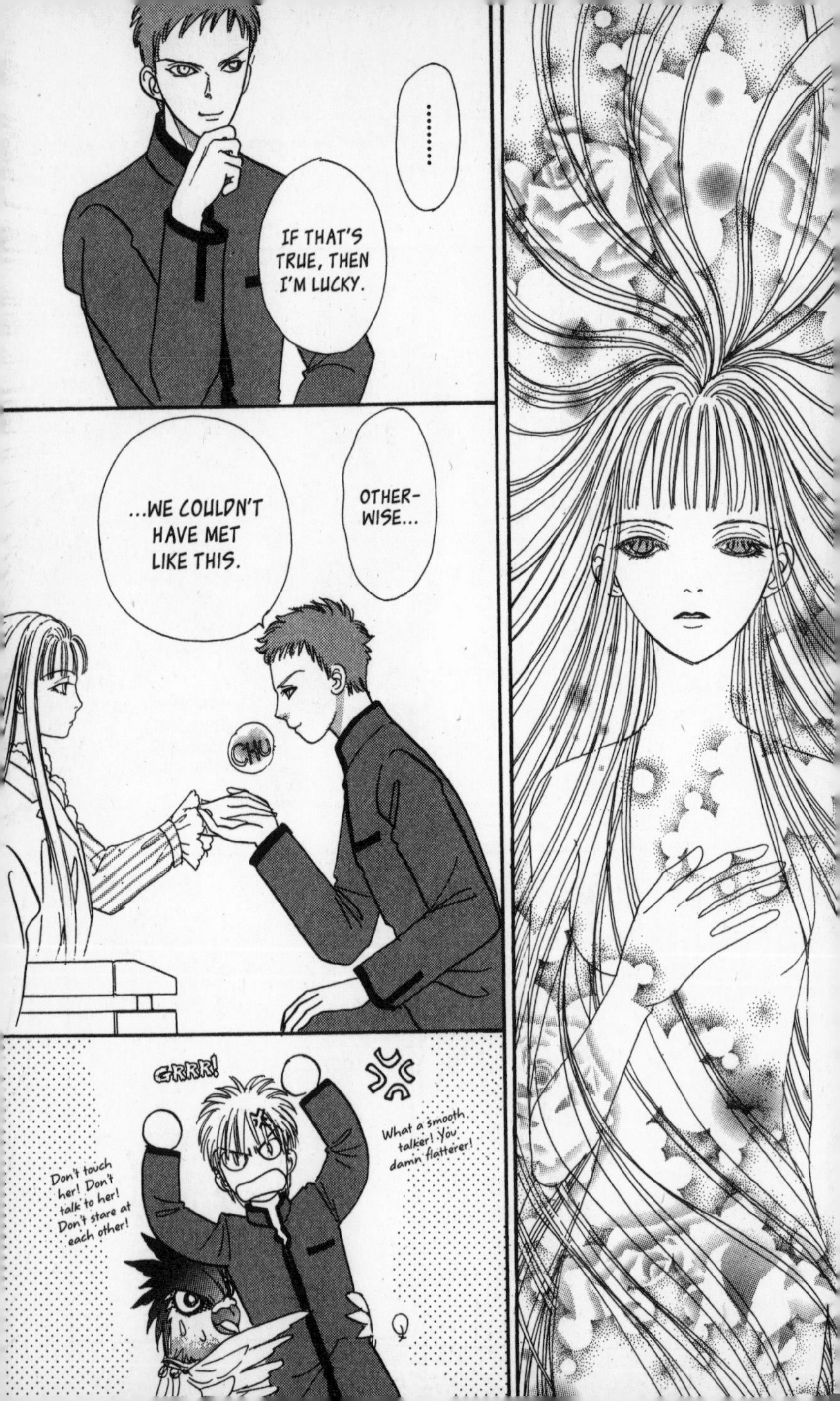
....
IF THAT'S TRUE, THEN I'M LUCKY.
OTHER-WISE...
...WE COULDN'T HAVE MET LIKE THIS.
CHU
GRRR!
What a smooth talker! You damn flatterer!
Don't touch her! Don't talk to her! Don't stare at each other!

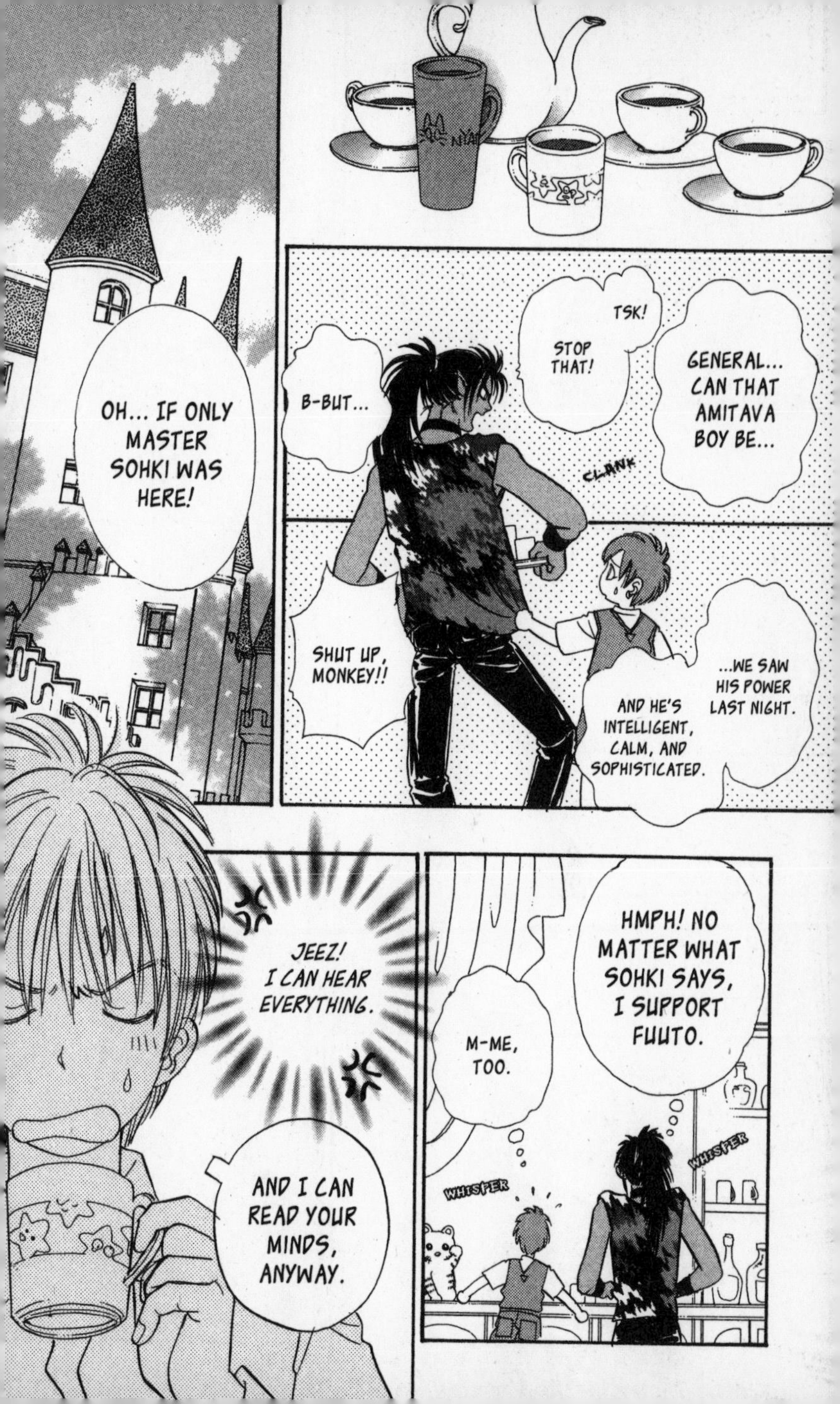
GENERAL... CAN THAT AMITAVA BOY BE...
TSK!
STOP THAT!
CLANK
B-BUT...
...WE SAW HIS POWER LAST NIGHT.
AND HE'S INTELLIGENT, CALM, AND SOPHISTICATED.
SHUT UP, MONKEY!!
OH... IF ONLY MASTER SOHKI WAS HERE!
HMPH! NO MATTER WHAT SOHKI SAYS, I SUPPORT FUUTO.
M-ME, TOO.
WHISPER
WHISPER
JEEZ! I CAN HEAR EVERYTHING.
AND I CAN READ YOUR MINDS, ANYWAY.

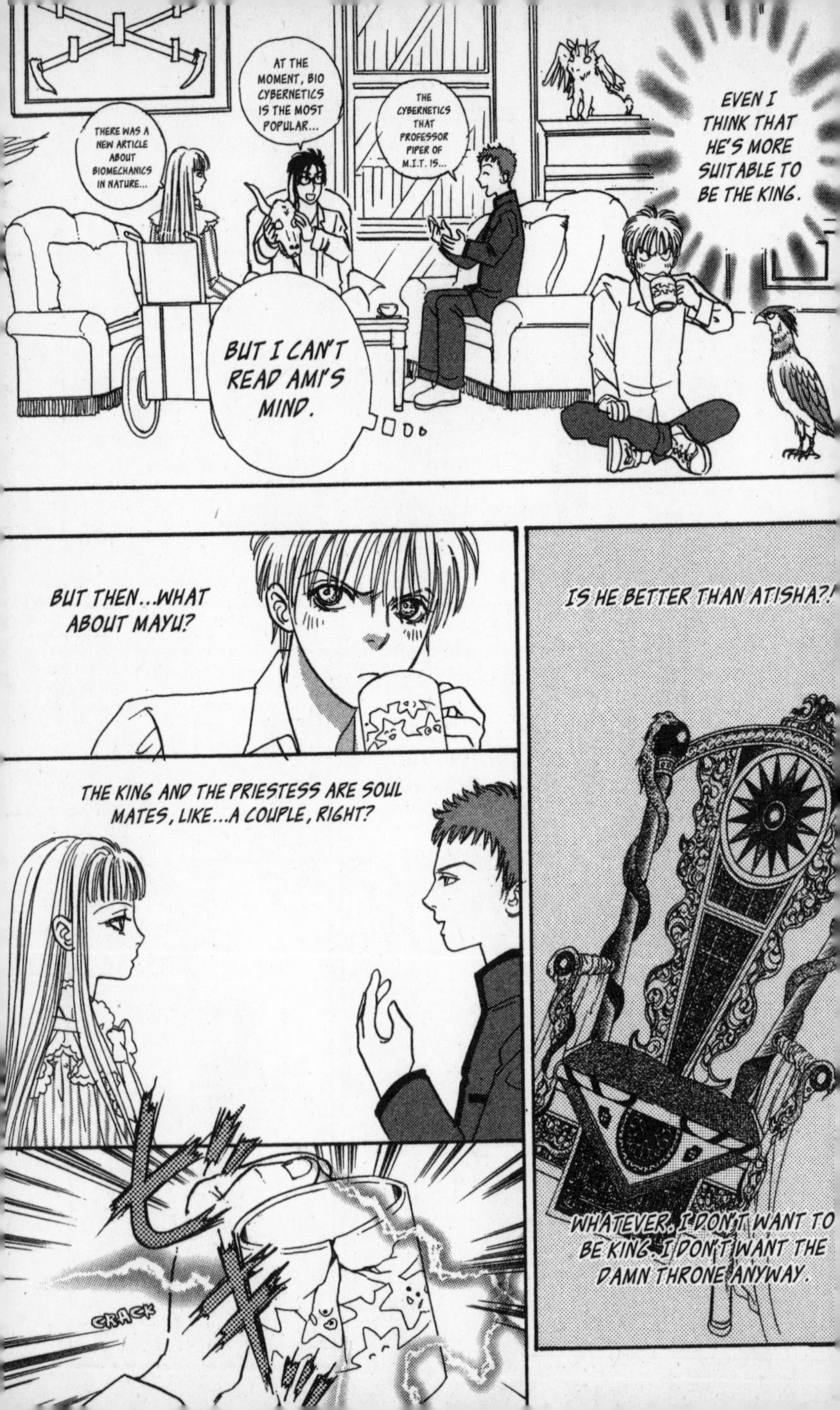
EVEN I THINK THAT HE'S MORE SUITABLE TO BE THE KING.
THE CYBERNETICS THAT PROFESSOR PIPER OF M.I.T. IS...
AT THE MOMENT, BIO CYBERNETICS IS THE MOST POPULAR...
THERE WAS A NEW ARTICLE ABOUT BIOMECHANICS IN NATURE...
BUT I CAN'T READ AMI'S MIND.
IS HE BETTER THAN ATISHA?!
WHATEVER. I DON'T WANT TO BE KING. I DON'T WANT THE DAMN THRONE ANYWAY.
BUT THEN...WHAT ABOUT MAYU?
THE KING AND THE PRIESTESS ARE SOUL MATES, LIKE...A COUPLE, RIGHT?
CRACK

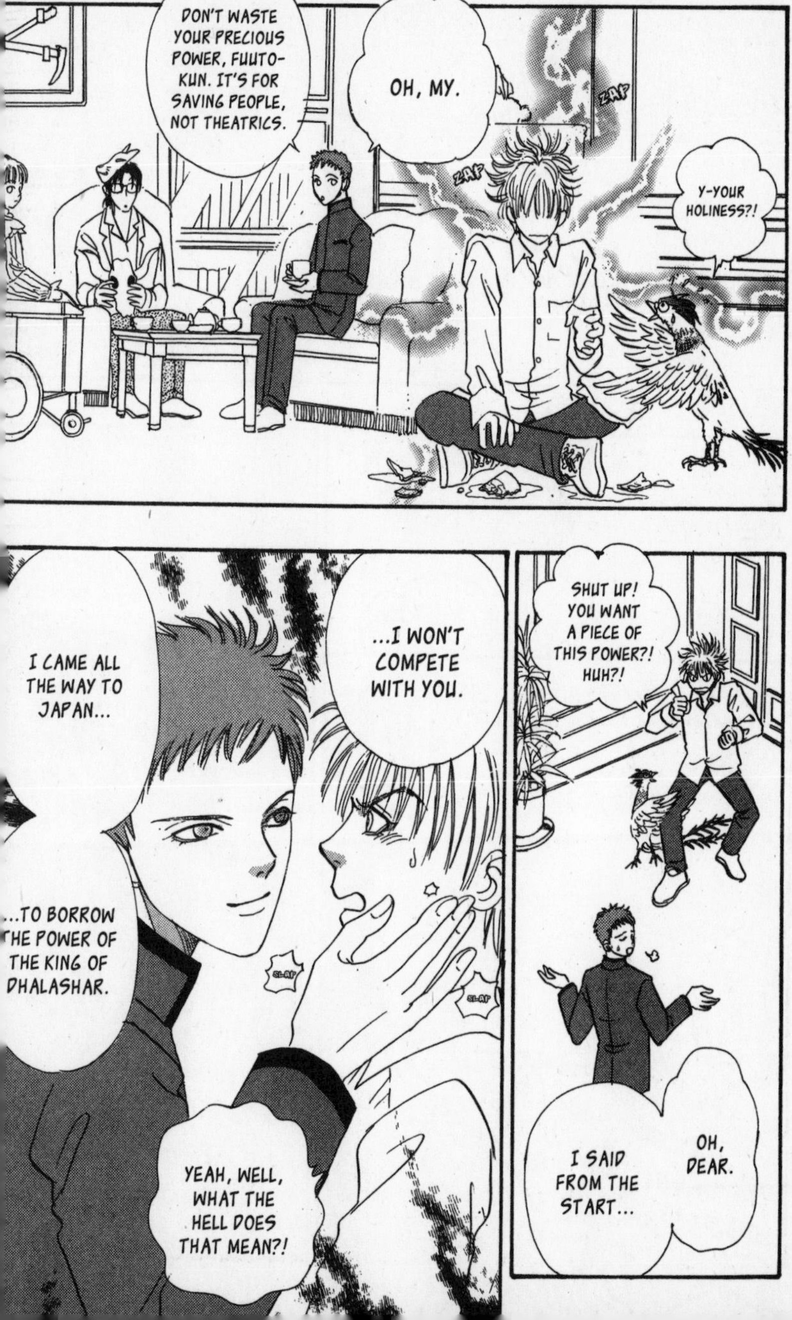
ZAP
Y-YOUR HOLINESS?!
ZAP
OH, MY.
DON'T WASTE YOUR PRECIOUS POWER, FUUTO-KUN. IT'S FOR SAVING PEOPLE, NOT THEATRICS.
SHUT UP! YOU WANT A PIECE OF THIS POWER?! HUH?!
OH, DEAR.
I SAID FROM THE START...
...I WON'T COMPETE WITH YOU.
I CAME ALL THE WAY TO JAPAN...
...TO BORROW THE POWER OF THE KING OF DHALASHAR.
SLAP
SLAP
YEAH, WELL, WHAT THE HELL DOES THAT MEAN?!

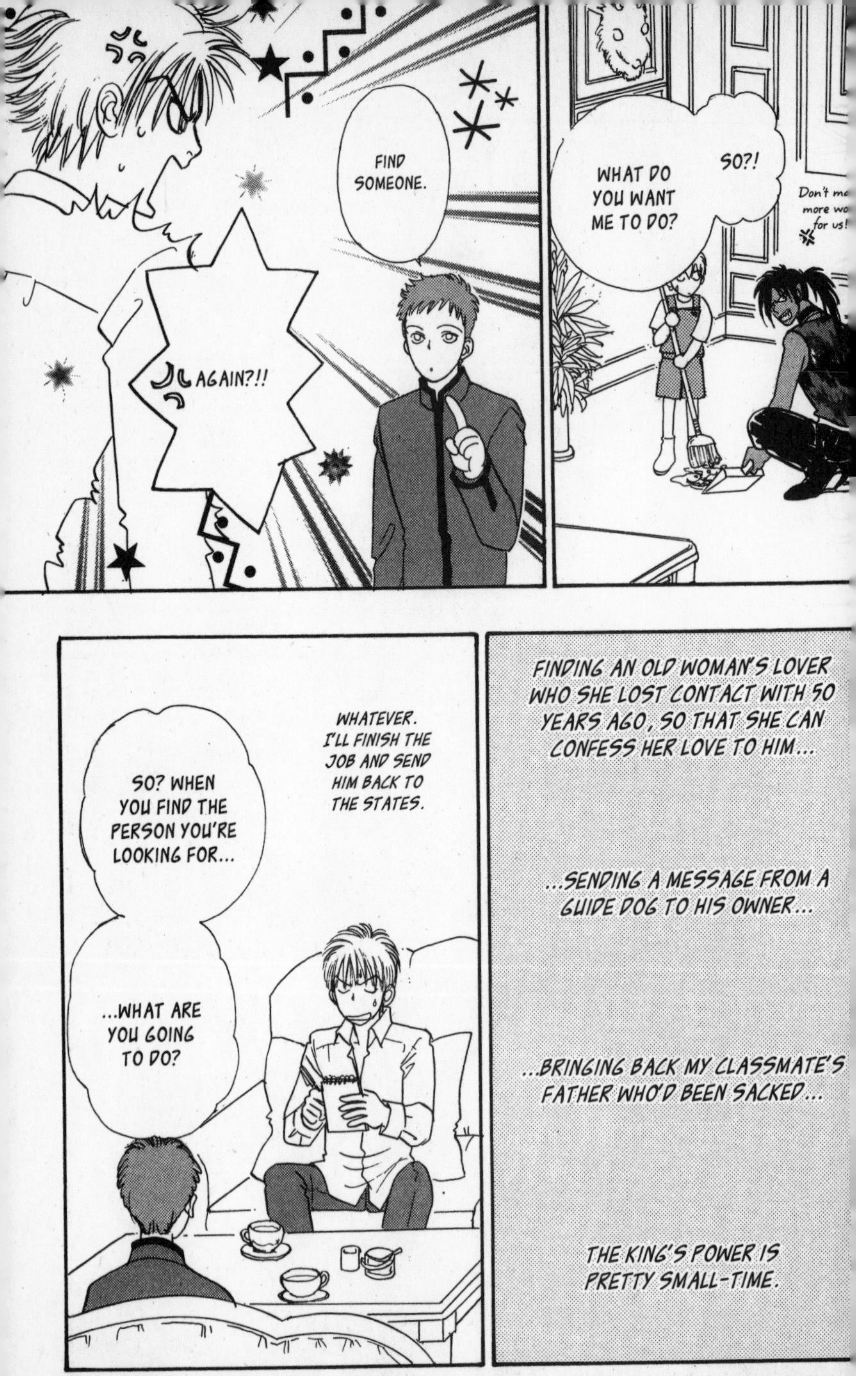
WHAT DO YOU WANT ME TO DO?
SO?!
Don't ma more wo for us!
FIND SOMEONE.
AGAIN?!!
FINDING AN OLD WOMAN'S LOVER WHO SHE LOST CONTACT WITH 50 YEARS AGO, SO THAT SHE CAN CONFESS HER LOVE TO HIM...
...SENDING A MESSAGE FROM A GUIDE DOG TO HIS OWNER...
...BRINGING BACK MY CLASSMATE'S FATHER WHO'D BEEN SACKED...
THE KING'S POWER IS PRETTY SMALL-TIME.
WHATEVER. I'LL FINISH THE JOB AND SEND HIM BACK TO THE STATES.
SO? WHEN YOU FIND THE PERSON YOU'RE LOOKING FOR...
...WHAT ARE YOU GOING TO DO?

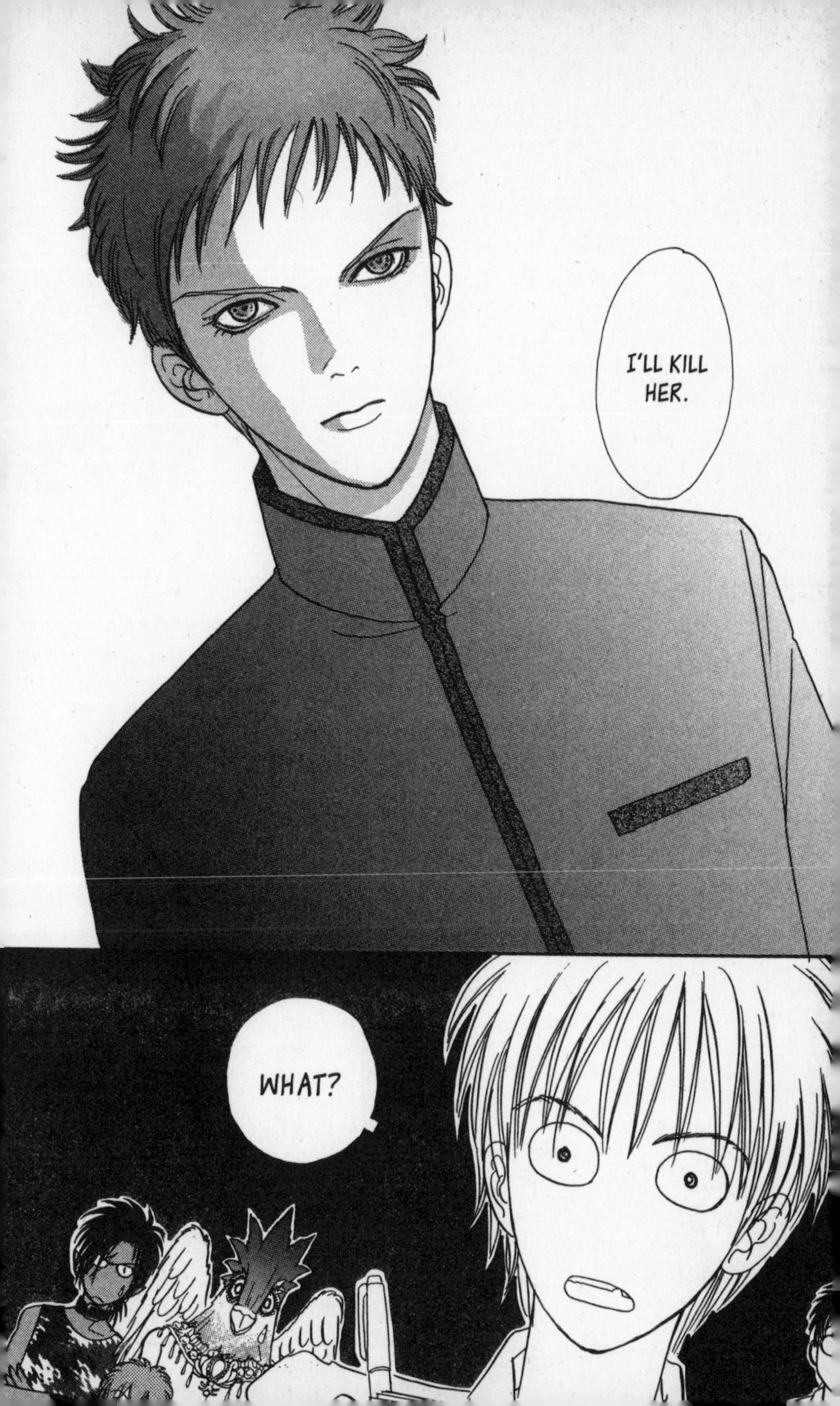
I'LL KILL HER.
WHAT?

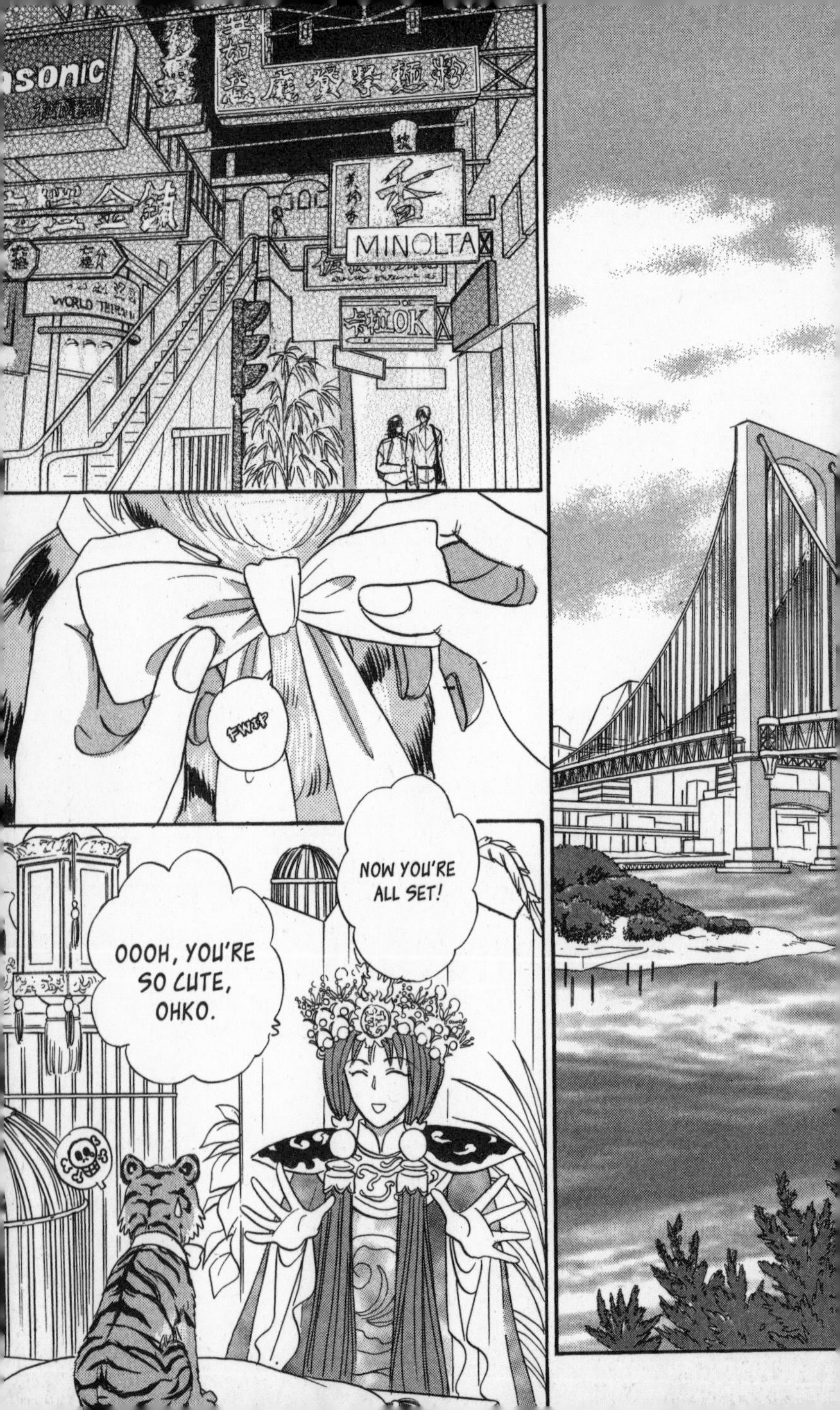
MINOLTA
NOW YOU'RE ALL SET!
OOOH, YOU'RE SO CUTE, OHKO.

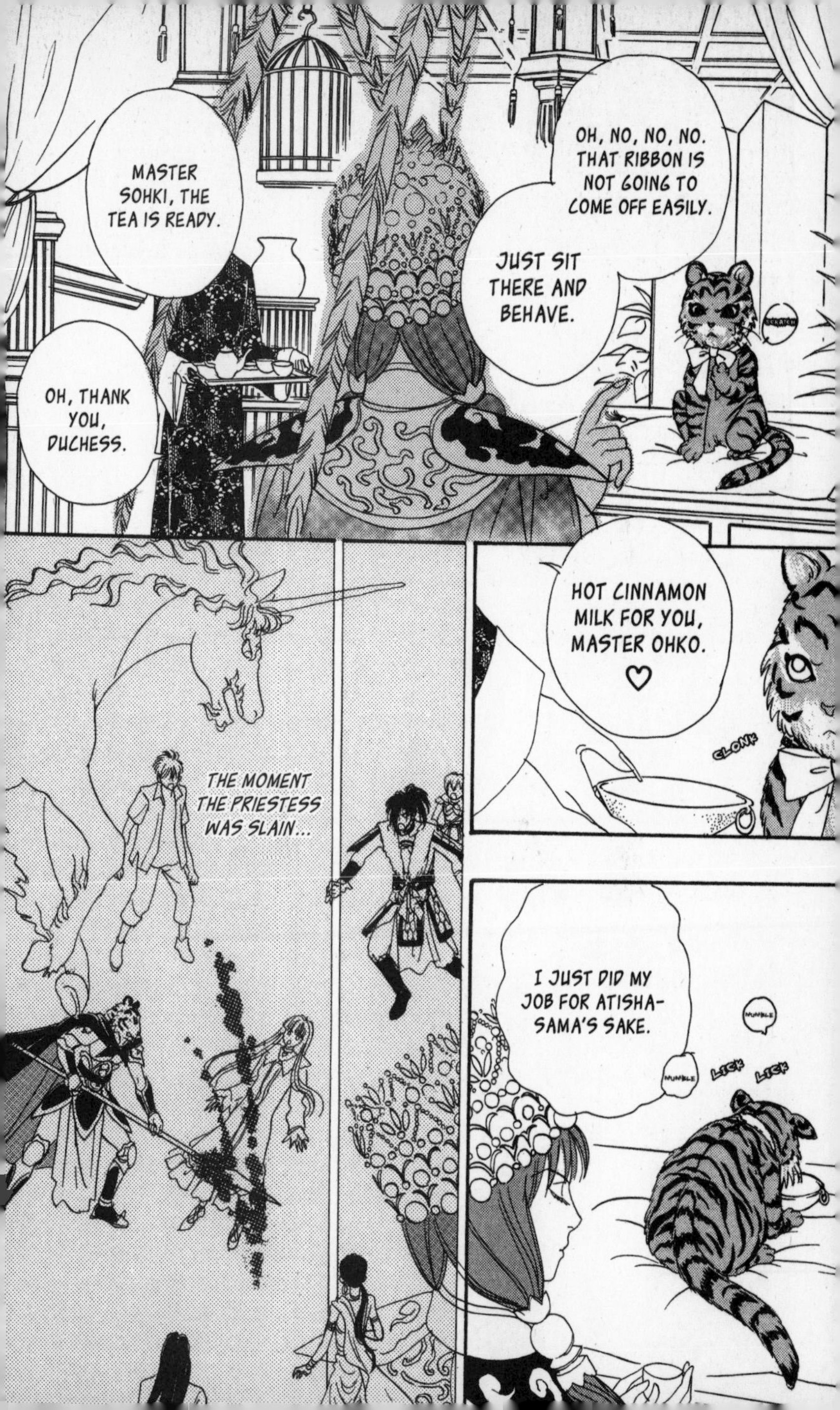
OH, NO, NO, NO. THAT RIBBON IS NOT GOING TO COME OFF EASILY.
JUST SIT THERE AND BEHAVE.
SCRATCH
MASTER SOHKI, THE TEA IS READY.
OH, THANK YOU, DUCHESS.
HOT CINNAMON MILK FOR YOU, MASTER OHKO. ♡
CLONK
I JUST DID MY JOB FOR ATISHA-SAMA'S SAKE.
MUMBLE
LICK LICK
MUMBLE
THE MOMENT THE PRIESTESS WAS SLAIN...

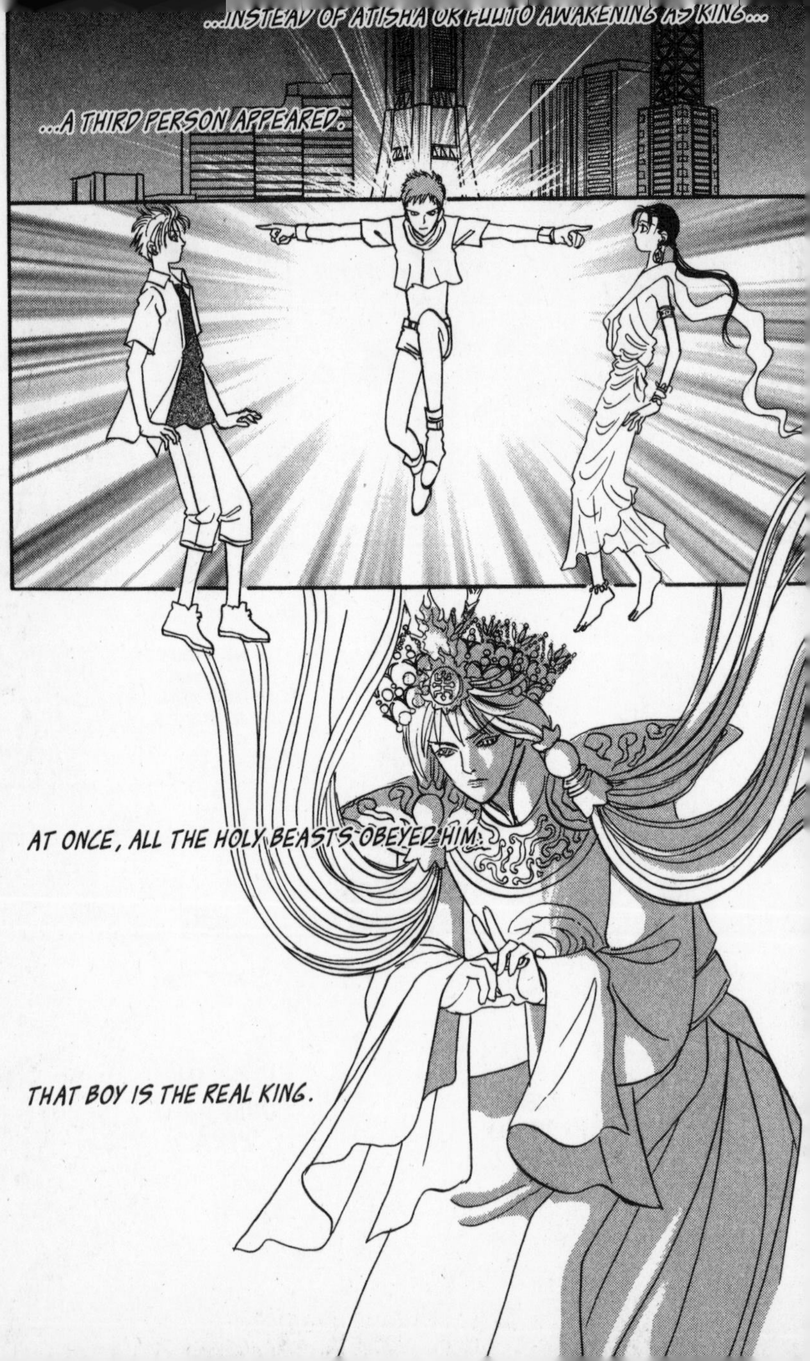
...INSTEAD OF ATISHA OR FUUTO AWAKENING AS KING...
...A THIRD PERSON APPEARED.
AT ONCE, ALL THE HOLY BEASTS OBEYED HIM.
THAT BOY IS THE REAL KING.

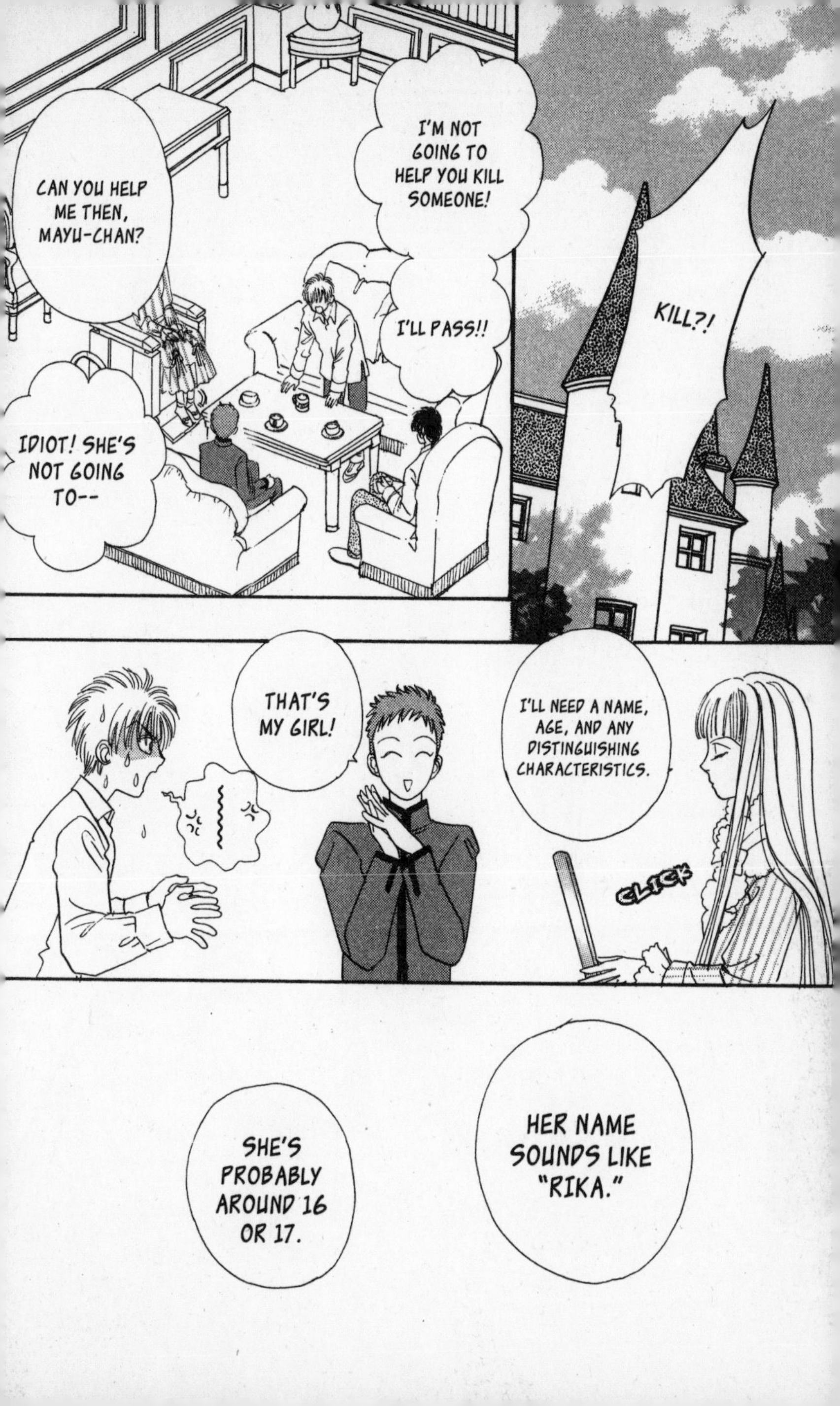
KILL?!
I'M NOT GOING TO HELP YOU KILL SOMEONE!
I'LL PASS!!
CAN YOU HELP ME THEN, MAYU-CHAN?
IDIOT! SHE'S NOT GOING TO--
I'LL NEED A NAME, AGE, AND ANY DISTINGUISHING CHARACTERISTICS.
CLICK
THAT'S MY GIRL!
HER NAME SOUNDS LIKE "RIKA."
SHE'S PROBABLY AROUND 16 OR 17.

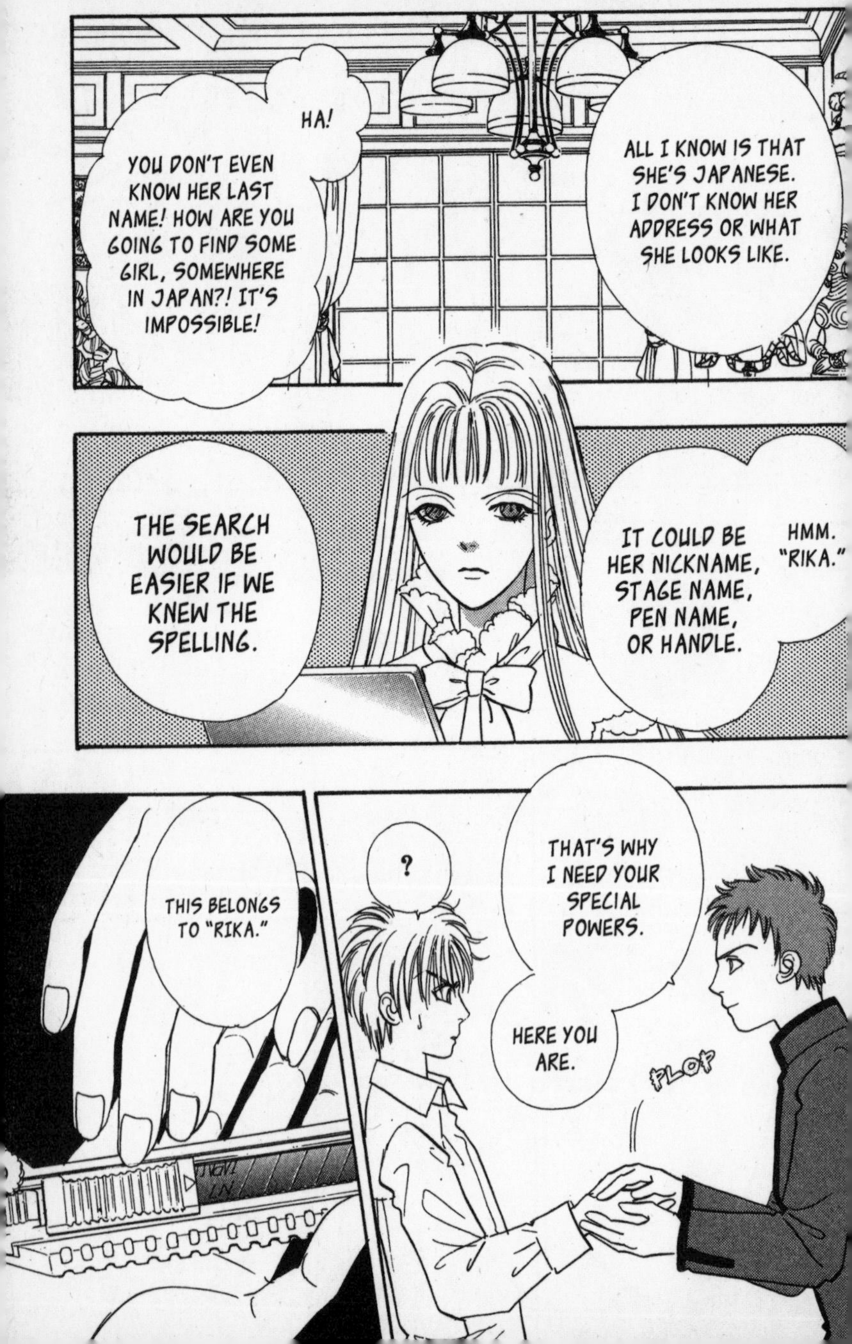
ALL I KNOW IS THAT SHE'S JAPANESE. I DON'T KNOW HER ADDRESS OR WHAT SHE LOOKS LIKE.
HA!
YOU DON'T EVEN KNOW HER LAST NAME! HOW ARE YOU GOING TO FIND SOME GIRL, SOMEWHERE IN JAPAN?! IT'S IMPOSSIBLE!
HMM. "RIKA."
IT COULD BE HER NICKNAME, STAGE NAME, PEN NAME, OR HANDLE.
THE SEARCH WOULD BE EASIER IF WE KNEW THE SPELLING.
THAT'S WHY I NEED YOUR SPECIAL POWERS.
?
HERE YOU ARE.
PLOP
THIS BELONGS TO "RIKA."

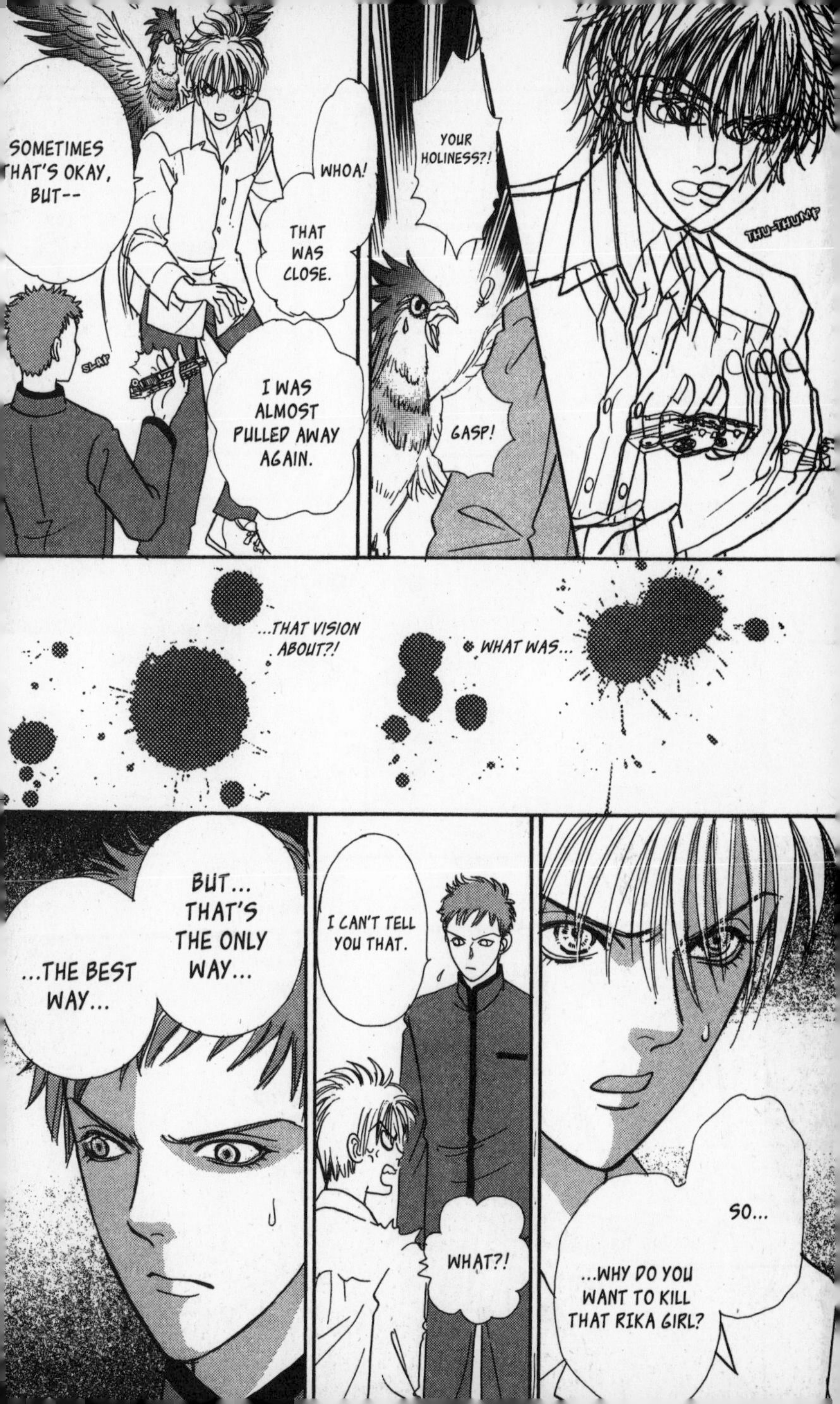
THU-THUMP
YOUR HOLINESS?!
GASP!
WHOA!
SOMETIMES THAT'S OKAY, BUT--
THAT WAS CLOSE.
SLAP
I WAS ALMOST PULLED AWAY AGAIN.
WHAT WAS...
...THAT VISION ABOUT?!
SO...
...WHY DO YOU WANT TO KILL THAT RIKA GIRL?
I CAN'T TELL YOU THAT.
WHAT?!
BUT... THAT'S THE ONLY WAY...
...THE BEST WAY...

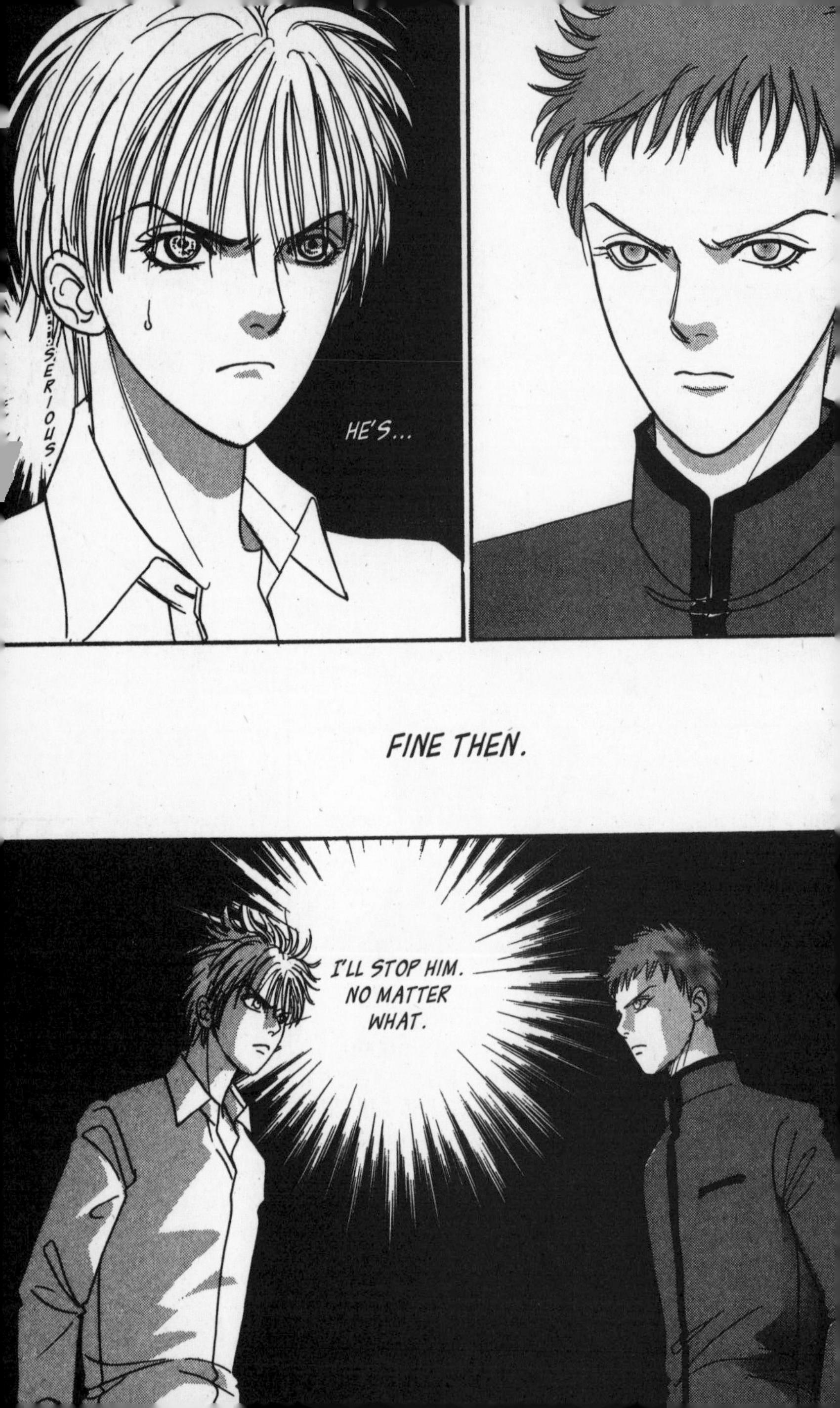

HE'S...
SERIOUS.
FINE THEN.
I'LL STOP HIM. NO MATTER WHAT.

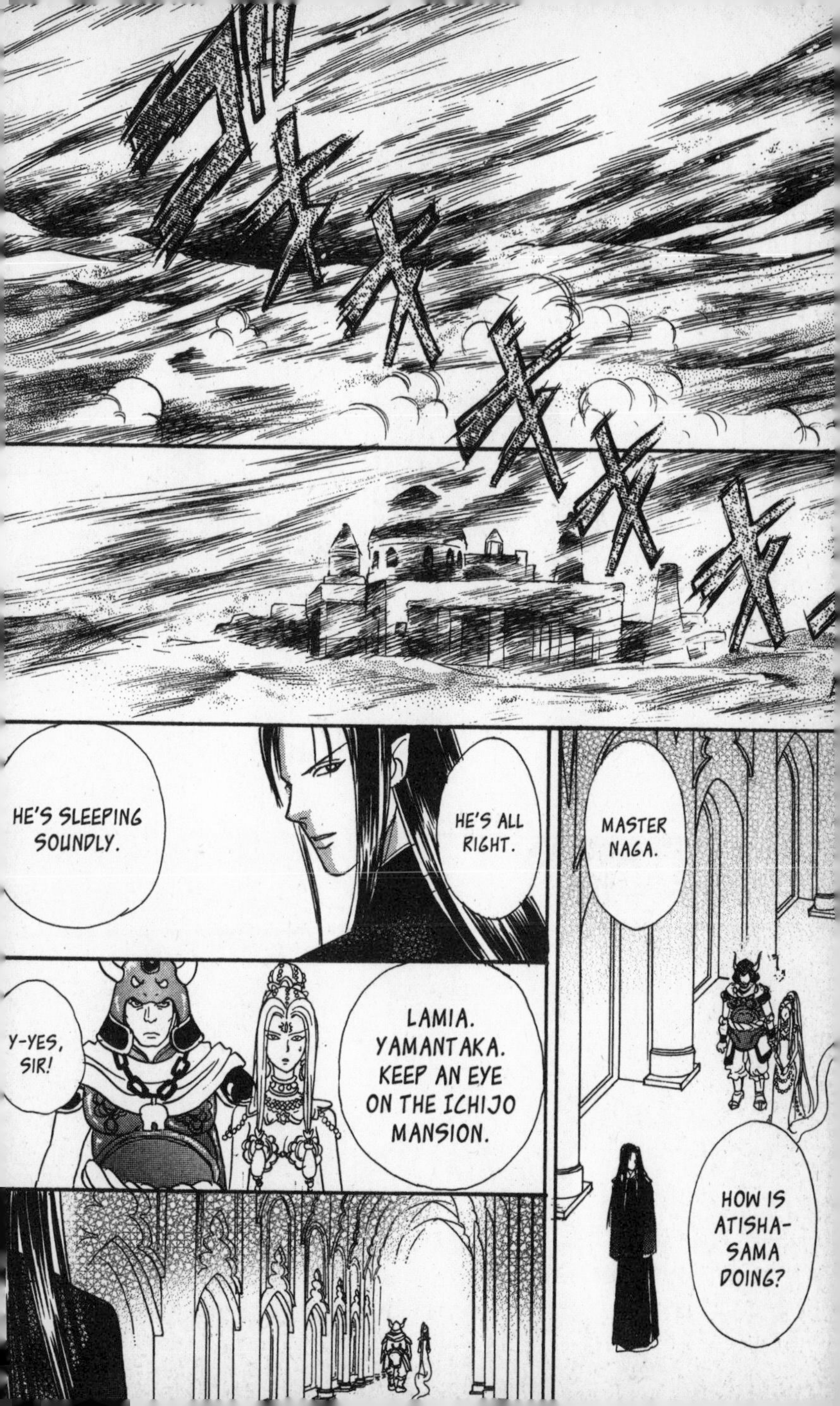
MASTER NAGA.
HOW IS ATISHA-SAMA DOING?
HE'S ALL RIGHT.
HE'S SLEEPING SOUNDLY.
LAMIA. YAMANTAKA. KEEP AN EYE ON THE ICHIJO MANSION.
Y-YES, SIR!

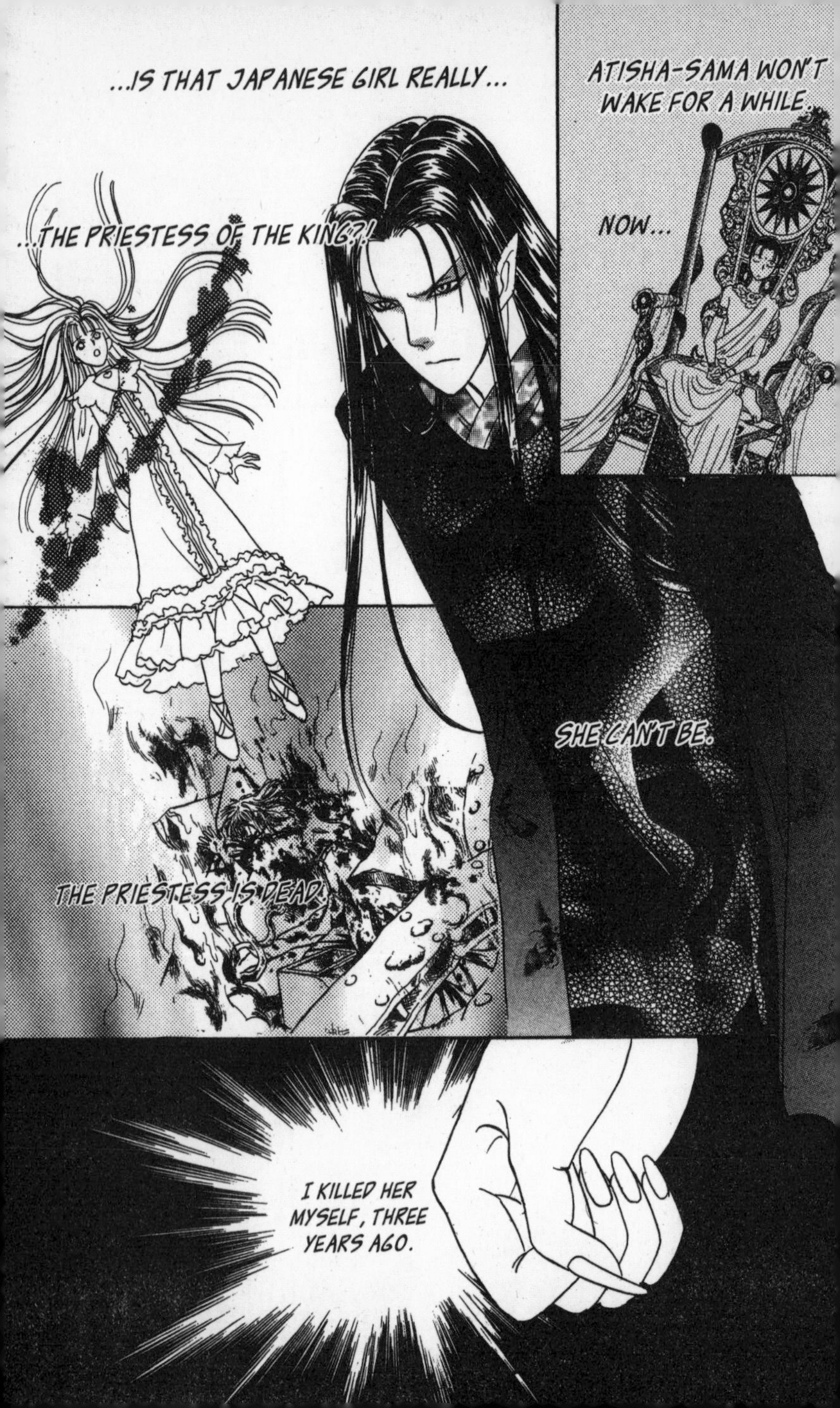
ATISHA-SAMA WON'T WAKE FOR A WHILE.
NOW...
...IS THAT JAPANESE GIRL REALLY...
...THE PRIESTESS OF THE KING?!
SHE CAN'T BE.
THE PRIESTESS IS DEAD.
I KILLED HER MYSELF, THREE YEARS AGO.

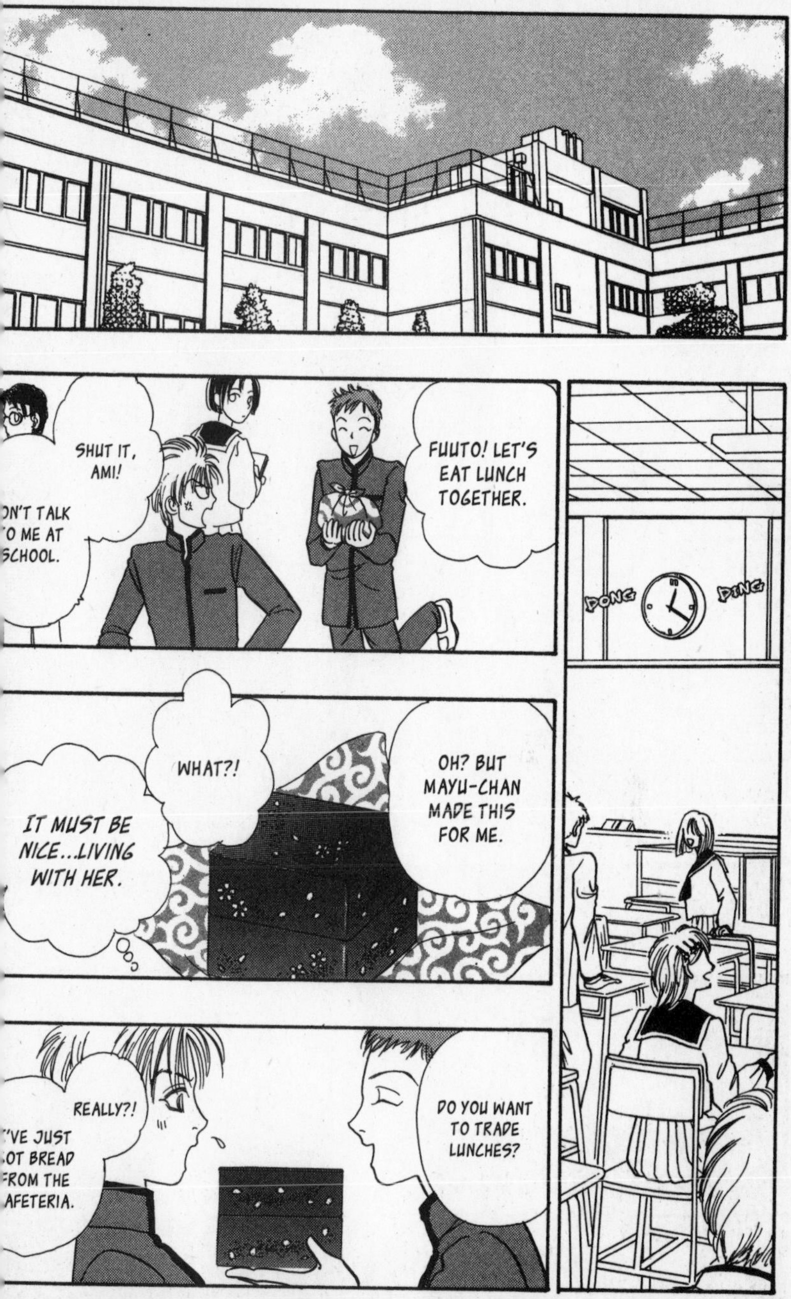
DING
DONG
FUUTO! LET'S EAT LUNCH TOGETHER.
SHUT IT, AMI!
ON'T TALK TO ME AT SCHOOL.
OH? BUT MAYU-CHAN MADE THIS FOR ME.
WHAT?!
IT MUST BE NICE...LIVING WITH HER.
DO YOU WANT TO TRADE LUNCHES?
REALLY?!
'VE JUST OT BREAD FROM THE AFETERIA.

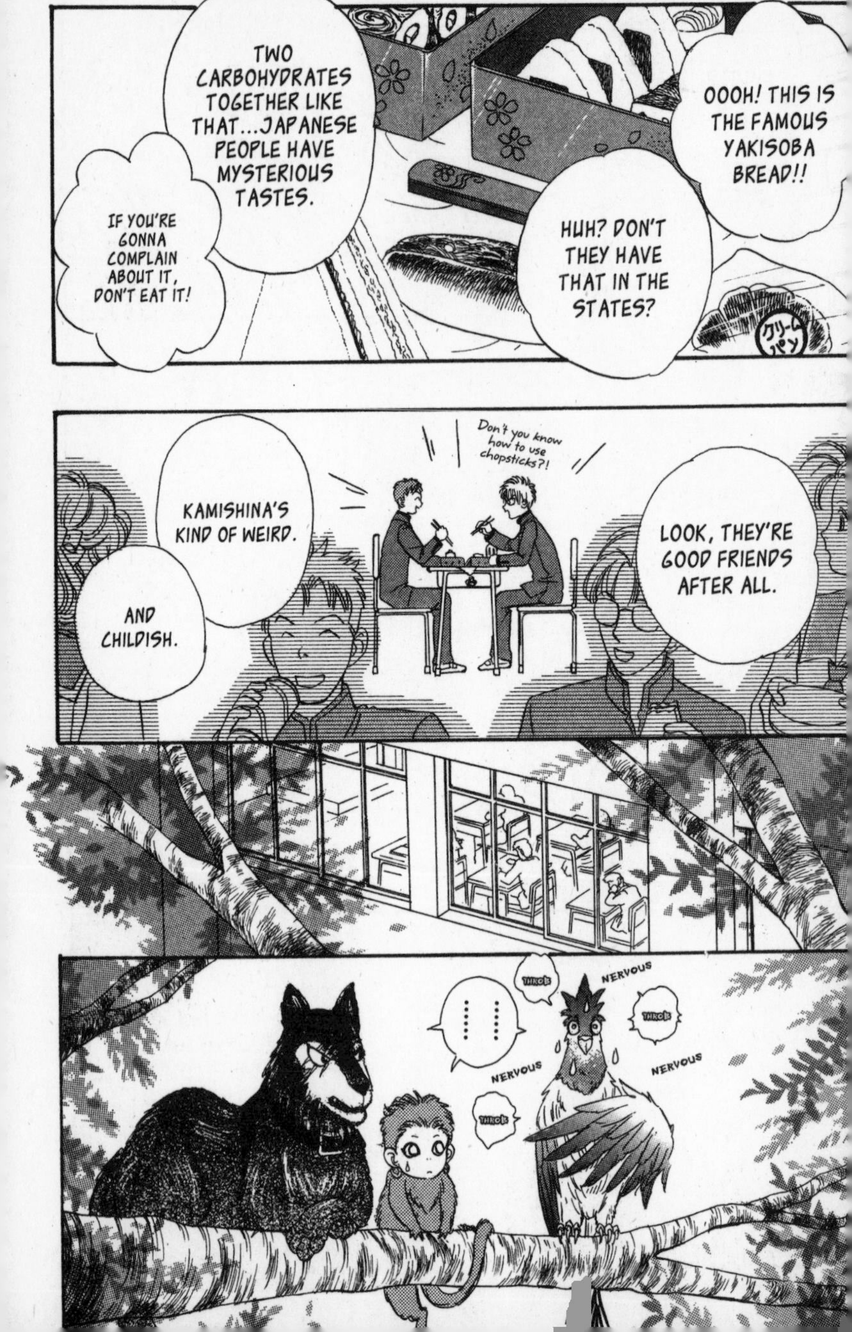

OOOH! THIS IS THE FAMOUS YAKISOBA BREAD!!
クリームパン
HUH? DON'T THEY HAVE THAT IN THE STATES?
TWO CARBOHYDRATES TOGETHER LIKE THAT...JAPANESE PEOPLE HAVE MYSTERIOUS TASTES.
IF YOU'RE GONNA COMPLAIN ABOUT IT, DON'T EAT IT!
LOOK, THEY'RE GOOD FRIENDS AFTER ALL.
Don't you know how to use chopsticks?!
KAMISHINA'S KIND OF WEIRD.
AND CHILDISH.
NERVOUS
THROB
THROB
NERVOUS
NERVOUS
......
THROB
NERVOUS

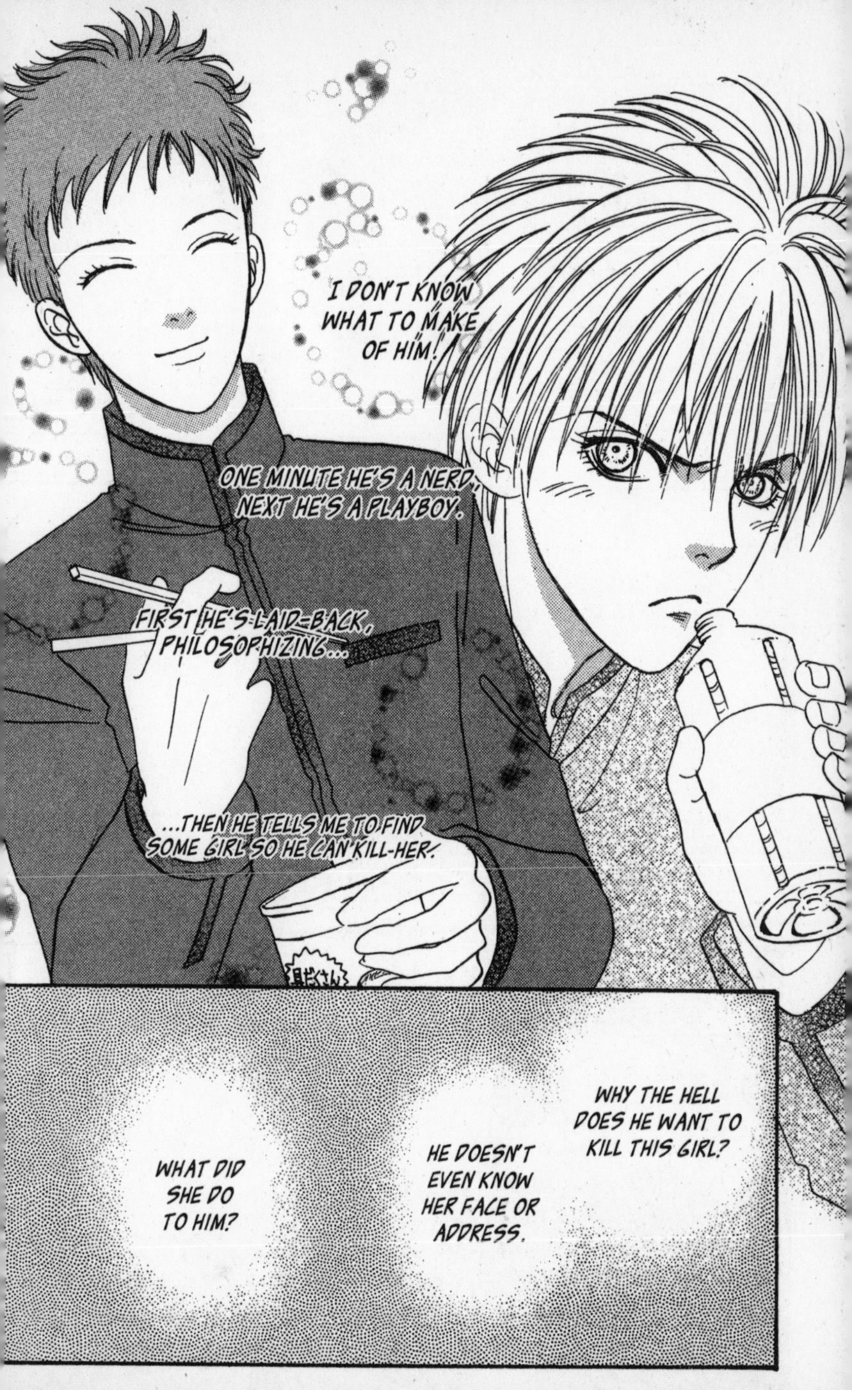

I DON'T KNOW WHAT TO MAKE OF HIM!
ONE MINUTE HE'S A NERD, NEXT HE'S A PLAYBOY.
FIRST HE'S LAID-BACK, PHILOSOPHIZING...
...THEN HE TELLS ME TO FIND SOME GIRL SO HE CAN KILL HER.
WHY THE HELL DOES HE WANT TO KILL THIS GIRL?
HE DOESN'T EVEN KNOW HER FACE OR ADDRESS.
WHAT DID SHE DO TO HIM?

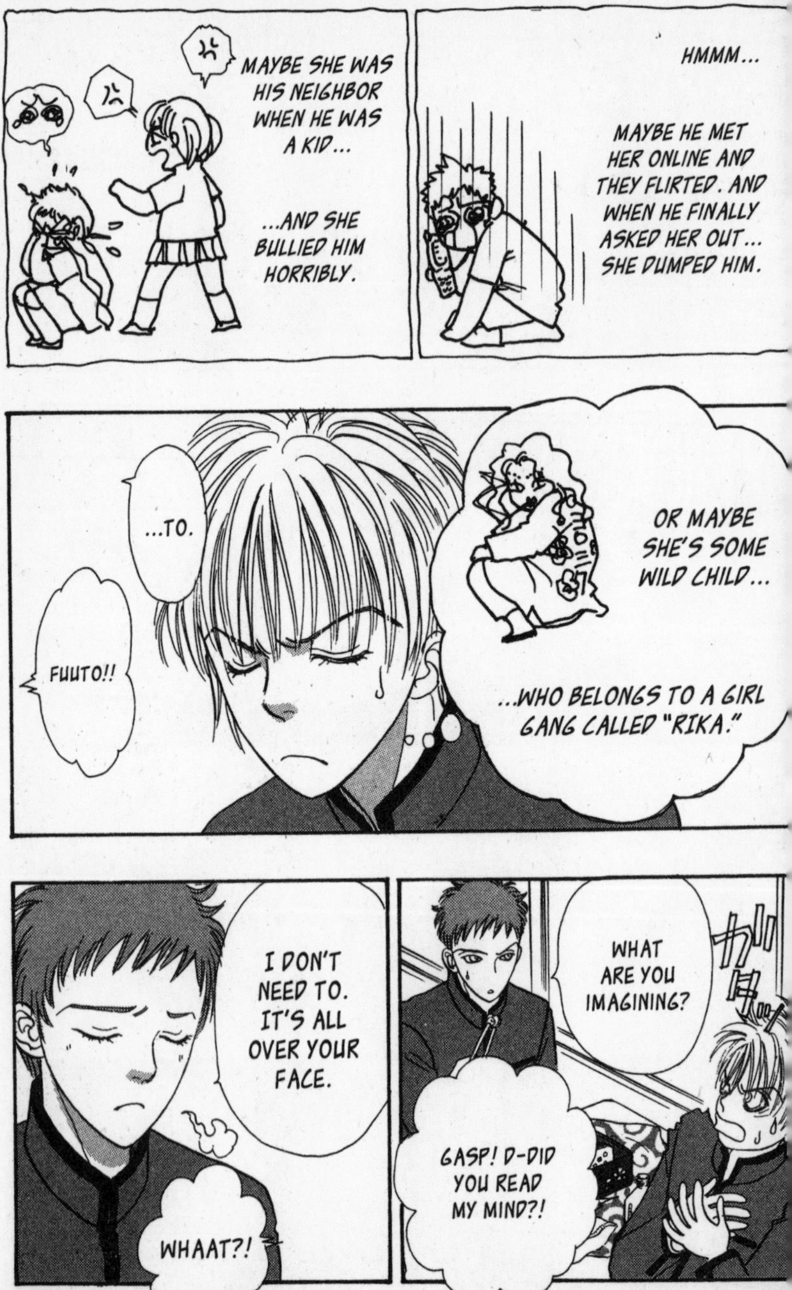
HMMM...
MAYBE HE MET HER ONLINE AND THEY FLIRTED. AND WHEN HE FINALLY ASKED HER OUT... SHE DUMPED HIM.
MAYBE SHE WAS HIS NEIGHBOR WHEN HE WAS A KID...
...AND SHE BULLIED HIM HORRIBLY.
OR MAYBE SHE'S SOME WILD CHILD...
...WHO BELONGS TO A GIRL GANG CALLED "RIKA."
...TO.
FUUTO!!
WHAT ARE YOU IMAGINING?
GASP! D-DID YOU READ MY MIND?!
I DON'T NEED TO. IT'S ALL OVER YOUR FACE.
WHAAT?!

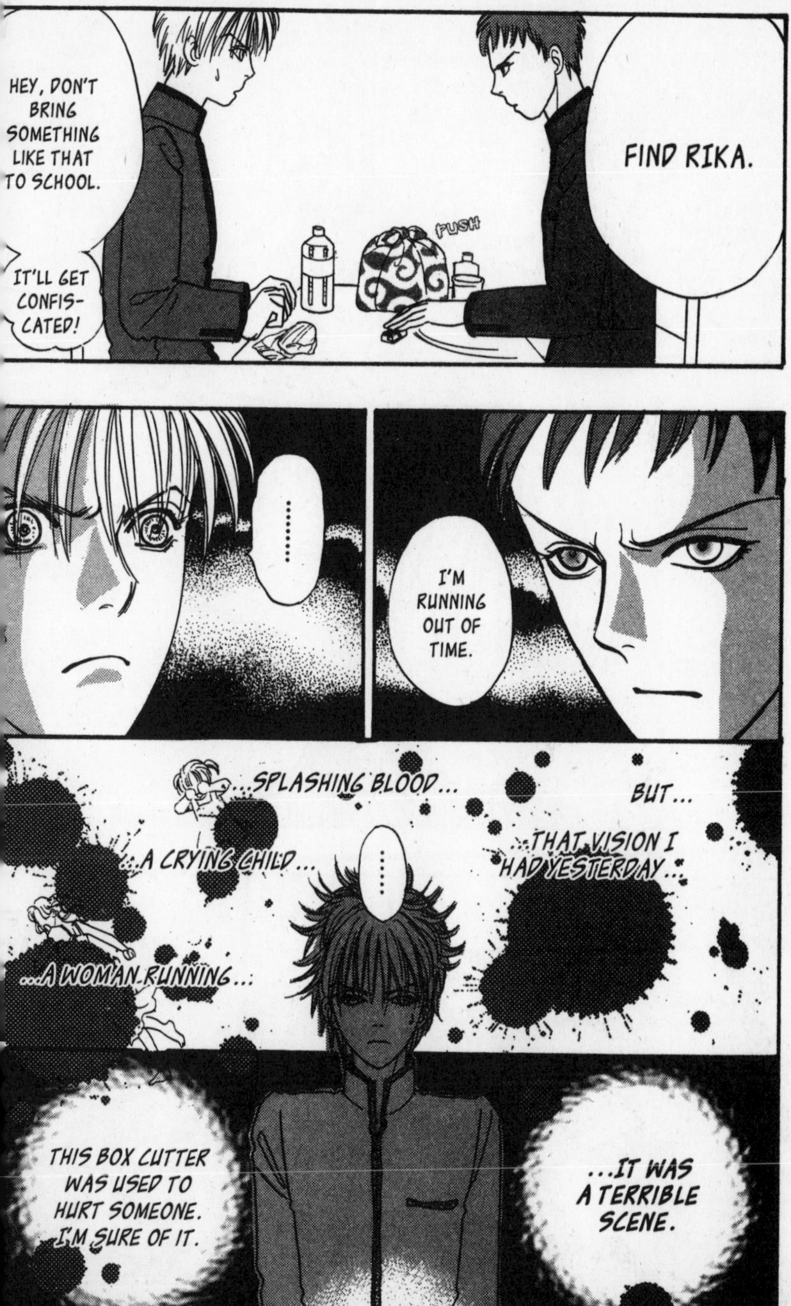
FIND RIKA.
PUSH
HEY, DON'T BRING SOMETHING LIKE THAT TO SCHOOL.
IT'LL GET CONFIS-CATED!
I'M RUNNING OUT OF TIME.
……
BUT...
...THAT VISION I HAD YESTERDAY...
……
...SPLASHING BLOOD...
...A CRYING CHILD...
...A WOMAN RUNNING...
...IT WAS A TERRIBLE SCENE.
THIS BOX CUTTER WAS USED TO HURT SOMEONE. I'M SURE OF IT.

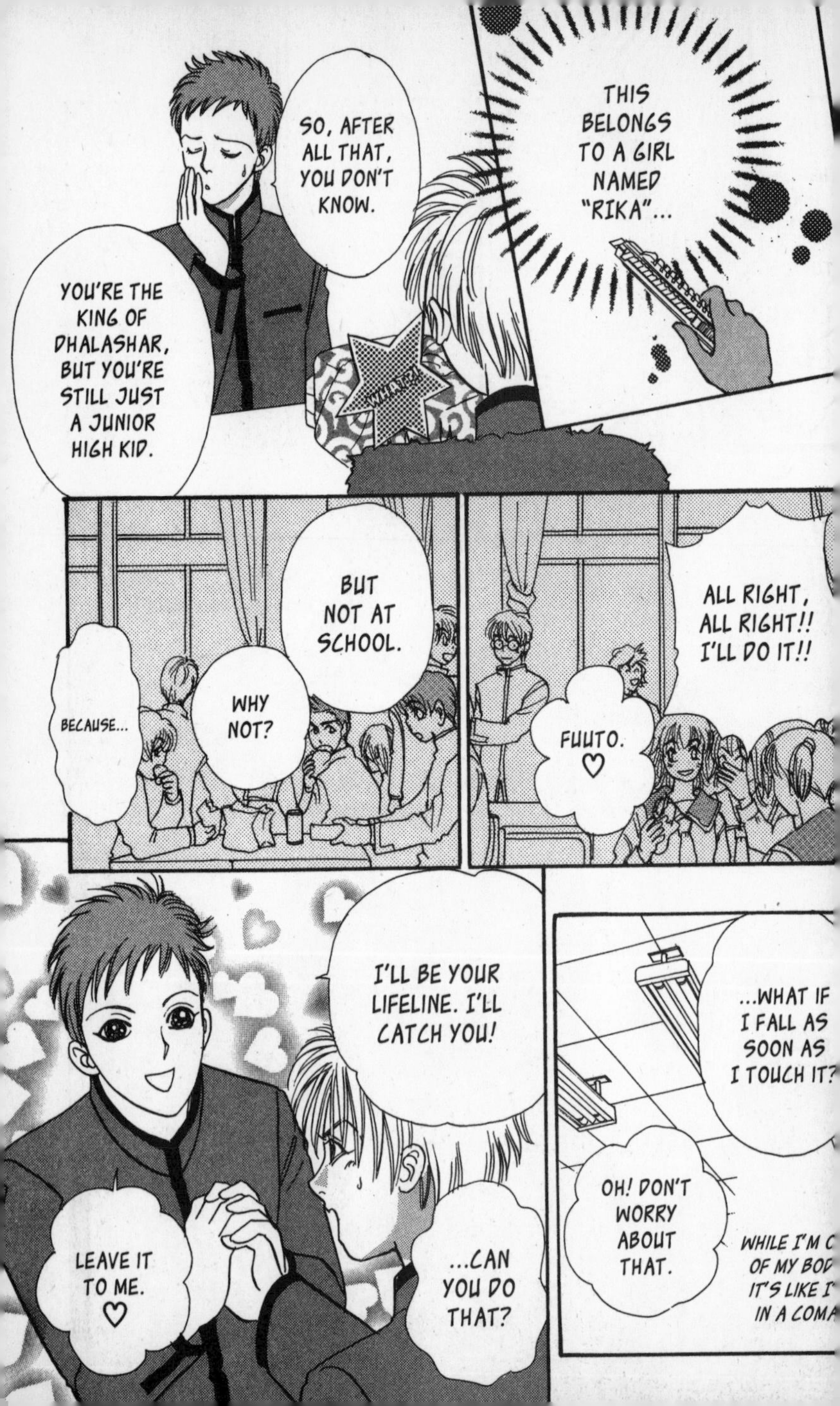
THIS BELONGS TO A GIRL NAMED "RIKA"...
SO, AFTER ALL THAT, YOU DON'T KNOW.
WHAT?!
YOU'RE THE KING OF DHALASHAR, BUT YOU'RE STILL JUST A JUNIOR HIGH KID.
ALL RIGHT, ALL RIGHT!! I'LL DO IT!!
FUUTO. ♡
BUT NOT AT SCHOOL.
WHY NOT?
BECAUSE...
...WHAT IF I FALL AS SOON AS I TOUCH IT?
OH! DON'T WORRY ABOUT THAT.
I'LL BE YOUR LIFELINE. I'LL CATCH YOU!
...CAN YOU DO THAT?
LEAVE IT TO ME. ♡

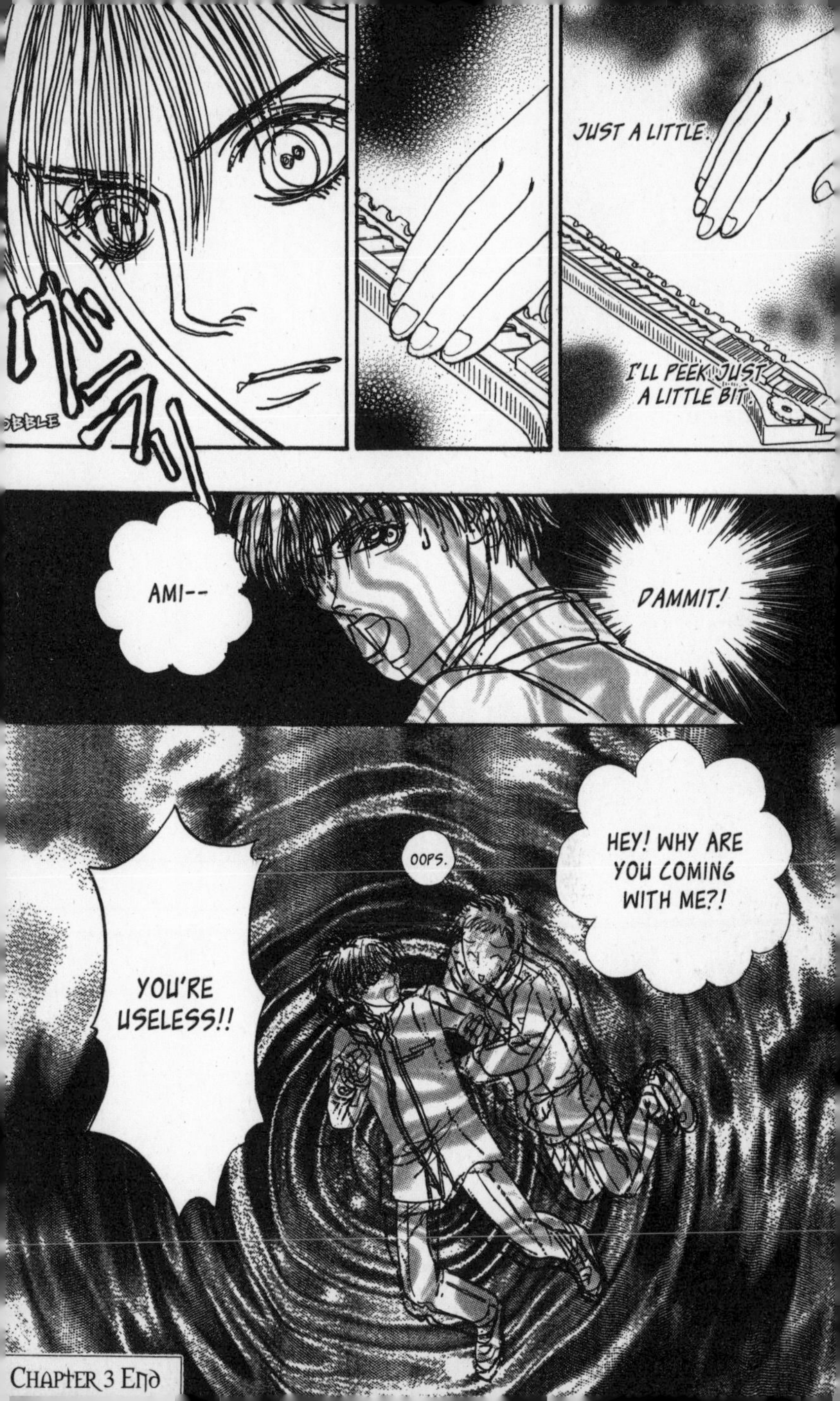
JUST A LITTLE.
I'LL PEEK JUST A LITTLE BIT.
OBBLE
DAMMIT!
AMI--
HEY! WHY ARE YOU COMING WITH ME?!
OOPS.
YOU'RE USELESS!!
CHAPTER 3 END

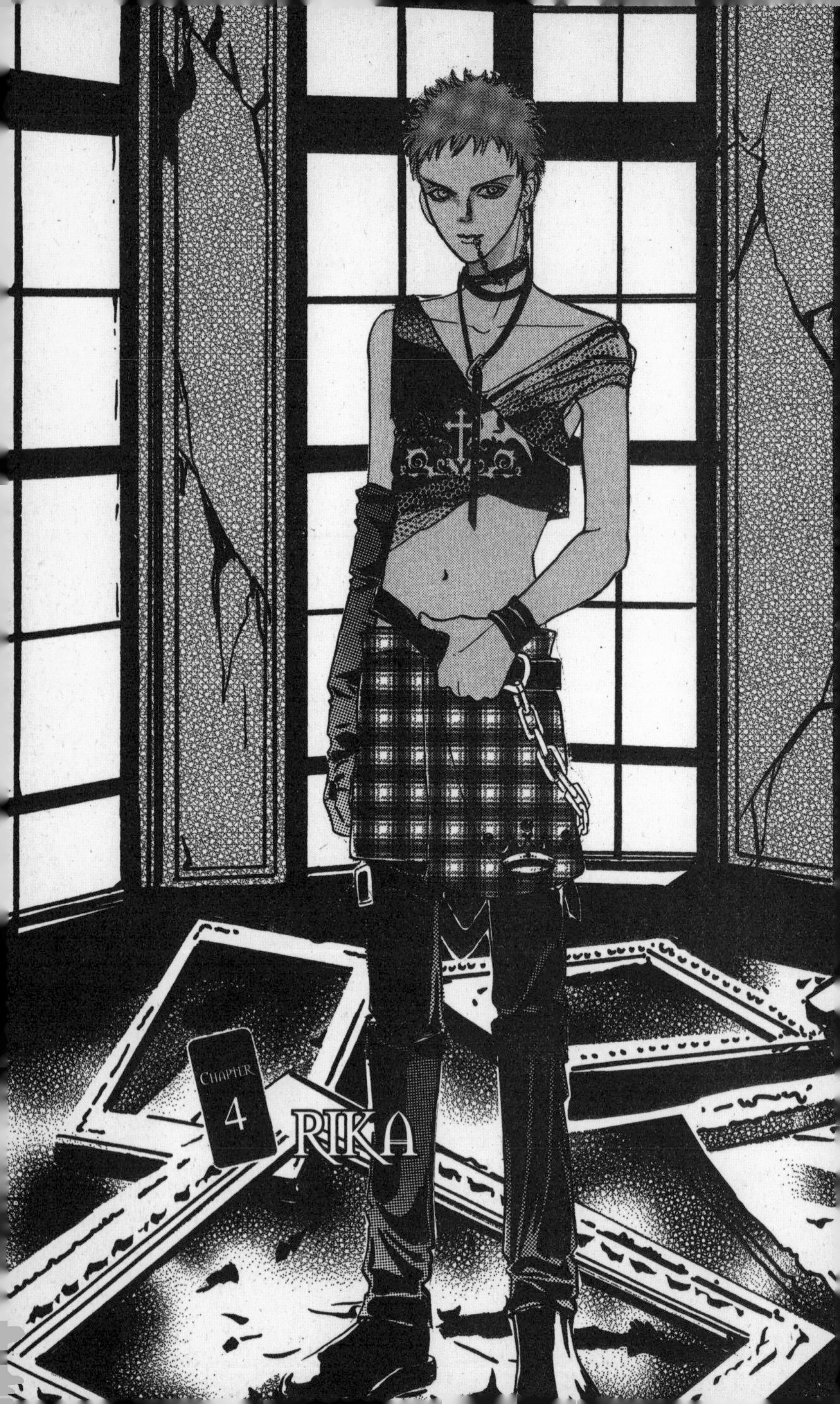
CHAPTER
4
RIKA

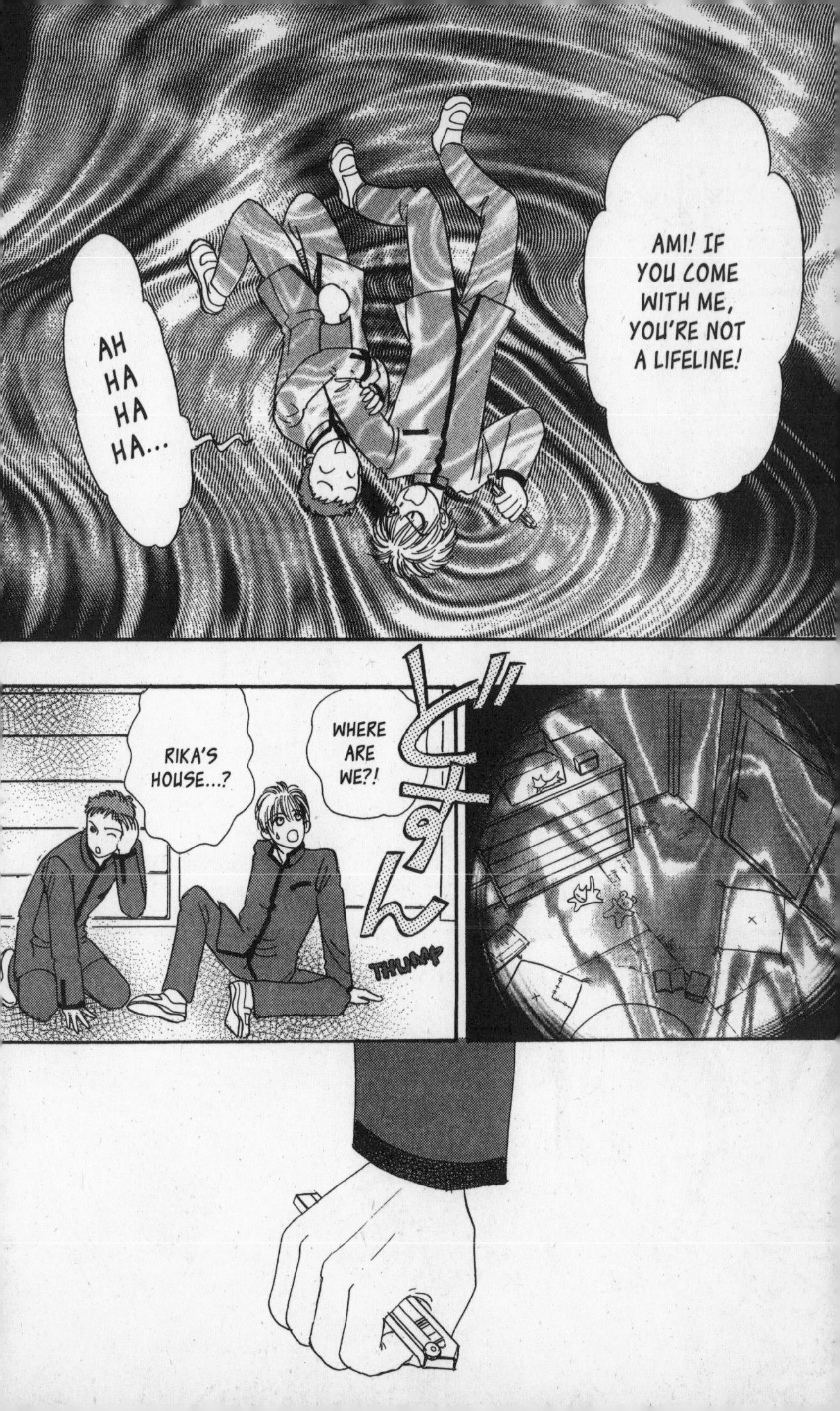
AMI! IF YOU COME WITH ME, YOU'RE NOT A LIFELINE!
AH HA HA HA...
どすん
THUMP
WHERE ARE WE?!
RIKA'S HOUSE...?

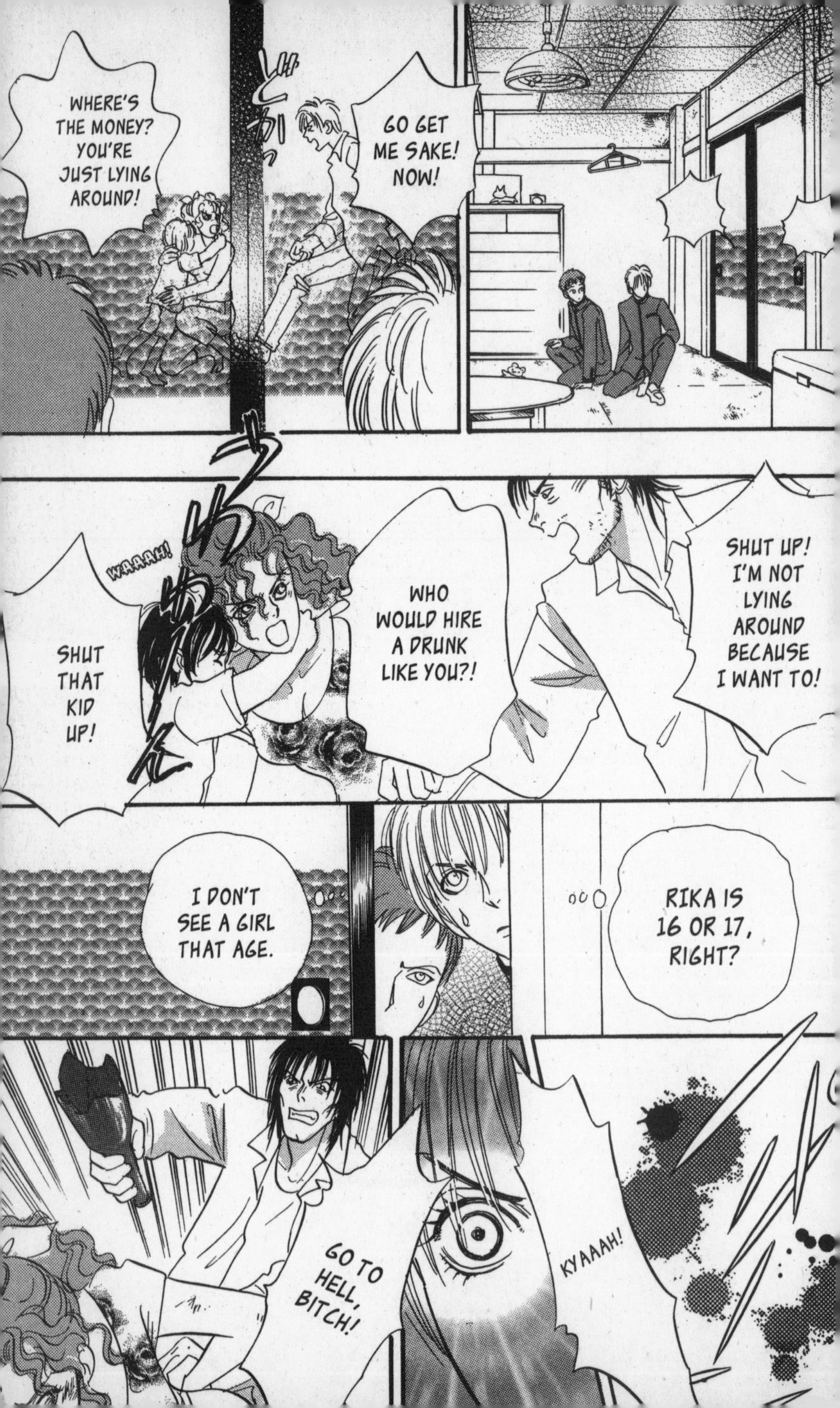
GO GET ME SAKE! NOW!
WHERE'S THE MONEY? YOU'RE JUST LYING AROUND!
SHUT UP! I'M NOT LYING AROUND BECAUSE I WANT TO!
WHO WOULD HIRE A DRUNK LIKE YOU?!
WAAAAH!
SHUT THAT KID UP!
RIKA IS 16 OR 17, RIGHT?
I DON'T SEE A GIRL THAT AGE.
KYAAAH!
GO TO HELL, BITCH!

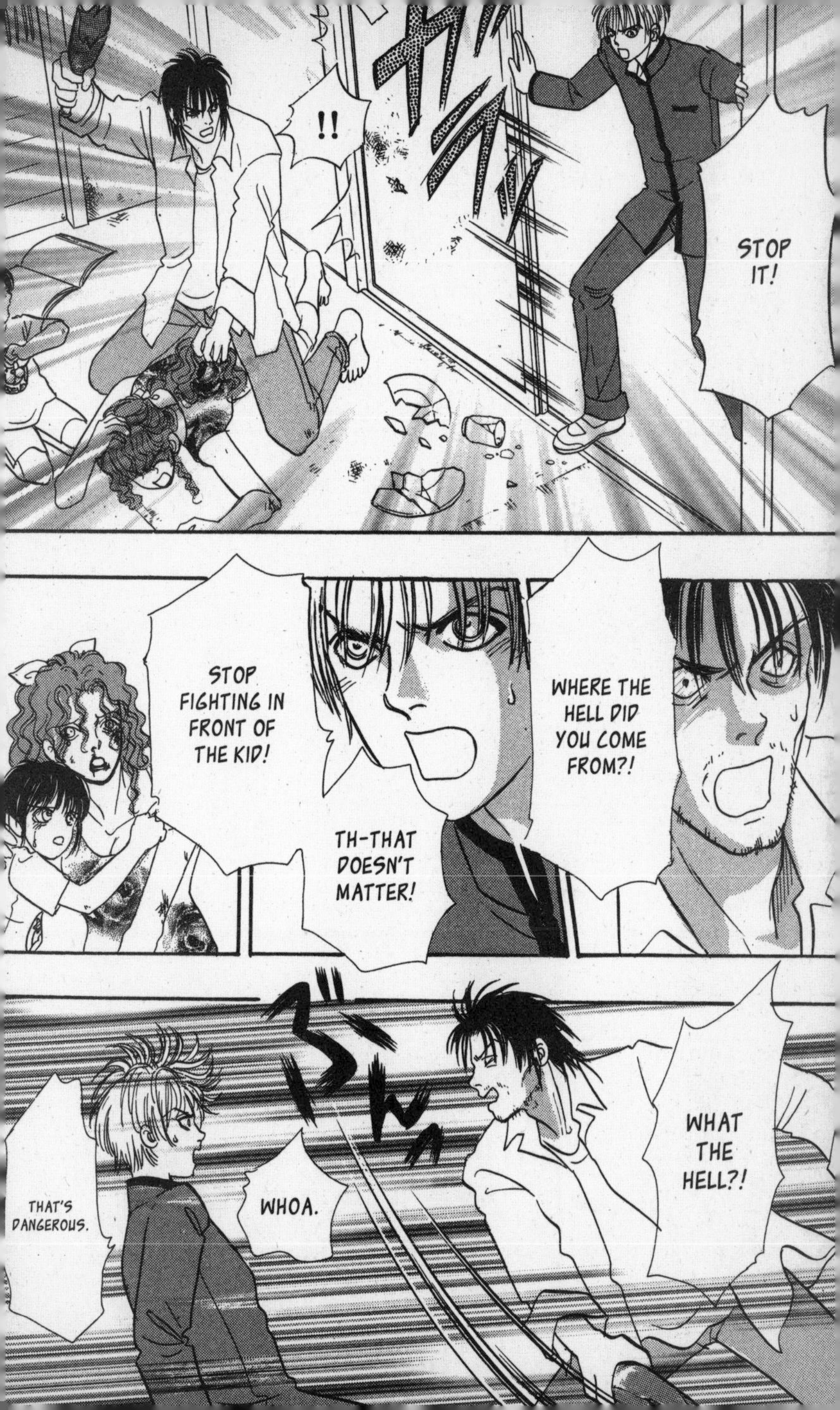
STOP IT!
!!
WHERE THE HELL DID YOU COME FROM?!
TH-THAT DOESN'T MATTER!
STOP FIGHTING IN FRONT OF THE KID!
WHAT THE HELL?!
WHOA.
THAT'S DANGEROUS.

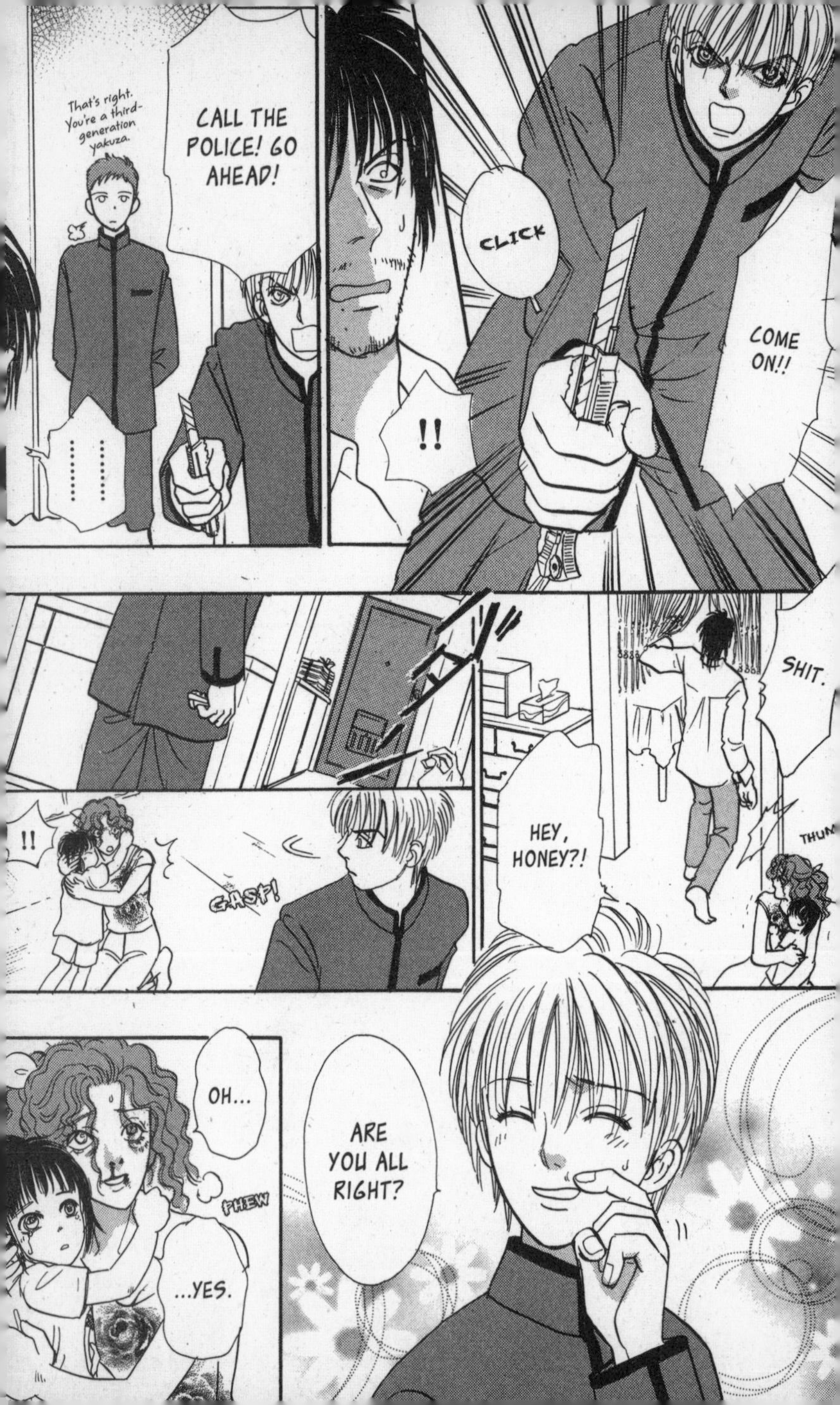

CLICK
COME ON!!
!!
CALL THE POLICE! GO AHEAD!
That's right. You're a third-generation yakuza.
......
SHIT.
THUN
HEY, HONEY?!
GASP!
!!
ARE YOU ALL RIGHT?
OH...
PHEW
...YES.

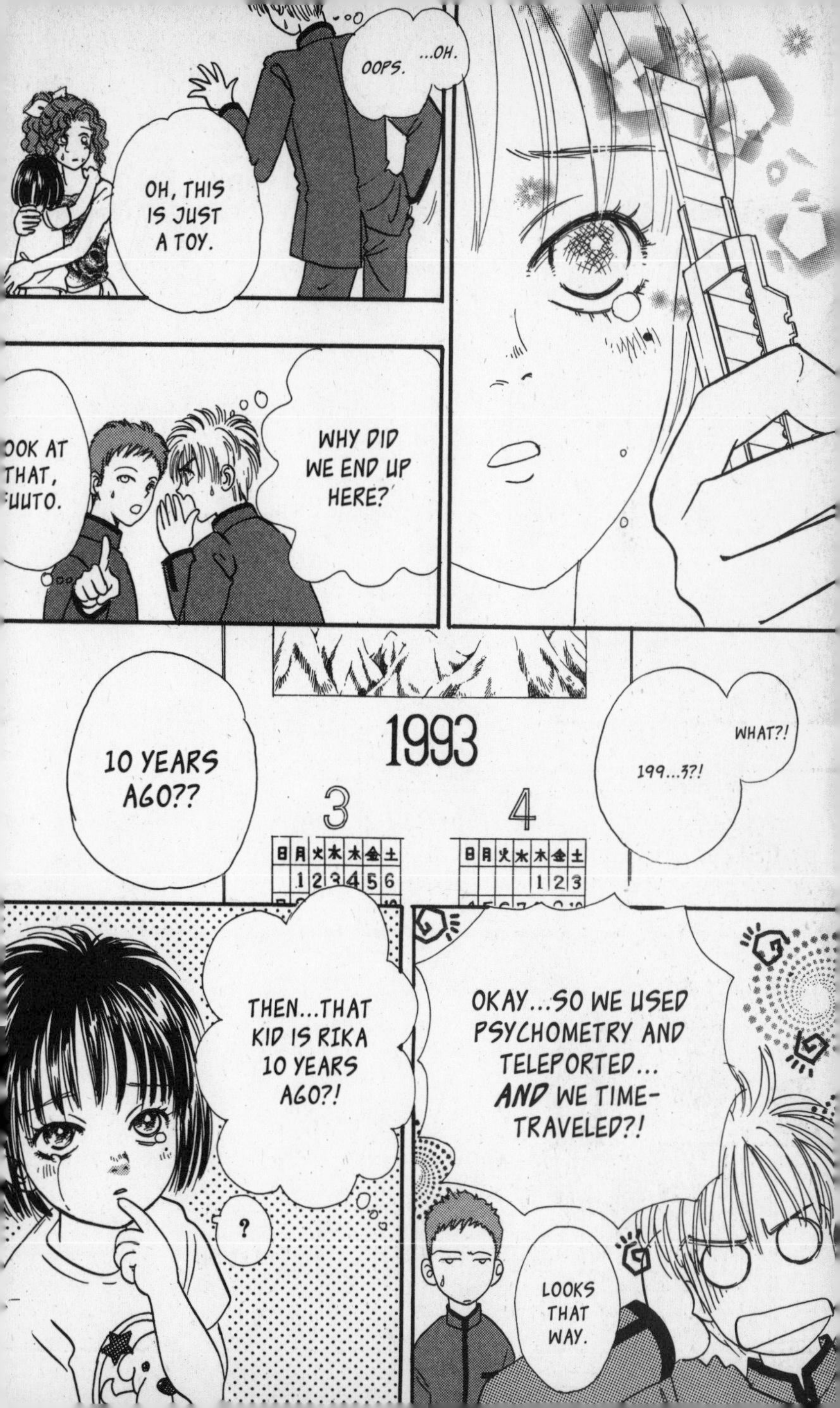
...OH.
OOPS.
OH, THIS IS JUST A TOY.
WHY DID WE END UP HERE?
OOK AT THAT, UUTO.
WHAT?!
199...3?!
1993
3
4
10 YEARS AGO??
OKAY...SO WE USED PSYCHOMETRY AND TELEPORTED... AND WE TIME-TRAVELED?!
LOOKS THAT WAY.
THEN...THAT KID IS RIKA 10 YEARS AGO?!
?

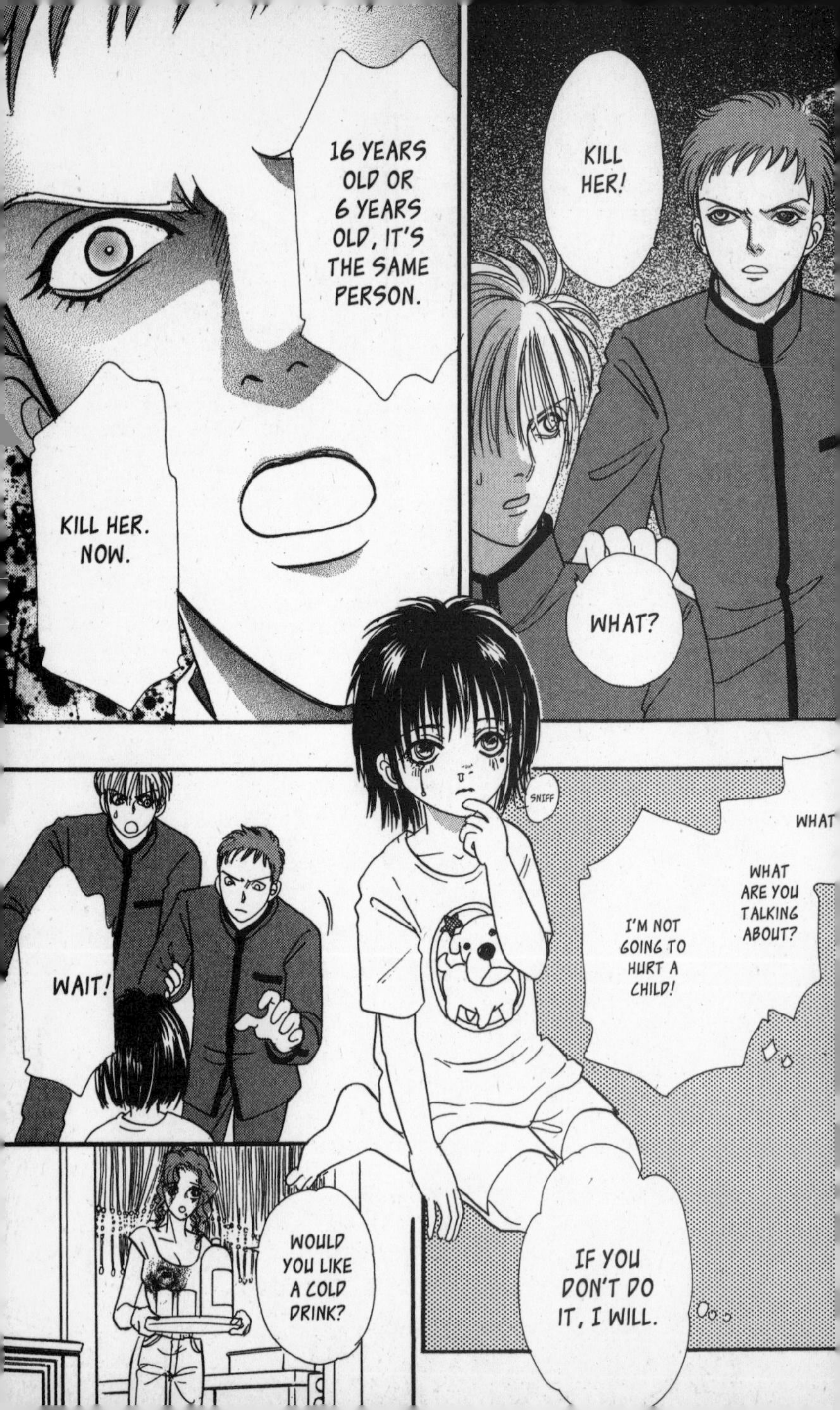
KILL HER!
WHAT?
16 YEARS OLD OR 6 YEARS OLD, IT'S THE SAME PERSON.
KILL HER. NOW.
WHAT
WHAT ARE YOU TALKING ABOUT?
I'M NOT GOING TO HURT A CHILD!
SNIFF
IF YOU DON'T DO IT, I WILL.
WAIT!
WOULD YOU LIKE A COLD DRINK?

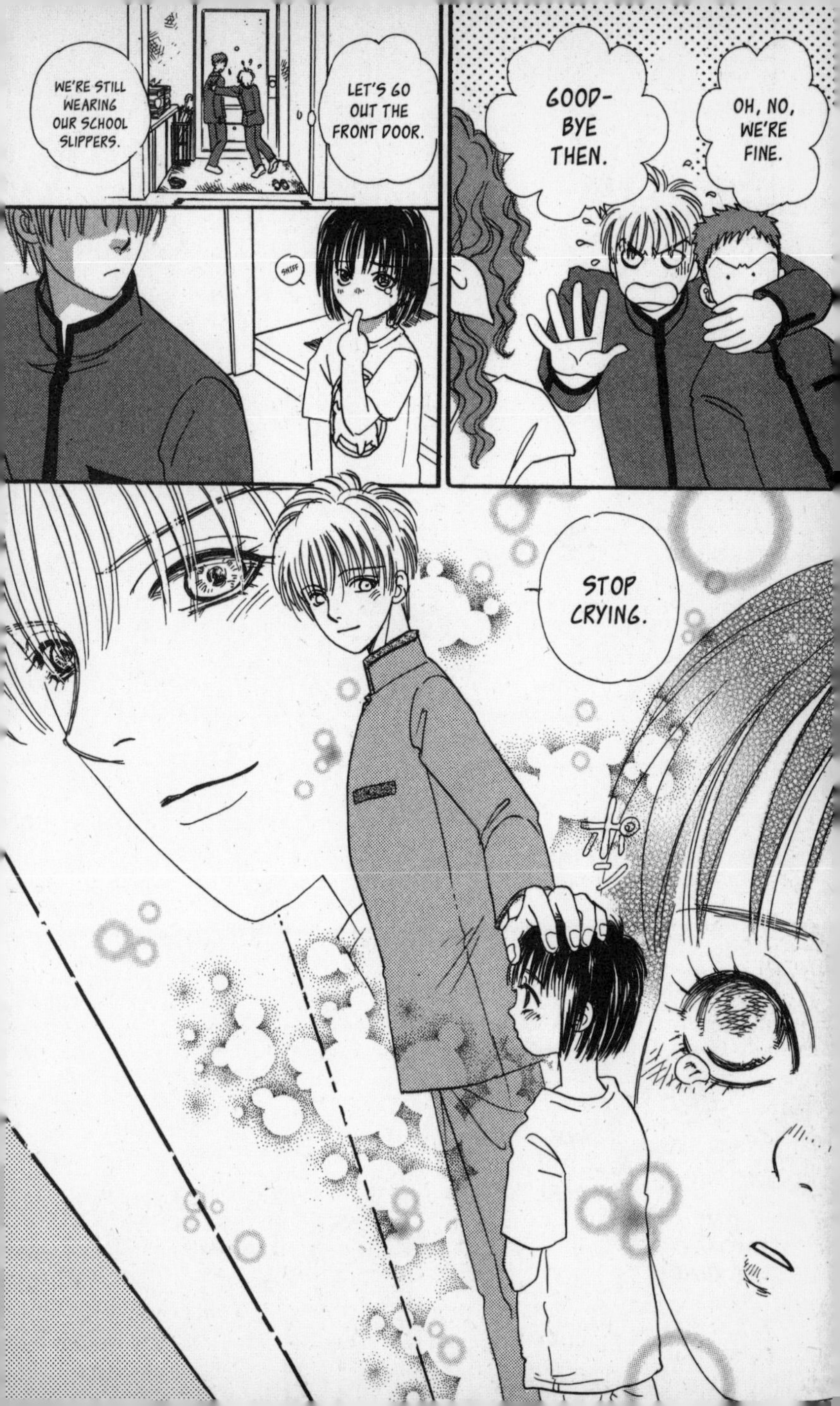

OH, NO, WE'RE FINE.
GOOD-BYE THEN.
LET'S GO OUT THE FRONT DOOR.
WE'RE STILL WEARING OUR SCHOOL SLIPPERS.
SNIFF
STOP CRYING.

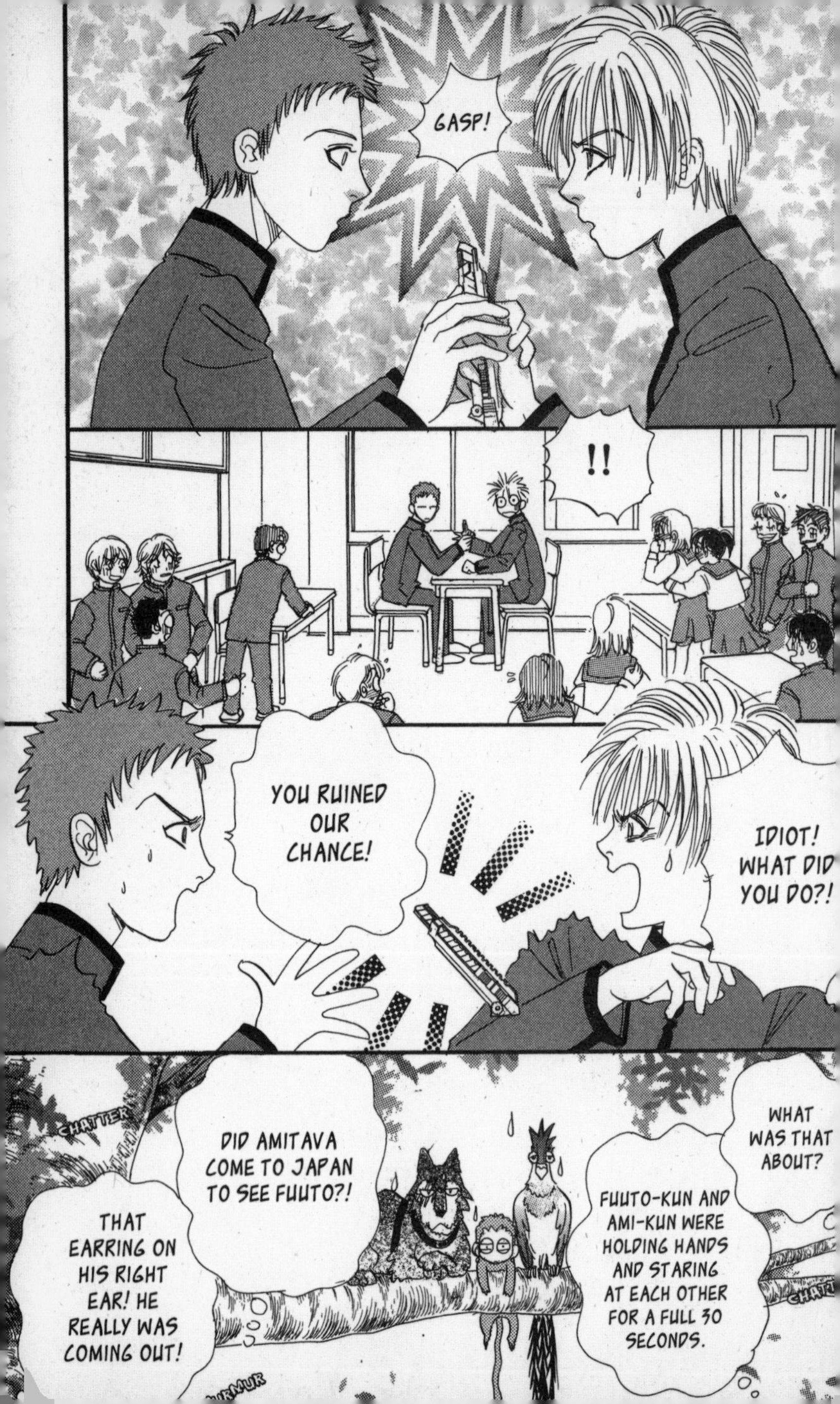
GASP!
!!
IDIOT! WHAT DID YOU DO?!
YOU RUINED OUR CHANCE!
WHAT WAS THAT ABOUT?
FUUTO-KUN AND AMI-KUN WERE HOLDING HANDS AND STARING AT EACH OTHER FOR A FULL 30 SECONDS.
DID AMITAVA COME TO JAPAN TO SEE FUUTO?!
THAT EARRING ON HIS RIGHT EAR! HE REALLY WAS COMING OUT!
CHATTER

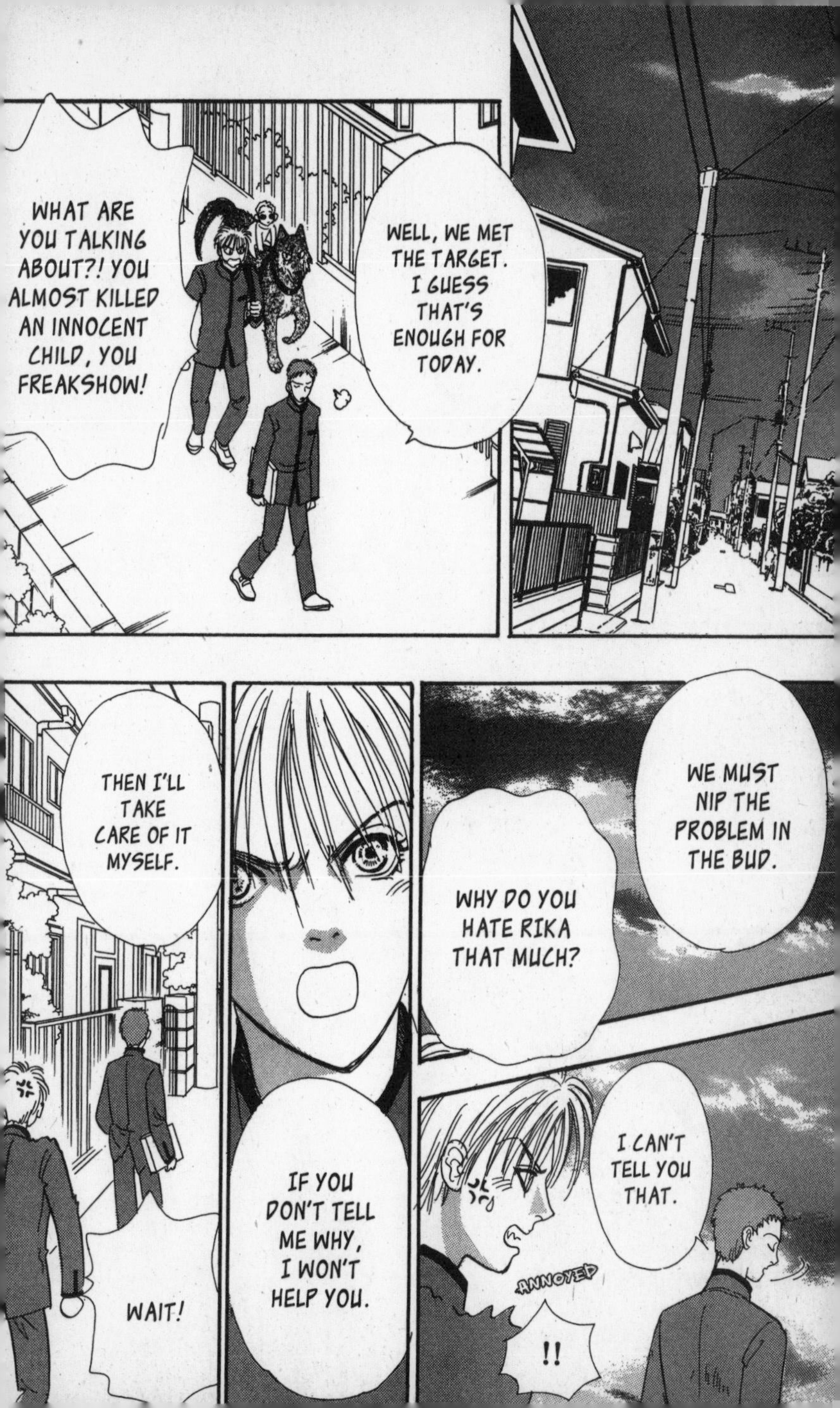
WELL, WE MET THE TARGET. I GUESS THAT'S ENOUGH FOR TODAY.
WHAT ARE YOU TALKING ABOUT?! YOU ALMOST KILLED AN INNOCENT CHILD, YOU FREAKSHOW!
WE MUST NIP THE PROBLEM IN THE BUD.
WHY DO YOU HATE RIKA THAT MUCH?
I CAN'T TELL YOU THAT.
ANNOYED
!!
IF YOU DON'T TELL ME WHY, I WON'T HELP YOU.
THEN I'LL TAKE CARE OF IT MYSELF.
WAIT!

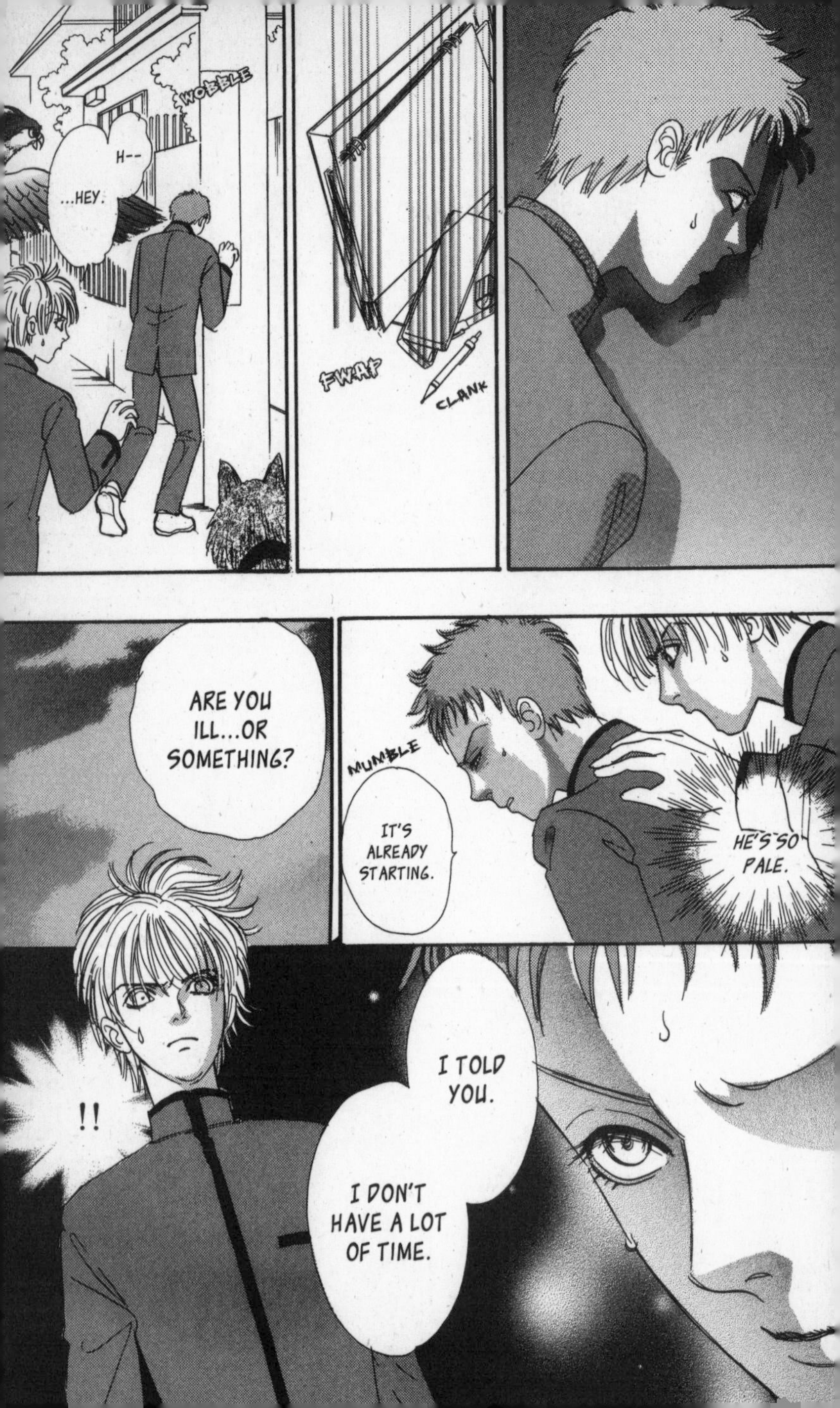
FWAP
CLANK
WOBBLE
H--
...HEY.
MUMBLE
IT'S ALREADY STARTING.
HE'S SO PALE.
ARE YOU ILL...OR SOMETHING?
I TOLD YOU.
I DON'T HAVE A LOT OF TIME.
!!

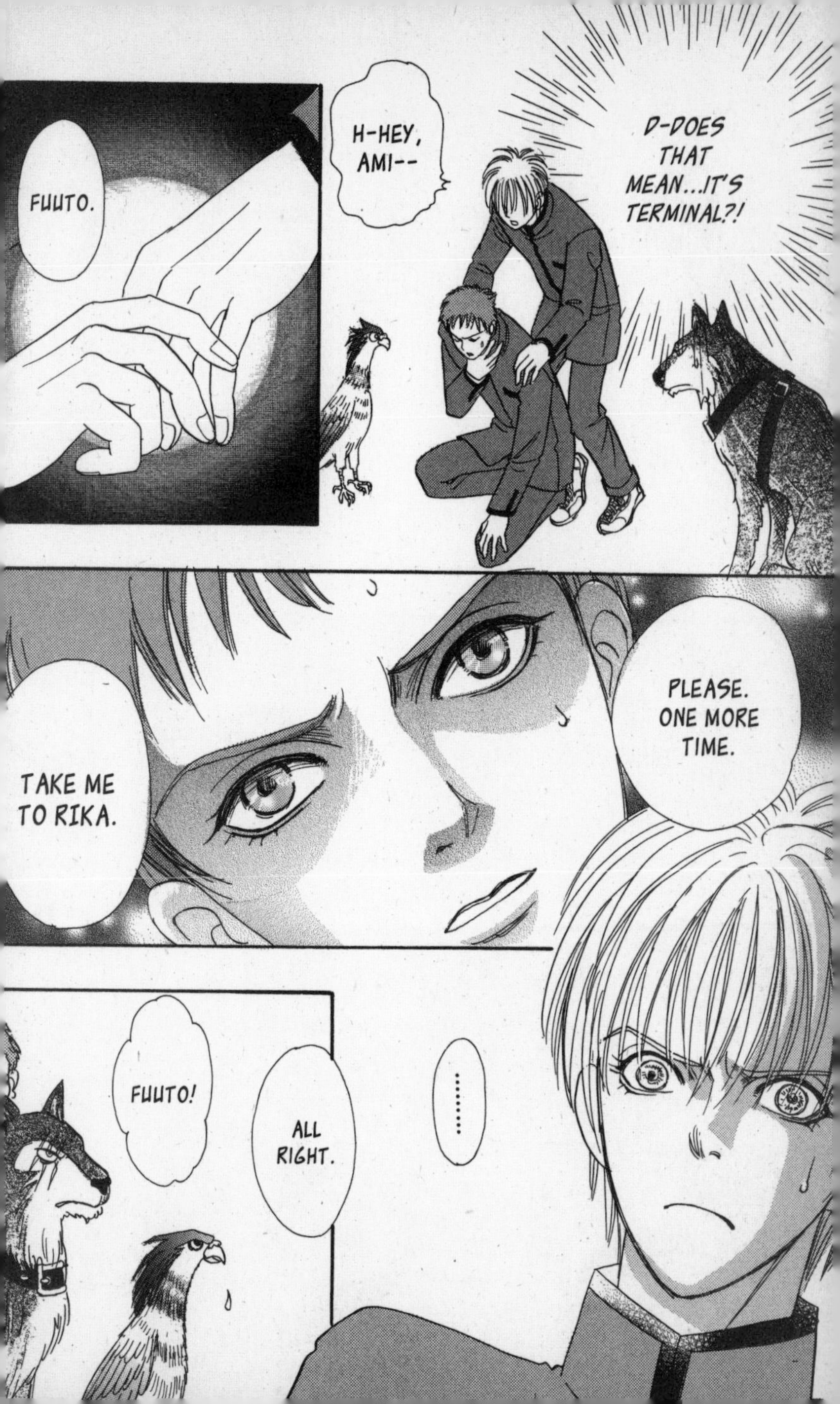
D-DOES THAT MEAN...IT'S TERMINAL?!
H-HEY, AMI--
FUUTO.
PLEASE. ONE MORE TIME.
TAKE ME TO RIKA.
......
ALL RIGHT.
FUUTO!

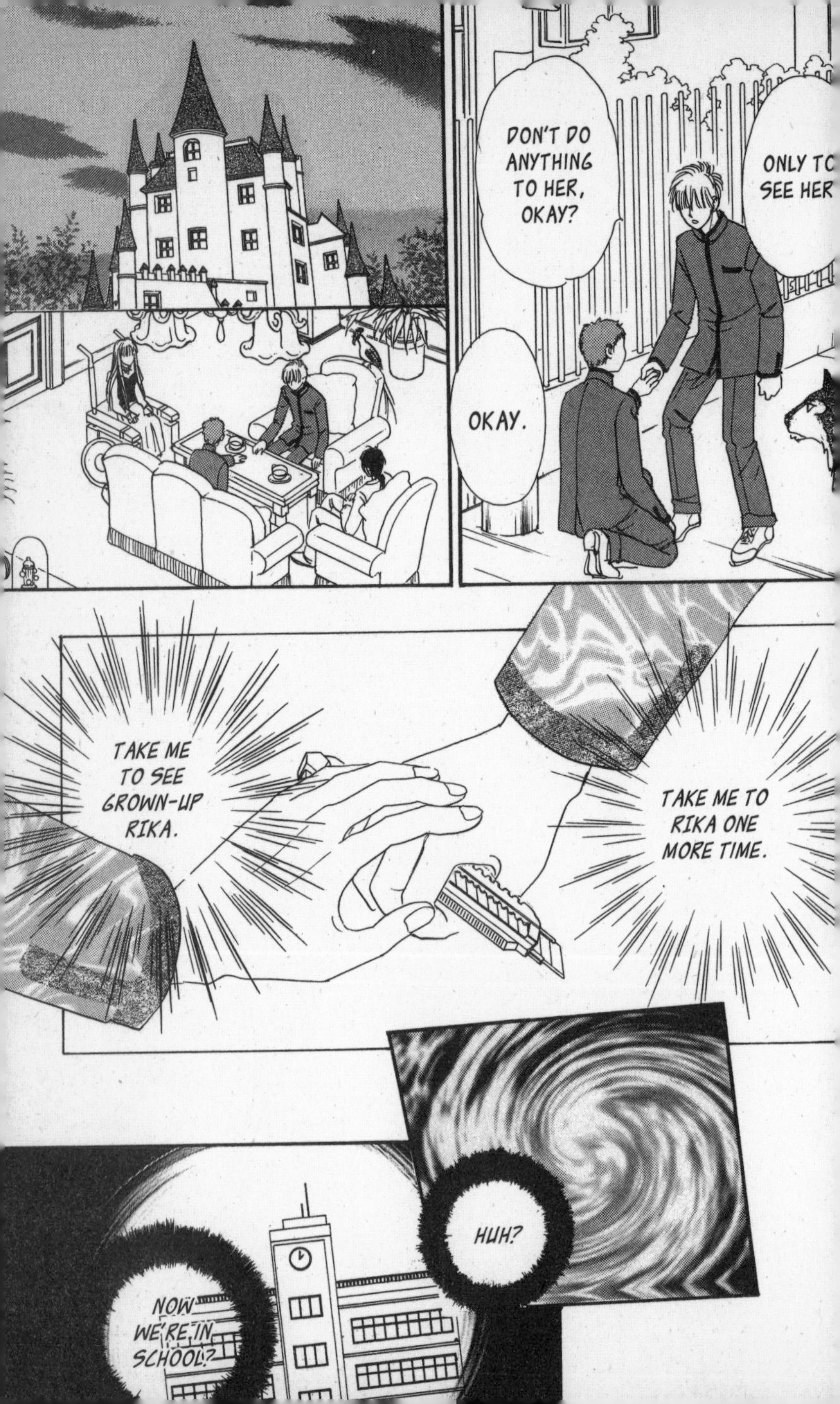

ONLY TO SEE HER
DON'T DO ANYTHING TO HER, OKAY?
OKAY.
TAKE ME TO RIKA ONE MORE TIME.
TAKE ME TO SEE GROWN-UP RIKA.
HUH?
NOW WE'RE IN SCHOOL?

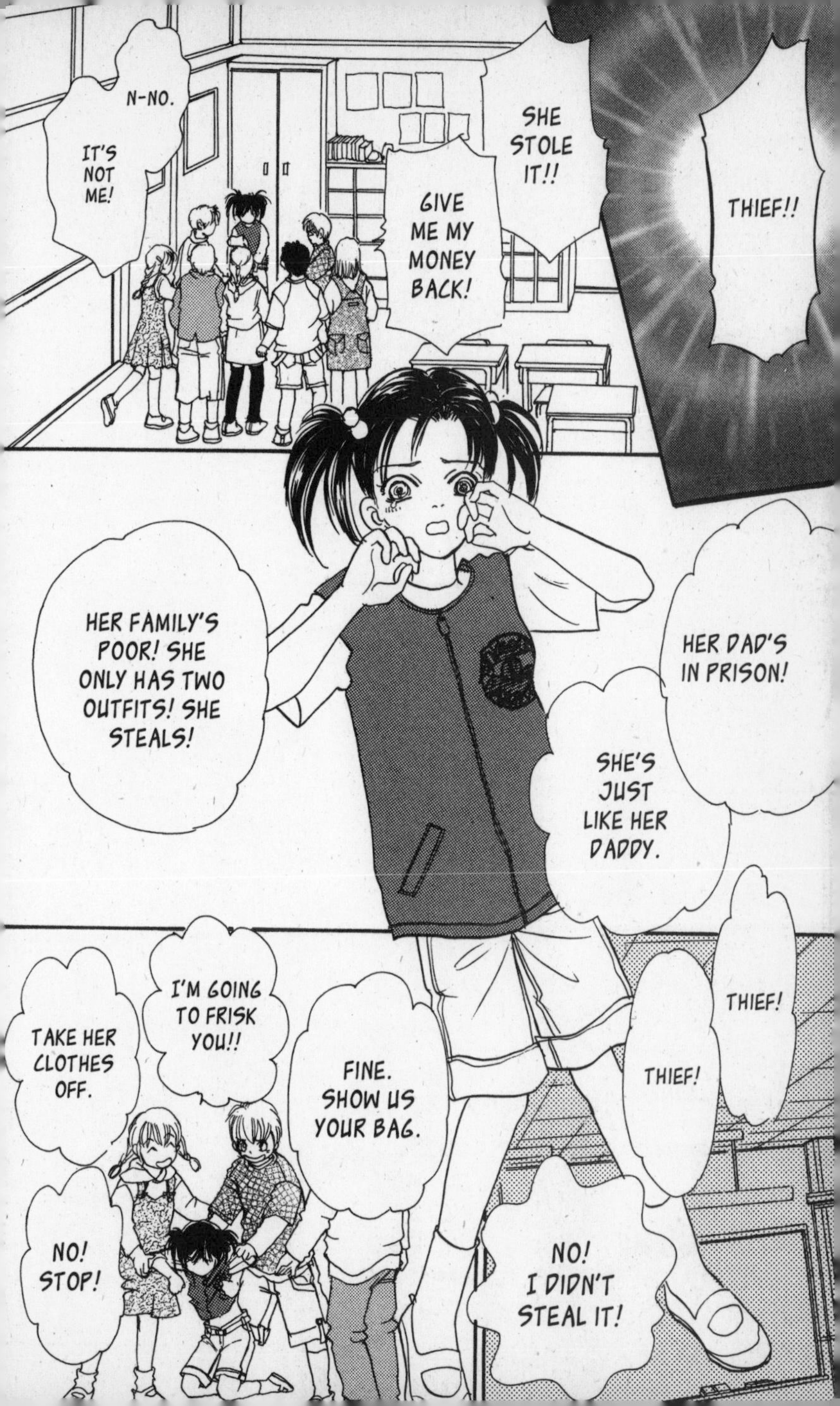
THIEF!!
SHE STOLE IT!!
GIVE ME MY MONEY BACK!
N-NO.
IT'S NOT ME!
HER DAD'S IN PRISON!
SHE'S JUST LIKE HER DADDY.
HER FAMILY'S POOR! SHE ONLY HAS TWO OUTFITS! SHE STEALS!
THIEF!
THIEF!
NO! I DIDN'T STEAL IT!
FINE. SHOW US YOUR BAG.
I'M GOING TO FRISK YOU!!
TAKE HER CLOTHES OFF.
NO! STOP!

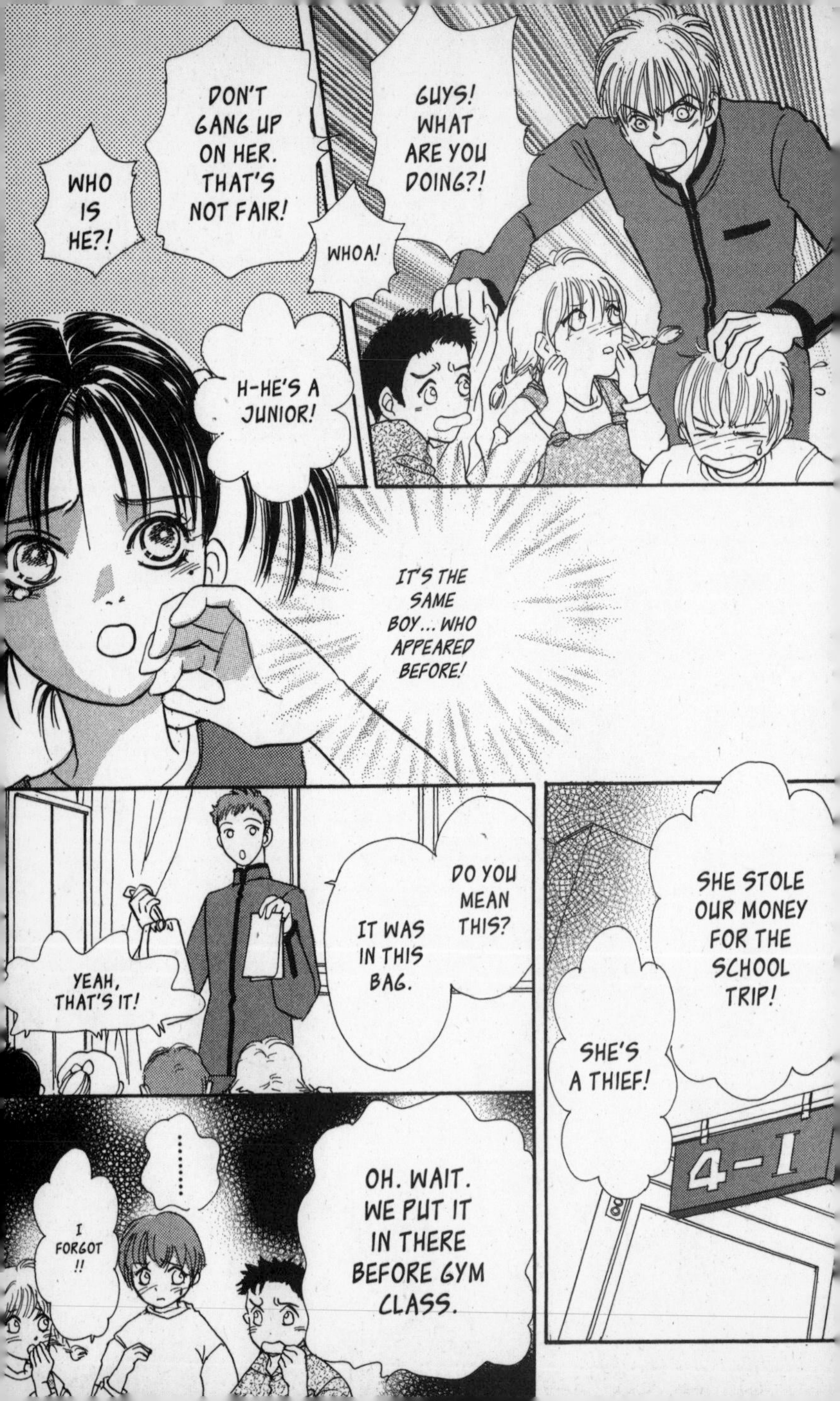
GUYS! WHAT ARE YOU DOING?!
WHOA!
DON'T GANG UP ON HER. THAT'S NOT FAIR!
WHO IS HE?!
H-HE'S A JUNIOR!
IT'S THE SAME BOY... WHO APPEARED BEFORE!
SHE STOLE OUR MONEY FOR THE SCHOOL TRIP!
SHE'S A THIEF!
4-1
DO YOU MEAN THIS?
IT WAS IN THIS BAG.
YEAH, THAT'S IT!
OH. WAIT. WE PUT IT IN THERE BEFORE GYM CLASS.
......
I FORGOT !!

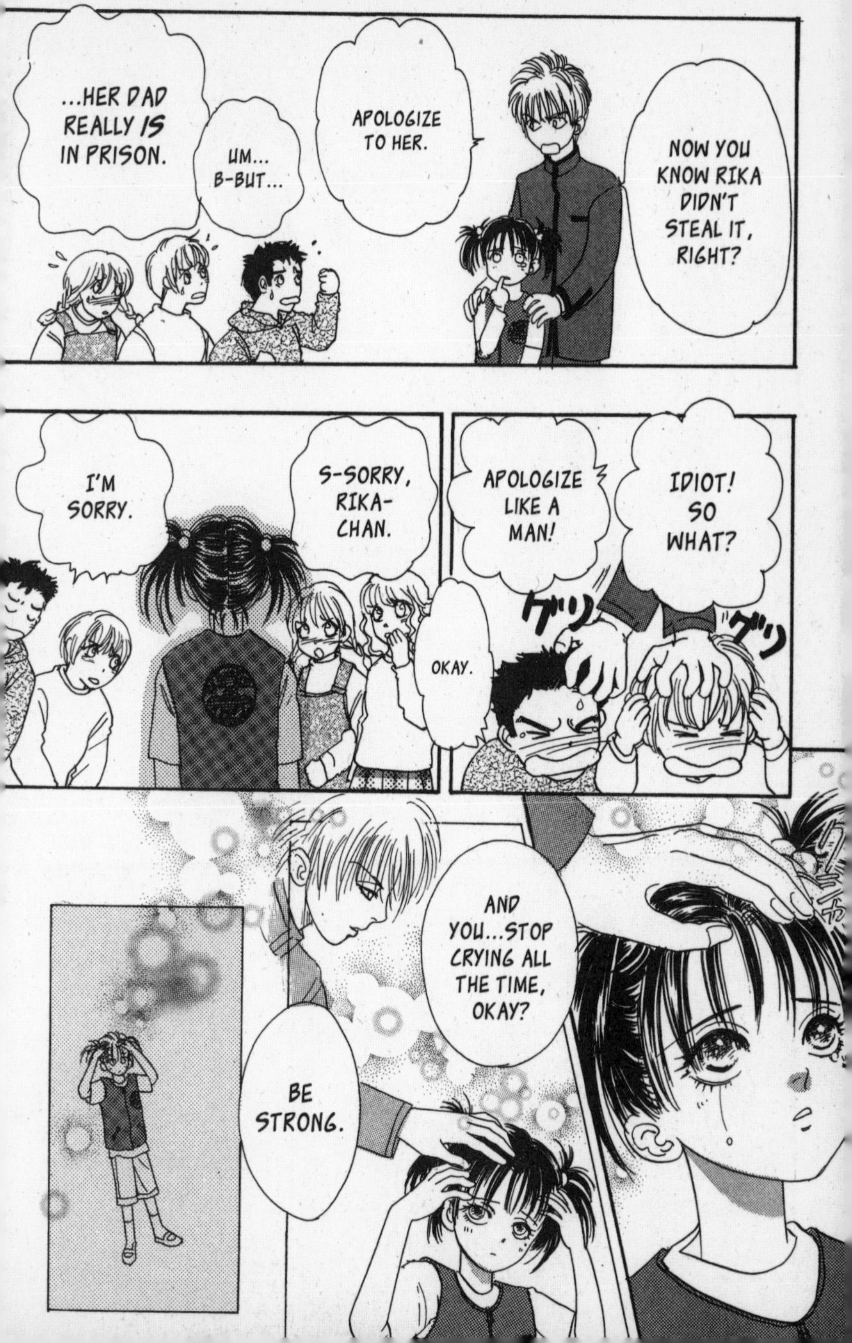
NOW YOU KNOW RIKA DIDN'T STEAL IT, RIGHT?
APOLOGIZE TO HER.
UM... B-BUT...
...HER DAD REALLY IS IN PRISON.
IDIOT! SO WHAT?
APOLOGIZE LIKE A MAN!
OKAY.
S-SORRY, RIKA-CHAN.
I'M SORRY.
AND YOU...STOP CRYING ALL THE TIME, OKAY?
BE STRONG.

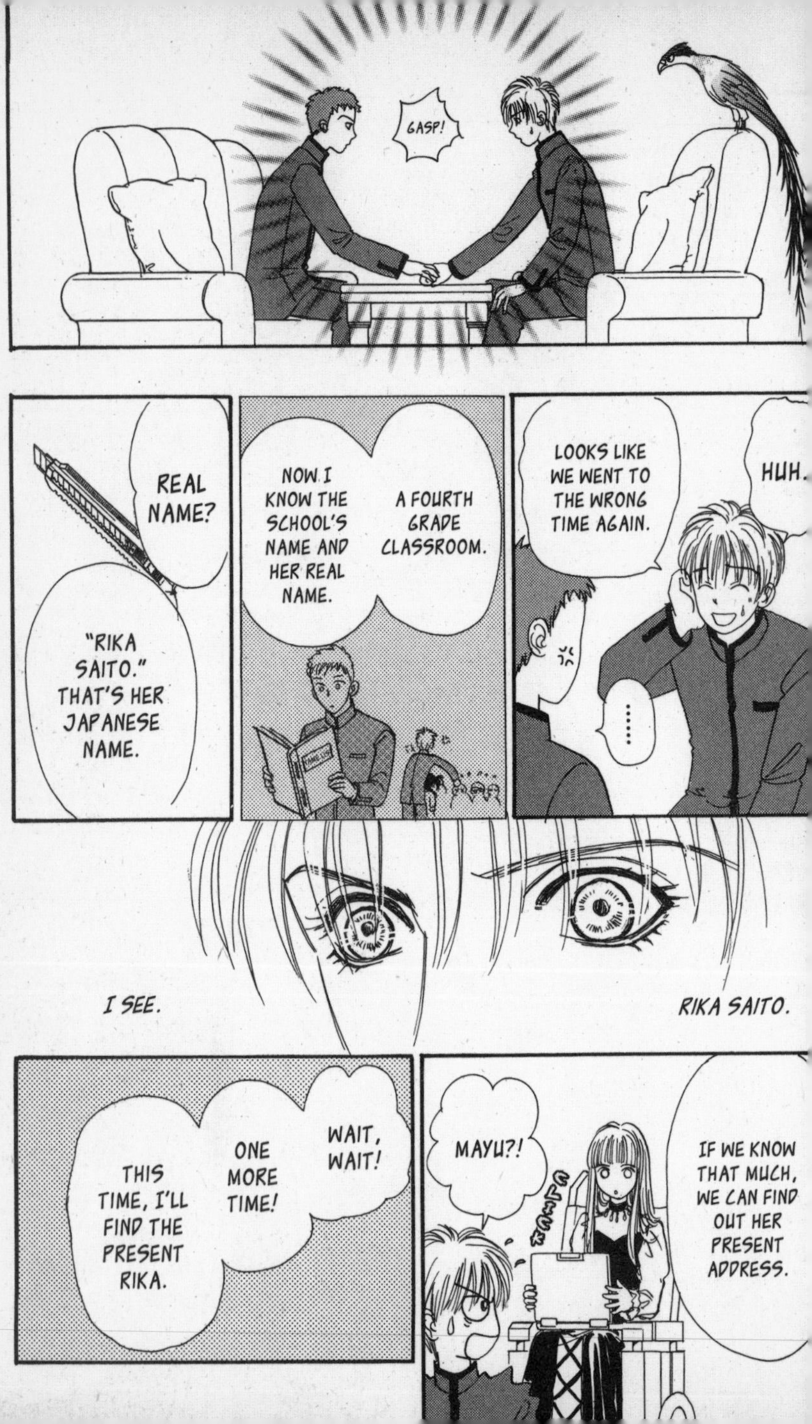
GASP!
HUH.
LOOKS LIKE WE WENT TO THE WRONG TIME AGAIN.
......
A FOURTH GRADE CLASSROOM.
NOW I KNOW THE SCHOOL'S NAME AND HER REAL NAME.
REAL NAME?
"RIKA SAITO." THAT'S HER JAPANESE NAME.
RIKA SAITO.
I SEE.
IF WE KNOW THAT MUCH, WE CAN FIND OUT HER PRESENT ADDRESS.
MAYU?!
WAIT, WAIT!
ONE MORE TIME!
THIS TIME, I'LL FIND THE PRESENT RIKA.

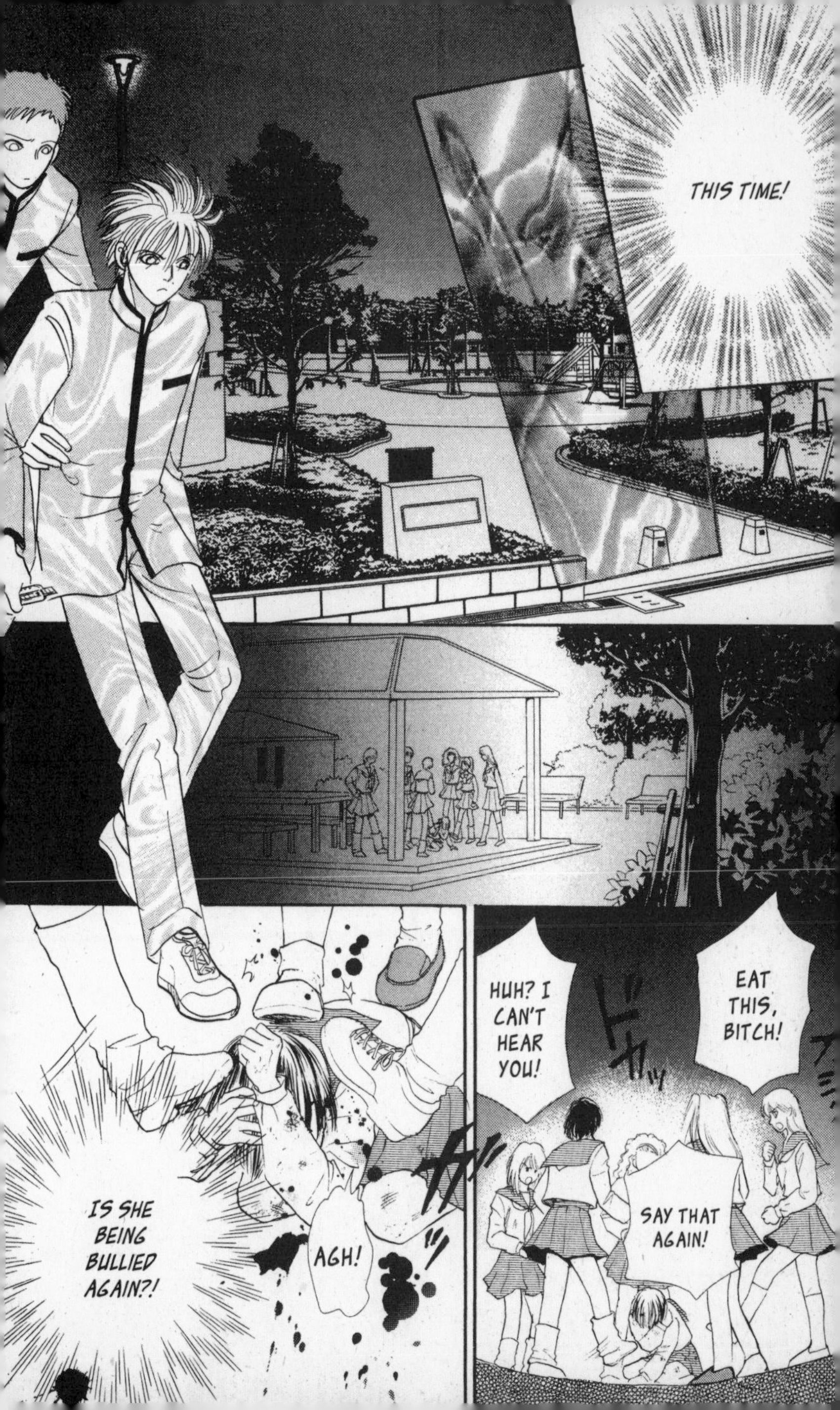
THIS TIME!
EAT THIS, BITCH!
HUH? I CAN'T HEAR YOU!
SAY THAT AGAIN!
AGH!
IS SHE BEING BULLIED AGAIN?!

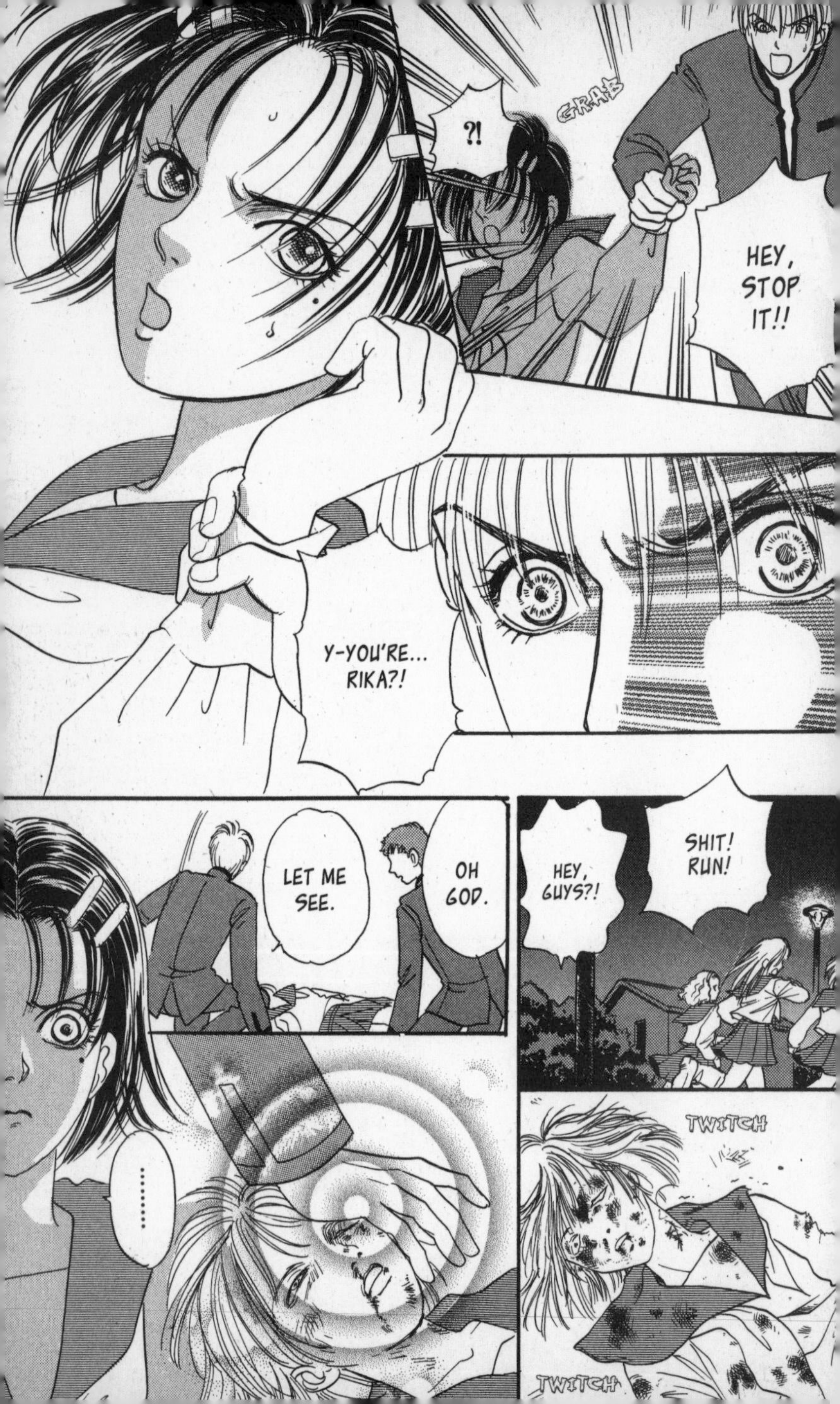
GRAB
?!
HEY, STOP IT!!
Y-YOU'RE... RIKA?!
SHIT! RUN!
HEY, GUYS?!
OH GOD.
LET ME SEE.
TWITCH
TWITCH
....

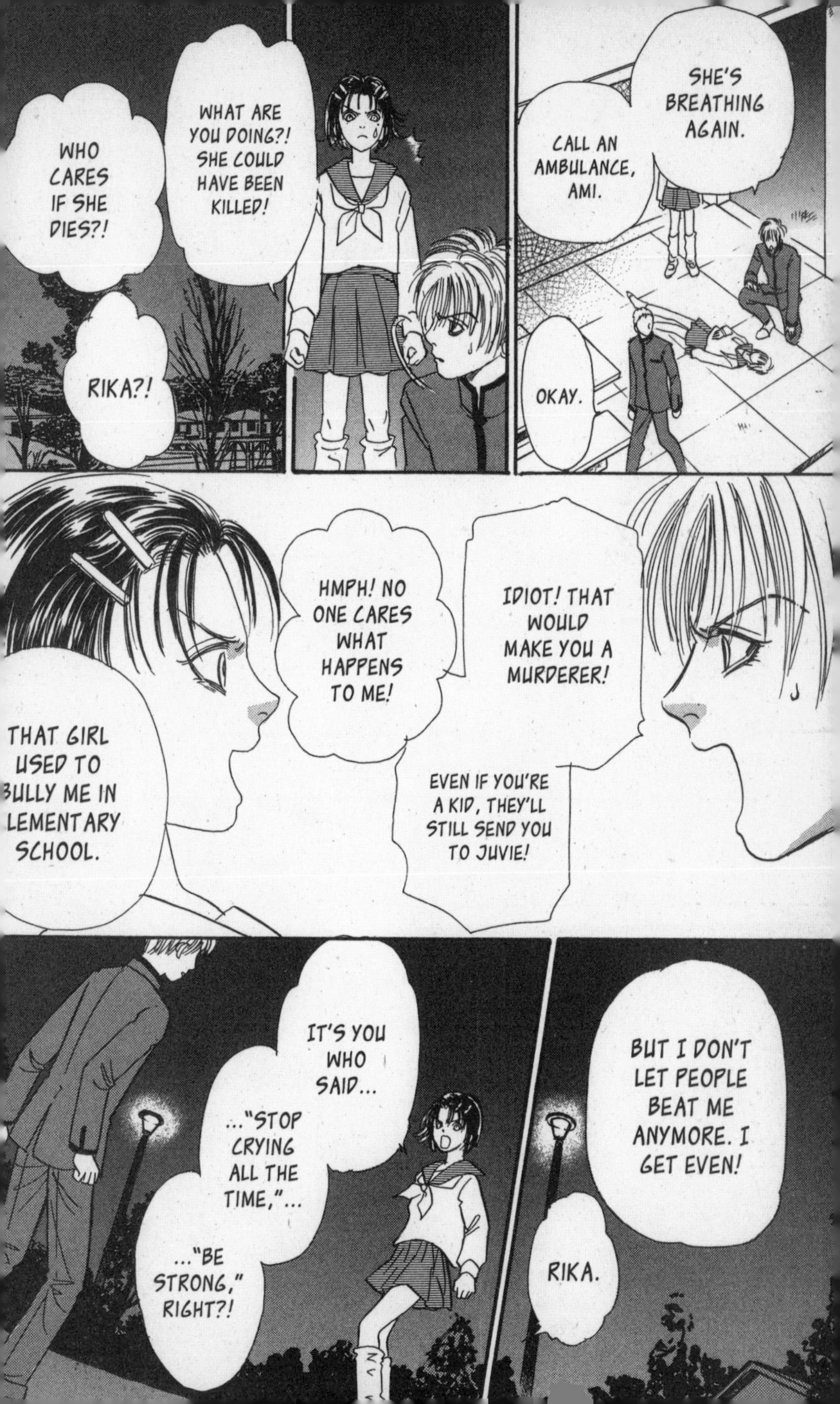
SHE'S BREATHING AGAIN.
CALL AN AMBULANCE, AMI.
OKAY.
WHAT ARE YOU DOING?! SHE COULD HAVE BEEN KILLED!
WHO CARES IF SHE DIES?!
RIKA?!
IDIOT! THAT WOULD MAKE YOU A MURDERER!
EVEN IF YOU'RE A KID, THEY'LL STILL SEND YOU TO JUVIE!
HMPH! NO ONE CARES WHAT HAPPENS TO ME!
THAT GIRL USED TO BULLY ME IN ELEMENTARY SCHOOL.
BUT I DON'T LET PEOPLE BEAT ME ANYMORE. I GET EVEN!
RIKA.
IT'S YOU WHO SAID...
..."STOP CRYING ALL THE TIME,"...
..."BE STRONG," RIGHT?!

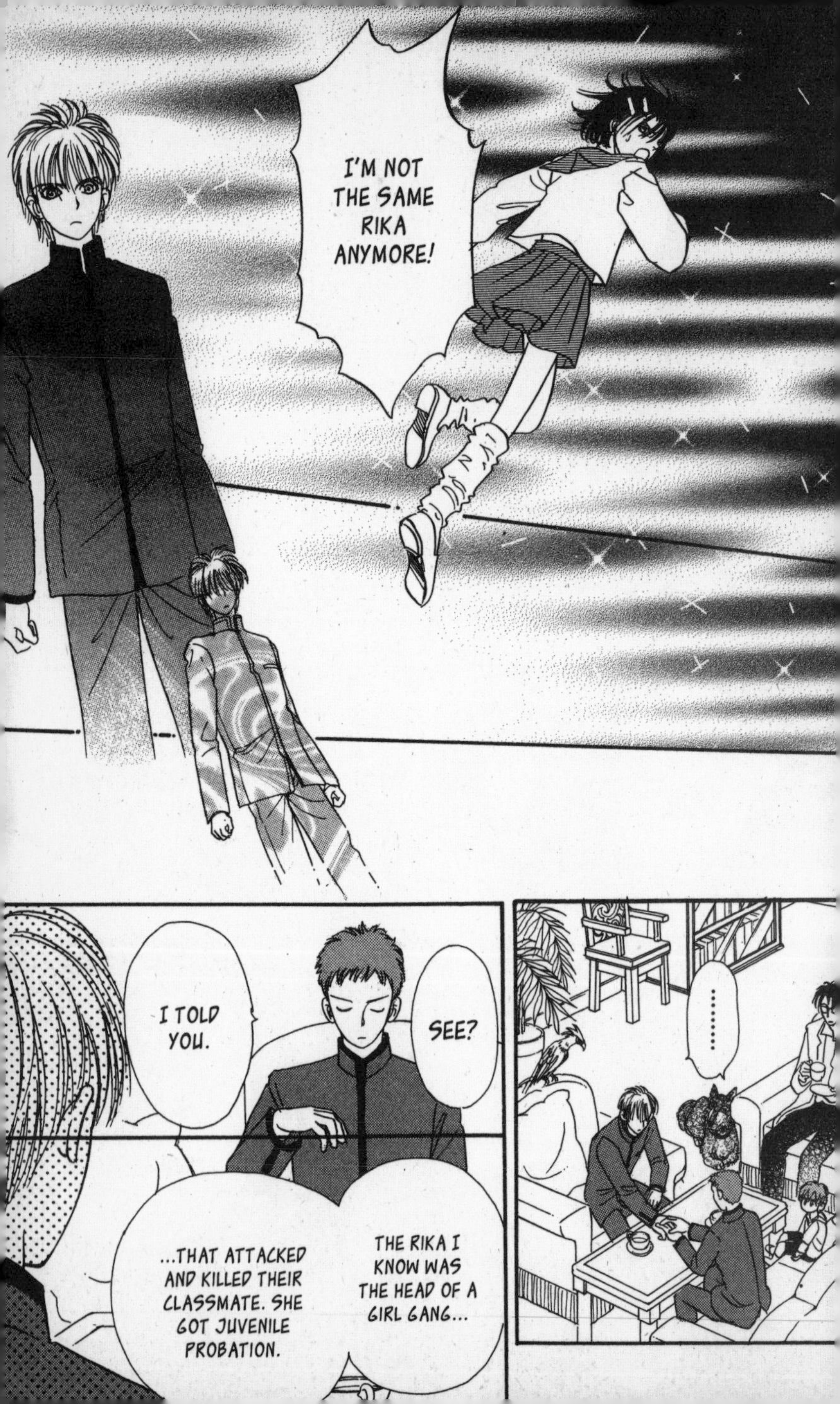
I'M NOT THE SAME RIKA ANYMORE!
......
SEE?
I TOLD YOU.
THE RIKA I KNOW WAS THE HEAD OF A GIRL GANG...
...THAT ATTACKED AND KILLED THEIR CLASSMATE. SHE GOT JUVENILE PROBATION.

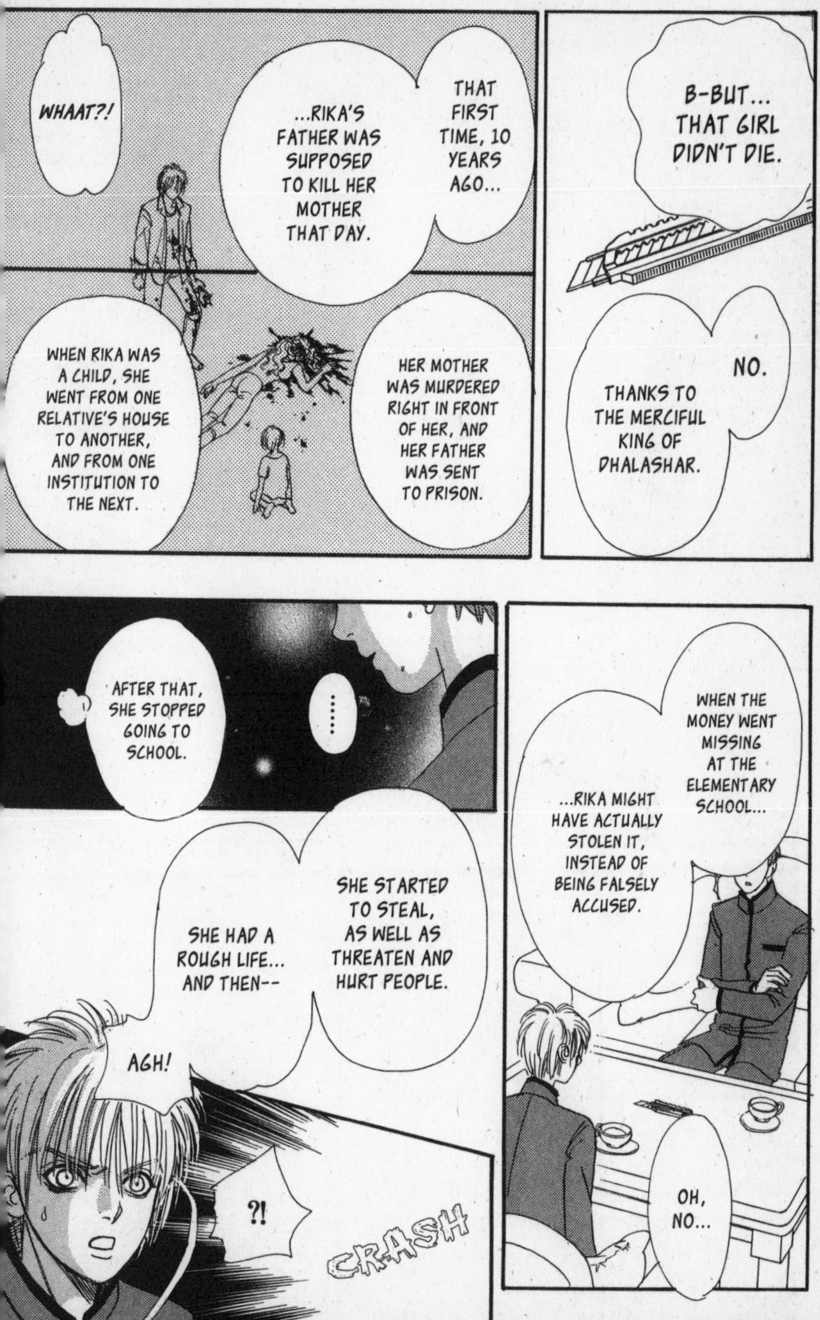

B-BUT... THAT GIRL DIDN'T DIE.
NO.
THANKS TO THE MERCIFUL KING OF DHALASHAR.
THAT FIRST TIME, 10 YEARS AGO...
...RIKA'S FATHER WAS SUPPOSED TO KILL HER MOTHER THAT DAY.
WHAAT?!
HER MOTHER WAS MURDERED RIGHT IN FRONT OF HER, AND HER FATHER WAS SENT TO PRISON.
WHEN RIKA WAS A CHILD, SHE WENT FROM ONE RELATIVE'S HOUSE TO ANOTHER, AND FROM ONE INSTITUTION TO THE NEXT.
WHEN THE MONEY WENT MISSING AT THE ELEMENTARY SCHOOL...
...RIKA MIGHT HAVE ACTUALLY STOLEN IT, INSTEAD OF BEING FALSELY ACCUSED.
OH, NO...
......
AFTER THAT, SHE STOPPED GOING TO SCHOOL.
SHE STARTED TO STEAL, AS WELL AS THREATEN AND HURT PEOPLE.
SHE HAD A ROUGH LIFE... AND THEN--
AGH!
?!
CRASH

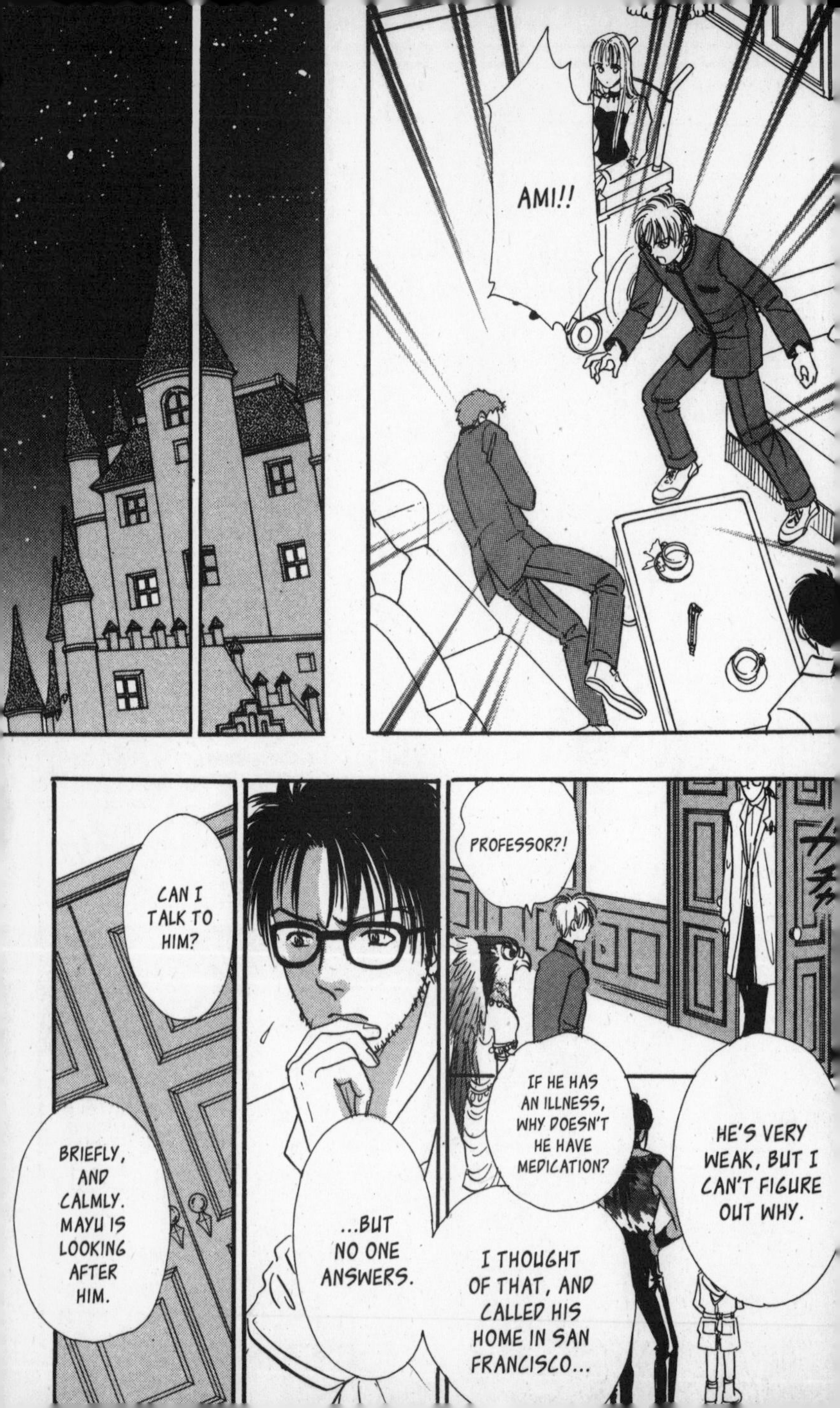
AMI!!
PROFESSOR?!
HE'S VERY WEAK, BUT I CAN'T FIGURE OUT WHY.
IF HE HAS AN ILLNESS, WHY DOESN'T HE HAVE MEDICATION?
I THOUGHT OF THAT, AND CALLED HIS HOME IN SAN FRANCISCO...
...BUT NO ONE ANSWERS.
CAN I TALK TO HIM?
BRIEFLY, AND CALMLY. MAYU IS LOOKING AFTER HIM.

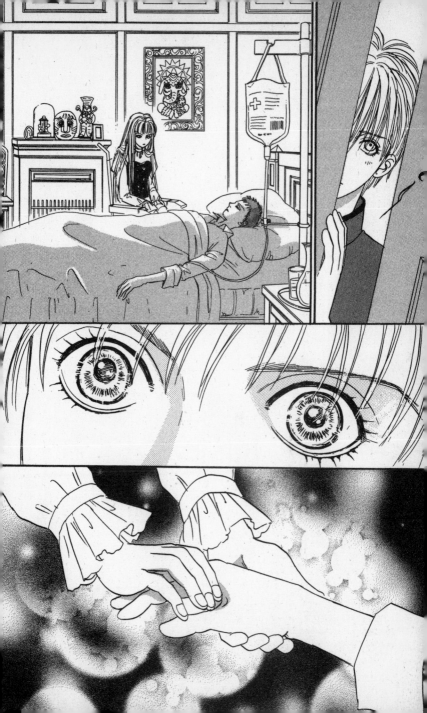

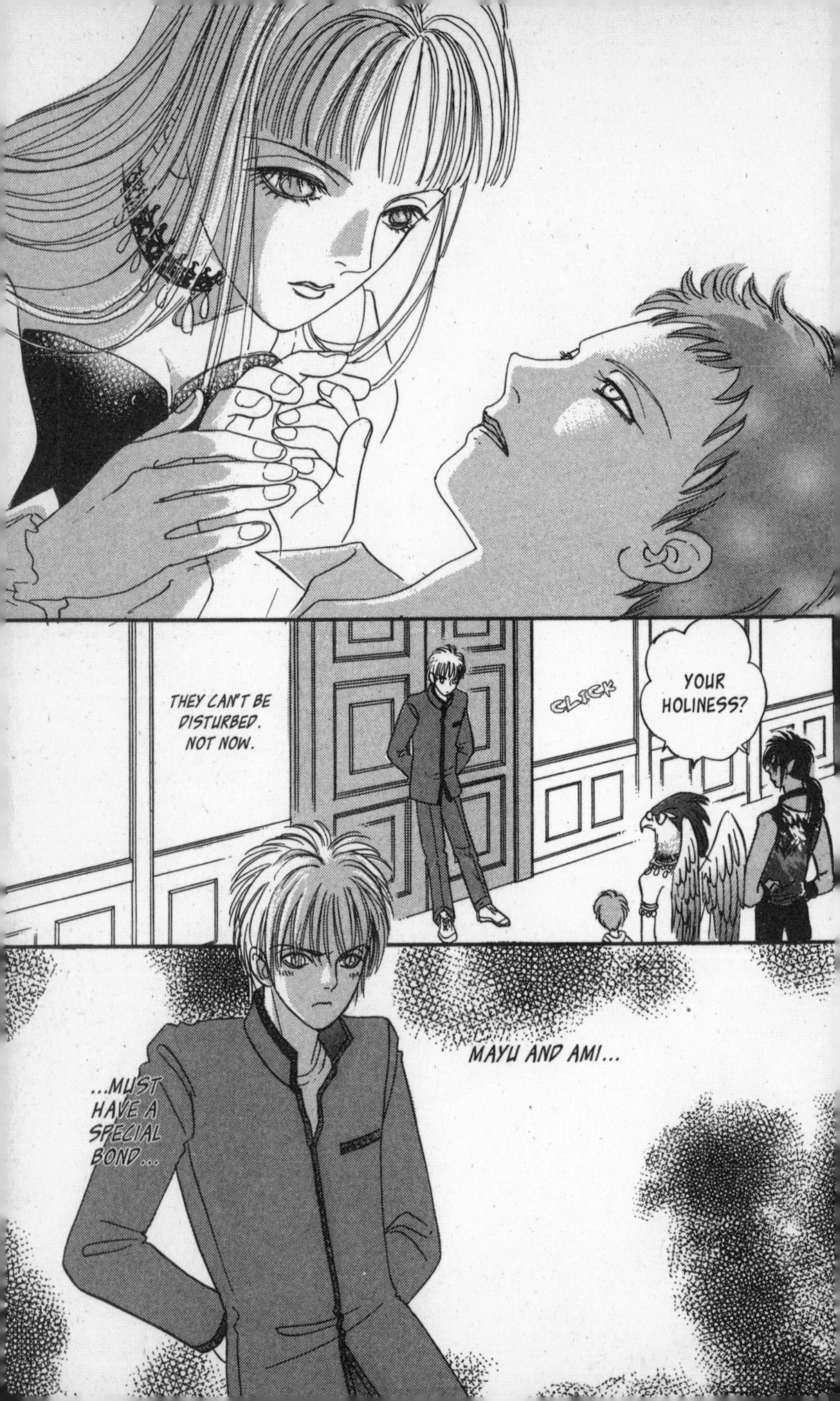

YOUR HOLINESS?
CLICK
THEY CAN'T BE DISTURBED. NOT NOW.
MAYU AND AMI...
...MUST HAVE A SPECIAL BOND...

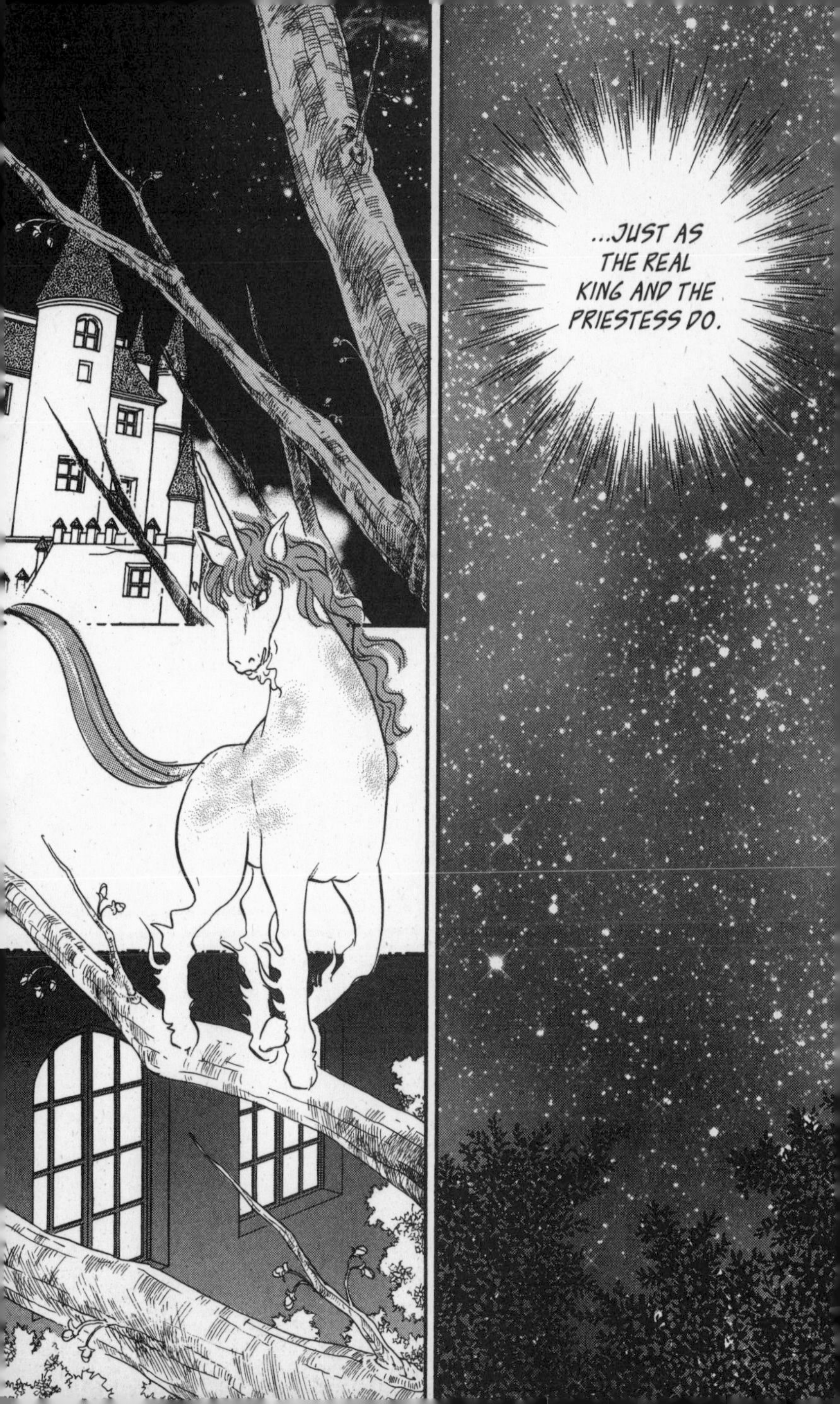
...JUST AS THE REAL KING AND THE PRIESTESS DO.

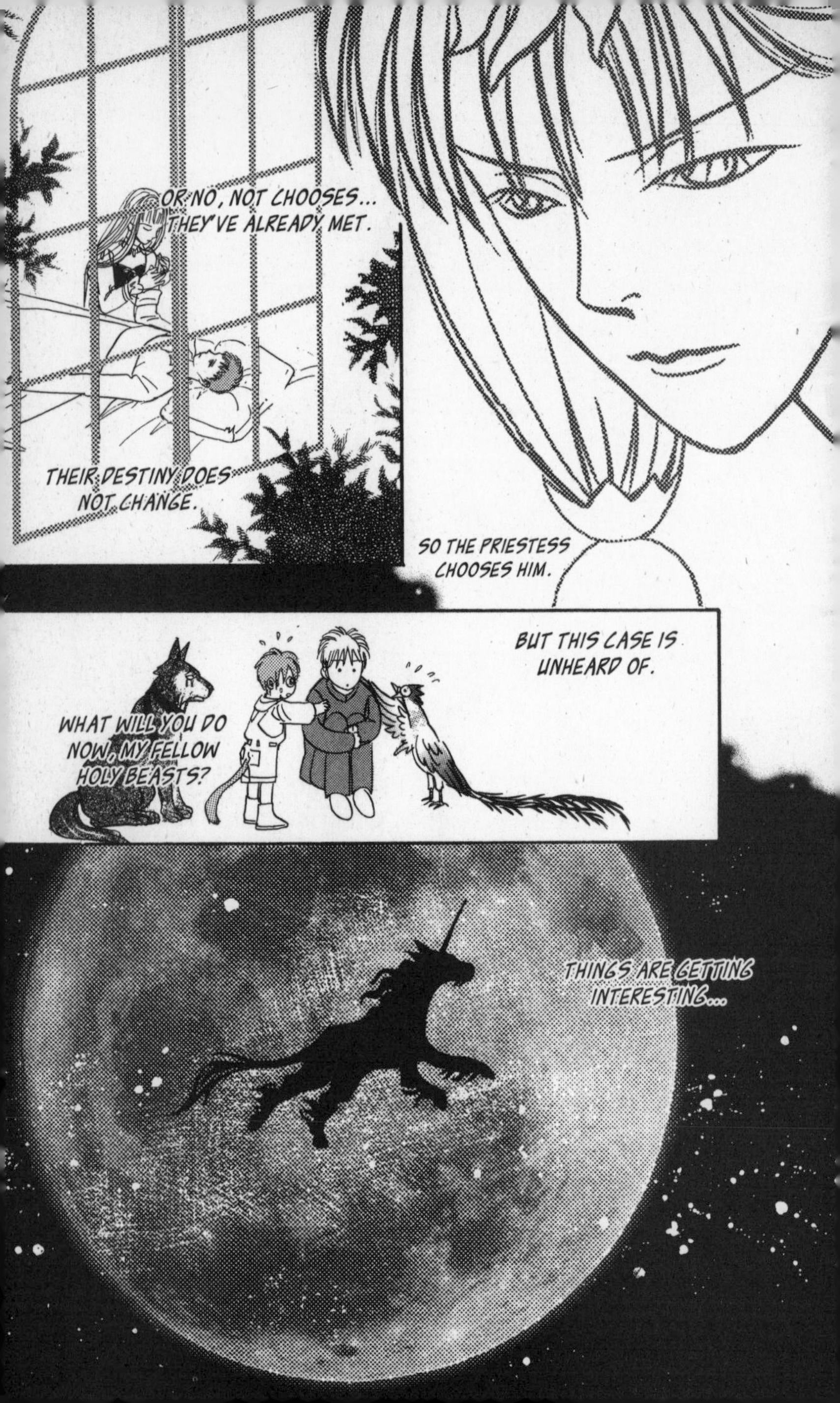
SO THE PRIESTESS CHOOSES HIM.
OR NO, NOT CHOOSES... THEY'VE ALREADY MET.
THEIR DESTINY DOES NOT CHANGE.
BUT THIS CASE IS UNHEARD OF.
WHAT WILL YOU DO NOW, MY FELLOW HOLY BEASTS?
THINGS ARE GETTING INTERESTING...

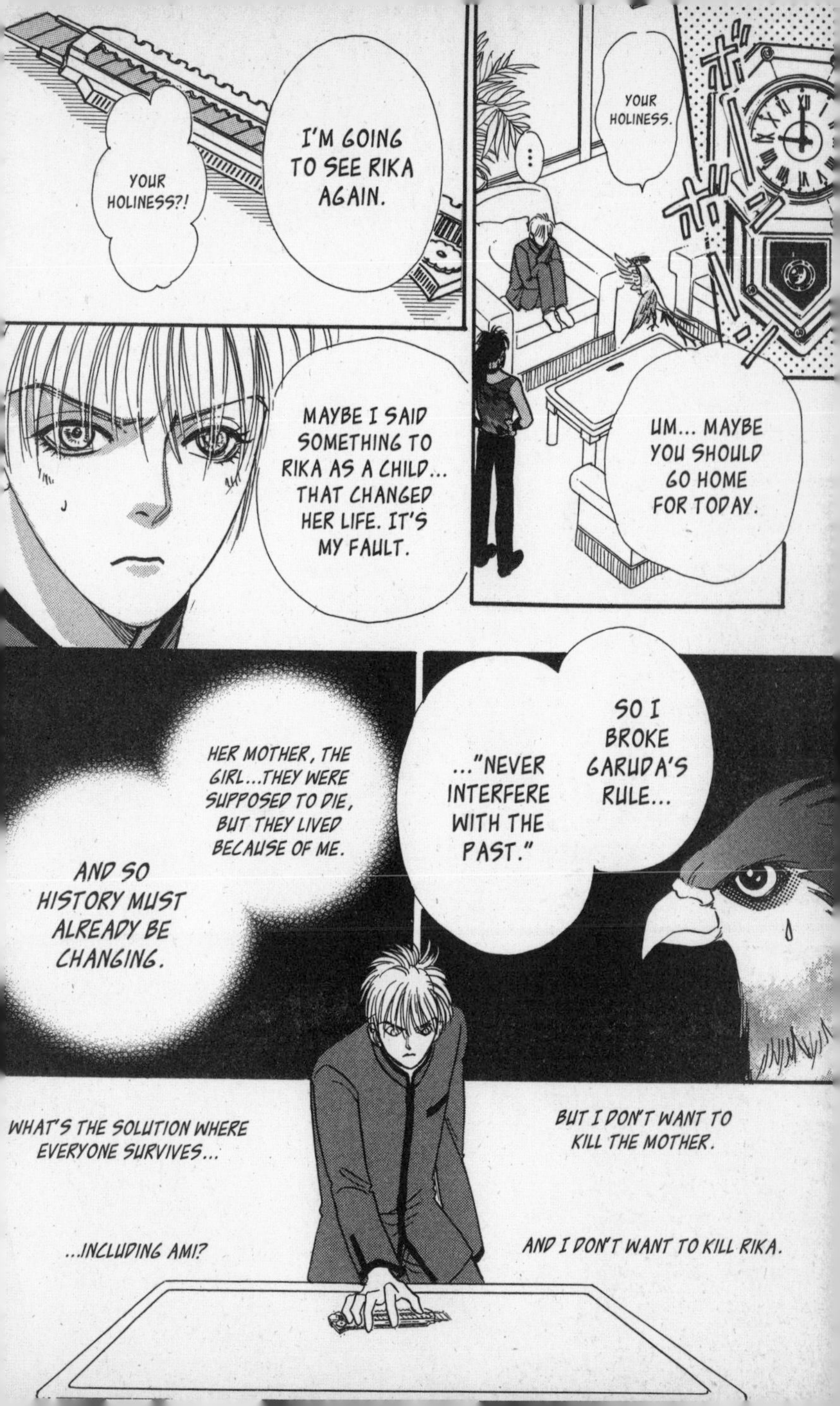
YOUR HOLINESS.
...
UM... MAYBE YOU SHOULD GO HOME FOR TODAY.
I'M GOING TO SEE RIKA AGAIN.
YOUR HOLINESS?!
MAYBE I SAID SOMETHING TO RIKA AS A CHILD... THAT CHANGED HER LIFE. IT'S MY FAULT.
SO I BROKE GARUDA'S RULE...
..."NEVER INTERFERE WITH THE PAST."
HER MOTHER, THE GIRL...THEY WERE SUPPOSED TO DIE, BUT THEY LIVED BECAUSE OF ME.
AND SO HISTORY MUST ALREADY BE CHANGING.
BUT I DON'T WANT TO KILL THE MOTHER.
AND I DON'T WANT TO KILL RIKA.
WHAT'S THE SOLUTION WHERE EVERYONE SURVIVES...
...INCLUDING AMI?

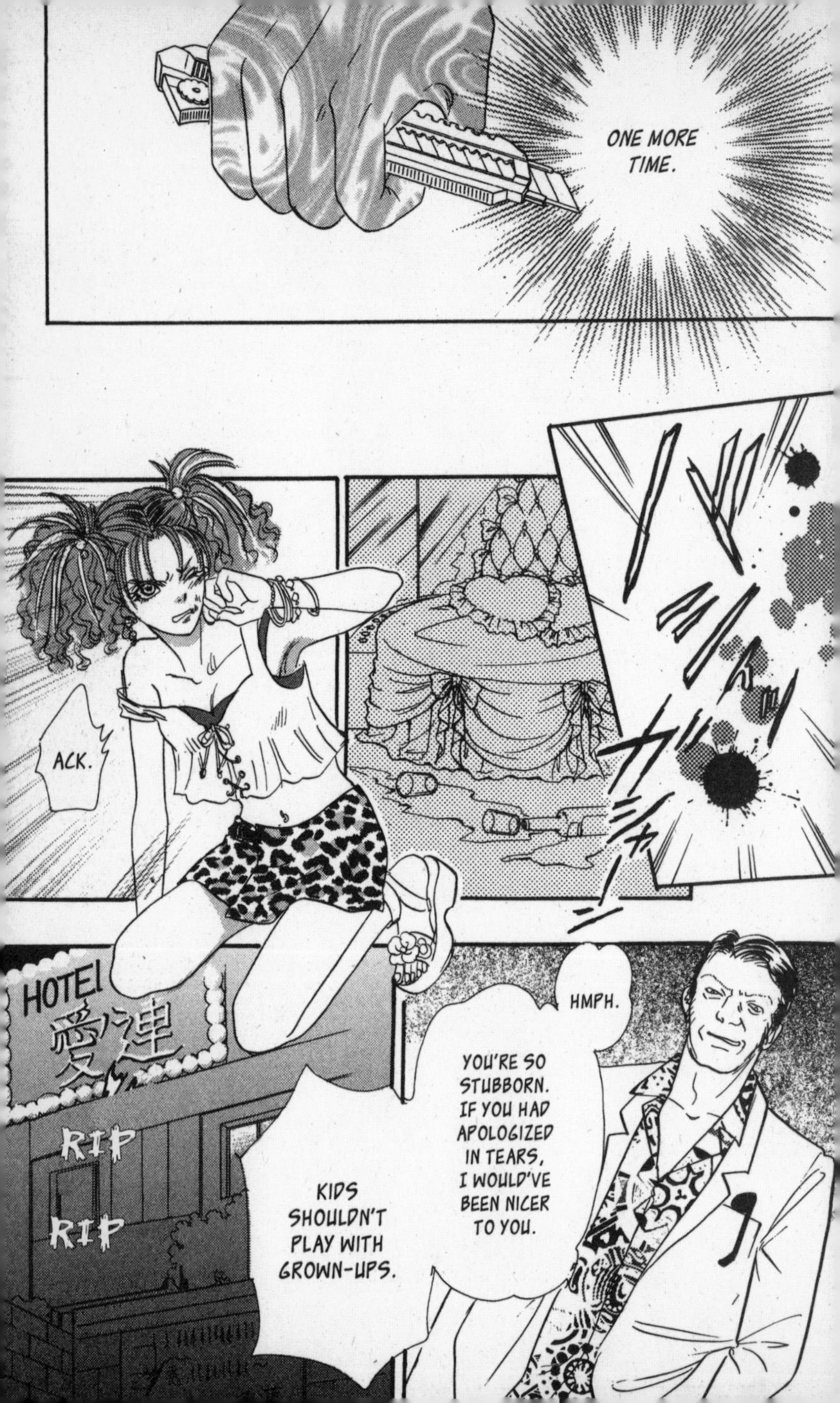
ONE MORE TIME.
ACK.
HMPH.
YOU'RE SO STUBBORN. IF YOU HAD APOLOGIZED IN TEARS, I WOULD'VE BEEN NICER TO YOU.
HOTEL
愛連
KIDS SHOULDN'T PLAY WITH GROWN-UPS.
RIP
RIP

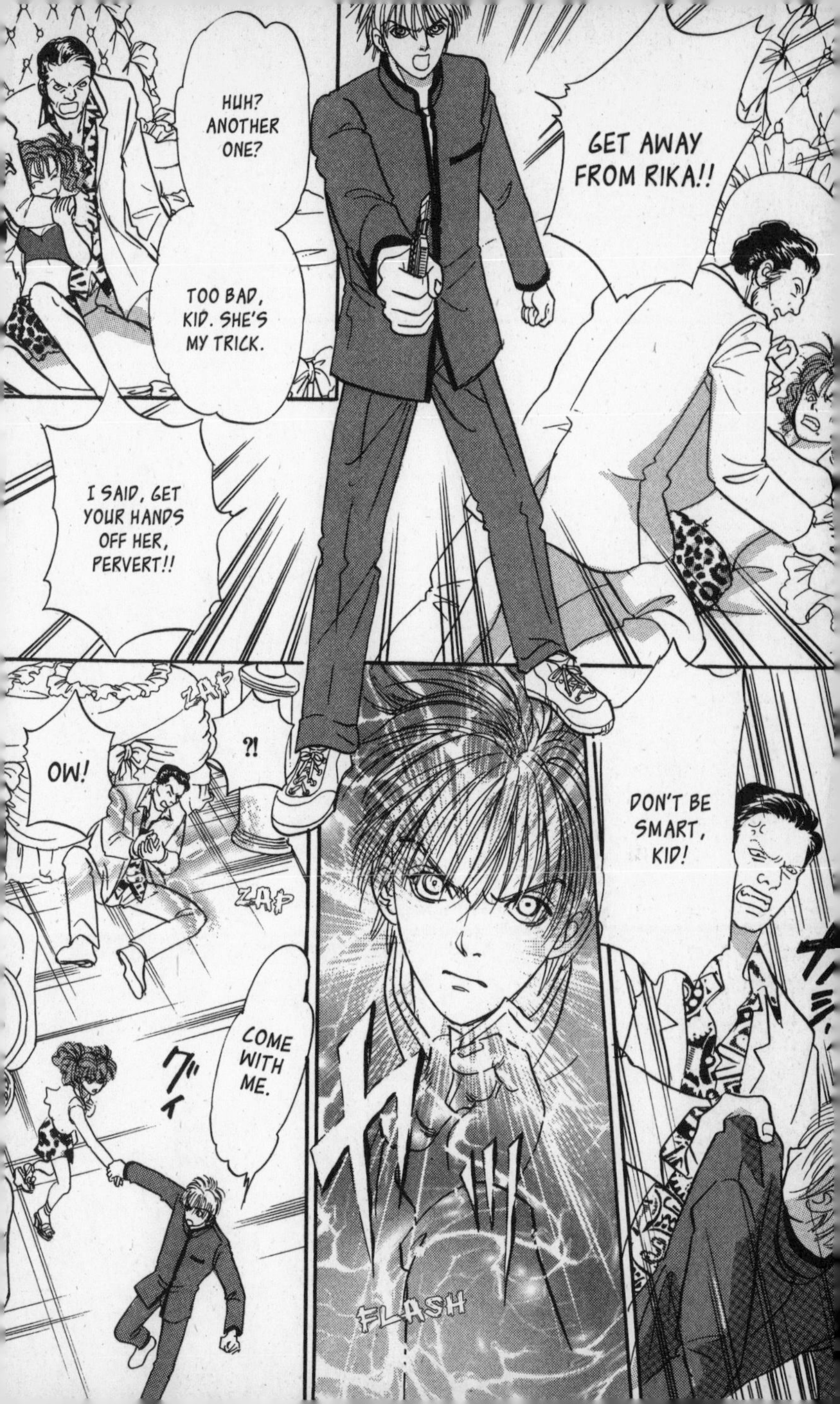
GET AWAY FROM RIKA!!
HUH? ANOTHER ONE?
TOO BAD, KID. SHE'S MY TRICK.
I SAID, GET YOUR HANDS OFF HER, PERVERT!!
DON'T BE SMART, KID!
FLASH
ZAP
OW!
?!
ZAP
COME WITH ME.
グイ

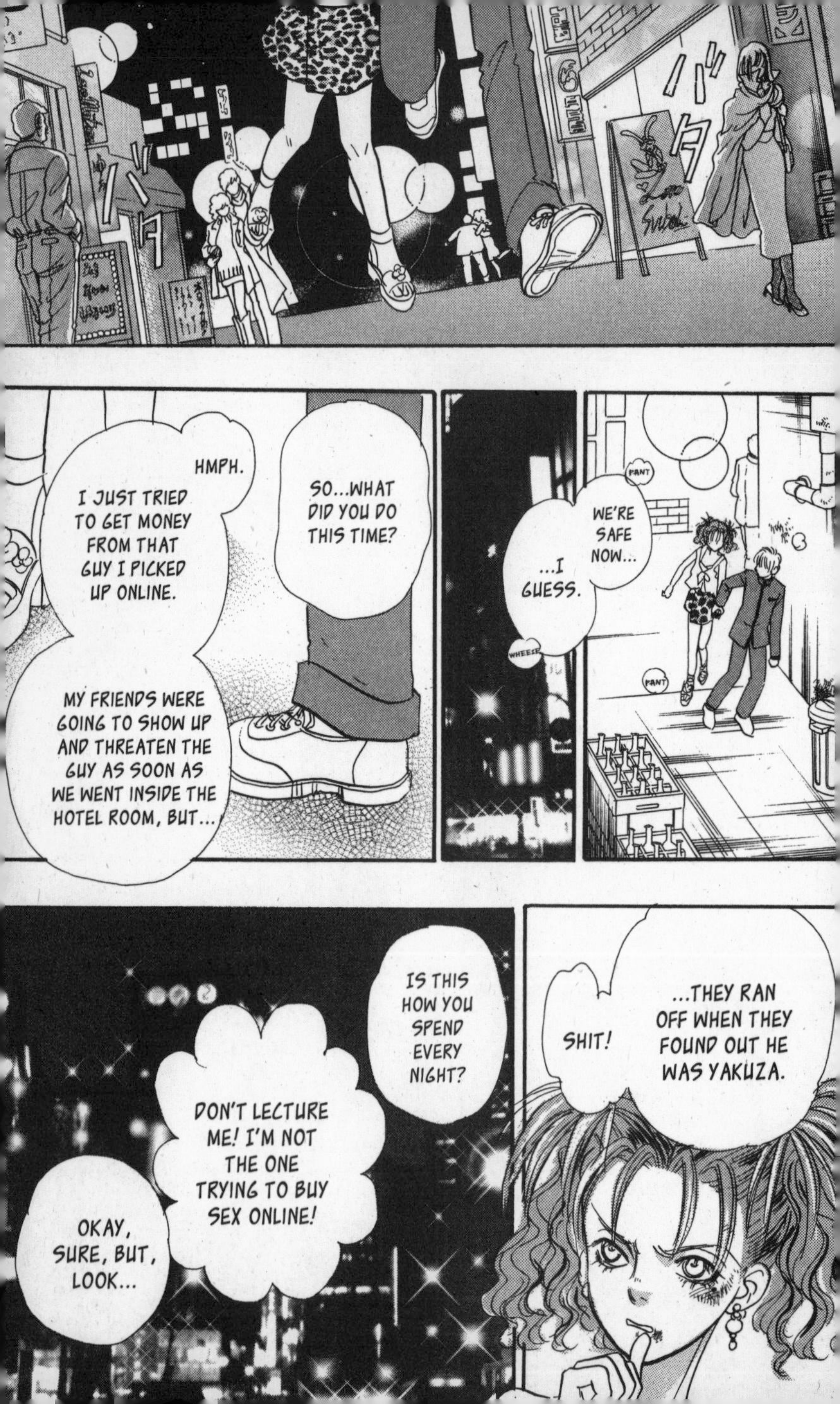
PANT
WE'RE SAFE NOW...
...I GUESS.
WHEEZE
PANT
SO...WHAT DID YOU DO THIS TIME?
HMPH.
I JUST TRIED TO GET MONEY FROM THAT GUY I PICKED UP ONLINE.
MY FRIENDS WERE GOING TO SHOW UP AND THREATEN THE GUY AS SOON AS WE WENT INSIDE THE HOTEL ROOM, BUT...
...THEY RAN OFF WHEN THEY FOUND OUT HE WAS YAKUZA.
SHIT!
IS THIS HOW YOU SPEND EVERY NIGHT?
DON'T LECTURE ME! I'M NOT THE ONE TRYING TO BUY SEX ONLINE!
OKAY, SURE, BUT, LOOK...

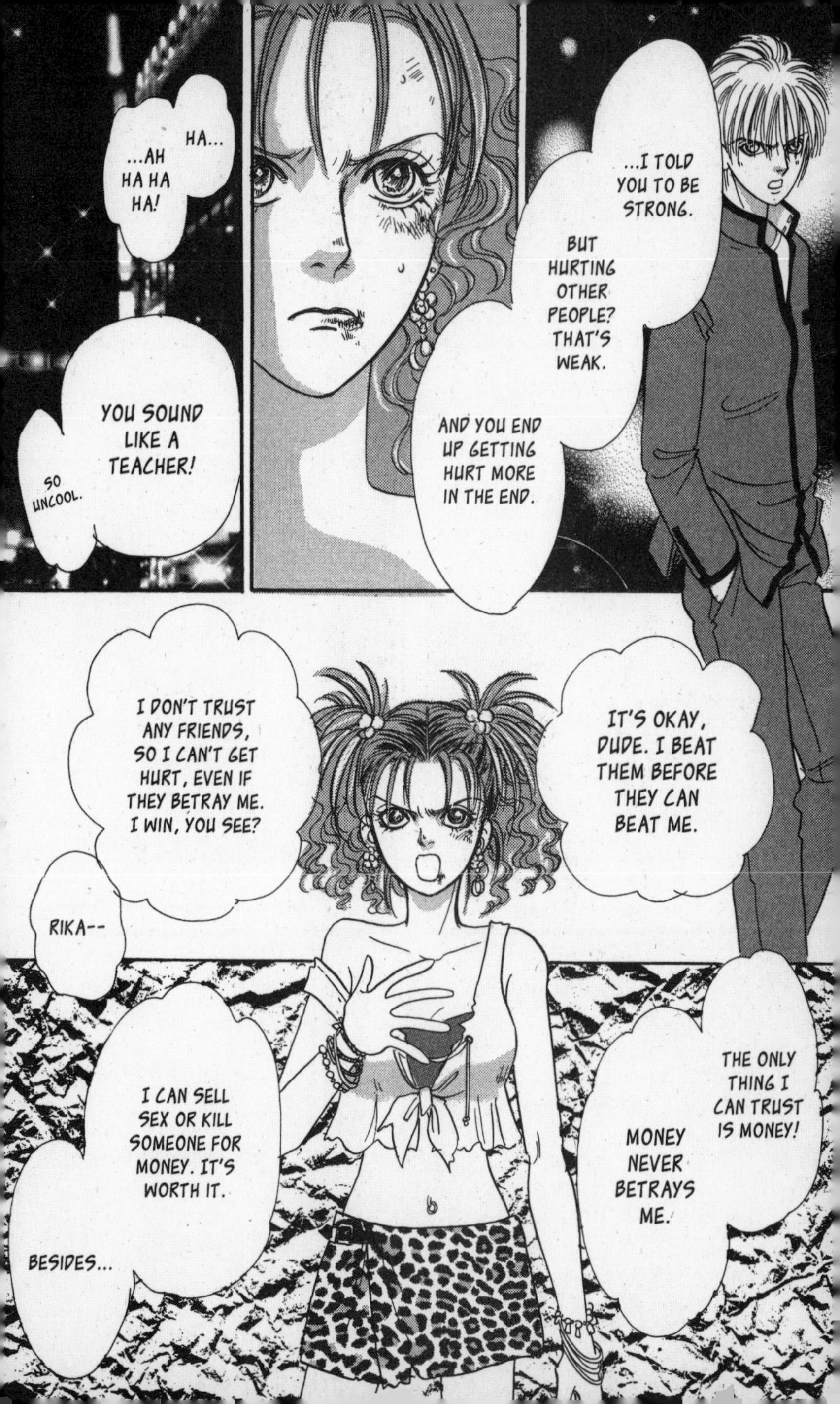
...I TOLD YOU TO BE STRONG.
BUT HURTING OTHER PEOPLE? THAT'S WEAK.
AND YOU END UP GETTING HURT MORE IN THE END.
HA...
...AH HA HA HA!
YOU SOUND LIKE A TEACHER!
SO UNCOOL.
IT'S OKAY, DUDE. I BEAT THEM BEFORE THEY CAN BEAT ME.
I DON'T TRUST ANY FRIENDS, SO I CAN'T GET HURT, EVEN IF THEY BETRAY ME. I WIN, YOU SEE?
RIKA--
THE ONLY THING I CAN TRUST IS MONEY!
MONEY NEVER BETRAYS ME.
I CAN SELL SEX OR KILL SOMEONE FOR MONEY. IT'S WORTH IT.
BESIDES...

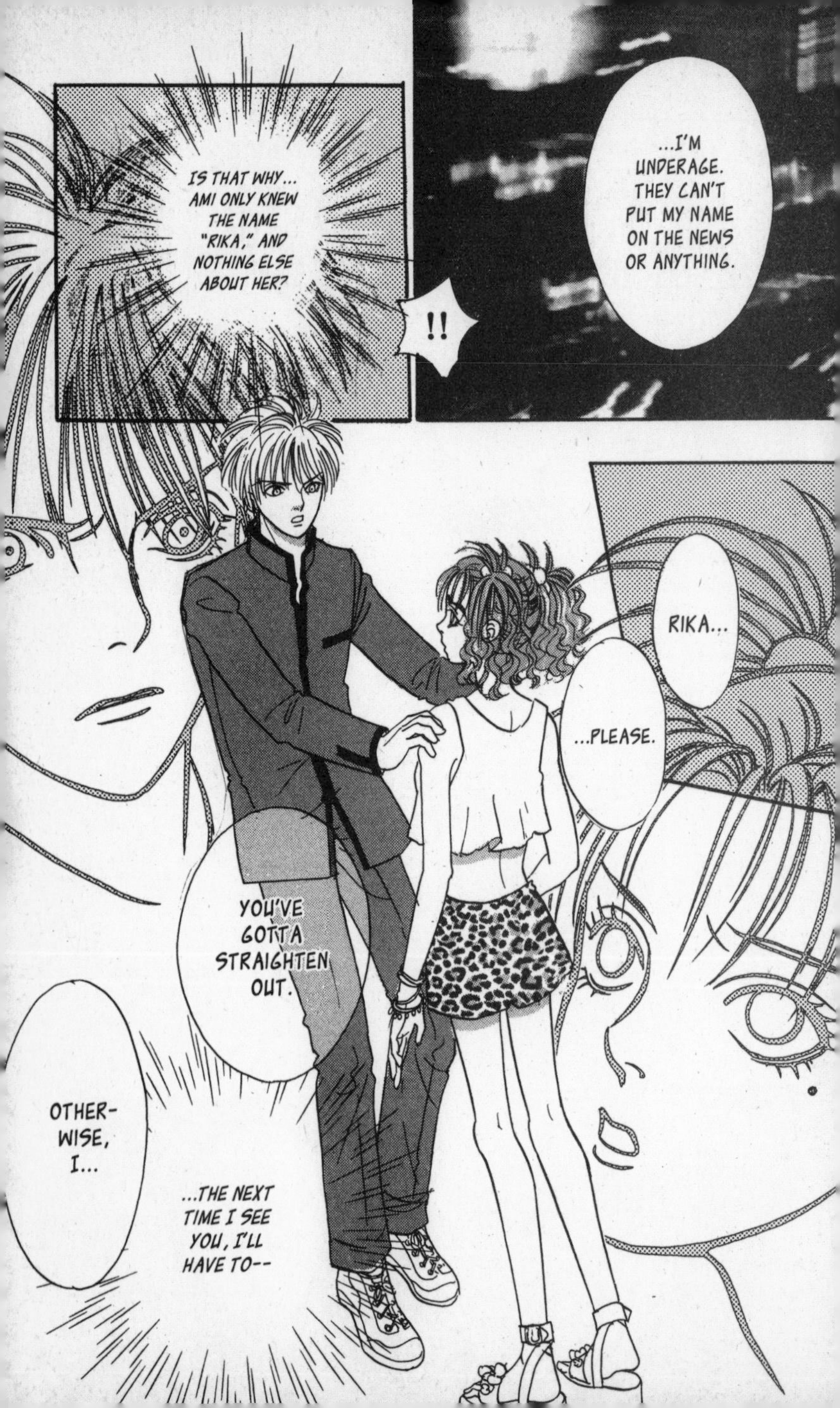
...I'M UNDERAGE. THEY CAN'T PUT MY NAME ON THE NEWS OR ANYTHING.
!!
IS THAT WHY... AMI ONLY KNEW THE NAME "RIKA," AND NOTHING ELSE ABOUT HER?
RIKA...
...PLEASE.
YOU'VE GOTTA STRAIGHTEN OUT.
OTHER-WISE, I...
...THE NEXT TIME I SEE YOU, I'LL HAVE TO--

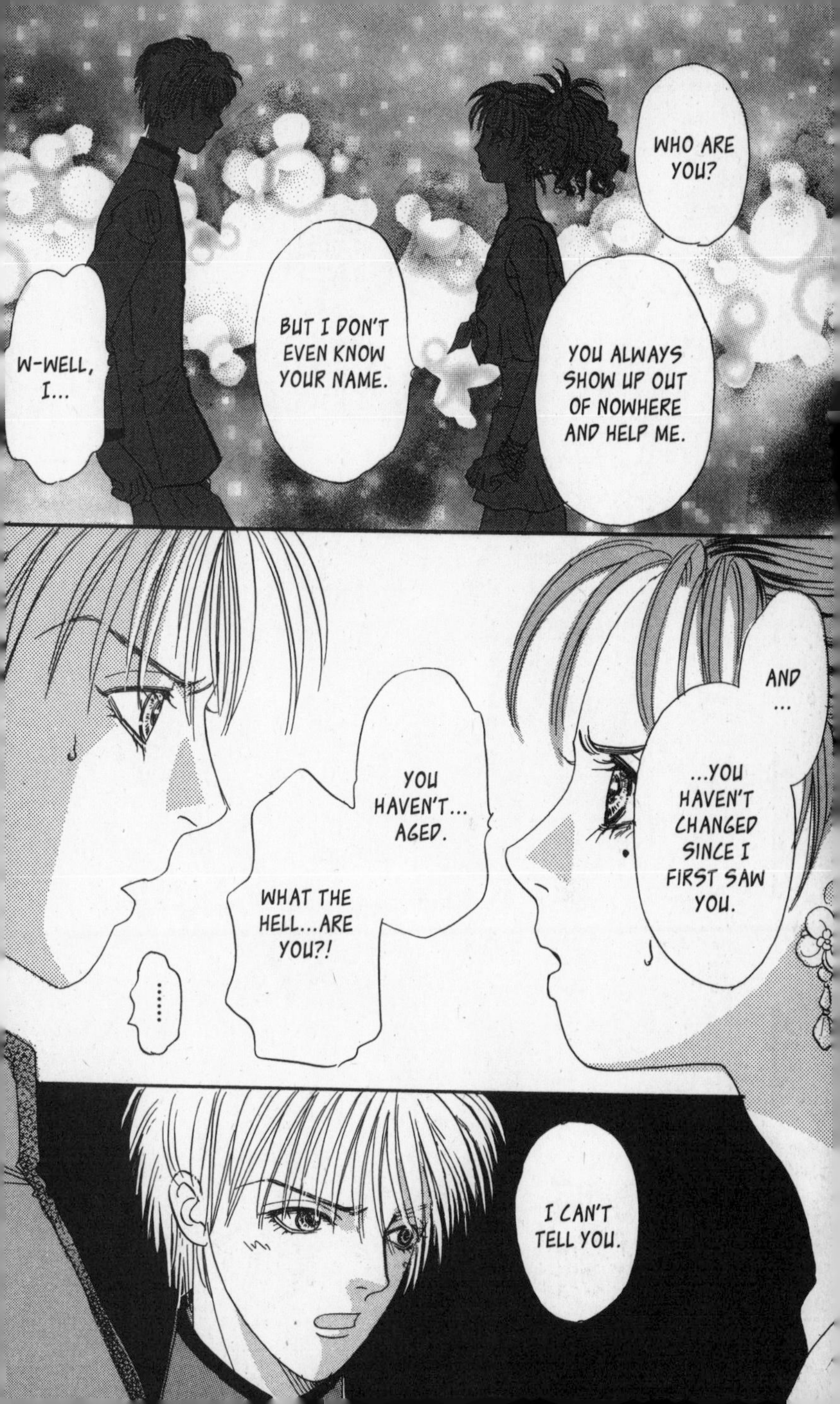
WHO ARE YOU?
YOU ALWAYS SHOW UP OUT OF NOWHERE AND HELP ME.
BUT I DON'T EVEN KNOW YOUR NAME.
W-WELL, I...
AND ...
...YOU HAVEN'T CHANGED SINCE I FIRST SAW YOU.
YOU HAVEN'T... AGED.
WHAT THE HELL...ARE YOU?!
......
I CAN'T TELL YOU.

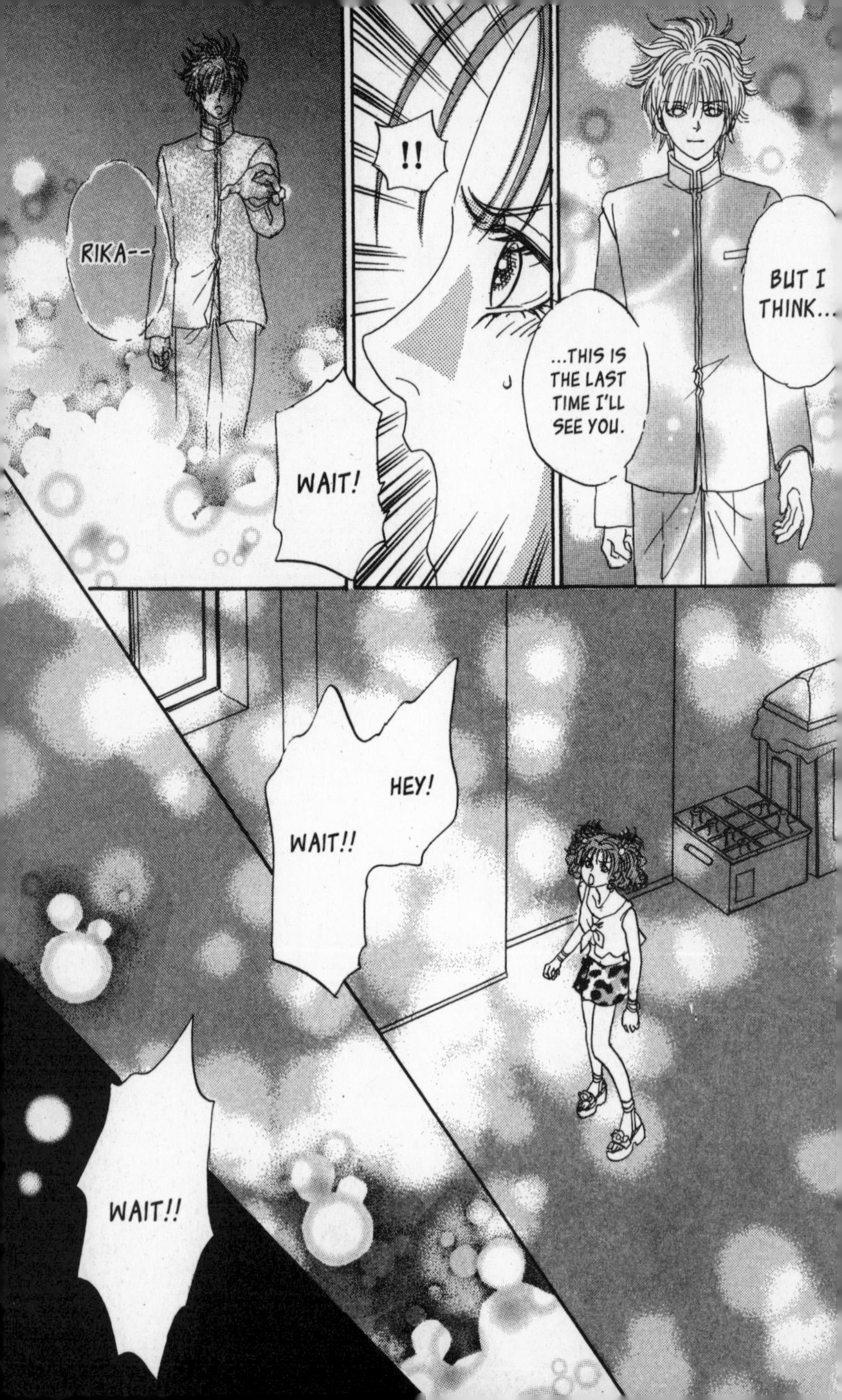
BUT I THINK...
...THIS IS THE LAST TIME I'LL SEE YOU.
!!
WAIT!
RIKA--
HEY!
WAIT!!
WAIT!!

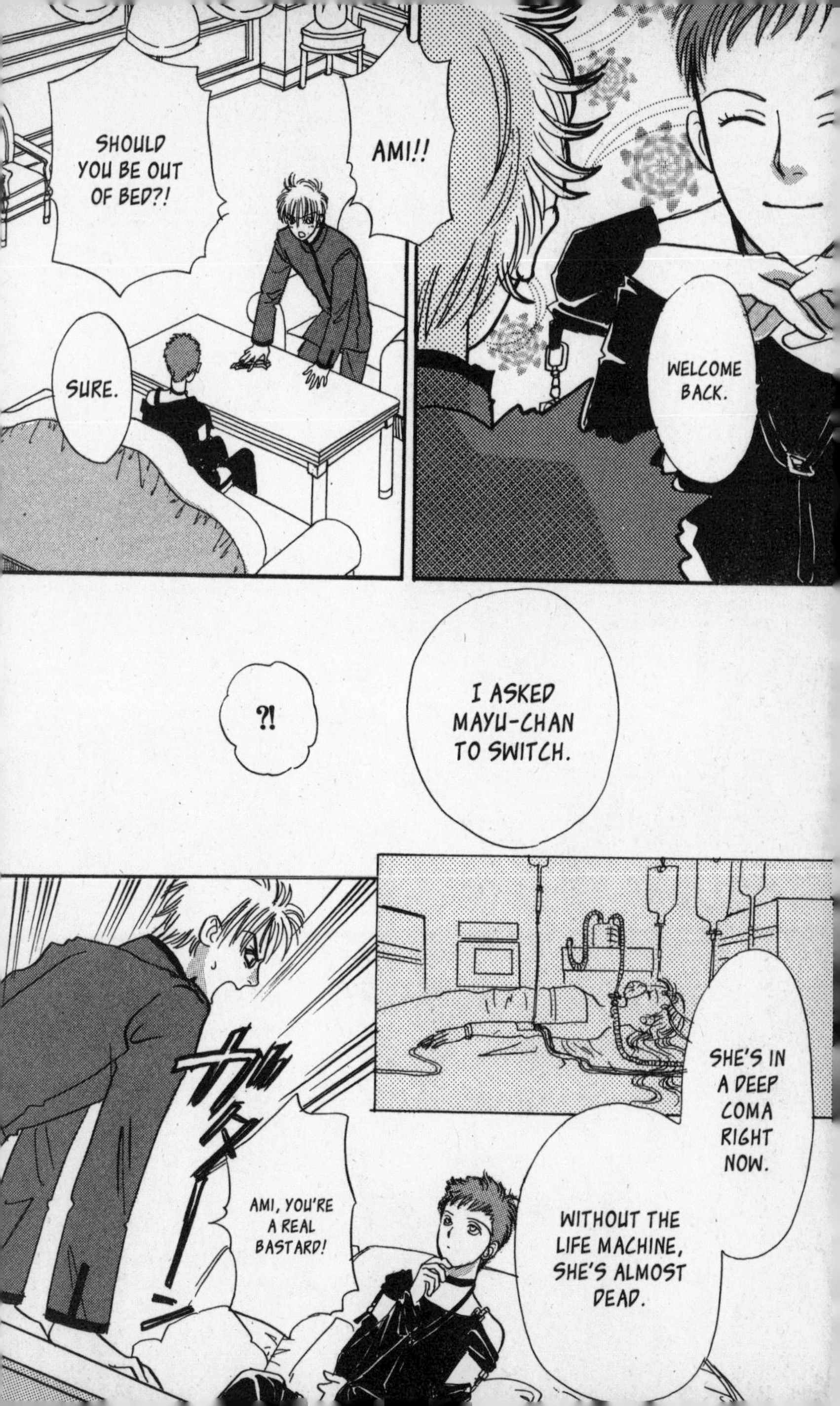
WELCOME BACK.
AMI!!
SHOULD YOU BE OUT OF BED?!
SURE.
I ASKED MAYU-CHAN TO SWITCH.
?!
SHE'S IN A DEEP COMA RIGHT NOW.
WITHOUT THE LIFE MACHINE, SHE'S ALMOST DEAD.
AMI, YOU'RE A REAL BASTARD!

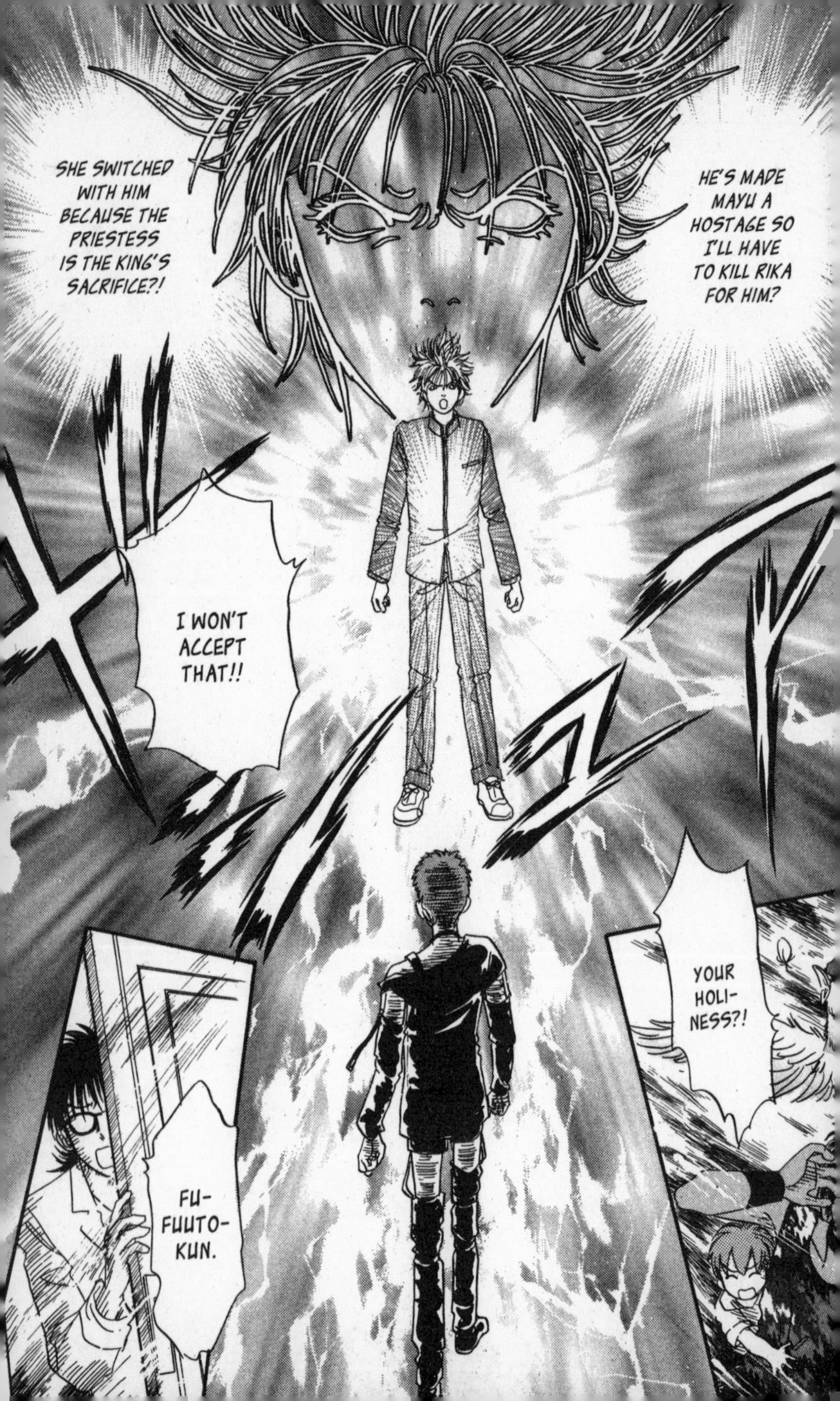
HE'S MADE MAYU A HOSTAGE SO I'LL HAVE TO KILL RIKA FOR HIM?
SHE SWITCHED WITH HIM BECAUSE THE PRIESTESS IS THE KING'S SACRIFICE?!
I WON'T ACCEPT THAT!!
YOUR HOLI-NESS?!
FU-FUUTO-KUN.

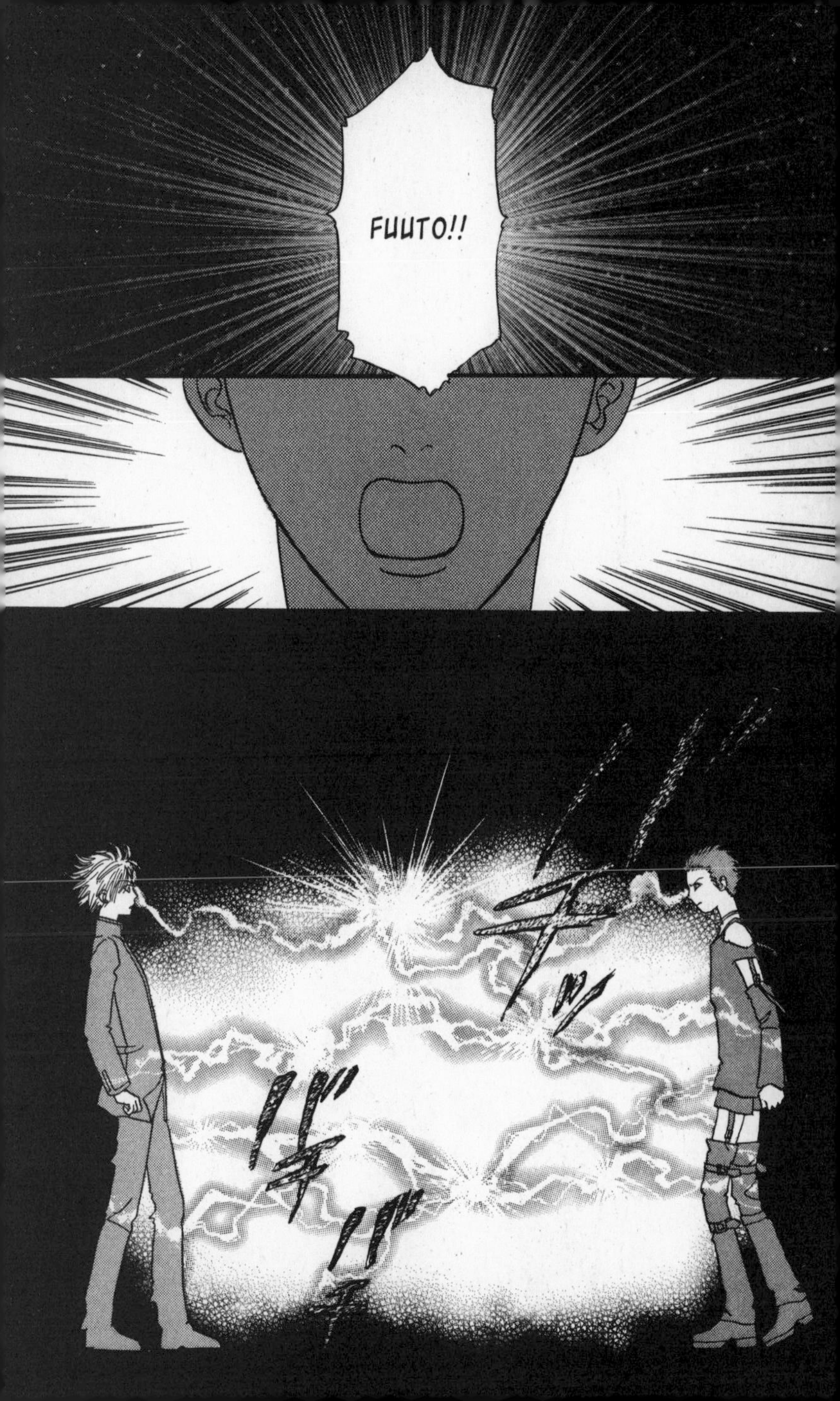
FUUTO!!

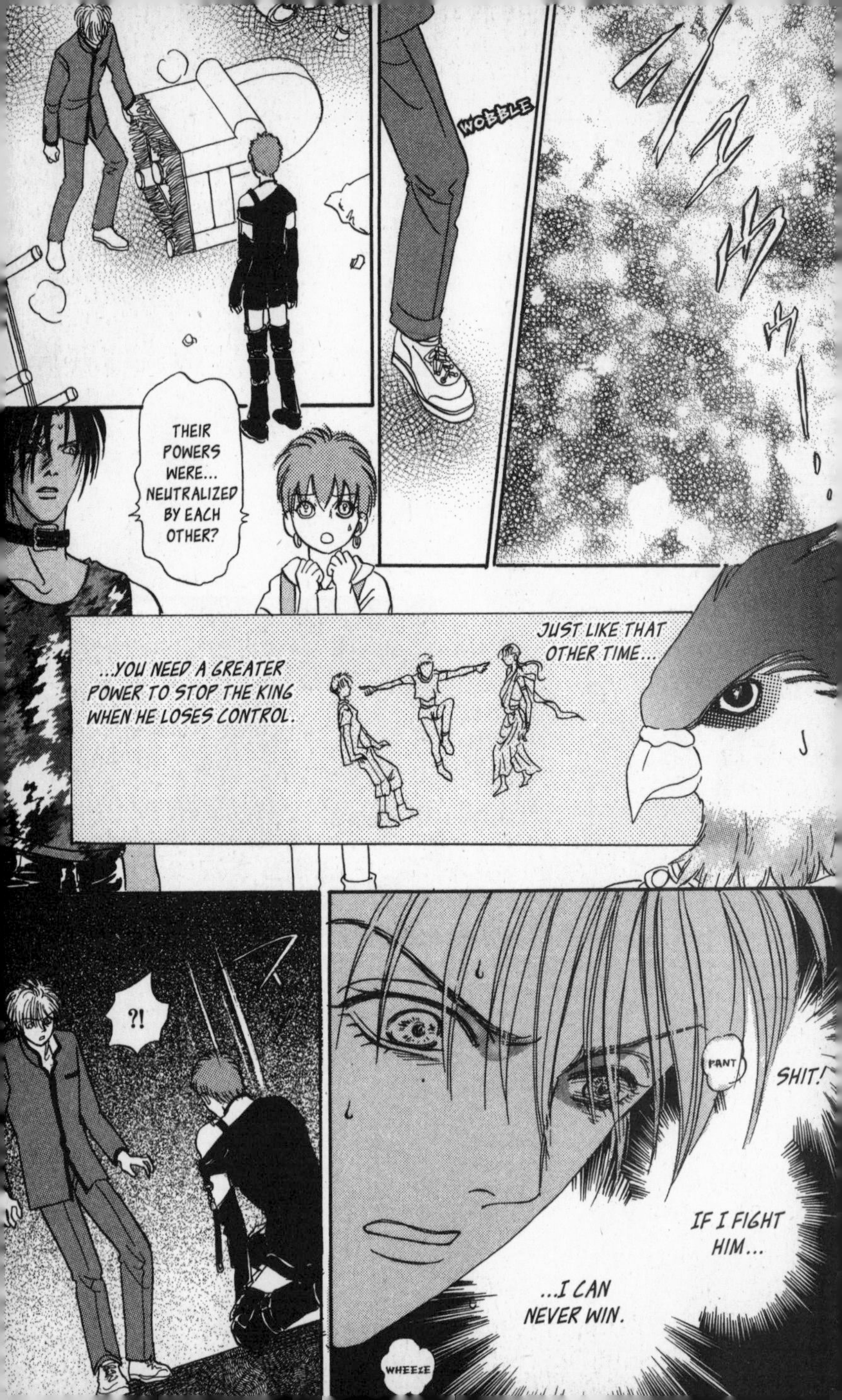
WOBBLE
THEIR POWERS WERE... NEUTRALIZED BY EACH OTHER?
JUST LIKE THAT OTHER TIME...
...YOU NEED A GREATER POWER TO STOP THE KING WHEN HE LOSES CONTROL.
PANT
SHIT!
IF I FIGHT HIM...
...I CAN NEVER WIN.
WHEEZE
?!

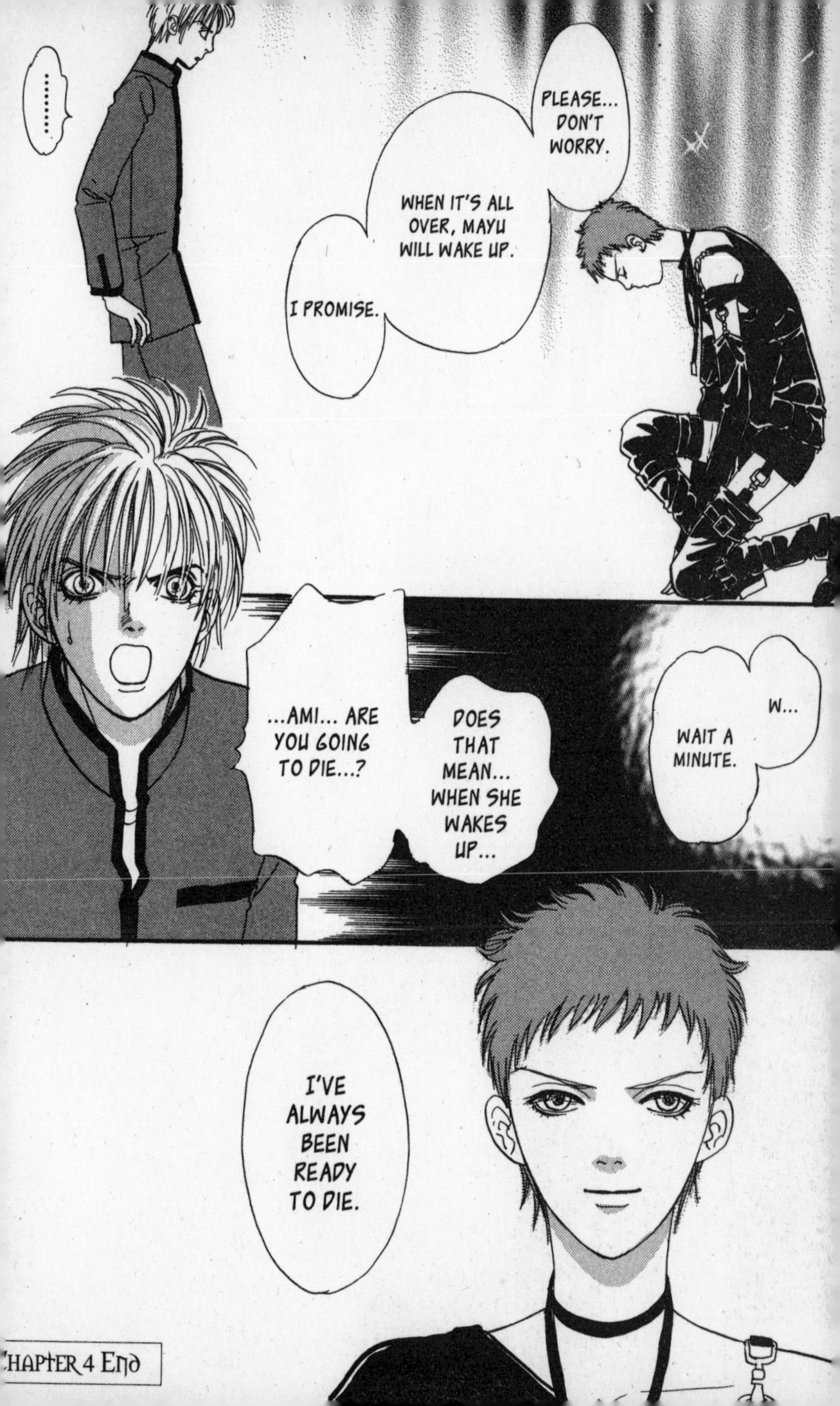
PLEASE... DON'T WORRY.
WHEN IT'S ALL OVER, MAYU WILL WAKE UP.
I PROMISE.
......
W...
WAIT A MINUTE.
DOES THAT MEAN... WHEN SHE WAKES UP...
...AMI... ARE YOU GOING TO DIE...?
I'VE ALWAYS BEEN READY TO DIE.
CHAPTER 4 END

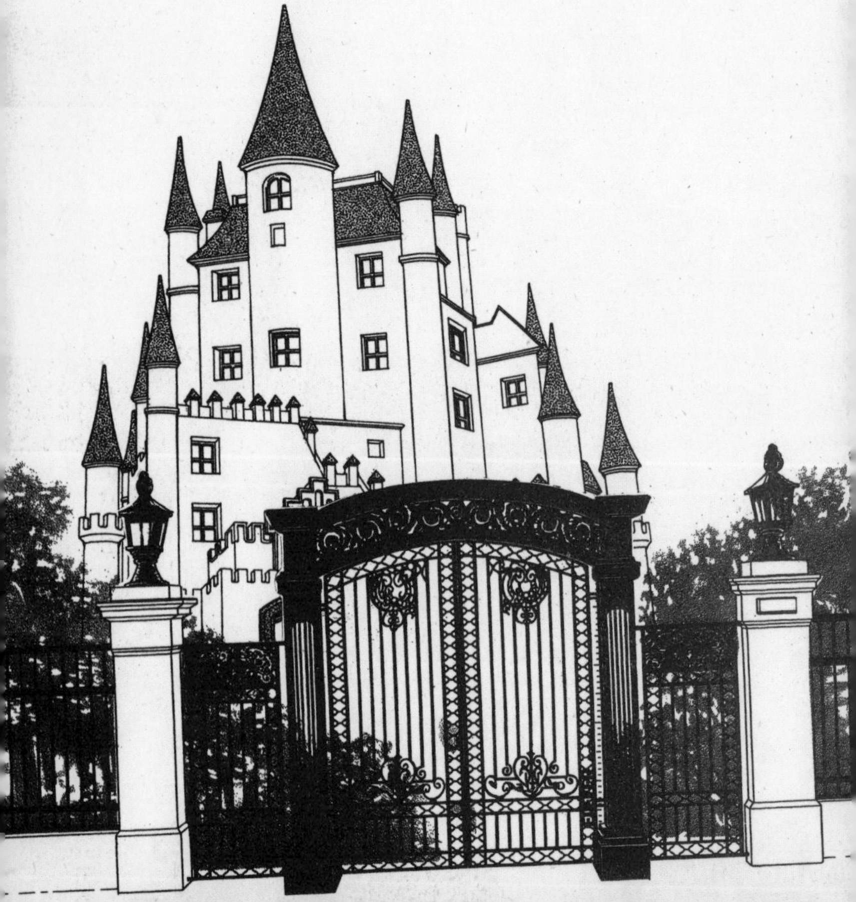

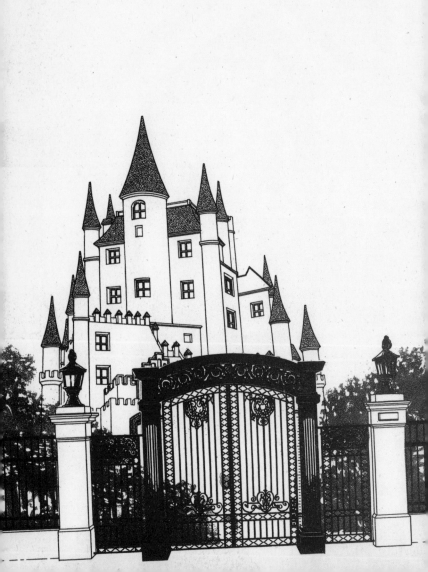

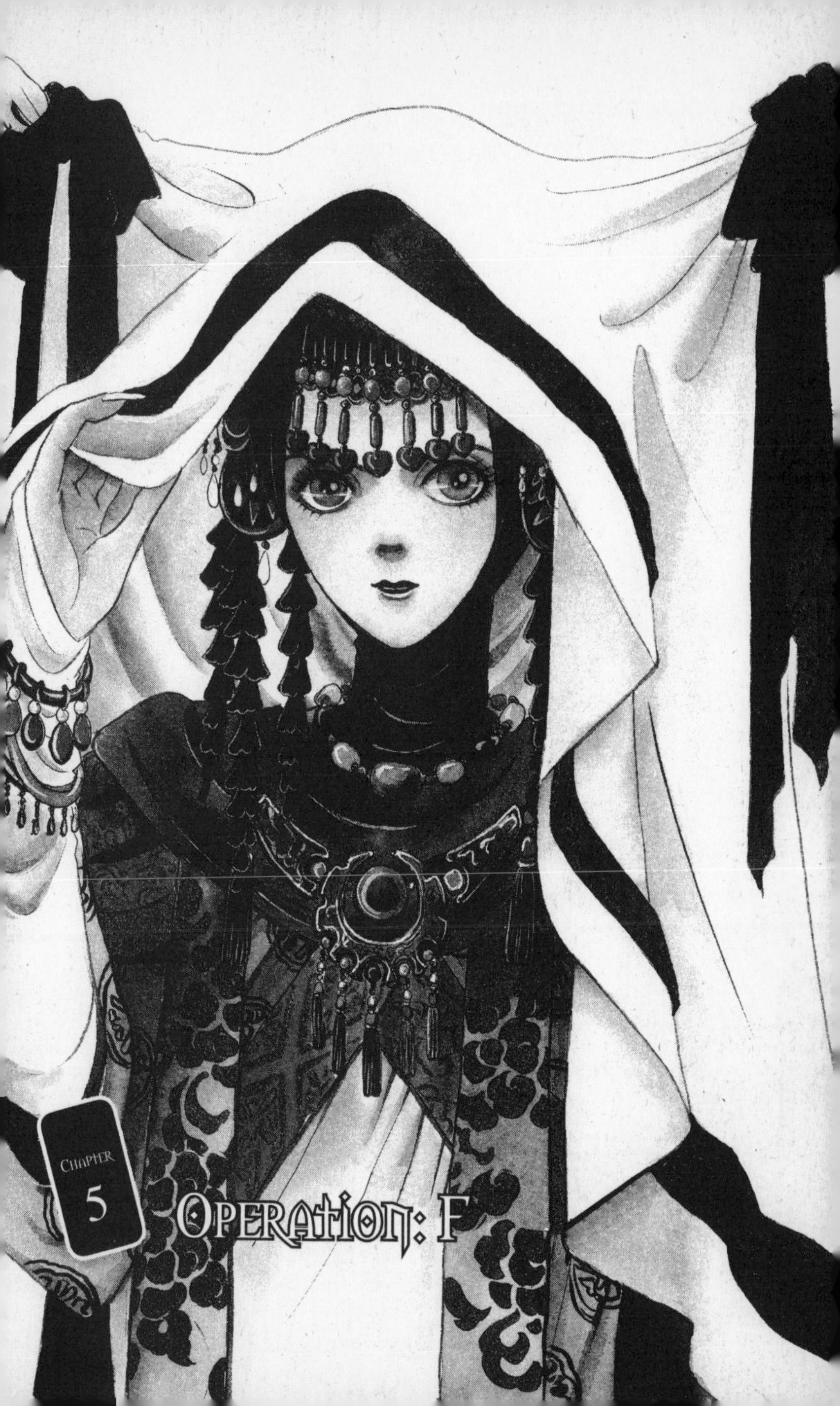
CHAPTER
5
OPERATION: F

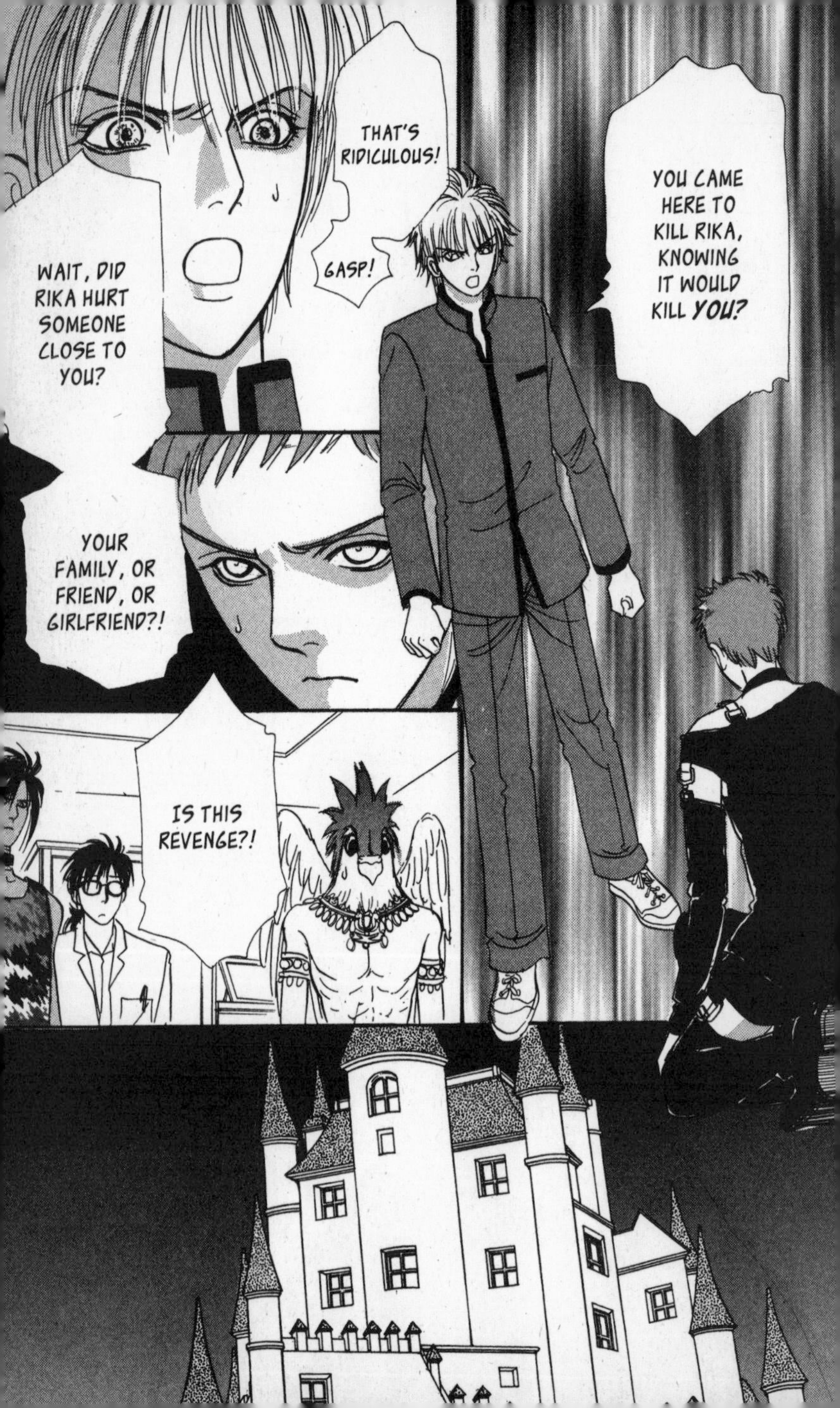
YOU CAME HERE TO KILL RIKA, KNOWING IT WOULD KILL *YOU?*
THAT'S RIDICULOUS!
GASP!
WAIT, DID RIKA HURT SOMEONE CLOSE TO YOU?
YOUR FAMILY, OR FRIEND, OR GIRLFRIEND?!
IS THIS REVENGE?!

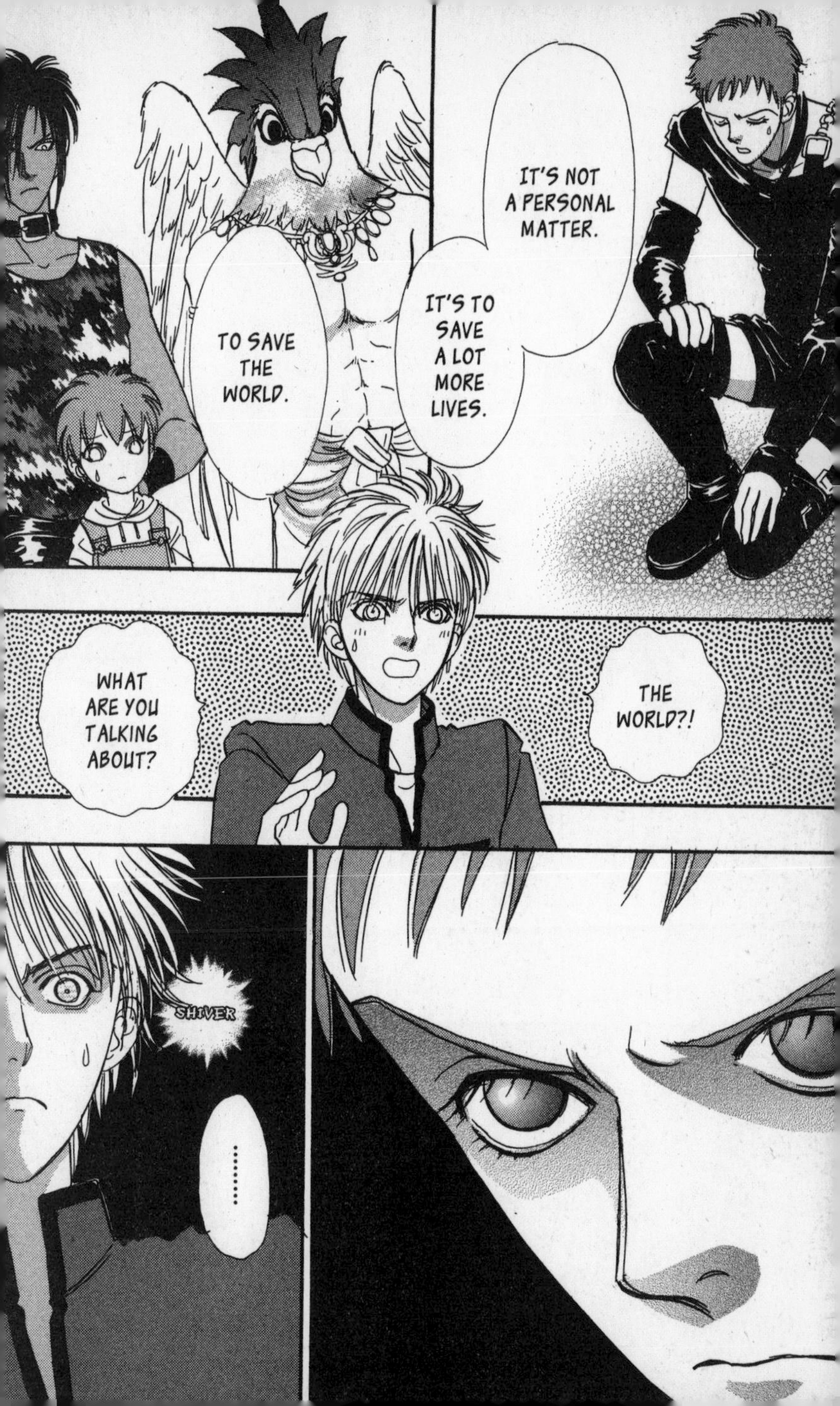
IT'S NOT A PERSONAL MATTER.
IT'S TO SAVE A LOT MORE LIVES.
TO SAVE THE WORLD.
THE WORLD?!
WHAT ARE YOU TALKING ABOUT?
SHIVER
......

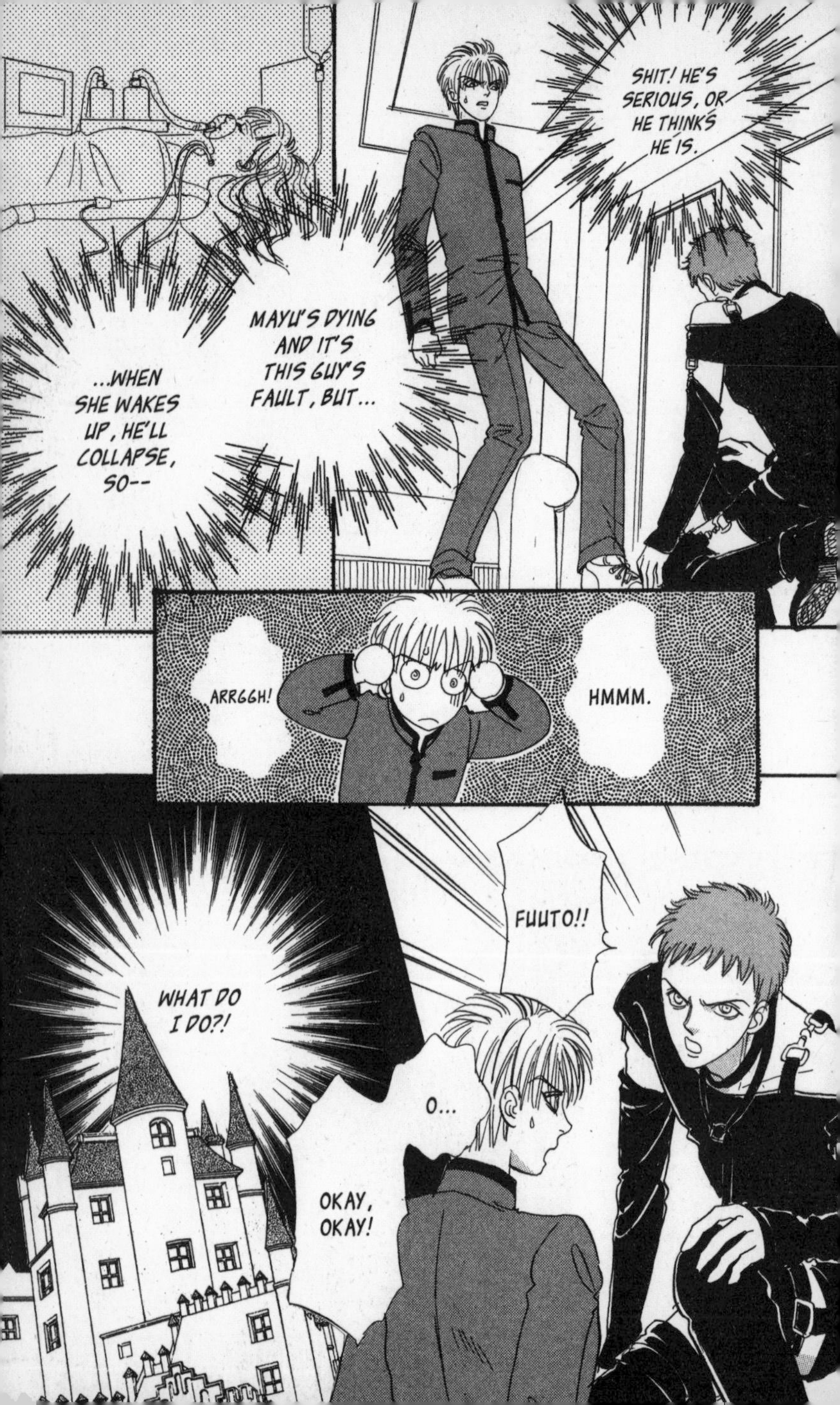
SHIT! HE'S SERIOUS, OR HE THINKS HE IS.
MAYU'S DYING AND IT'S THIS GUY'S FAULT, BUT...
...WHEN SHE WAKES UP, HE'LL COLLAPSE, SO--
HMMM.
ARRGGH!
FUUTO!!
O...
OKAY, OKAY!
WHAT DO I DO?!

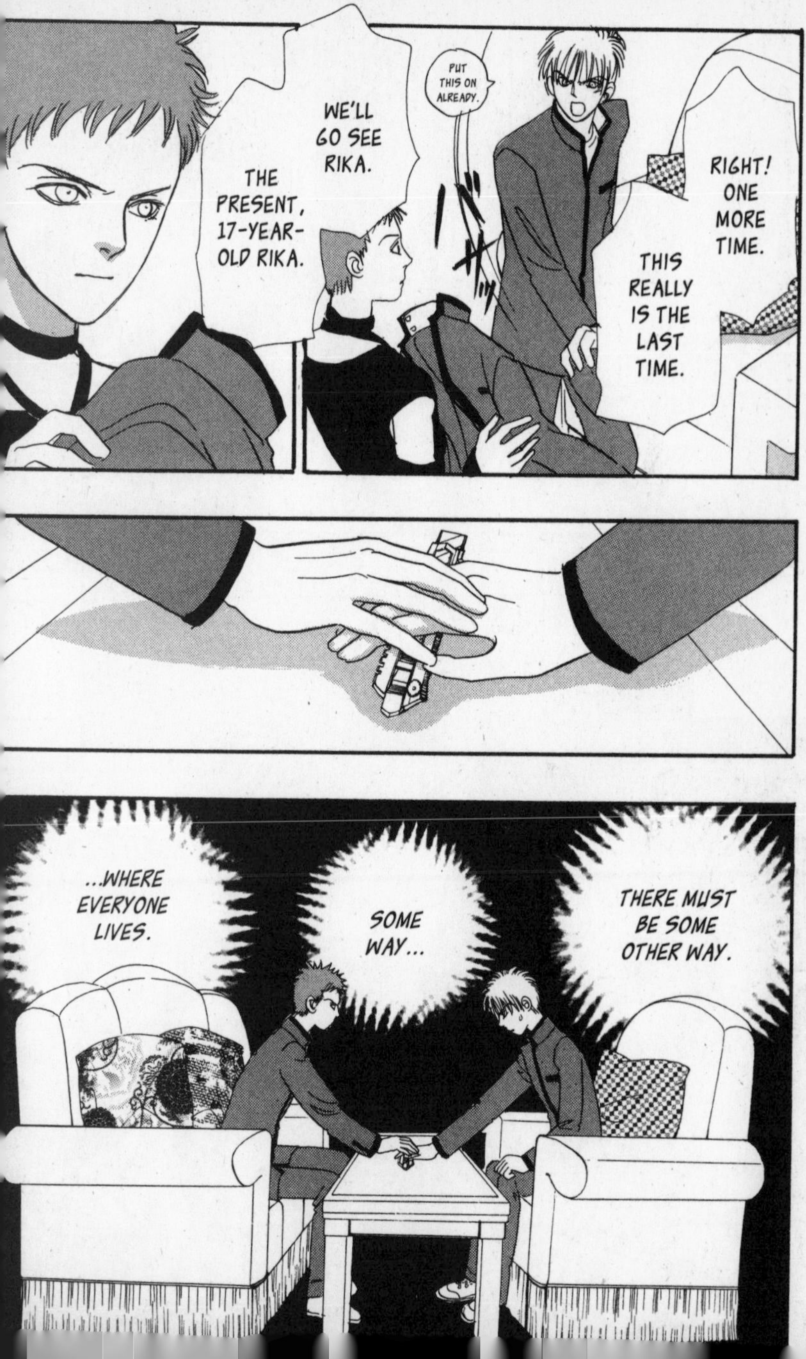
RIGHT! ONE MORE TIME.
PUT THIS ON ALREADY.
THIS REALLY IS THE LAST TIME.
WE'LL GO SEE RIKA.
THE PRESENT, 17-YEAR-OLD RIKA.
THERE MUST BE SOME OTHER WAY.
SOME WAY...
...WHERE EVERYONE LIVES.

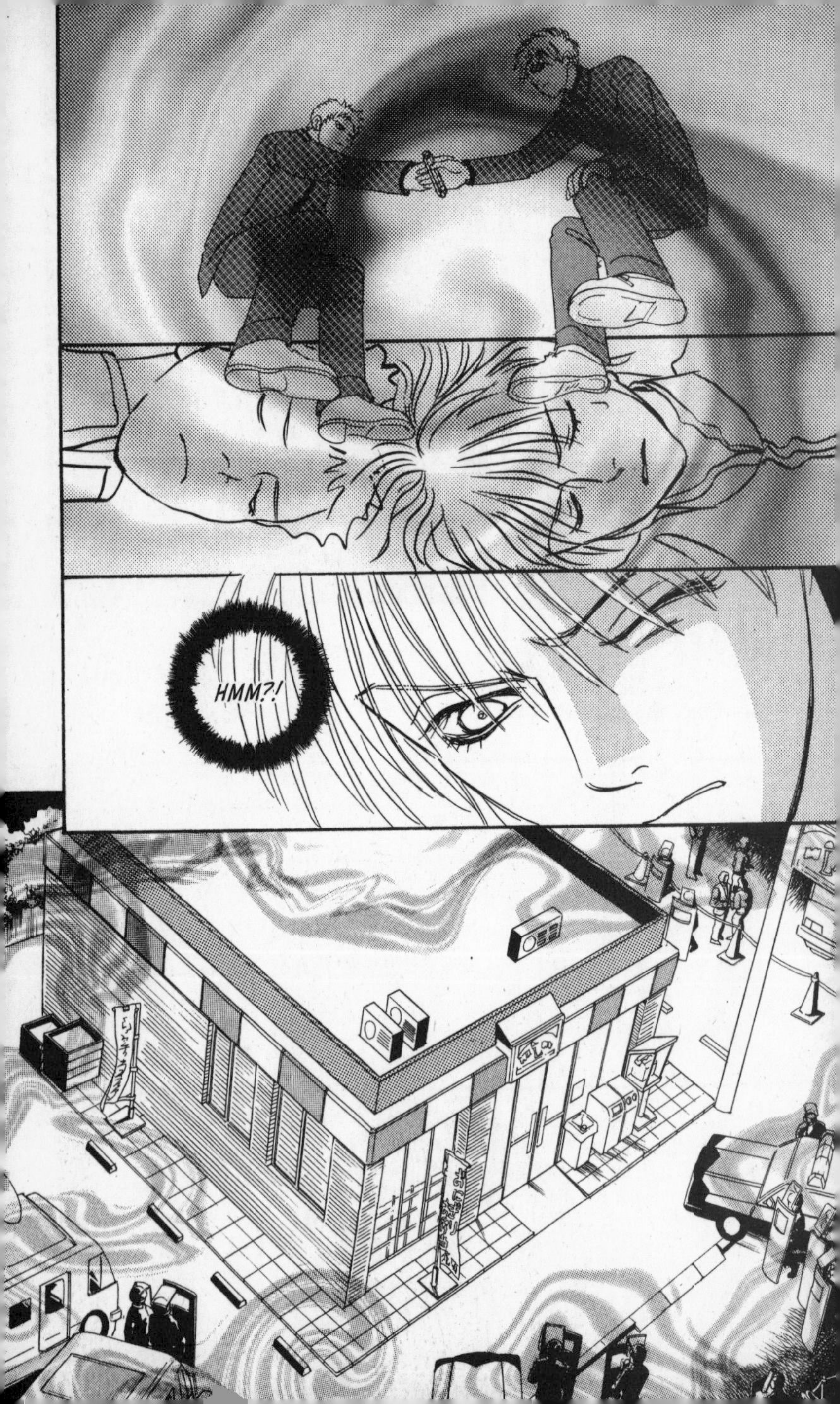
HMM?!

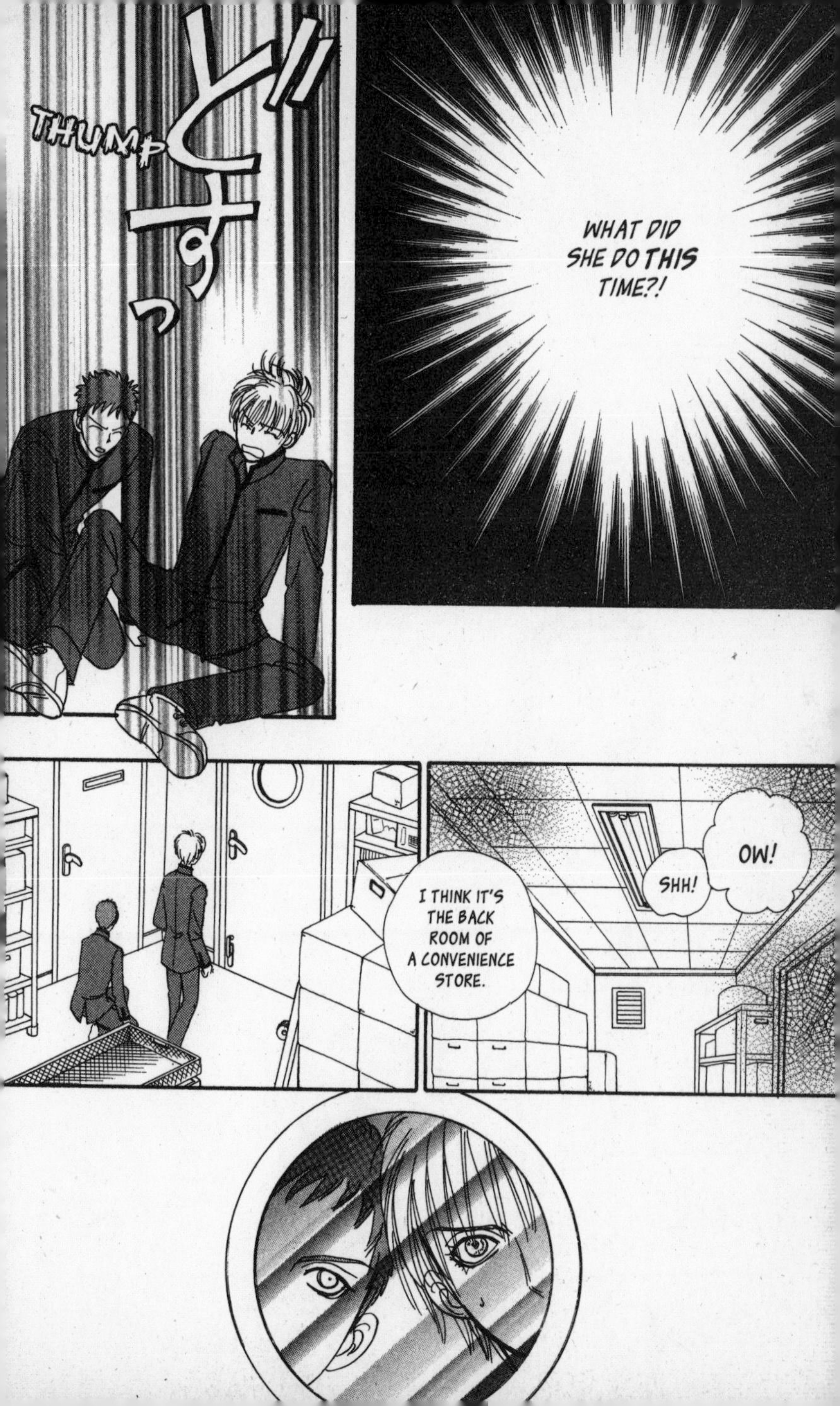
WHAT DID SHE DO THIS TIME?!
どすっ
THUMP
OW!
SHH!
I THINK IT'S THE BACK ROOM OF A CONVENIENCE STORE.

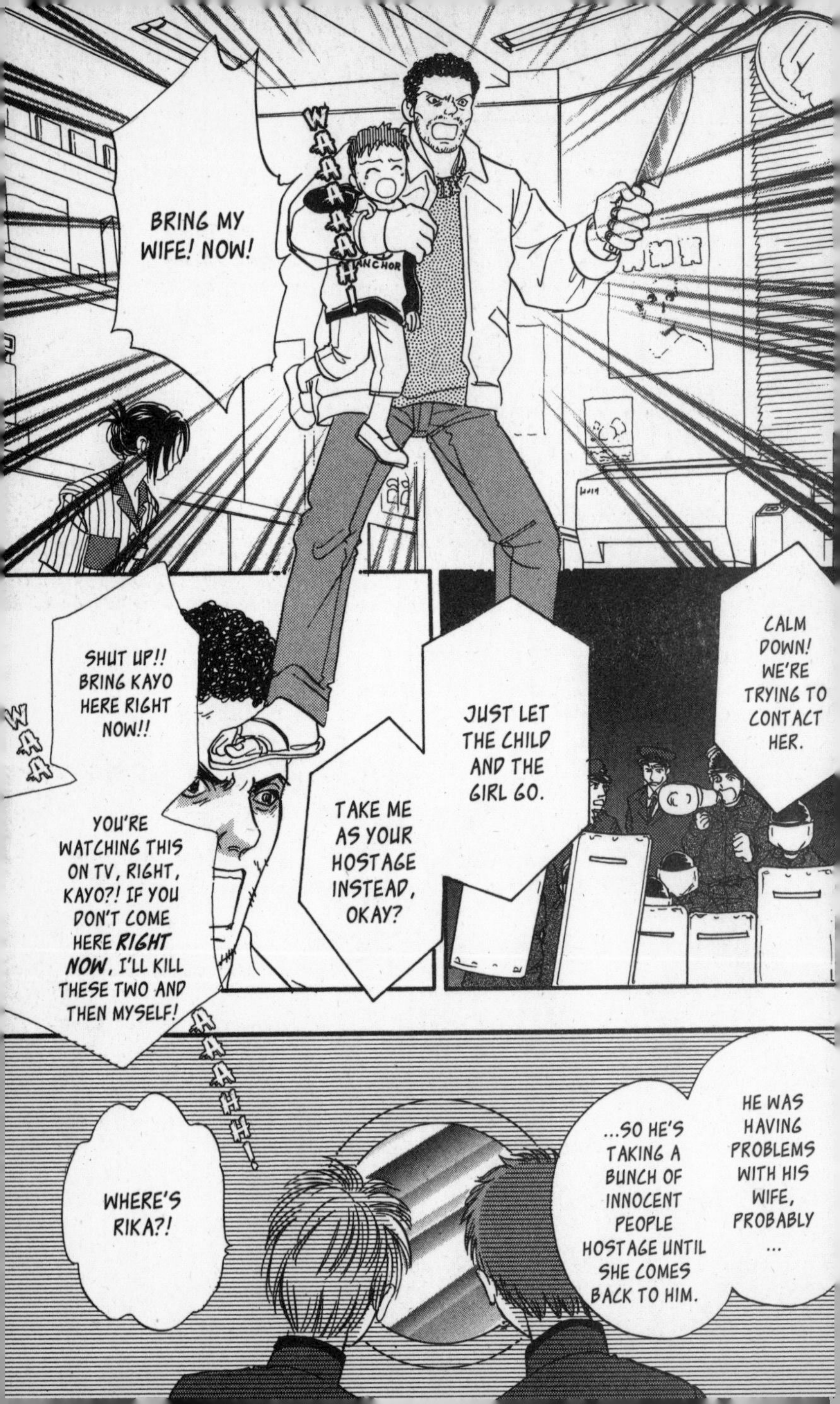
WAAAAAH!
BRING MY WIFE! NOW!
CALM DOWN! WE'RE TRYING TO CONTACT HER.
JUST LET THE CHILD AND THE GIRL GO.
TAKE ME AS YOUR HOSTAGE INSTEAD, OKAY?
SHUT UP!! BRING KAYO HERE RIGHT NOW!!
WAA
YOU'RE WATCHING THIS ON TV, RIGHT, KAYO?! IF YOU DON'T COME HERE **RIGHT NOW**, I'LL KILL THESE TWO AND THEN MYSELF!
AAAAHH!
HE WAS HAVING PROBLEMS WITH HIS WIFE, PROBABLY ...
...SO HE'S TAKING A BUNCH OF INNOCENT PEOPLE HOSTAGE UNTIL SHE COMES BACK TO HIM.
WHERE'S RIKA?!

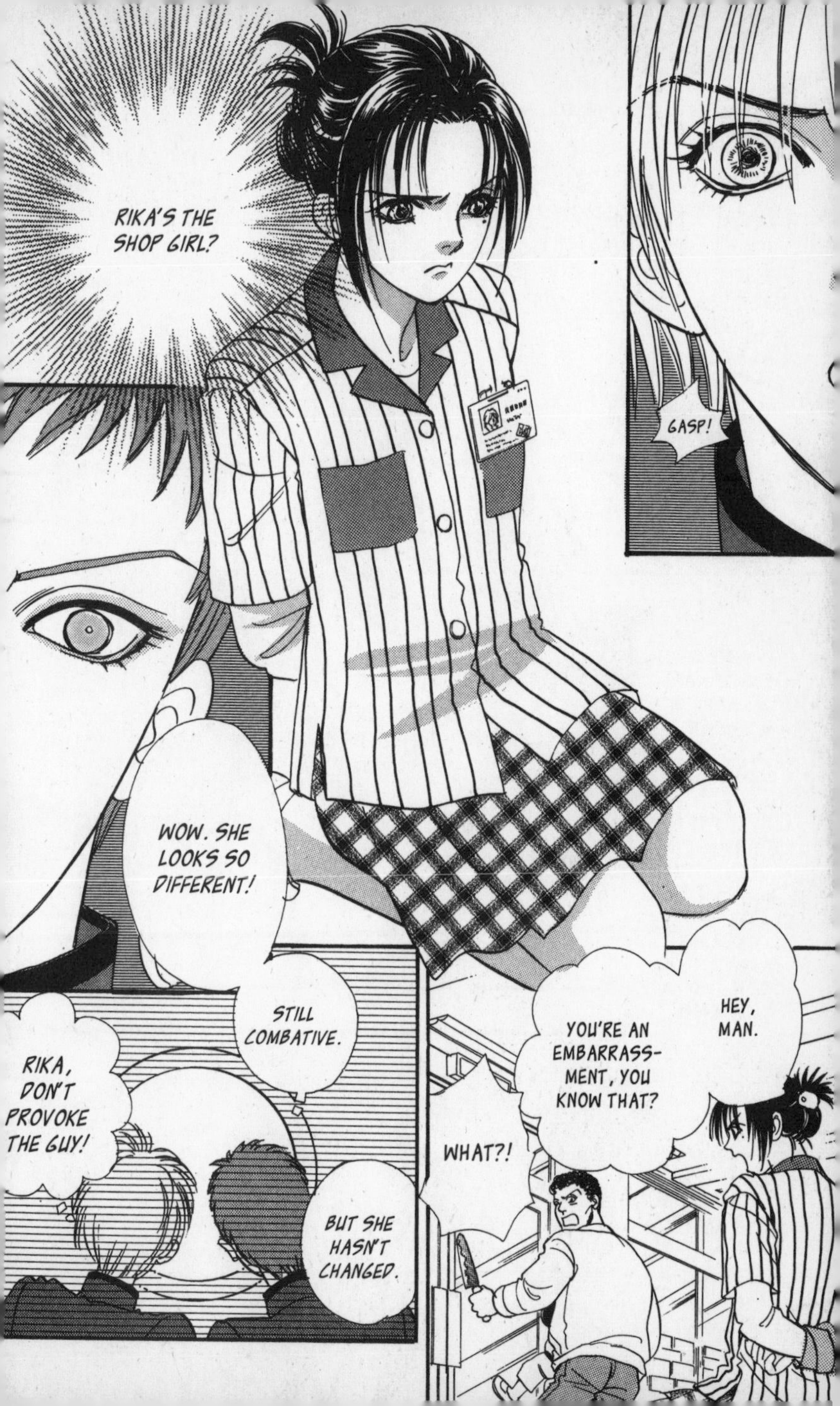
GASP!
RIKA'S THE SHOP GIRL?
WOW. SHE LOOKS SO DIFFERENT!
HEY, MAN.
YOU'RE AN EMBARRASS-MENT, YOU KNOW THAT?
WHAT?!
STILL COMBATIVE.
RIKA, DON'T PROVOKE THE GUY!
BUT SHE HASN'T CHANGED.

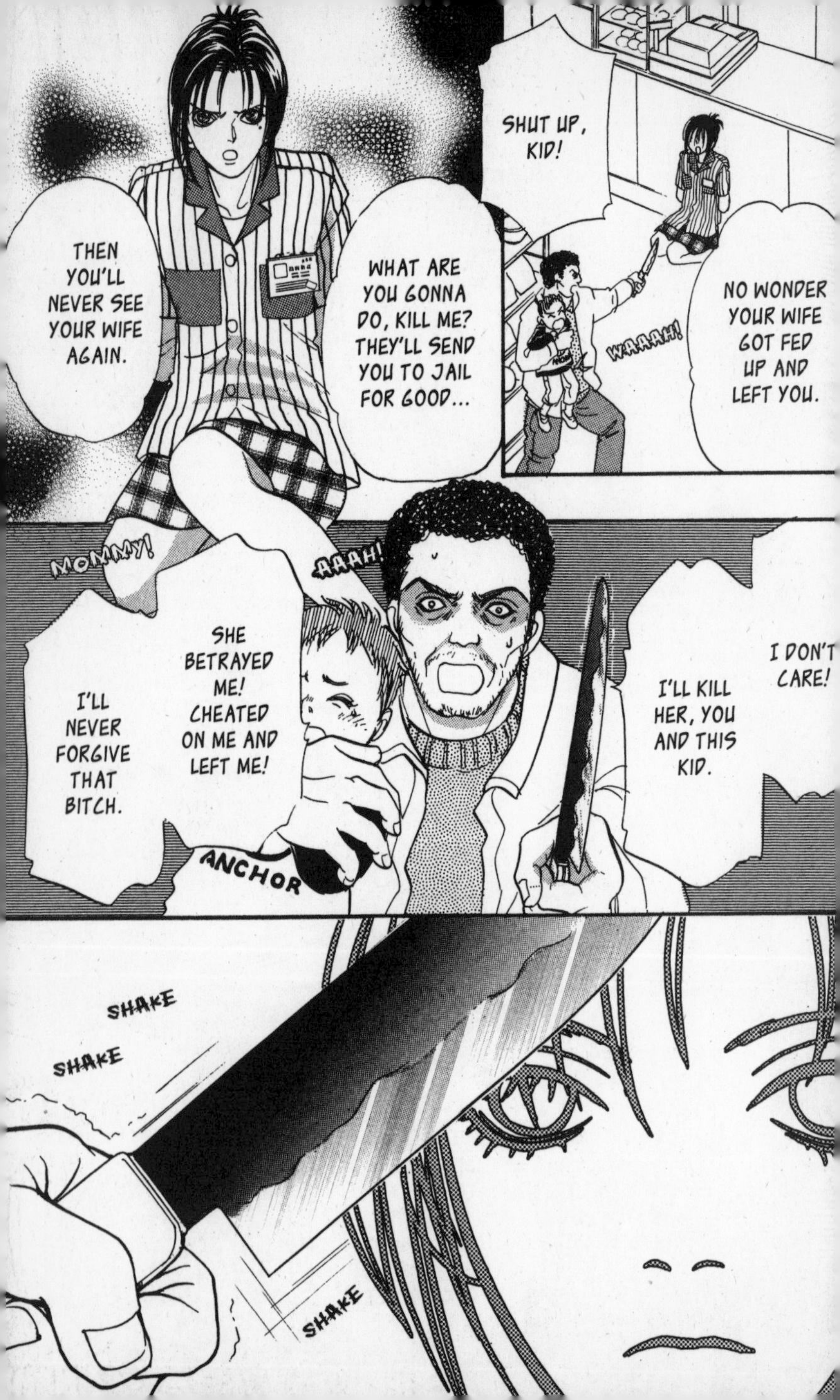
SHUT UP, KID!
WAAAAH!
NO WONDER YOUR WIFE GOT FED UP AND LEFT YOU.
WHAT ARE YOU GONNA DO, KILL ME? THEY'LL SEND YOU TO JAIL FOR GOOD...
THEN YOU'LL NEVER SEE YOUR WIFE AGAIN.
I DON'T CARE!
I'LL KILL HER, YOU AND THIS KID.
AAAH!
SHE BETRAYED ME! CHEATED ON ME AND LEFT ME!
I'LL NEVER FORGIVE THAT BITCH.
MOMMY!
ANCHOR
SHAKE
SHAKE
SHAKE

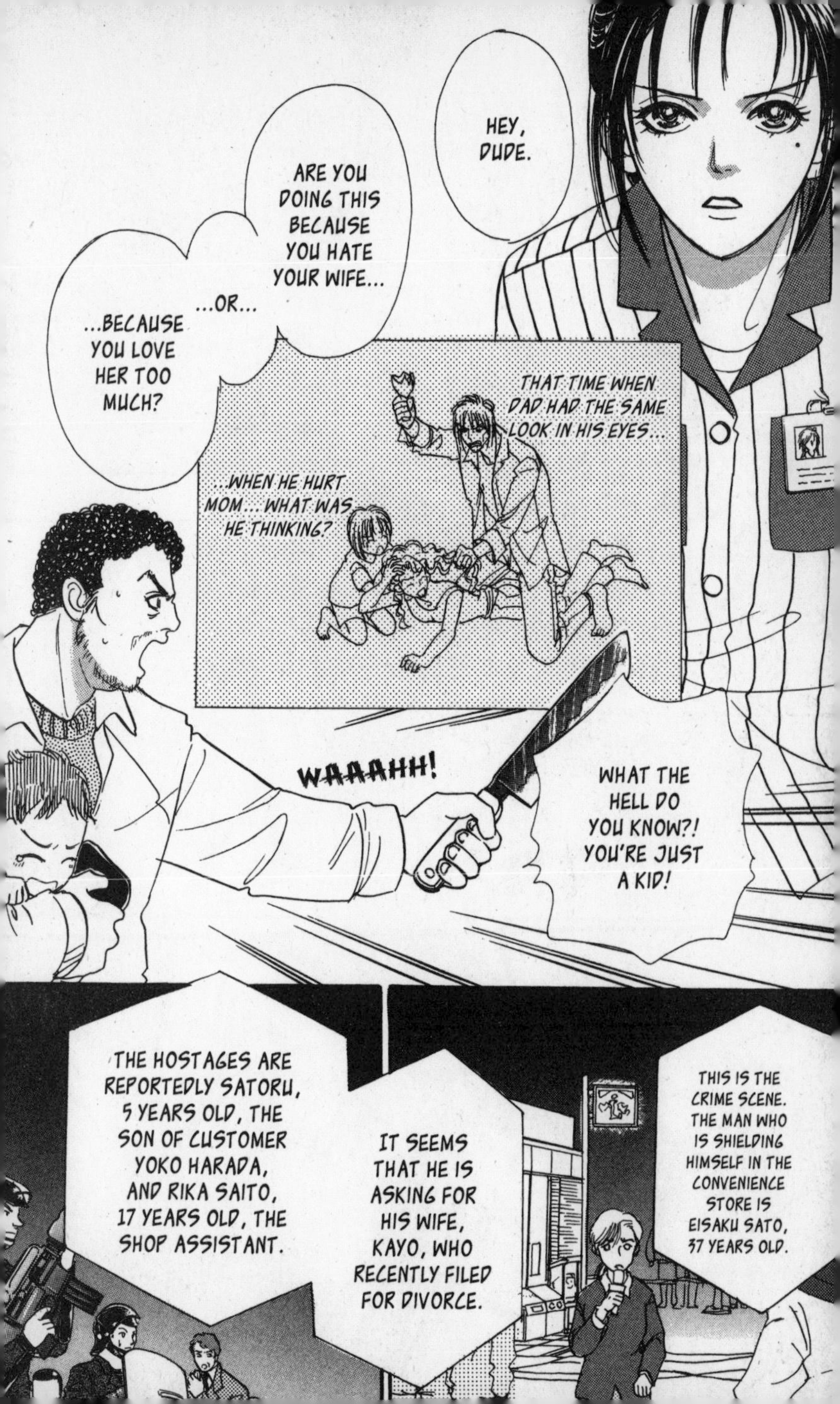
HEY, DUDE.
ARE YOU DOING THIS BECAUSE YOU HATE YOUR WIFE...
...OR...
...BECAUSE YOU LOVE HER TOO MUCH?
THAT TIME WHEN DAD HAD THE SAME LOOK IN HIS EYES...
...WHEN HE HURT MOM... WHAT WAS HE THINKING?
WHAT THE HELL DO YOU KNOW?! YOU'RE JUST A KID!
WAAAHH!
THIS IS THE CRIME SCENE. THE MAN WHO IS SHIELDING HIMSELF IN THE CONVENIENCE STORE IS EISAKU SATO, 37 YEARS OLD.
IT SEEMS THAT HE IS ASKING FOR HIS WIFE, KAYO, WHO RECENTLY FILED FOR DIVORCE.
THE HOSTAGES ARE REPORTEDLY SATORU, 5 YEARS OLD, THE SON OF CUSTOMER YOKO HARADA, AND RIKA SAITO, 17 YEARS OLD, THE SHOP ASSISTANT.

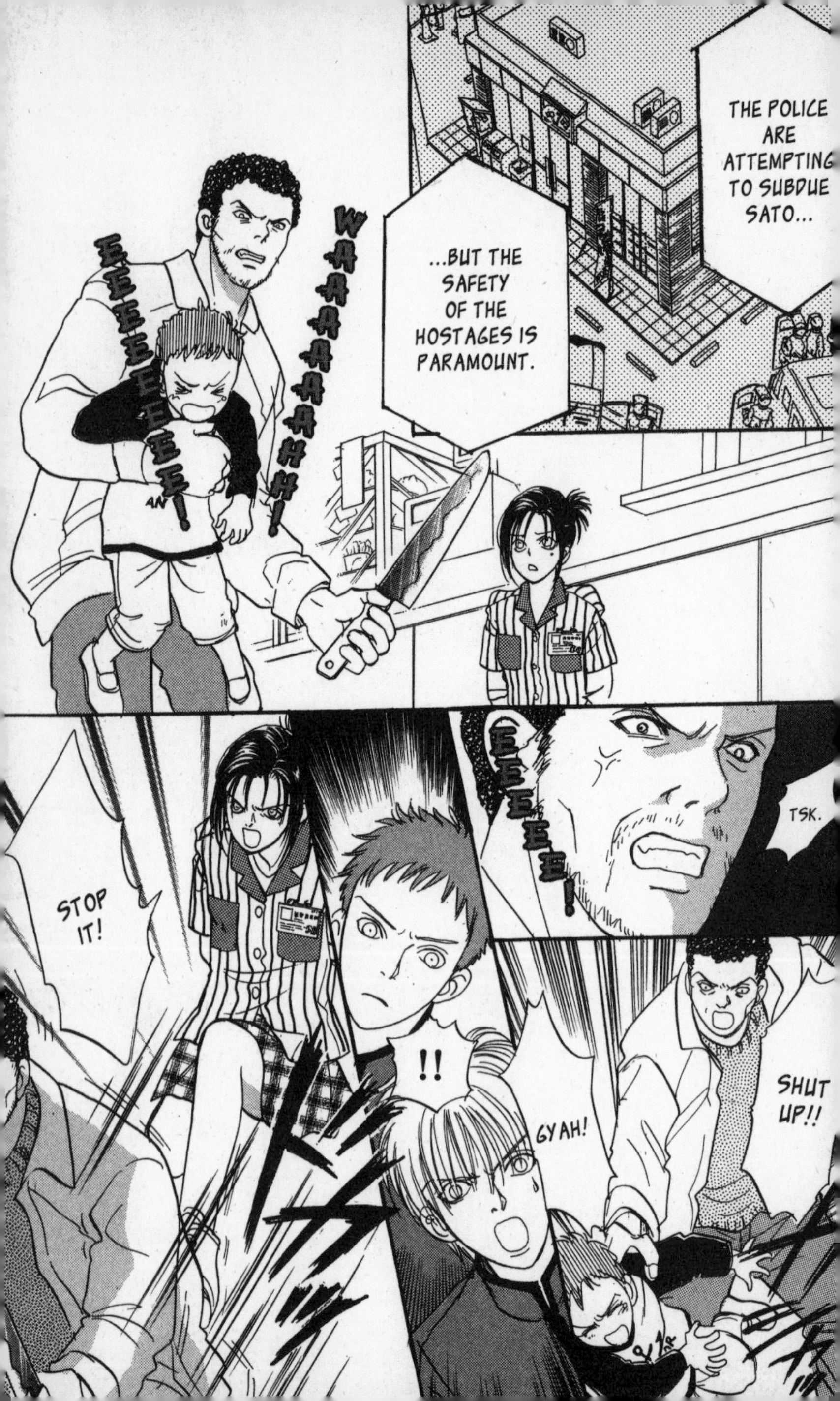
THE POLICE ARE ATTEMPTING TO SUBDUE SATO...
...BUT THE SAFETY OF THE HOSTAGES IS PARAMOUNT.
WAAAAAAHH!
EEEEEEEE!
AN
TSK.
EEEEE!
STOP IT!
SHUT UP!!
GYAH!
!!

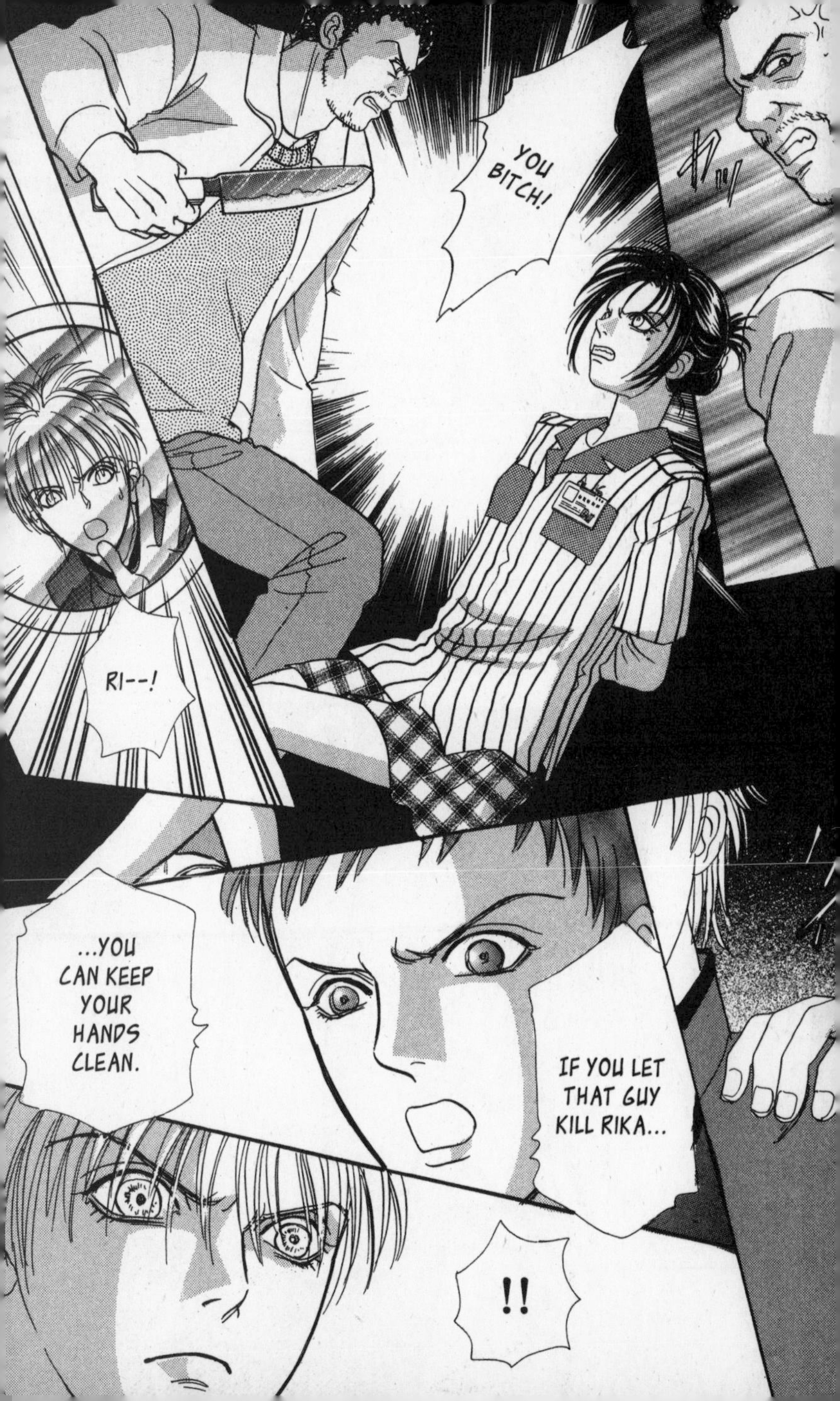
YOU BITCH!
RI--!
IF YOU LET THAT GUY KILL RIKA...
...YOU CAN KEEP YOUR HANDS CLEAN.
!!

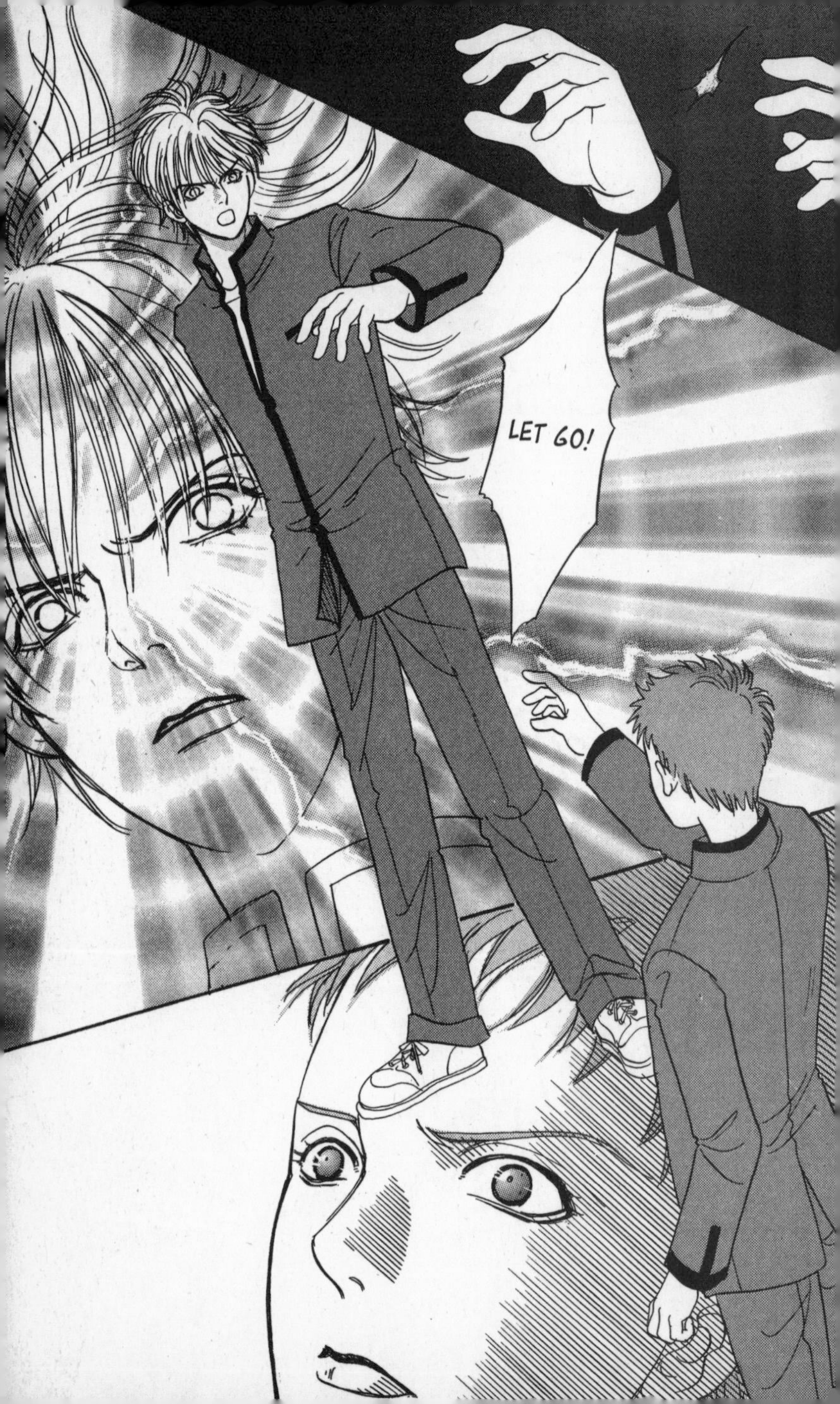
LET GO!

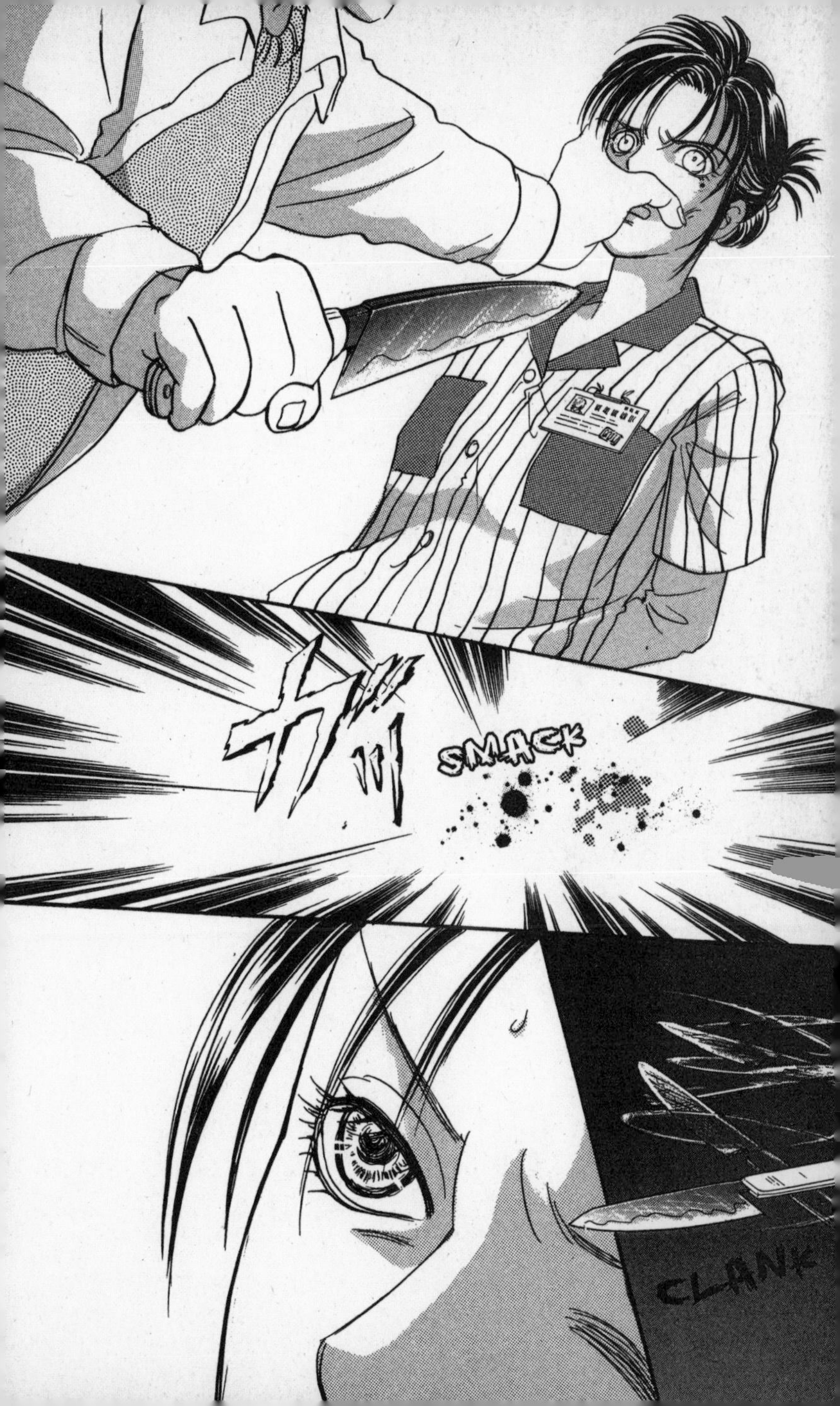
ガッ
SMACK
CLANK

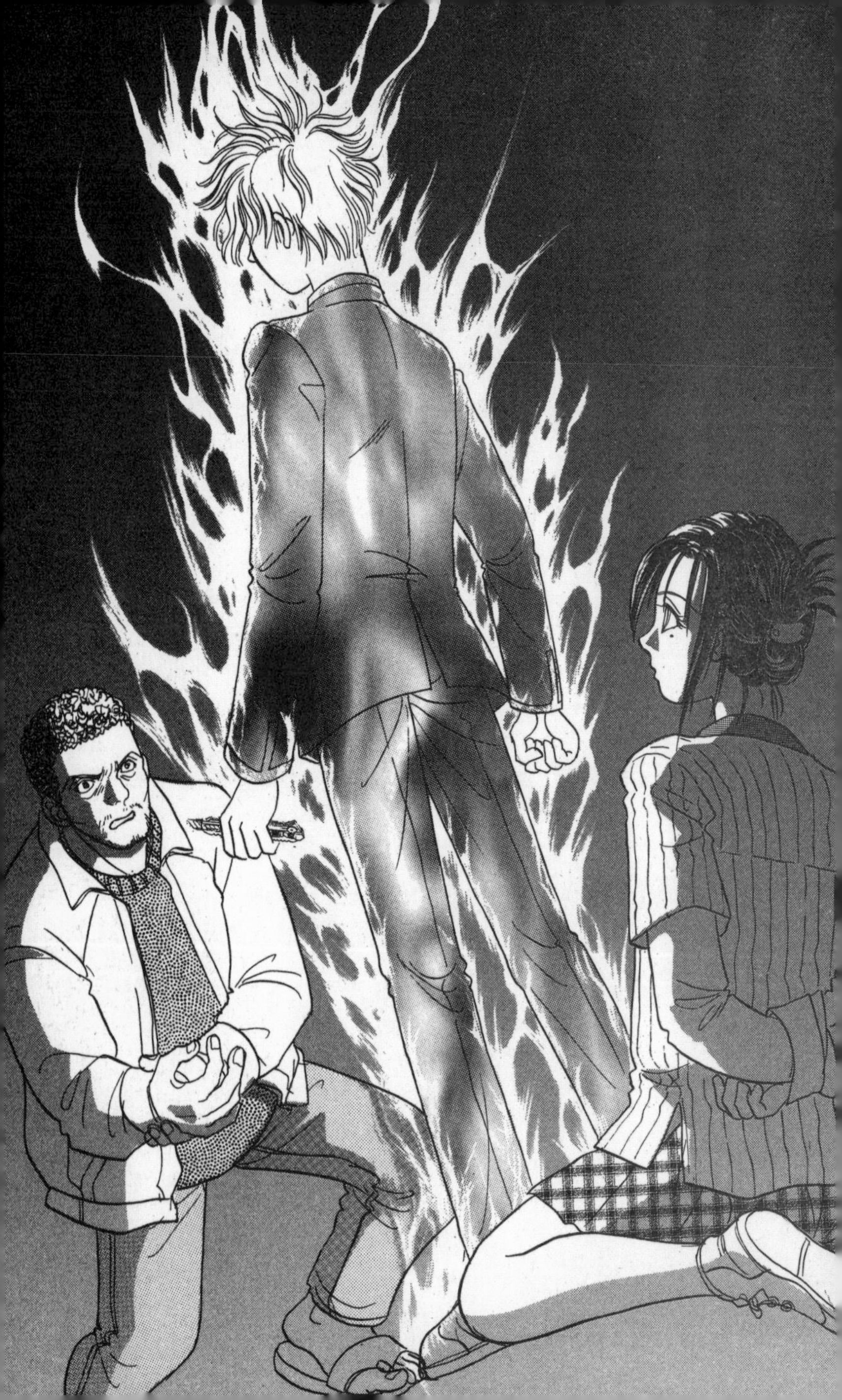

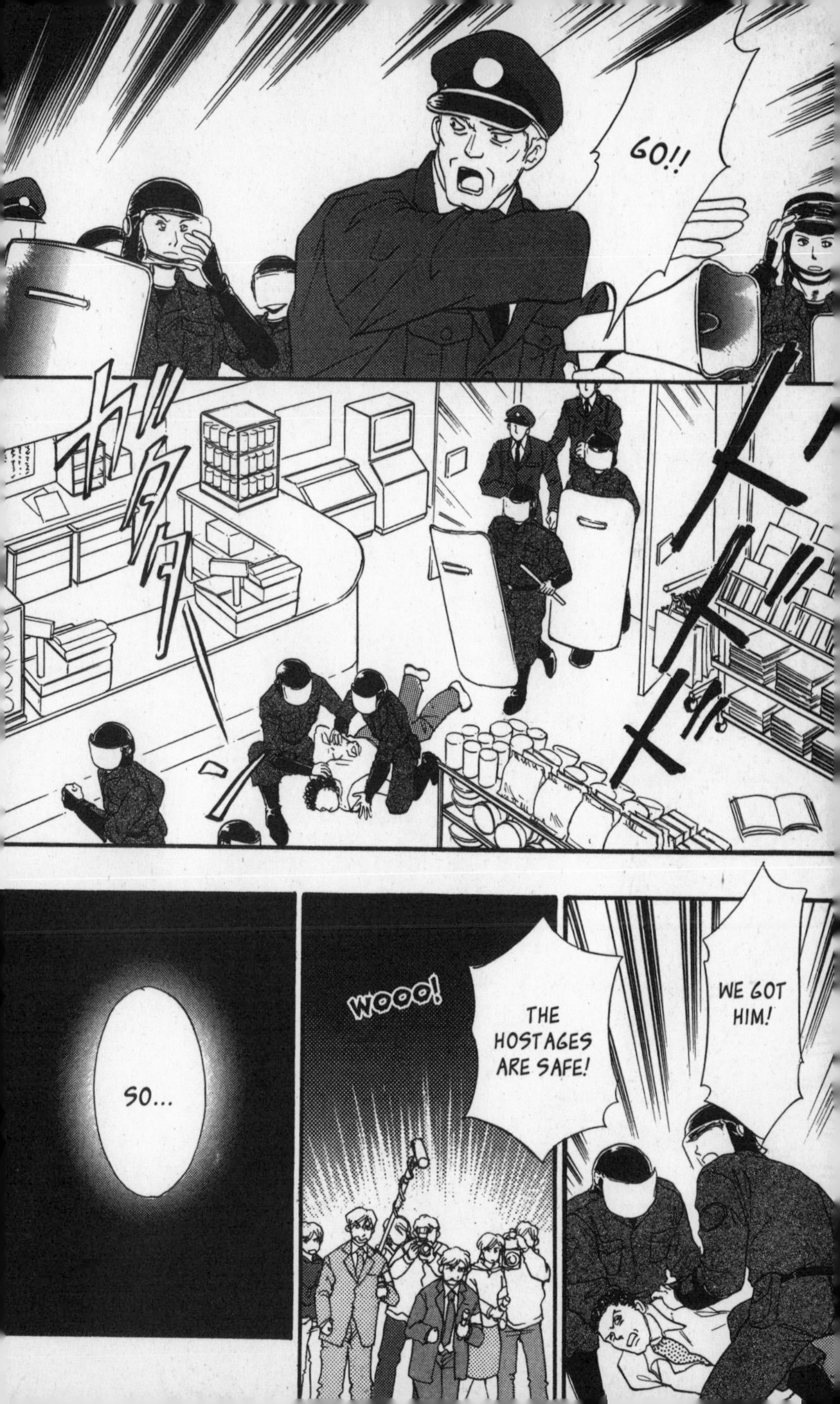
GO!!
WE GOT HIM!
THE HOSTAGES ARE SAFE!
WOOO!
SO...

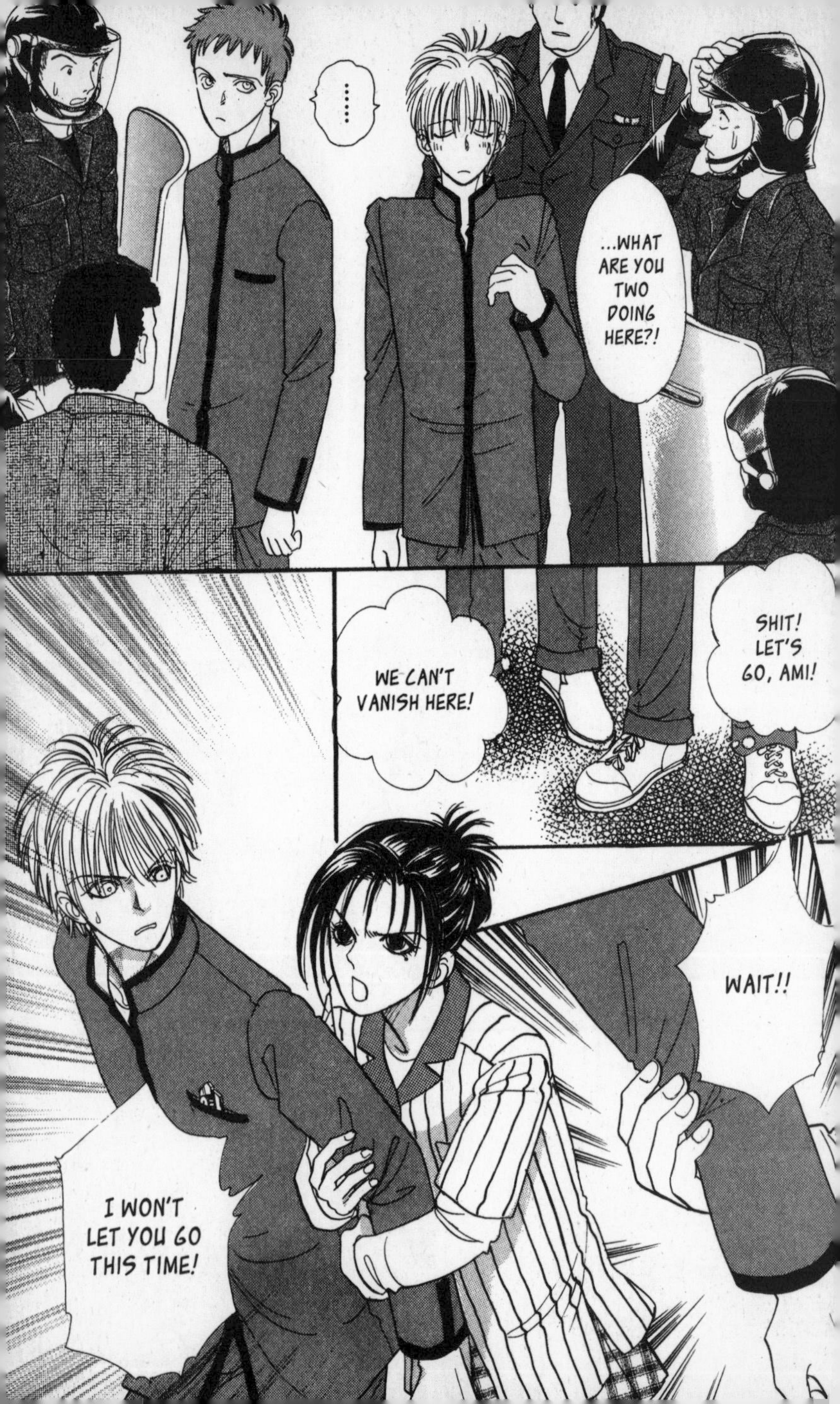

...WHAT ARE YOU TWO DOING HERE?!
......
SHIT! LET'S GO, AMI!
WE CAN'T VANISH HERE!
WAIT!!
I WON'T LET YOU GO THIS TIME!

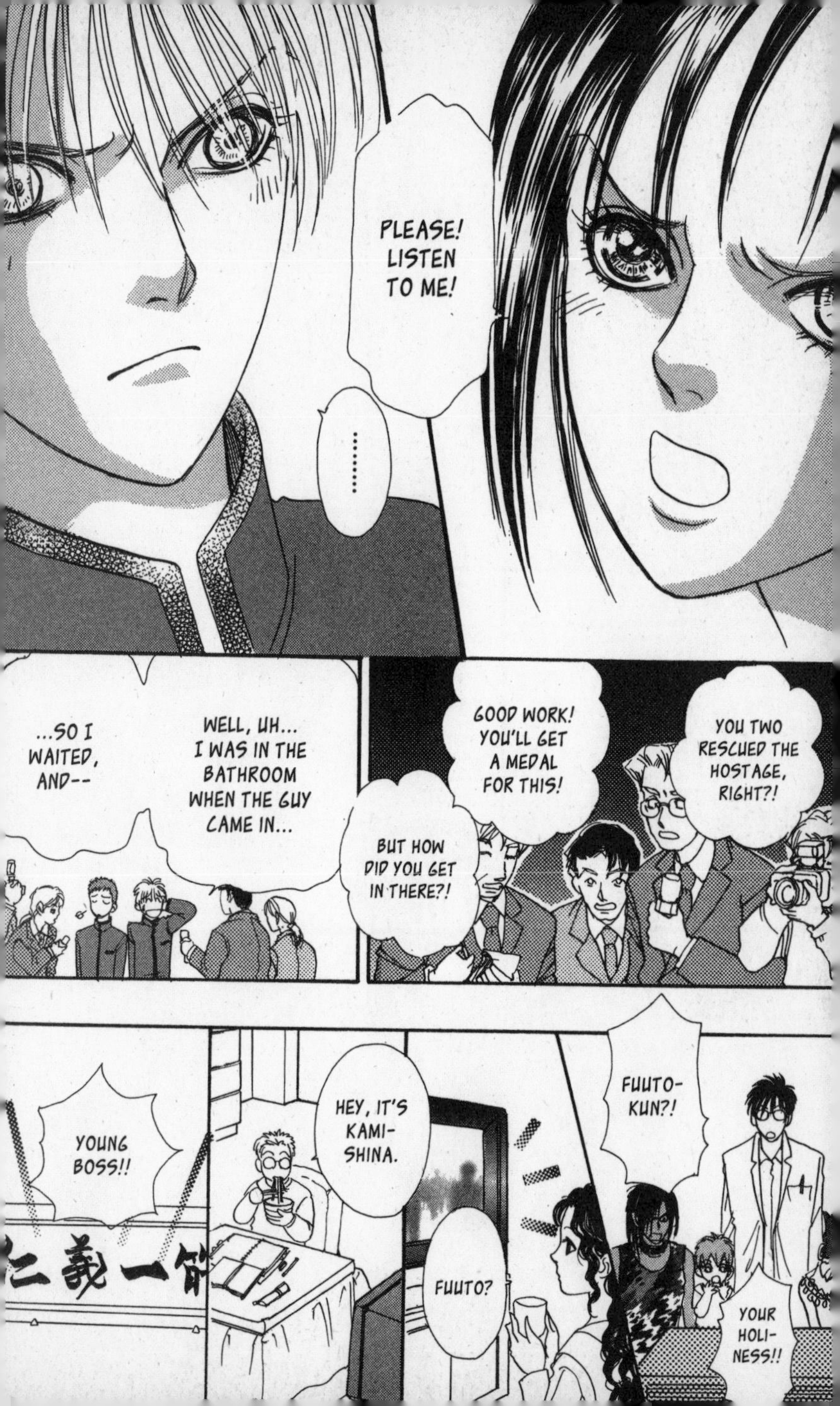
PLEASE! LISTEN TO ME!
......
YOU TWO RESCUED THE HOSTAGE, RIGHT?!
GOOD WORK! YOU'LL GET A MEDAL FOR THIS!
BUT HOW DID YOU GET IN THERE?!
WELL, UH... I WAS IN THE BATHROOM WHEN THE GUY CAME IN...
...SO I WAITED, AND--
FUUTO-KUN?!
YOUR HOLI-NESS!!
HEY, IT'S KAMI-SHINA.
FUUTO?
YOUNG BOSS!!

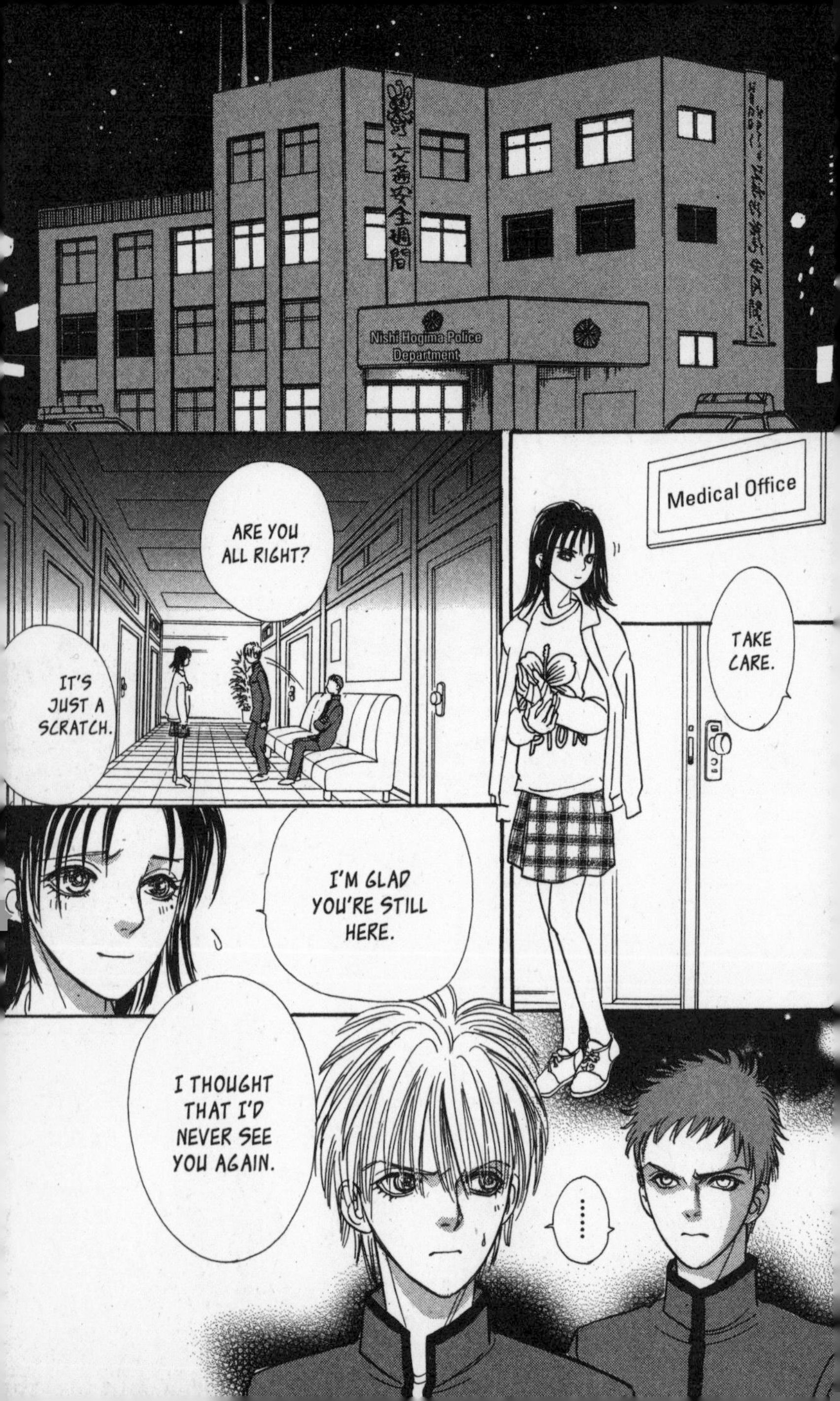

Nishi Hogima Police Department
Medical Office
TAKE CARE.
ARE YOU ALL RIGHT?
IT'S JUST A SCRATCH.
I'M GLAD YOU'RE STILL HERE.
I THOUGHT THAT I'D NEVER SEE YOU AGAIN.
......

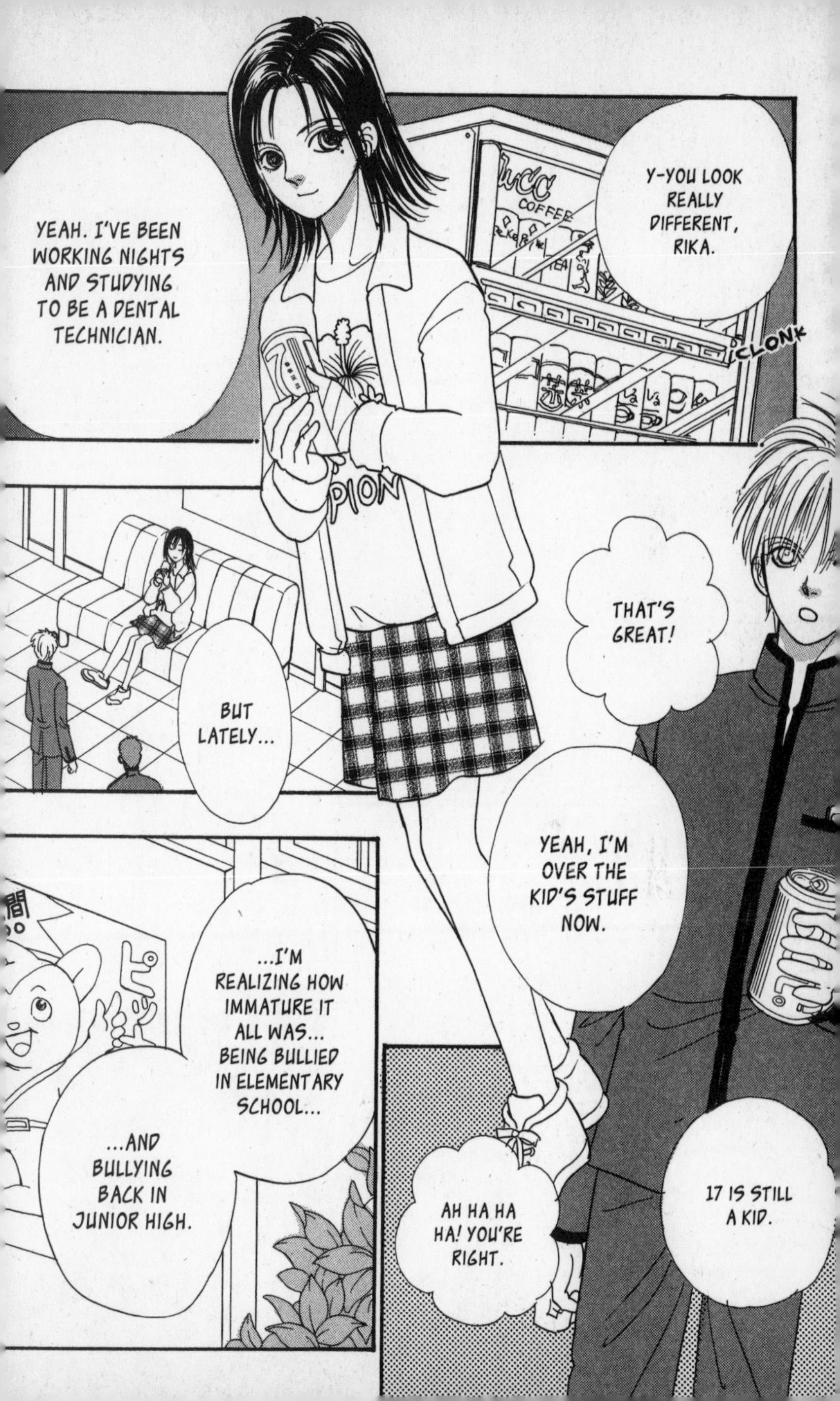

Y-YOU LOOK REALLY DIFFERENT, RIKA.
CLONK
YEAH. I'VE BEEN WORKING NIGHTS AND STUDYING TO BE A DENTAL TECHNICIAN.
THAT'S GREAT!
BUT LATELY...
...I'M REALIZING HOW IMMATURE IT ALL WAS... BEING BULLIED IN ELEMENTARY SCHOOL...
...AND BULLYING BACK IN JUNIOR HIGH.
YEAH, I'M OVER THE KID'S STUFF NOW.
17 IS STILL A KID.
AH HA HA HA! YOU'RE RIGHT.

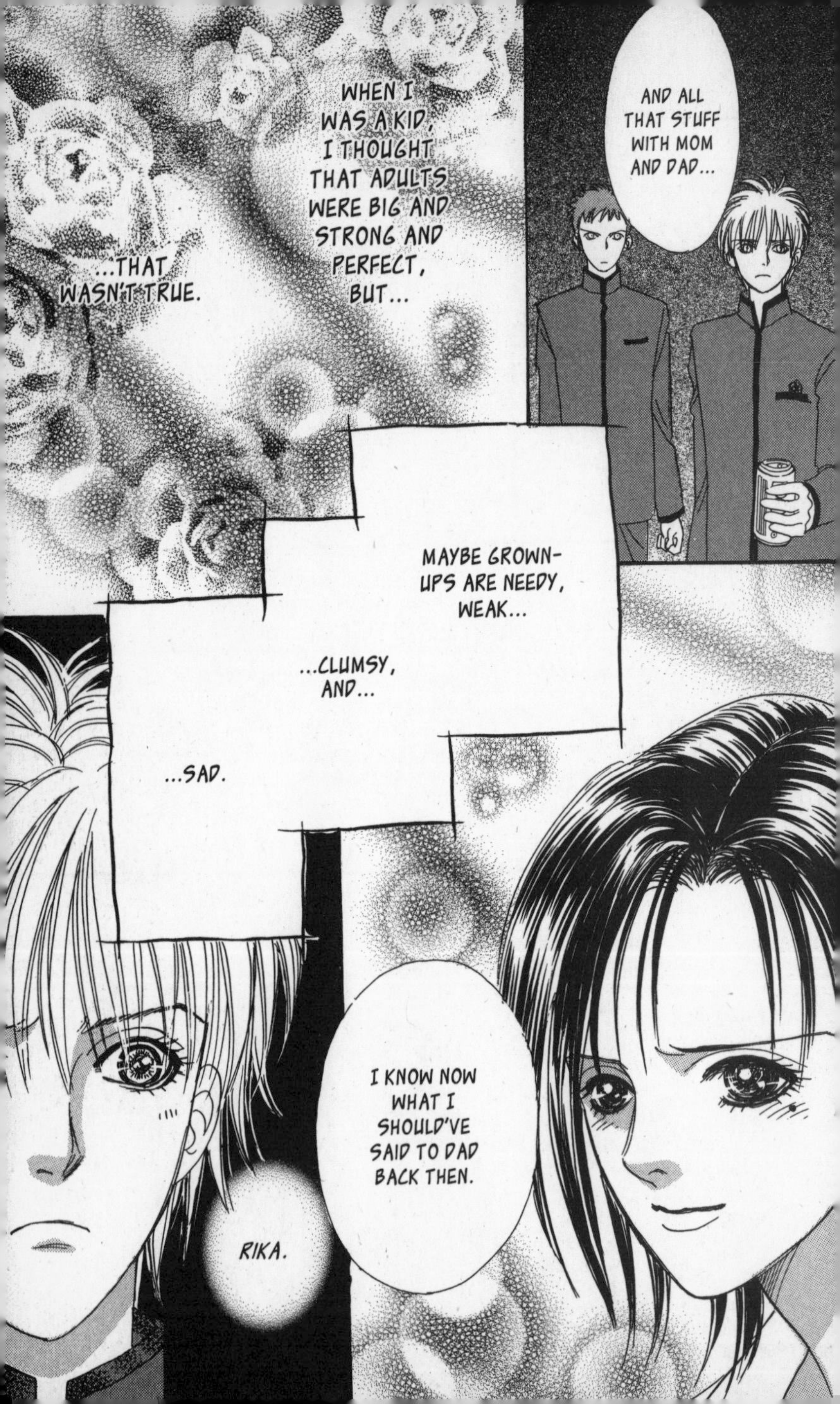
AND ALL THAT STUFF WITH MOM AND DAD...
WHEN I WAS A KID, I THOUGHT THAT ADULTS WERE BIG AND STRONG AND PERFECT, BUT...
...THAT WASN'T TRUE.
MAYBE GROWN-UPS ARE NEEDY, WEAK...
...CLUMSY, AND...
...SAD.
I KNOW NOW WHAT I SHOULD'VE SAID TO DAD BACK THEN.
RIKA.

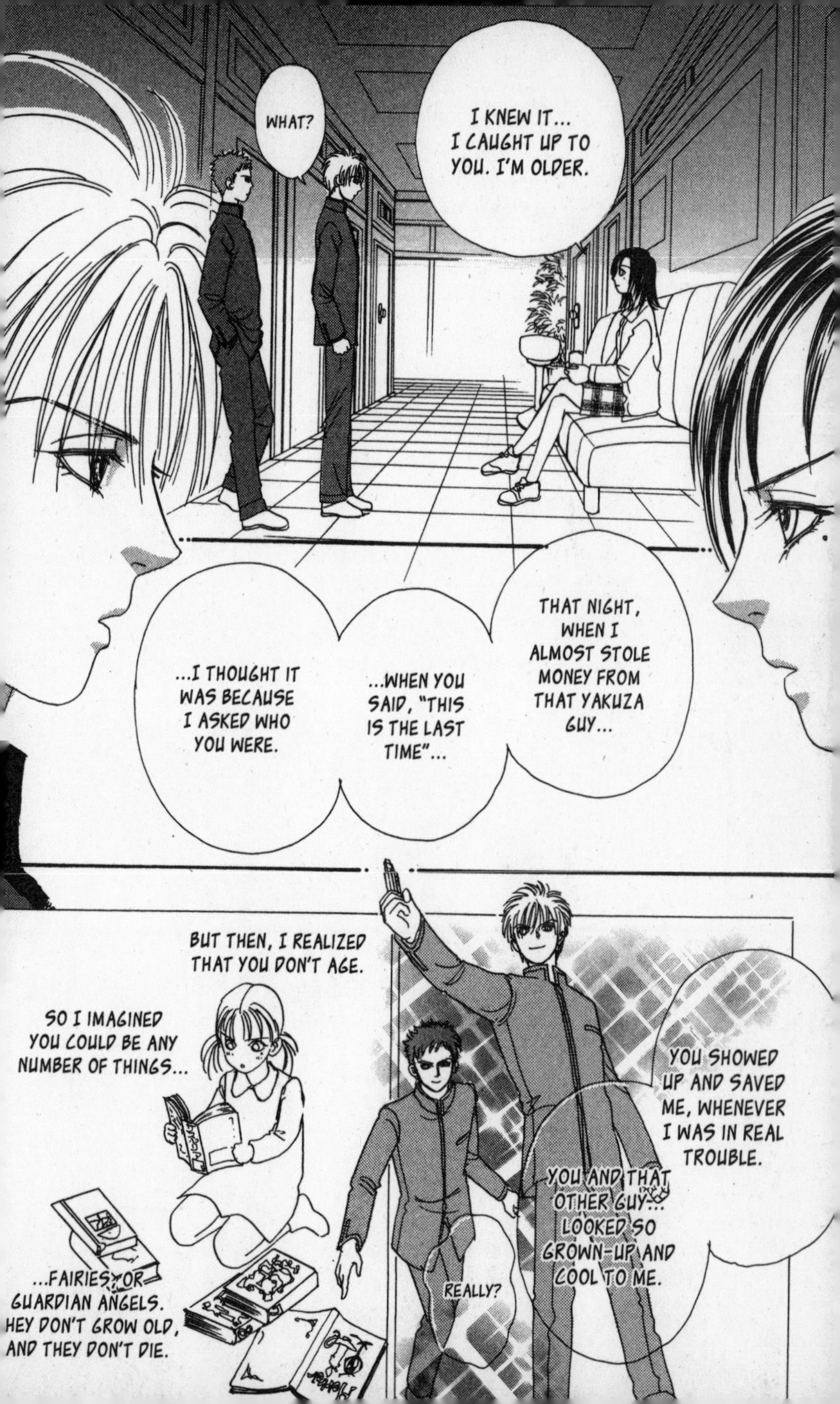
I KNEW IT... I CAUGHT UP TO YOU. I'M OLDER.
WHAT?
THAT NIGHT, WHEN I ALMOST STOLE MONEY FROM THAT YAKUZA GUY...
...WHEN YOU SAID, "THIS IS THE LAST TIME"...
...I THOUGHT IT WAS BECAUSE I ASKED WHO YOU WERE.
YOU SHOWED UP AND SAVED ME, WHENEVER I WAS IN REAL TROUBLE.
YOU AND THAT OTHER GUY... LOOKED SO GROWN-UP AND COOL TO ME.
BUT THEN, I REALIZED THAT YOU DON'T AGE.
REALLY?
SO I IMAGINED YOU COULD BE ANY NUMBER OF THINGS...
...FAIRIES OR GUARDIAN ANGELS. HEY DON'T GROW OLD, AND THEY DON'T DIE.

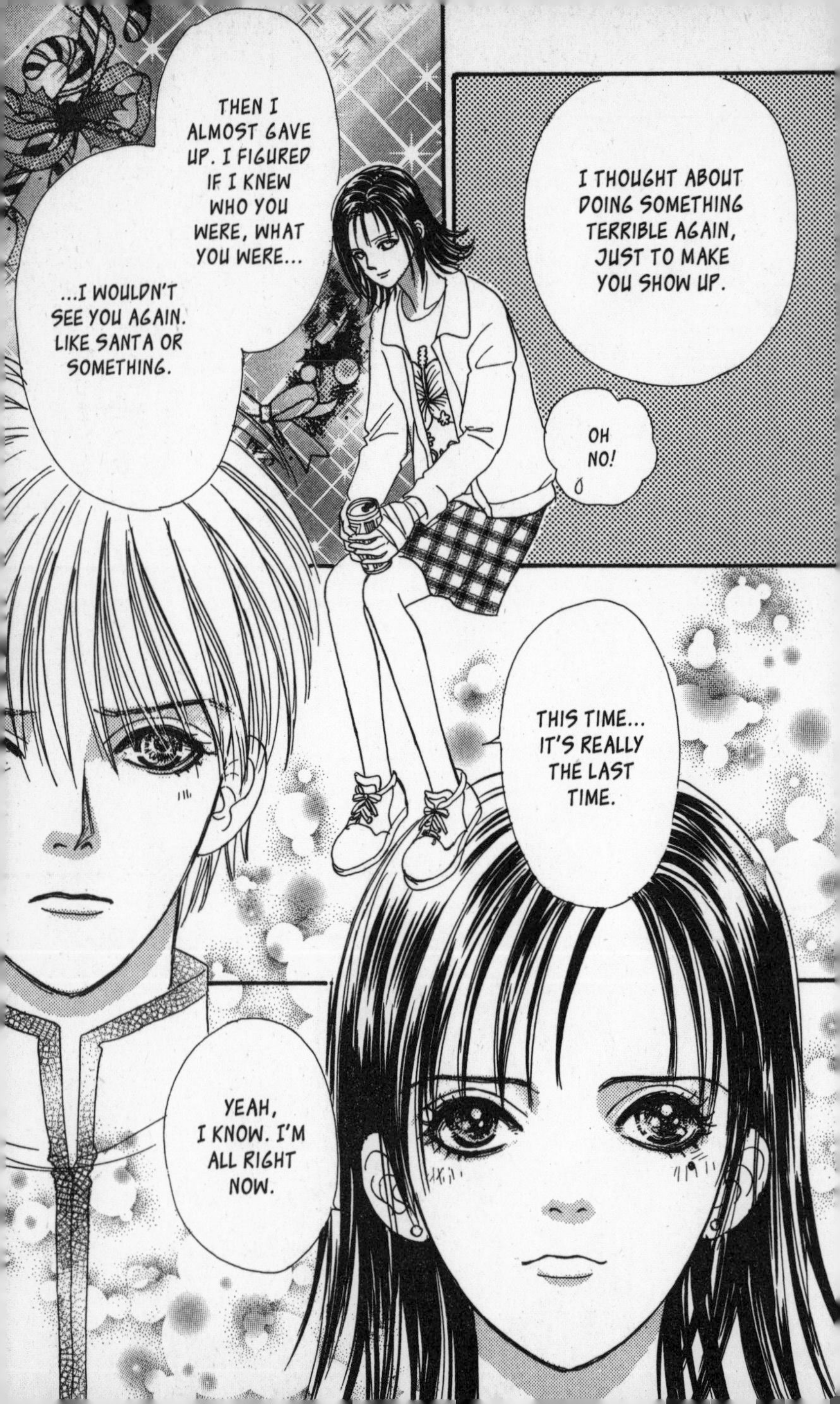
I THOUGHT ABOUT DOING SOMETHING TERRIBLE AGAIN, JUST TO MAKE YOU SHOW UP.
OH NO!
THEN I ALMOST GAVE UP. I FIGURED IF I KNEW WHO YOU WERE, WHAT YOU WERE...
...I WOULDN'T SEE YOU AGAIN. LIKE SANTA OR SOMETHING.
THIS TIME... IT'S REALLY THE LAST TIME.
YEAH, I KNOW. I'M ALL RIGHT NOW.

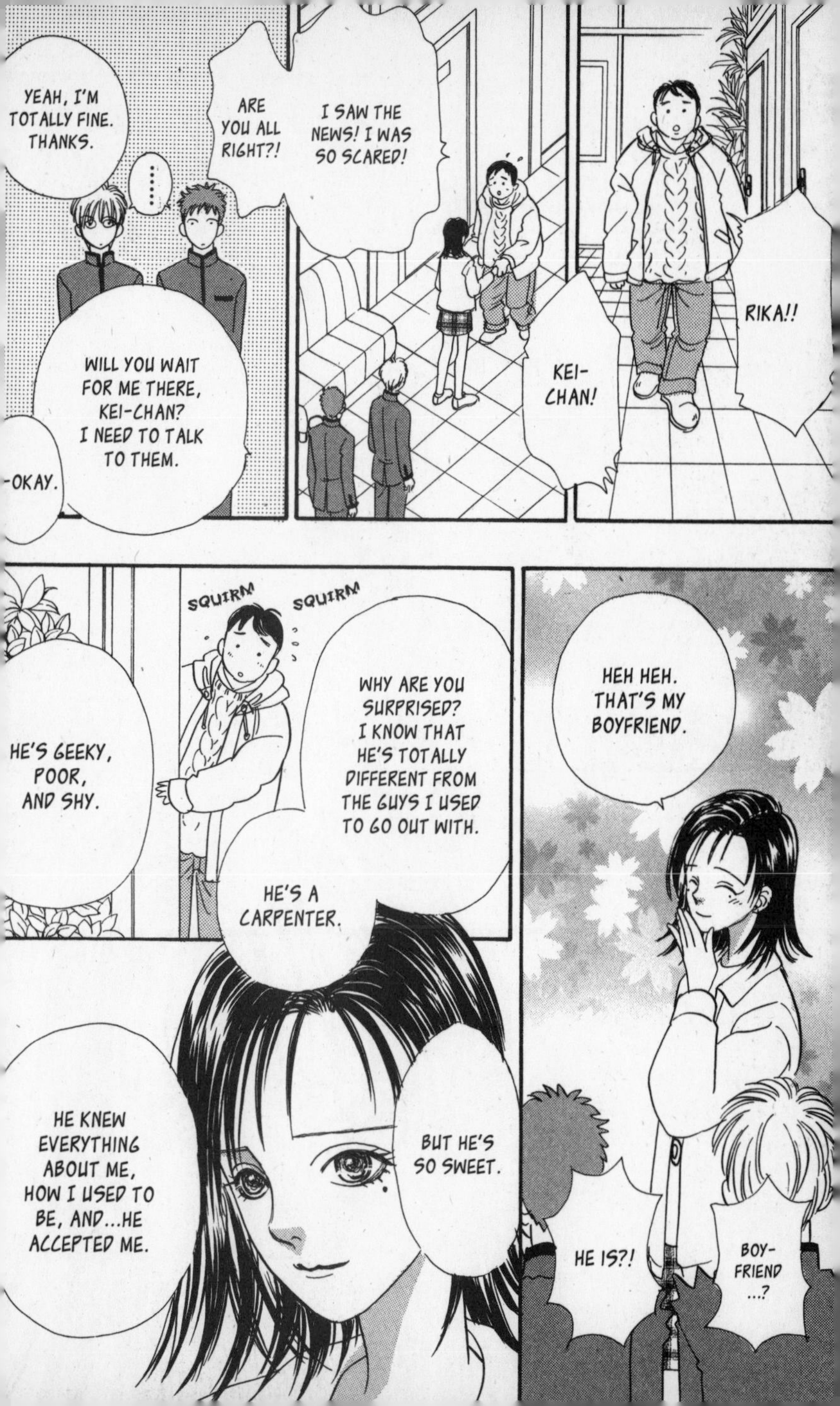
RIKA!!
KEI-CHAN!
ARE YOU ALL RIGHT?! I SAW THE NEWS! I WAS SO SCARED!
YEAH, I'M TOTALLY FINE. THANKS.
......
WILL YOU WAIT FOR ME THERE, KEI-CHAN? I NEED TO TALK TO THEM.
-OKAY.
HEH HEH. THAT'S MY BOYFRIEND.
BOY-FRIEND ...?
HE IS?!
SQUIRM SQUIRM
WHY ARE YOU SURPRISED? I KNOW THAT HE'S TOTALLY DIFFERENT FROM THE GUYS I USED TO GO OUT WITH.
HE'S GEEKY, POOR, AND SHY.
HE'S A CARPENTER.
BUT HE'S SO SWEET.
HE KNEW EVERYTHING ABOUT ME, HOW I USED TO BE, AND...HE ACCEPTED ME.

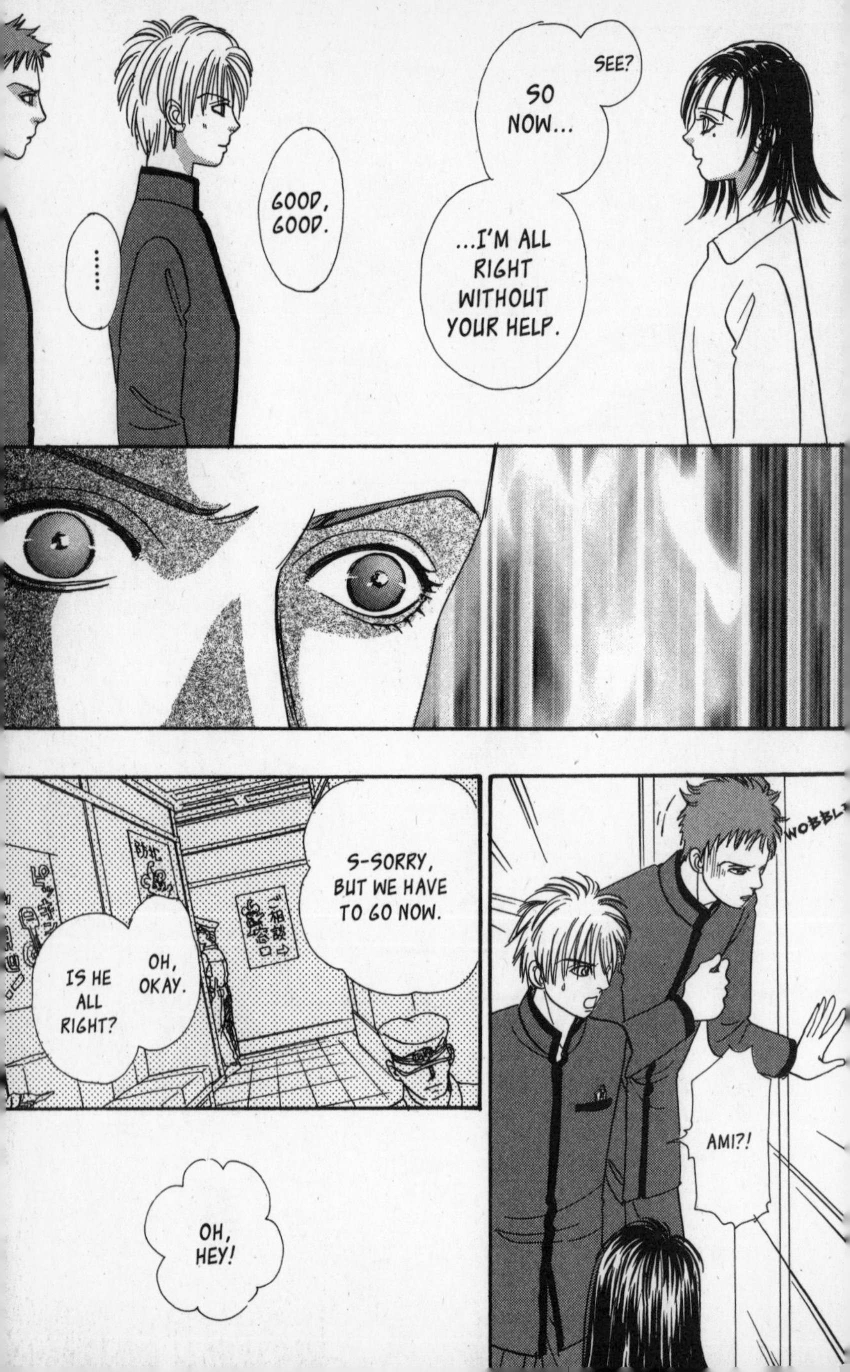
SEE?
SO NOW...
...I'M ALL RIGHT WITHOUT YOUR HELP.
GOOD, GOOD.
......
WOBBL
AMI?!
S-SORRY, BUT WE HAVE TO GO NOW.
OH, OKAY.
IS HE ALL RIGHT?
OH, HEY!

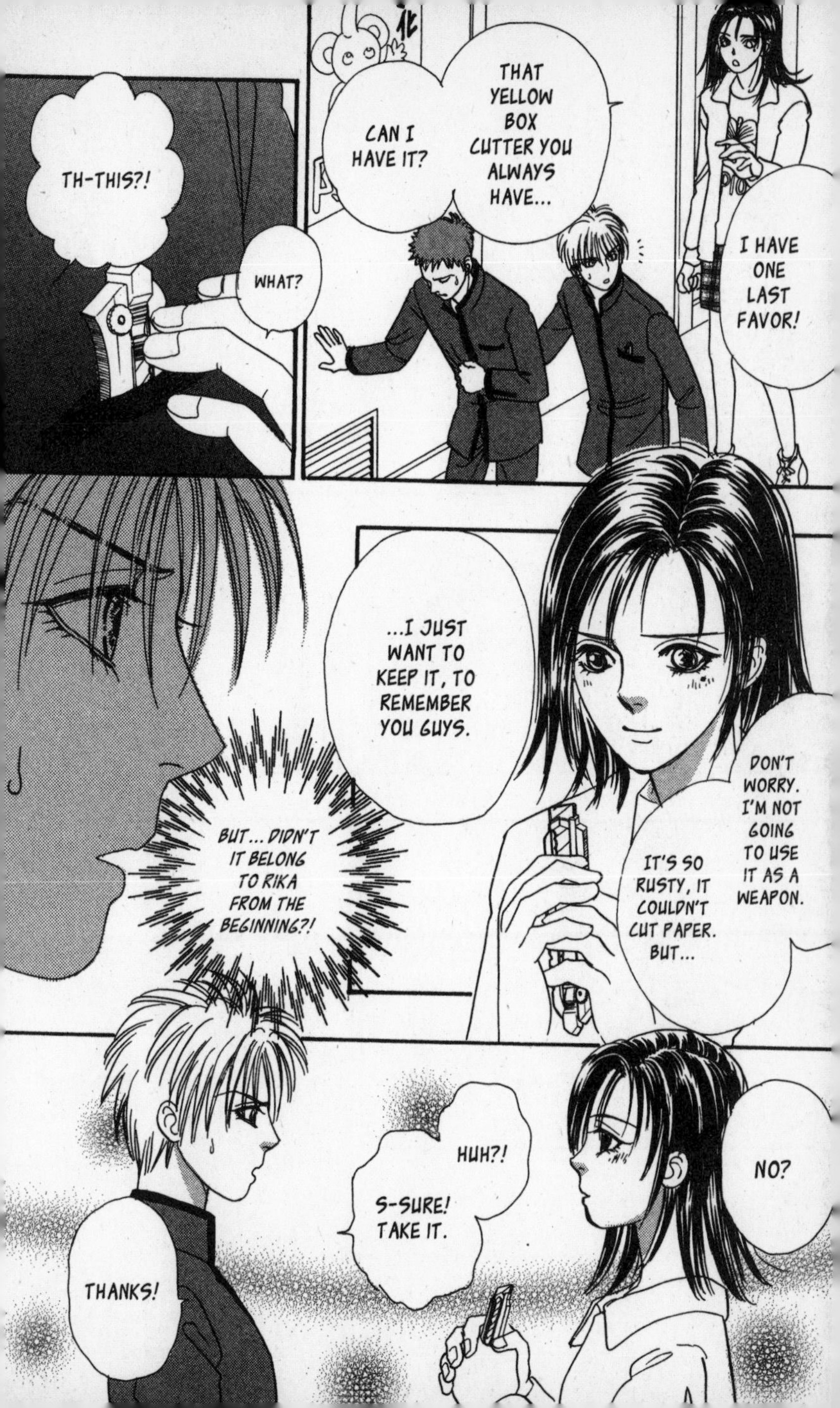
I HAVE ONE LAST FAVOR!
THAT YELLOW BOX CUTTER YOU ALWAYS HAVE...
CAN I HAVE IT?
WHAT?
TH-THIS?!
DON'T WORRY. I'M NOT GOING TO USE IT AS A WEAPON.
IT'S SO RUSTY, IT COULDN'T CUT PAPER. BUT...
...I JUST WANT TO KEEP IT, TO REMEMBER YOU GUYS.
BUT... DIDN'T IT BELONG TO RIKA FROM THE BEGINNING?!
NO?
HUH?!
S-SURE! TAKE IT.
THANKS!

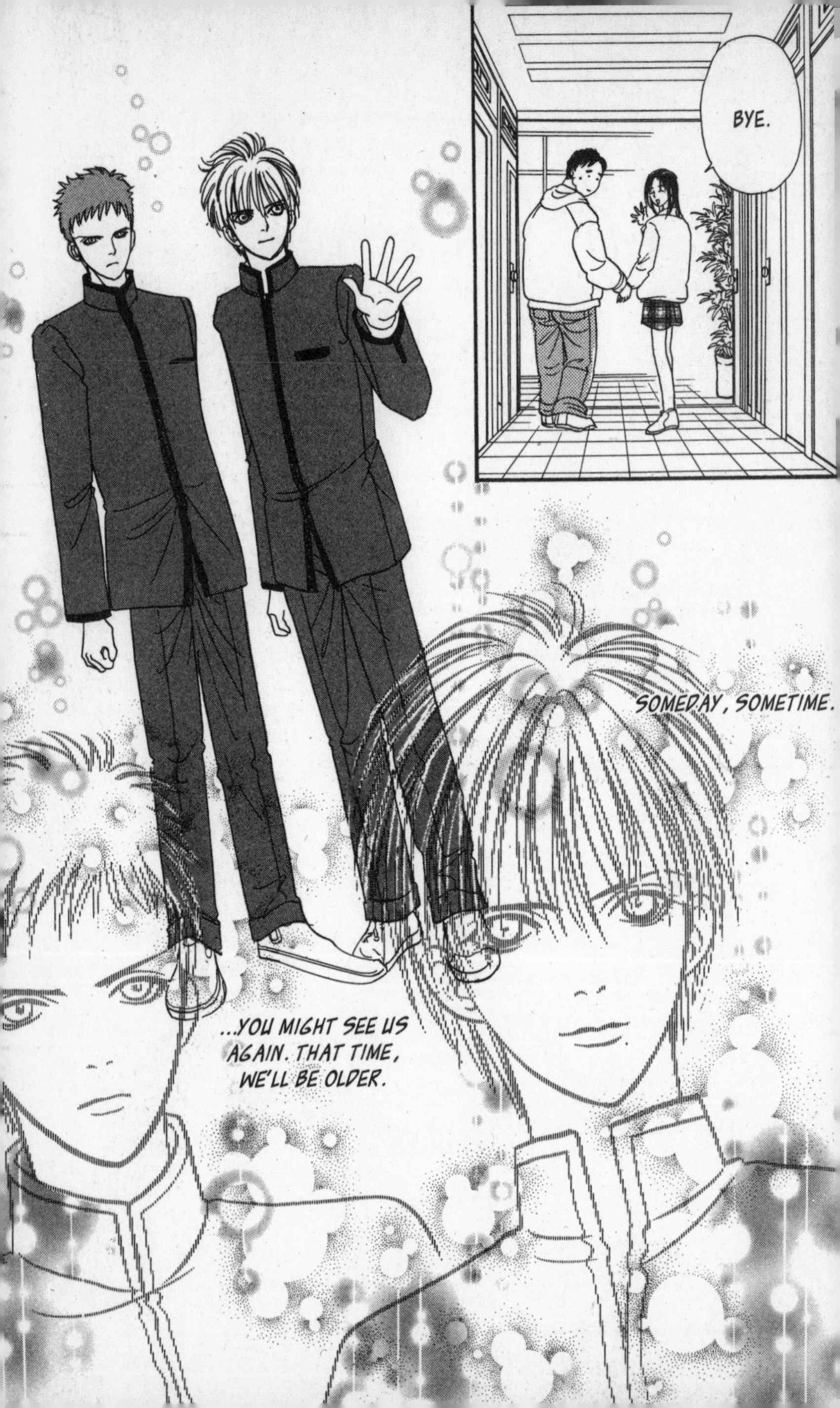
BYE.
SOMEDAY, SOMETIME.
...YOU MIGHT SEE US AGAIN. THAT TIME, WE'LL BE OLDER.

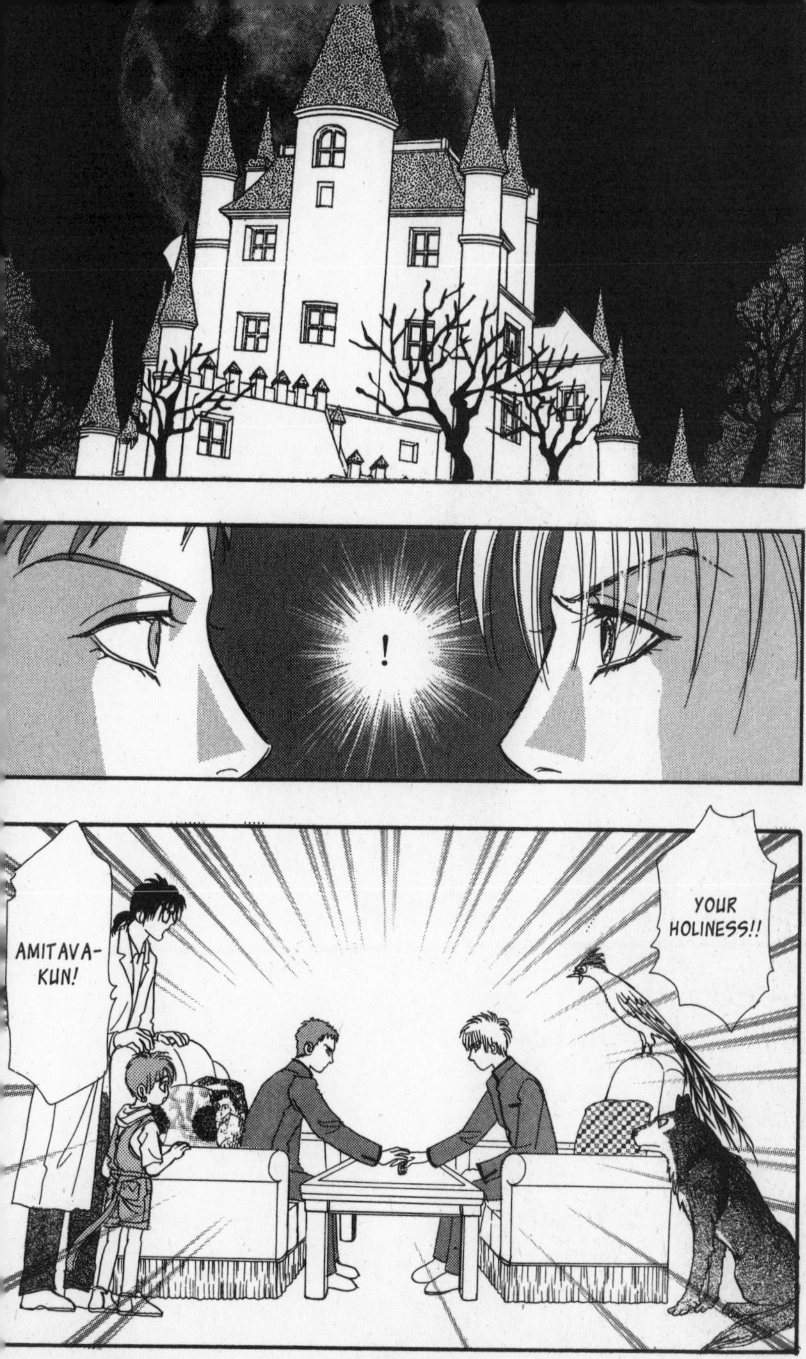
!
YOUR HOLINESS!!
AMITAVA-KUN!

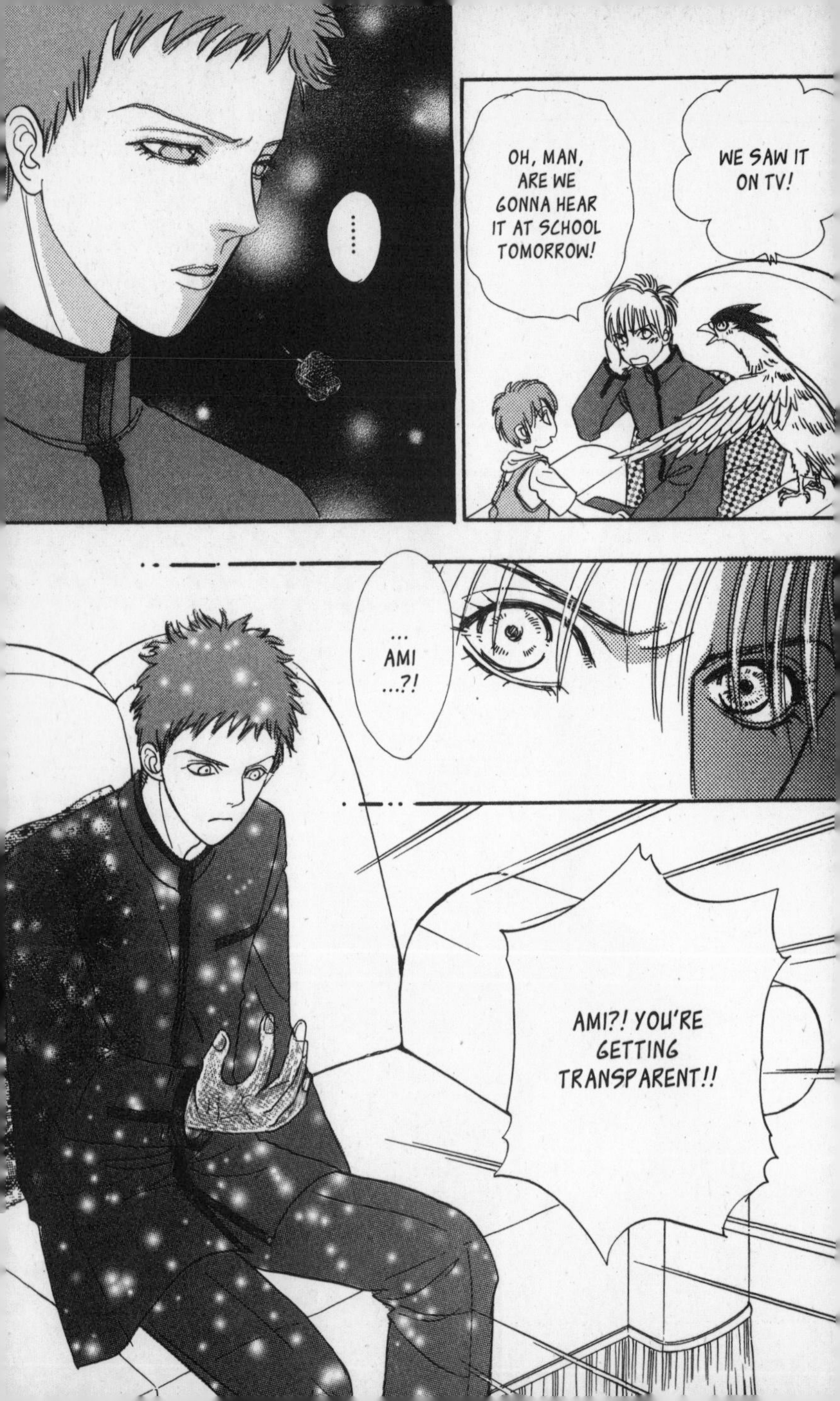
WE SAW IT ON TV!
OH, MAN, ARE WE GONNA HEAR IT AT SCHOOL TOMORROW!
......
... AMI ...?!
AMI?! YOU'RE GETTING TRANSPARENT!!

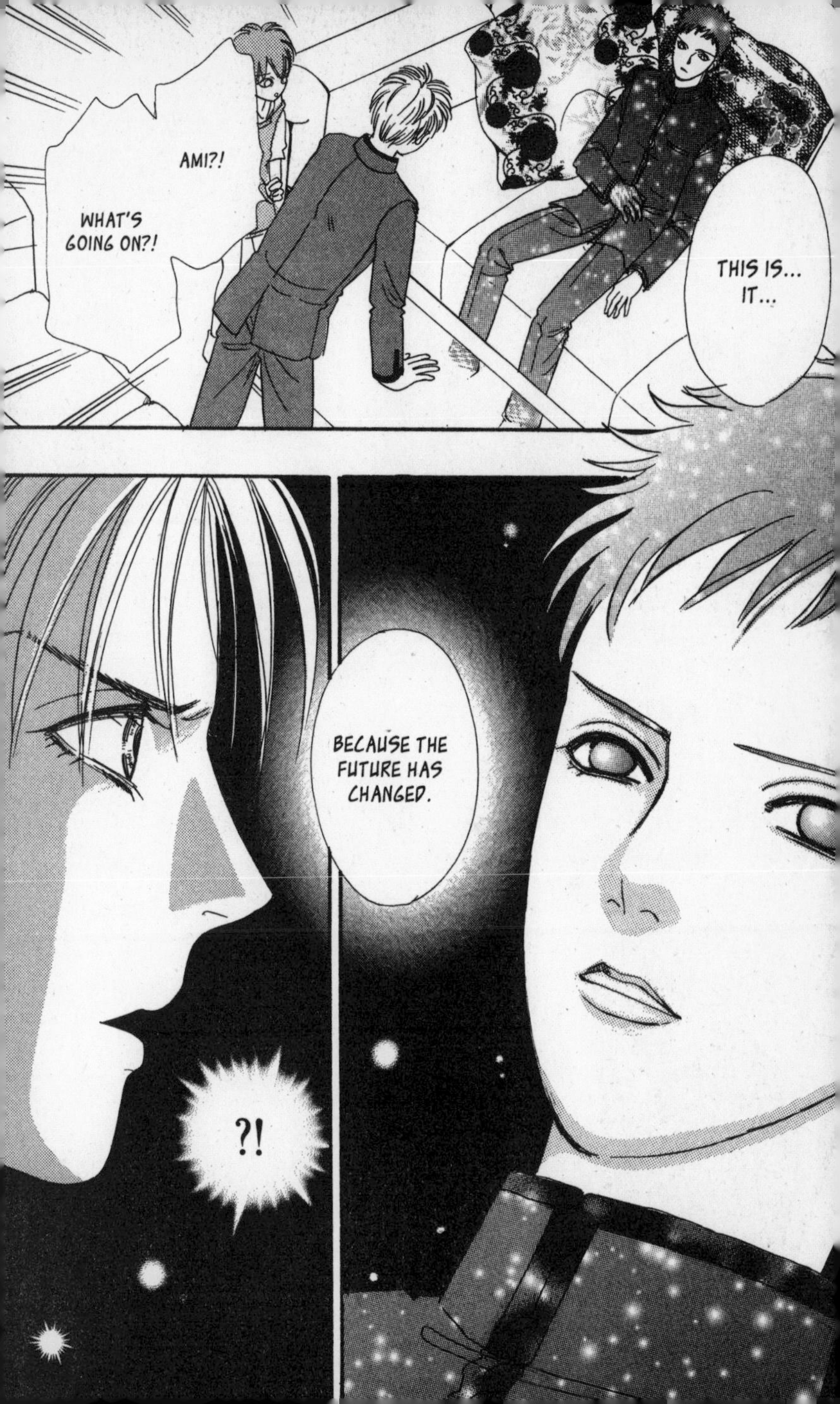
AMI?!
WHAT'S GOING ON?!
THIS IS... IT...
BECAUSE THE FUTURE HAS CHANGED.
?!

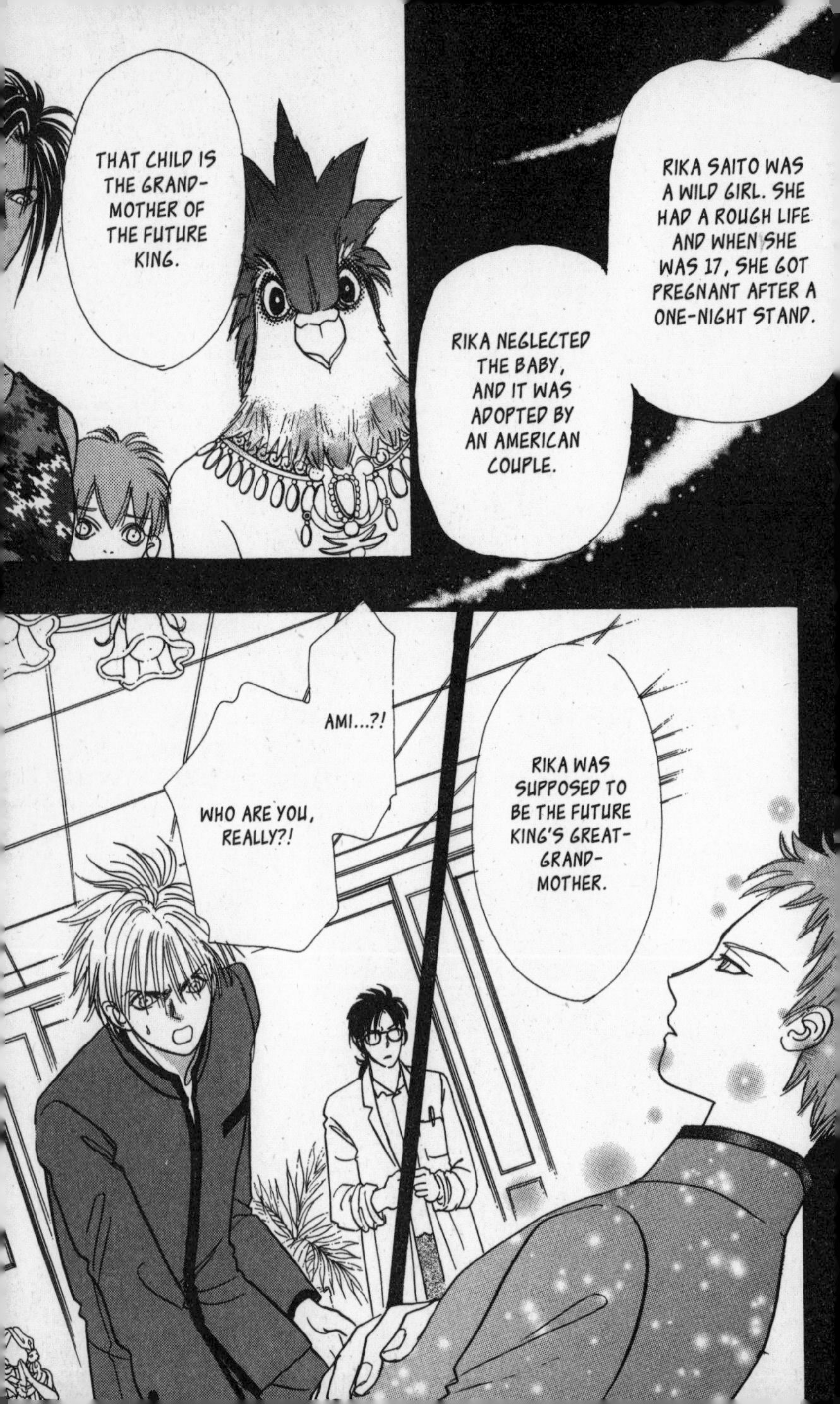

RIKA SAITO WAS A WILD GIRL. SHE HAD A ROUGH LIFE AND WHEN SHE WAS 17, SHE GOT PREGNANT AFTER A ONE-NIGHT STAND.
RIKA NEGLECTED THE BABY, AND IT WAS ADOPTED BY AN AMERICAN COUPLE.
THAT CHILD IS THE GRAND-MOTHER OF THE FUTURE KING.
RIKA WAS SUPPOSED TO BE THE FUTURE KING'S GREAT-GRAND-MOTHER.
AMI...?!
WHO ARE YOU, REALLY?!

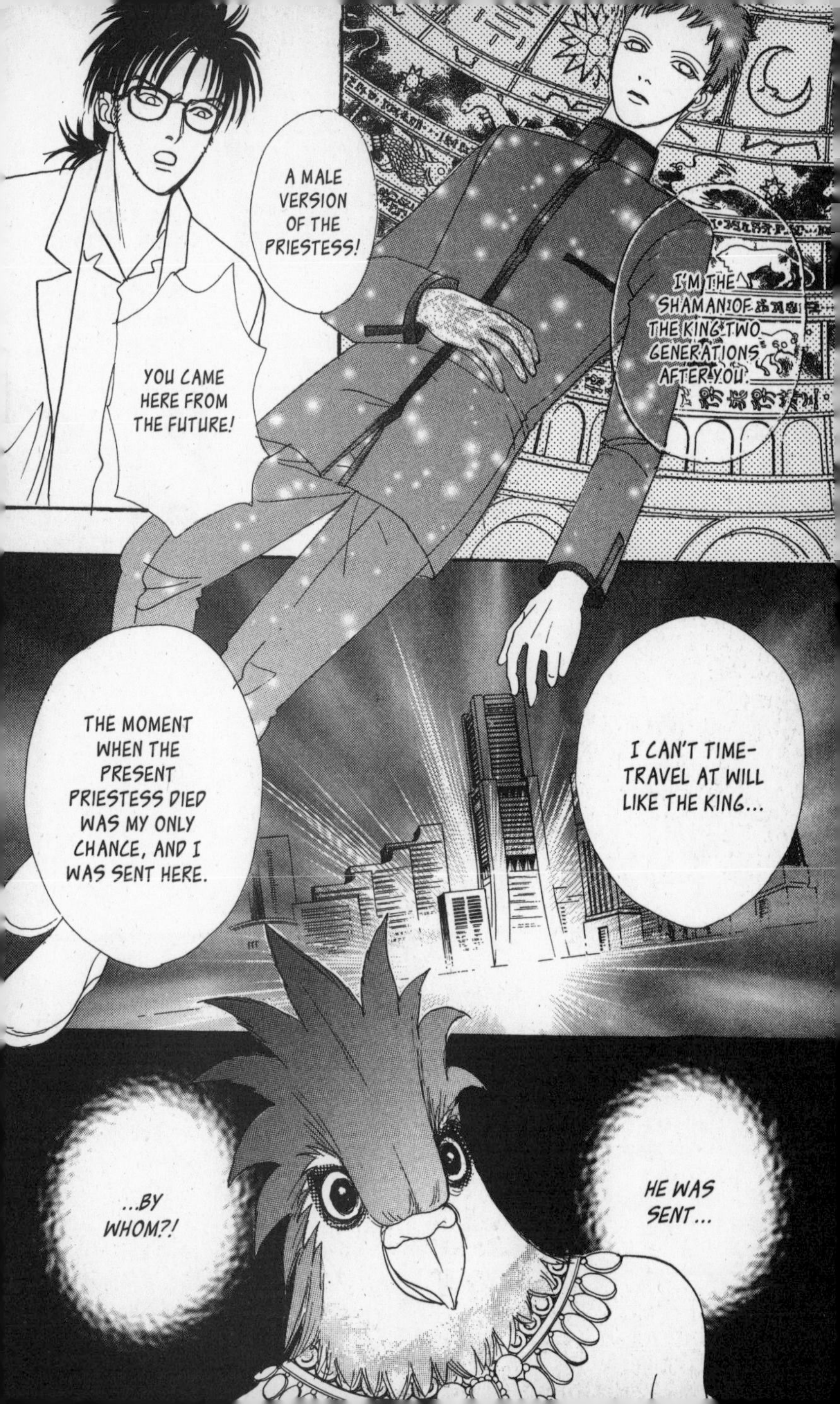
I'M THE SHAMAN OF THE KING TWO GENERATIONS AFTER YOU.
A MALE VERSION OF THE PRIESTESS!
YOU CAME HERE FROM THE FUTURE!
I CAN'T TIME-TRAVEL AT WILL LIKE THE KING...
THE MOMENT WHEN THE PRESENT PRIESTESS DIED WAS MY ONLY CHANCE, AND I WAS SENT HERE.
HE WAS SENT...
...BY WHOM?!

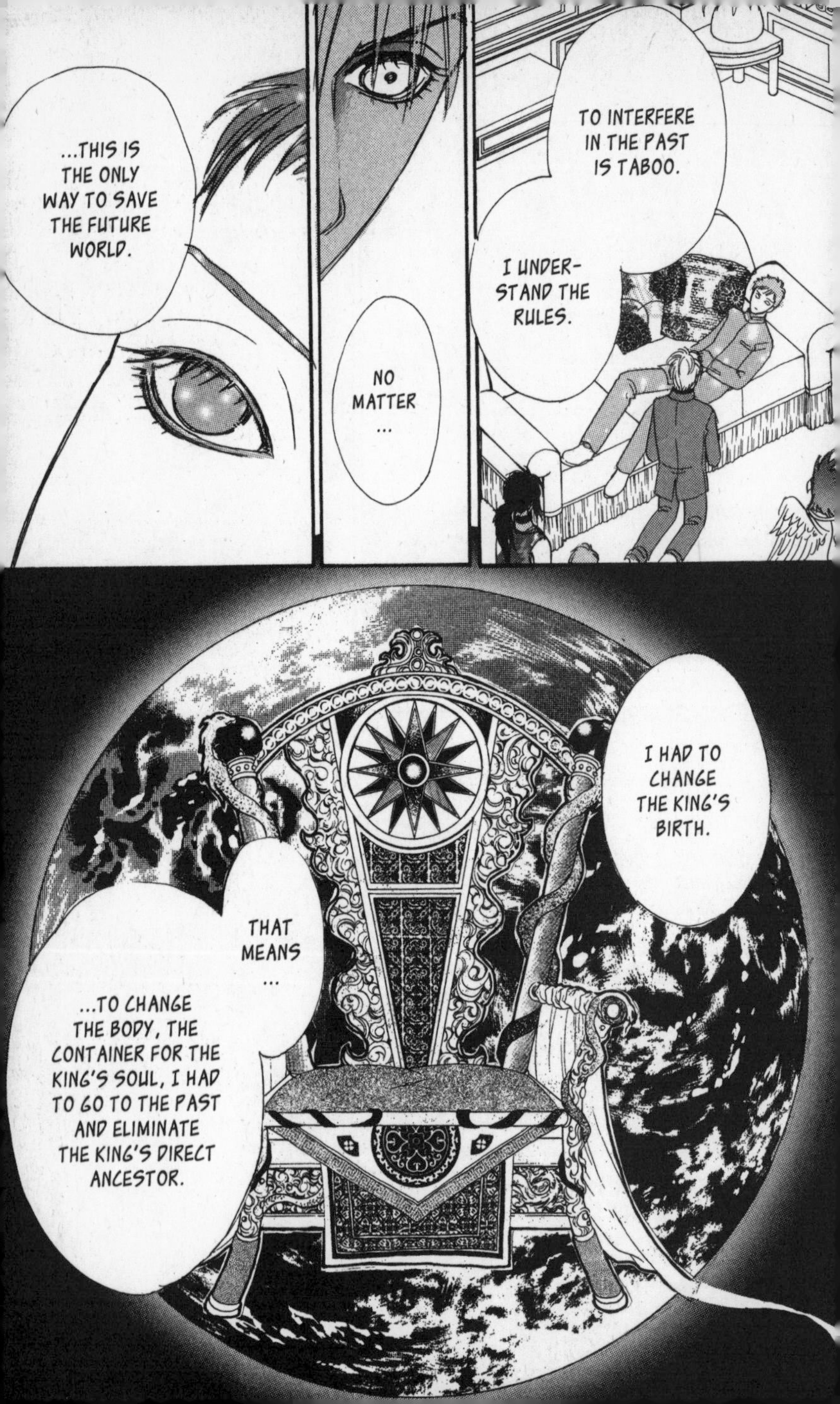
TO INTERFERE IN THE PAST IS TABOO.
I UNDER-STAND THE RULES.
NO MATTER ...
...THIS IS THE ONLY WAY TO SAVE THE FUTURE WORLD.
I HAD TO CHANGE THE KING'S BIRTH.
THAT MEANS ...
...TO CHANGE THE BODY, THE CONTAINER FOR THE KING'S SOUL, I HAD TO GO TO THE PAST AND ELIMINATE THE KING'S DIRECT ANCESTOR.

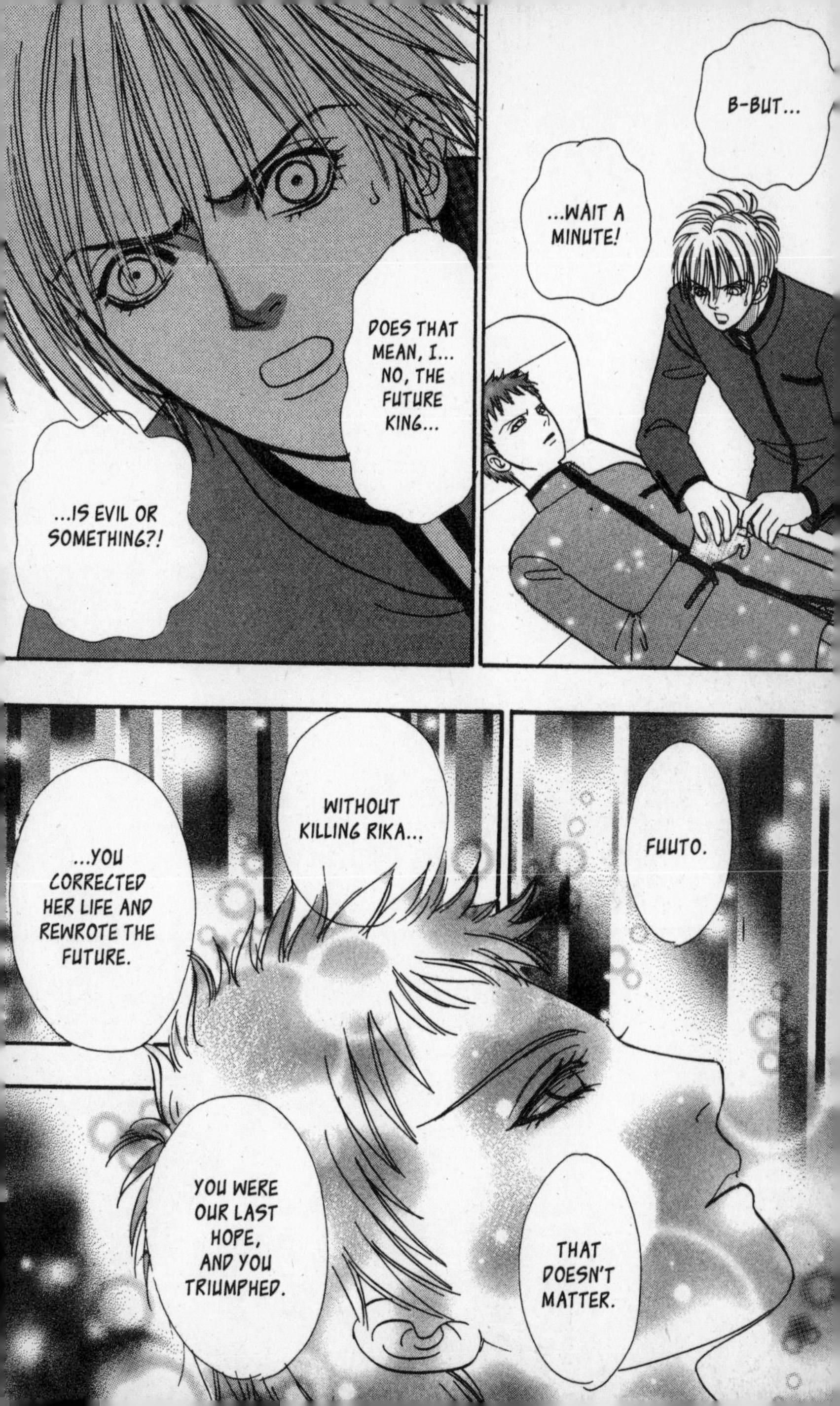
B-BUT...
...WAIT A MINUTE!
DOES THAT MEAN, I... NO, THE FUTURE KING...
...IS EVIL OR SOMETHING?!
FUUTO.
WITHOUT KILLING RIKA...
...YOU CORRECTED HER LIFE AND REWROTE THE FUTURE.
YOU WERE OUR LAST HOPE, AND YOU TRIUMPHED.
THAT DOESN'T MATTER.

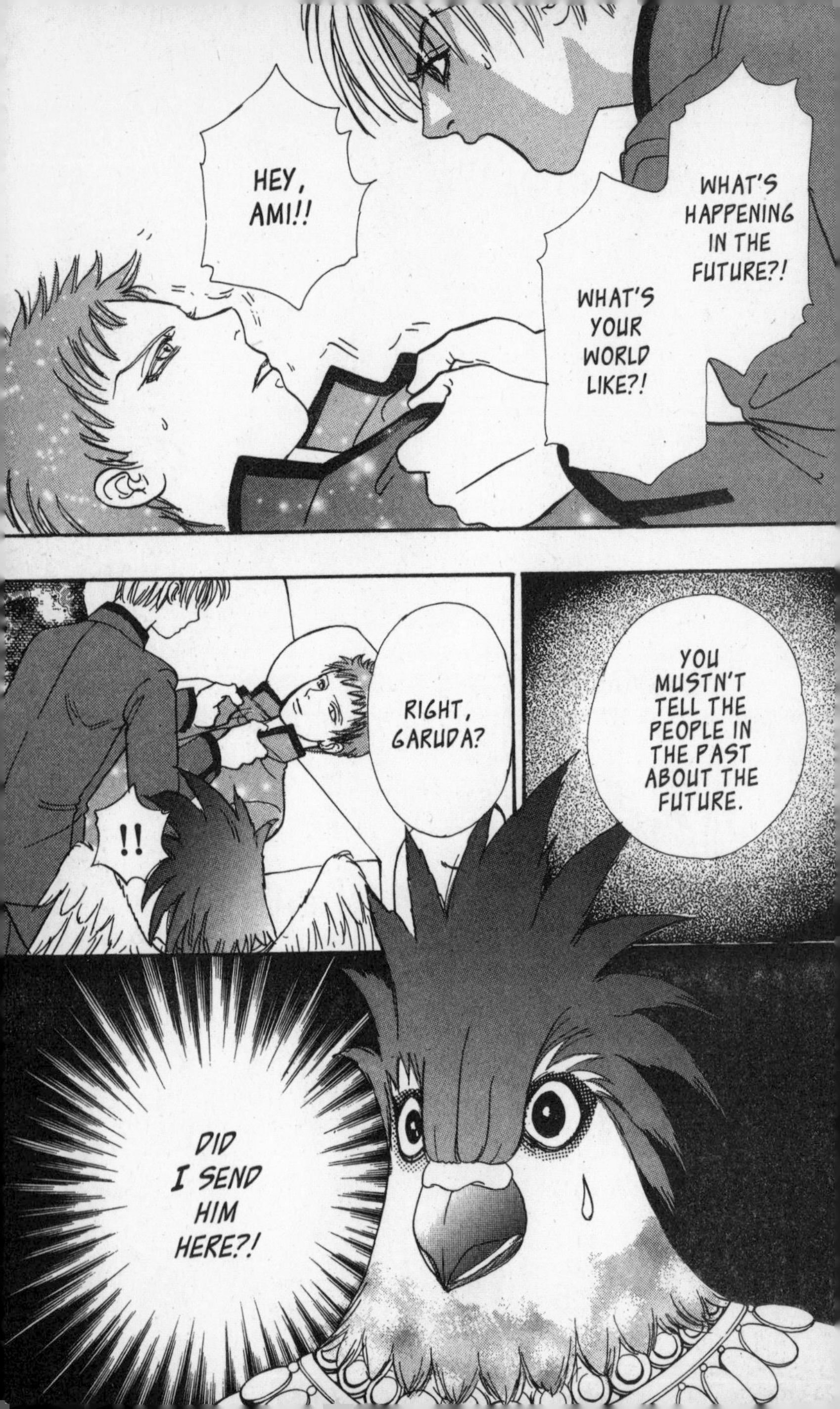
HEY, AMI!!
WHAT'S HAPPENING IN THE FUTURE?!
WHAT'S YOUR WORLD LIKE?!
YOU MUSTN'T TELL THE PEOPLE IN THE PAST ABOUT THE FUTURE.
RIGHT, GARUDA?
!!
DID I SEND HIM HERE?!

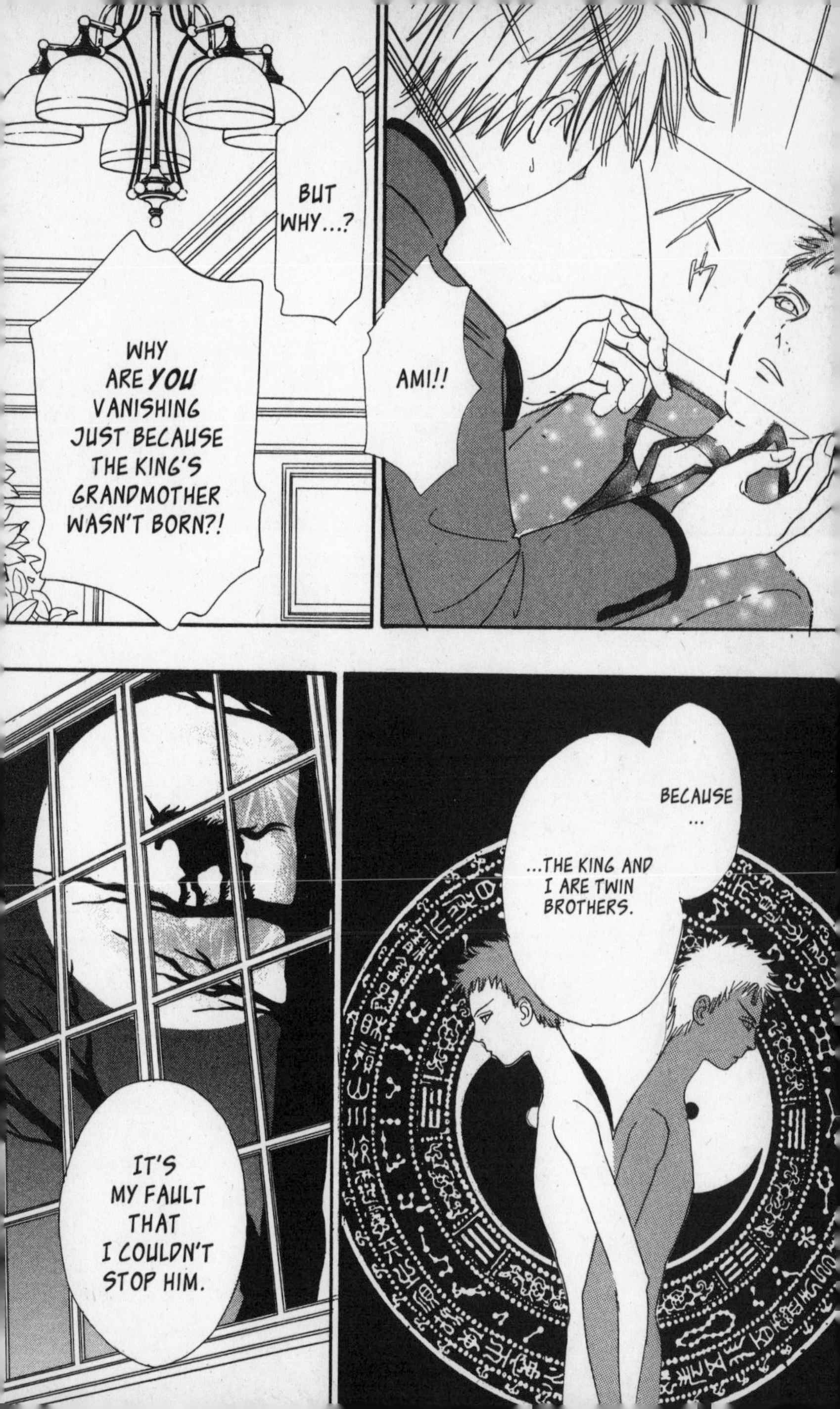
AMI!!
BUT WHY...?
WHY ARE YOU VANISHING JUST BECAUSE THE KING'S GRANDMOTHER WASN'T BORN?!
BECAUSE ...
...THE KING AND I ARE TWIN BROTHERS.
IT'S MY FAULT THAT I COULDN'T STOP HIM.

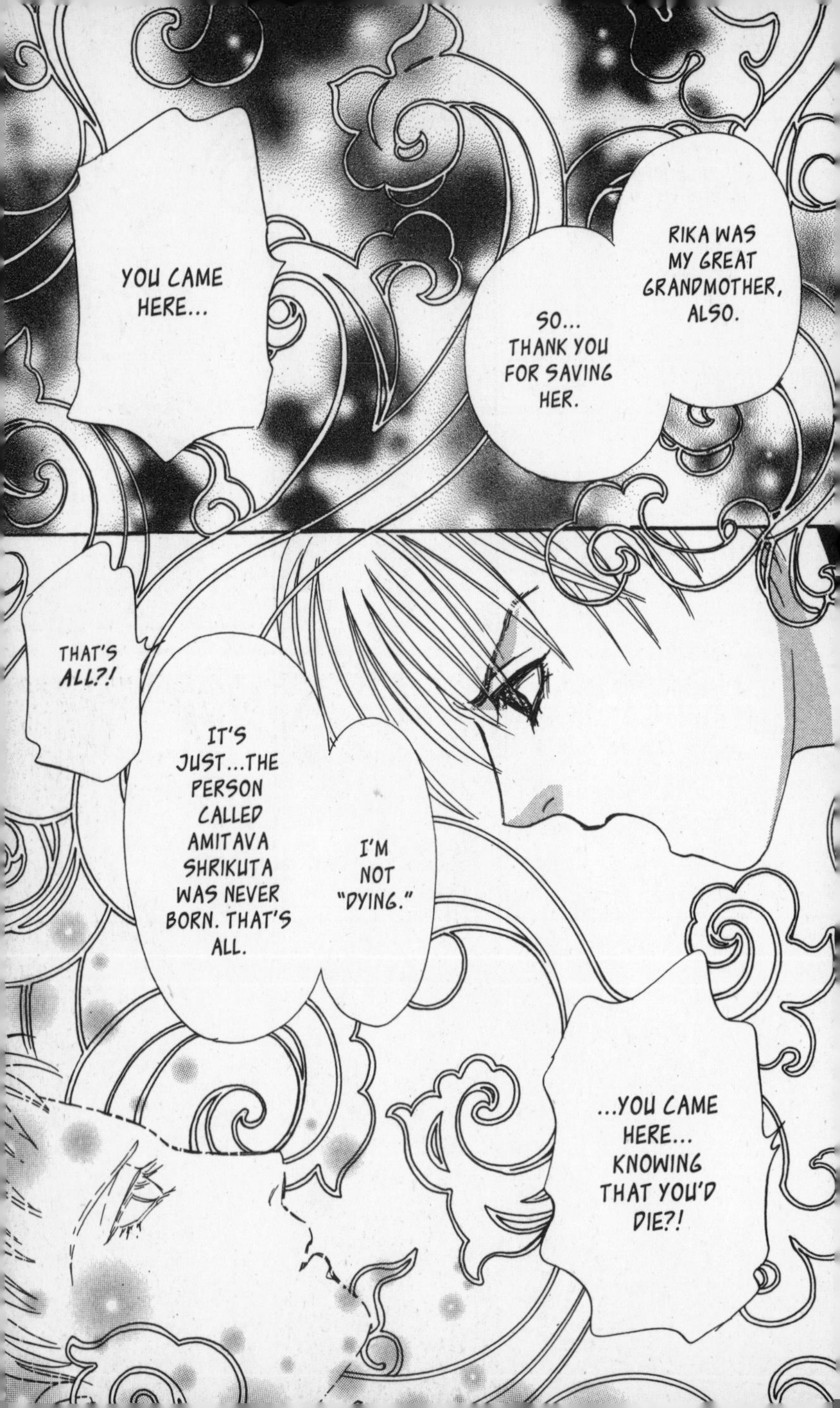
RIKA WAS MY GREAT GRANDMOTHER, ALSO.
SO... THANK YOU FOR SAVING HER.
YOU CAME HERE...
...YOU CAME HERE... KNOWING THAT YOU'D DIE?!
I'M NOT "DYING."
IT'S JUST...THE PERSON CALLED AMITAVA SHRIKUTA WAS NEVER BORN. THAT'S ALL.
THAT'S *ALL?!*

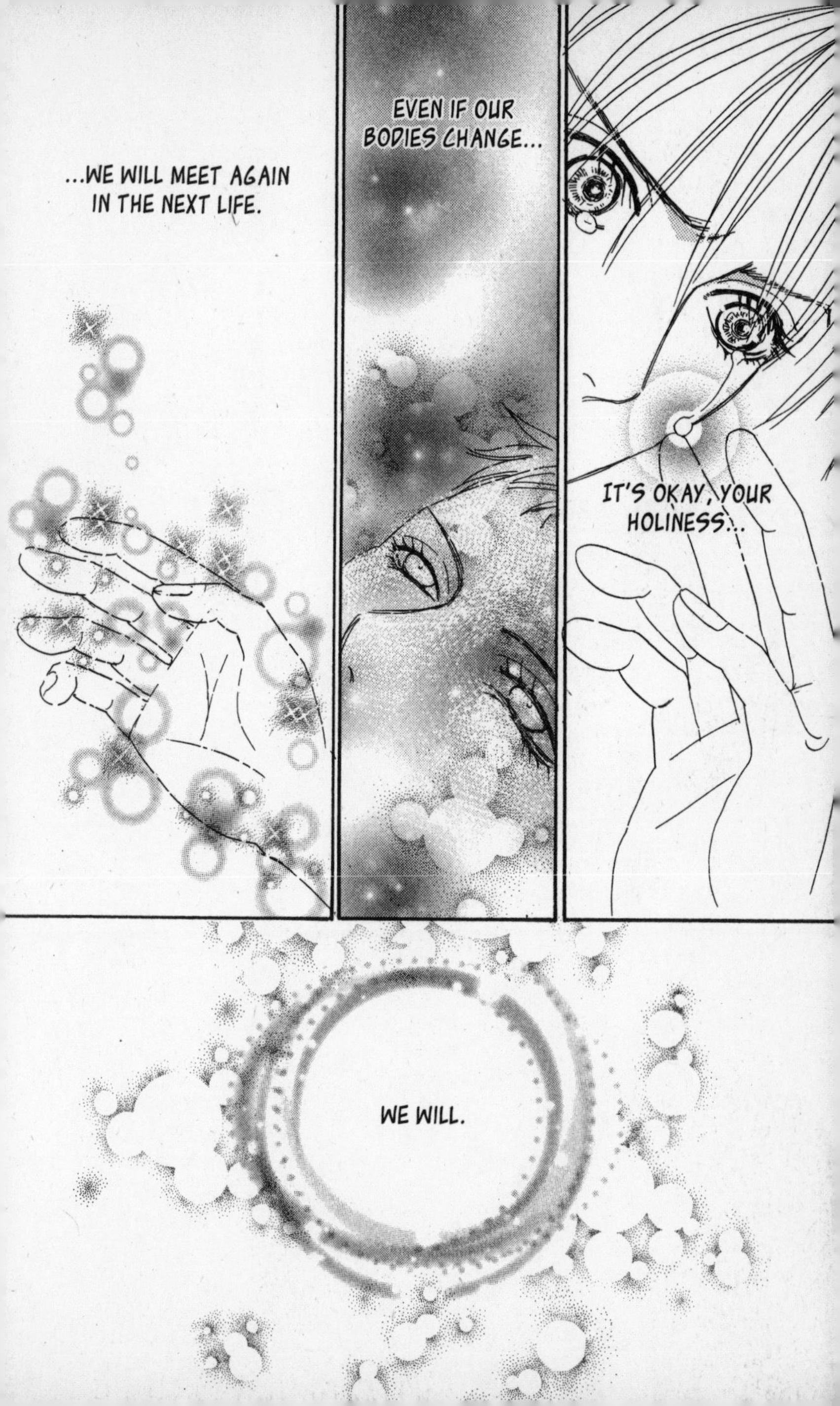
IT'S OKAY, YOUR HOLINESS...
EVEN IF OUR BODIES CHANGE...
...WE WILL MEET AGAIN IN THE NEXT LIFE.
WE WILL.

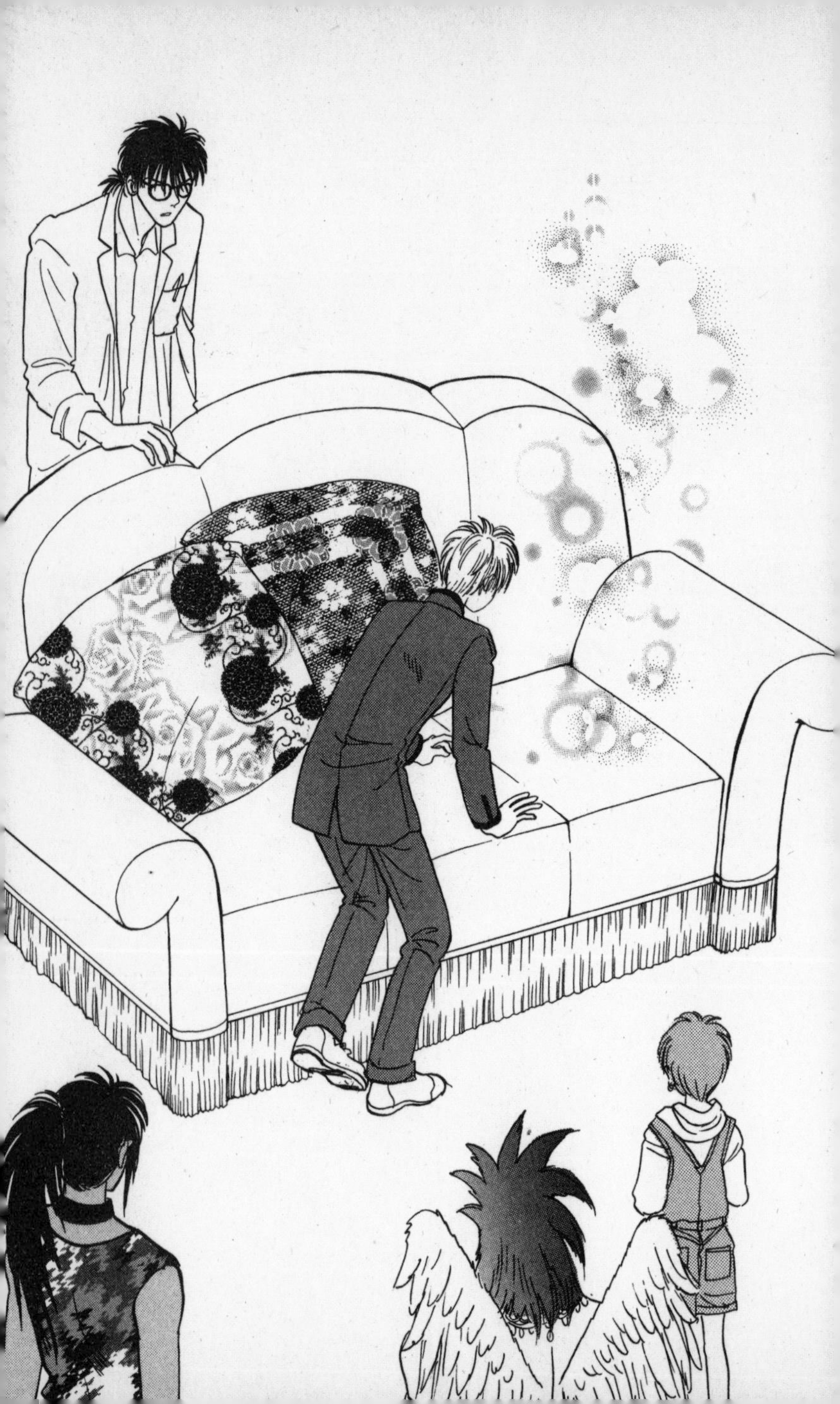

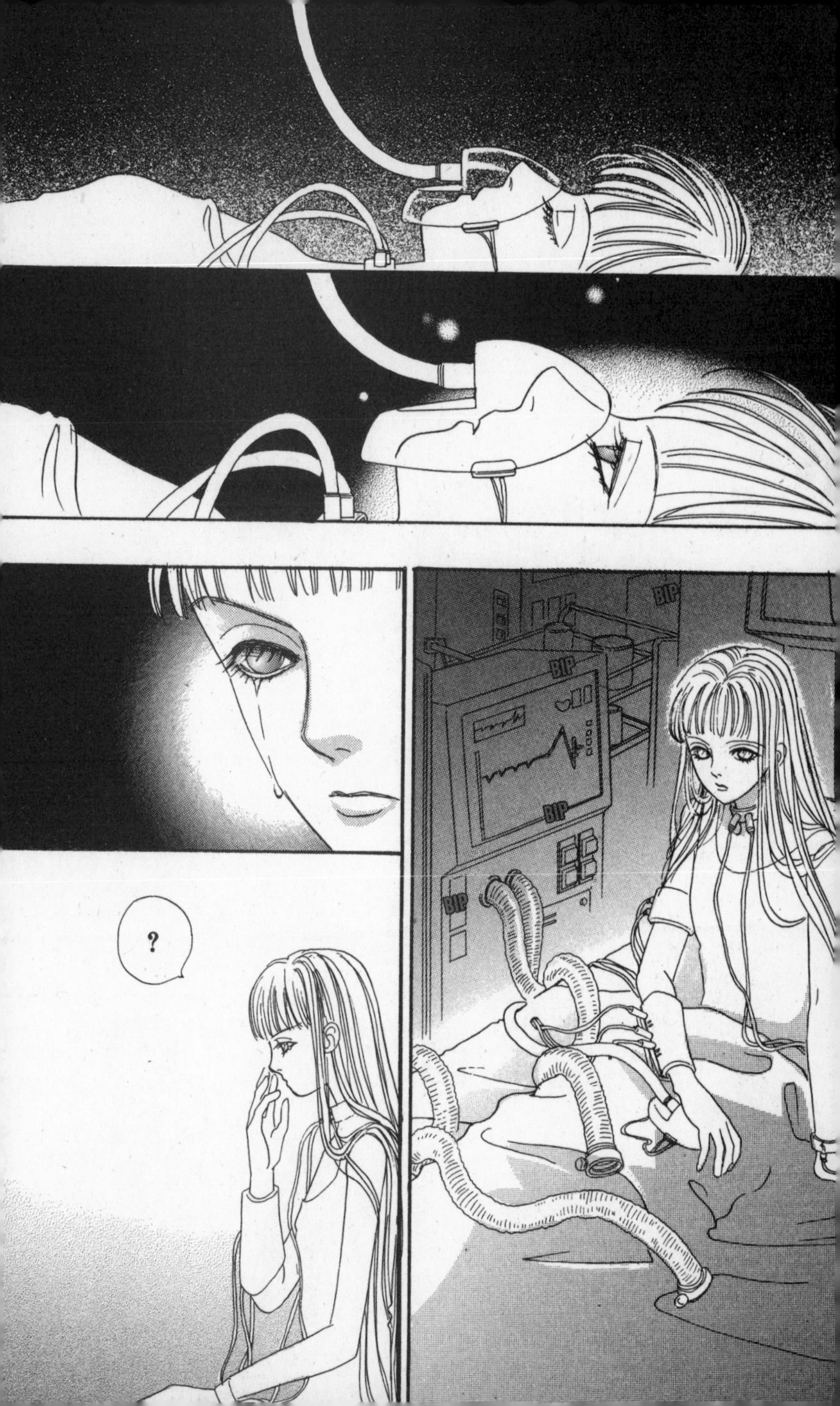
BIP
BIP
BIP
BIP
?

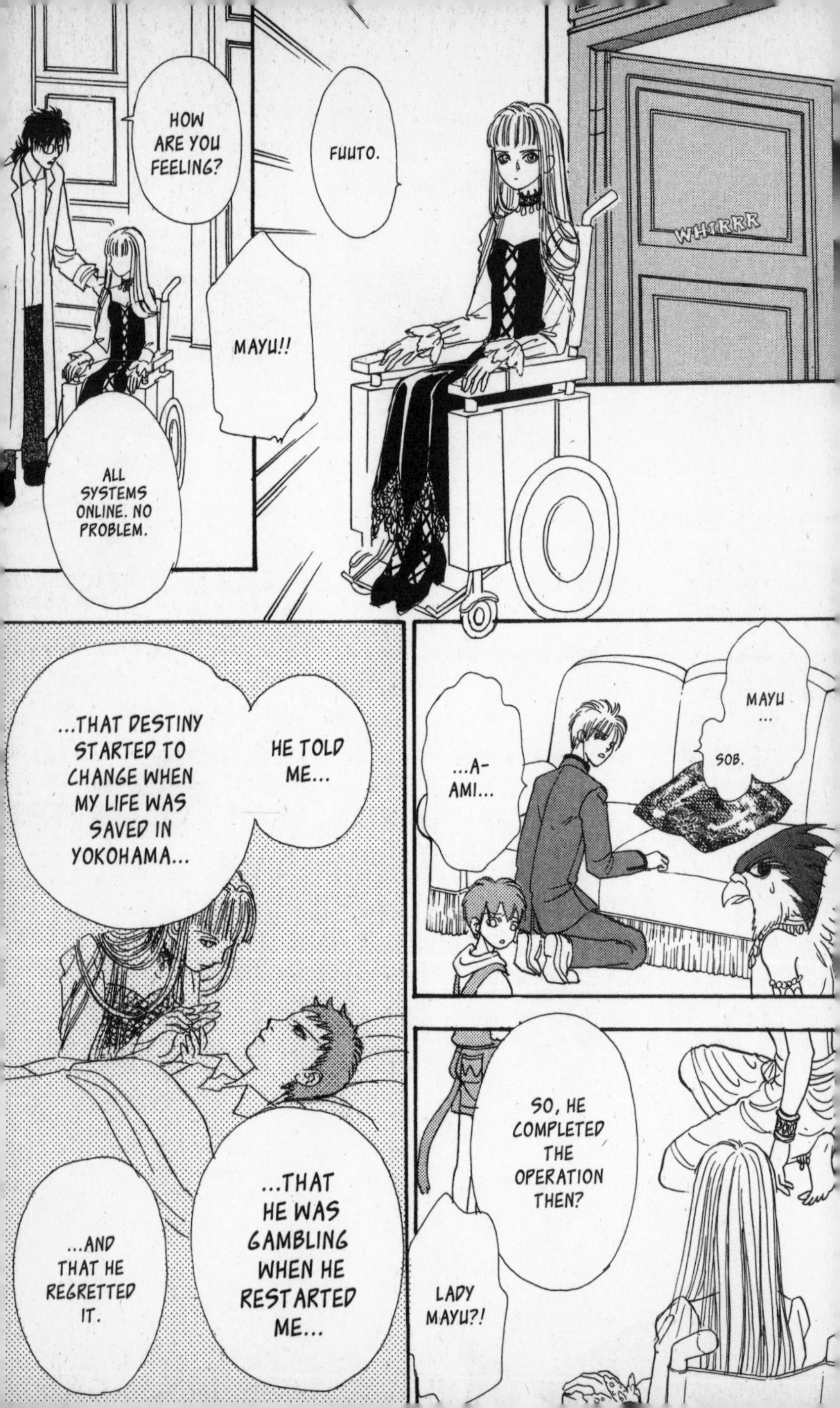
WHIRRR
FUUTO.
MAYU!!
HOW ARE YOU FEELING?
ALL SYSTEMS ONLINE. NO PROBLEM.
MAYU... SOB.
...A-AMI...
SO, HE COMPLETED THE OPERATION THEN?
LADY MAYU?!
HE TOLD ME...
...THAT DESTINY STARTED TO CHANGE WHEN MY LIFE WAS SAVED IN YOKOHAMA...
...THAT HE WAS GAMBLING WHEN HE RESTARTED ME...
...AND THAT HE REGRETTED IT.

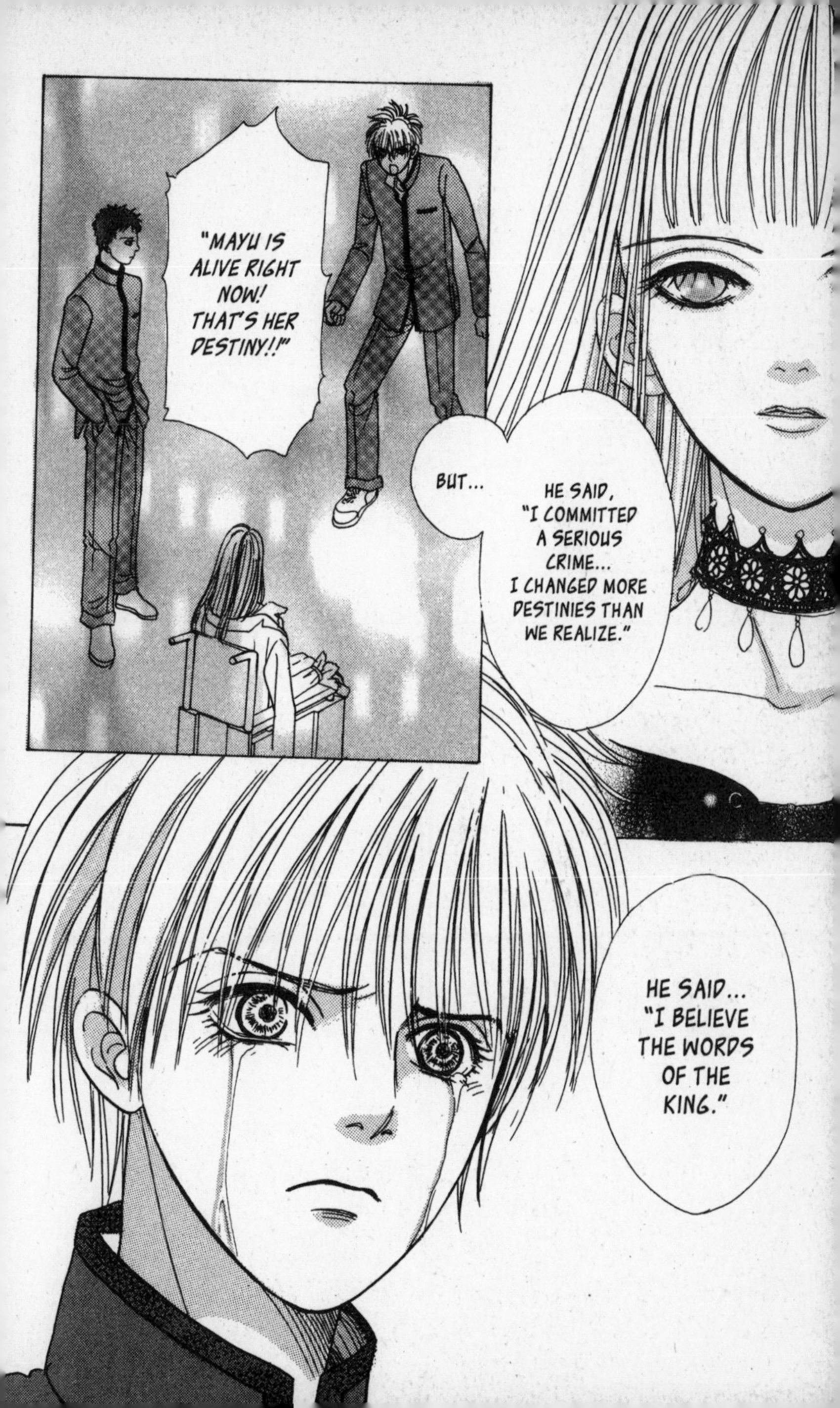

BUT...
HE SAID, "I COMMITTED A SERIOUS CRIME... I CHANGED MORE DESTINIES THAN WE REALIZE."
"MAYU IS ALIVE RIGHT NOW! THAT'S HER DESTINY!!"
HE SAID... "I BELIEVE THE WORDS OF THE KING."

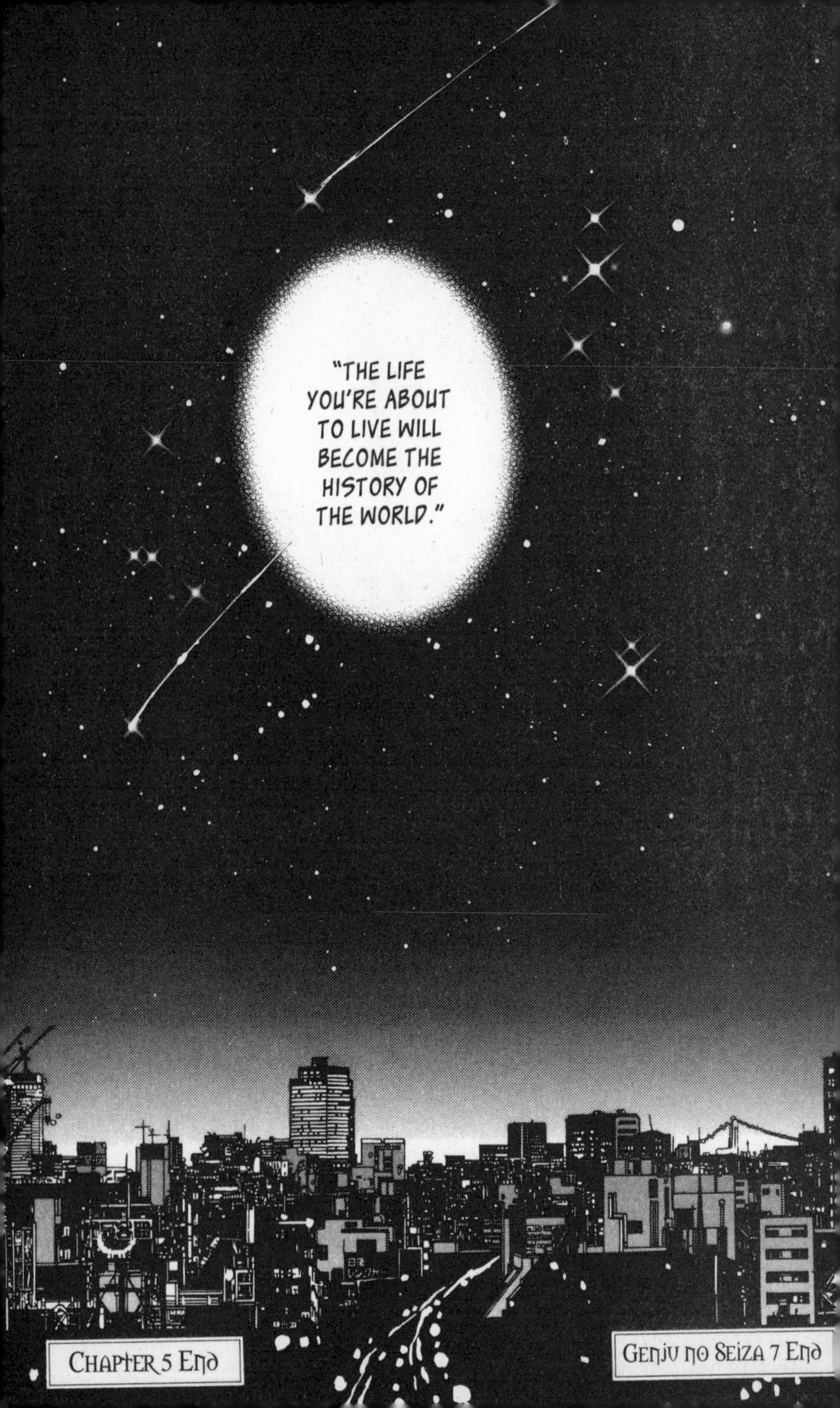
"THE LIFE YOU'RE ABOUT TO LIVE WILL BECOME THE HISTORY OF THE WORLD."
Genju no Seiza 7 End
Chapter 5 End

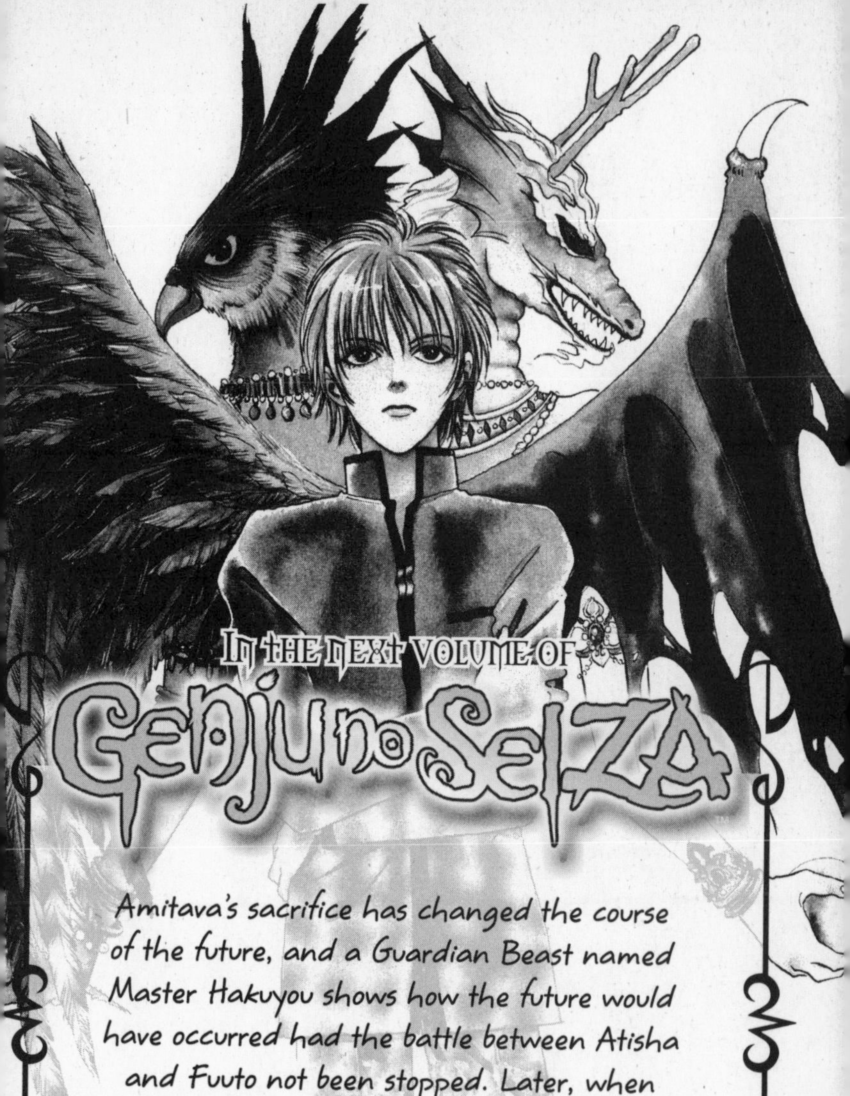

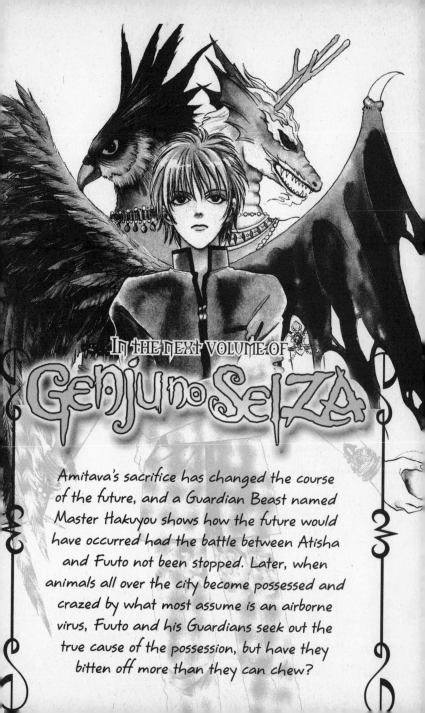

In the next volume of

Genju no Seiza

Amitava's sacrifice has changed the course of the future, and a Guardian Beast named Master Hakuyou shows how the future would have occurred had the battle between Atisha and Fuuto not been stopped. Later, when animals all over the city become possessed and crazed by what most assume is an airborne virus, Fuuto and his Guardians seek out the true cause of the possession, but have they bitten off more than they can chew?

TOKYOPOP.COM

WHERE MANGA LIVES!

▶ **JOIN** the **TOKYOPOP community:**
www.TOKYOPOP.com

**COME AND PREVIEW THE
HOTTEST MANGA AROUND!**

CREATE...
UPLOAD...
DOWNLOAD...
BLOG...
CHAT...
VOTE...
LIVE!!!!

WWW.TOKYOPOP.COM HAS:

- Exclusives
- Manga Pilot Program
- Contests
- Games
- Rising Stars of Manga
- iManga
- and more...

TOKYOPOP.COM
NOW LIVE!

Pet Shop of Horrors

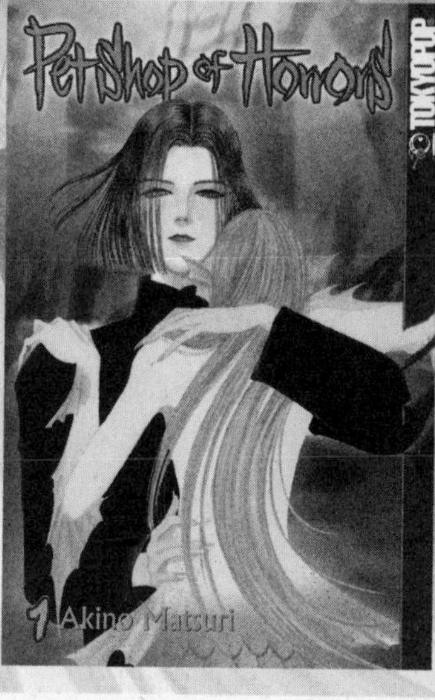

Pet Shop of Horrors
TOKYOPOP
1 Akino Matsuri

Akino-sensei's first and still her most famous manga series, Pet Shop of Horrors introduced us to the iconic Count D and his friend and occasional foil, Officer Leon Orcot. The appeal of Pet Shop's cautionary horror stories can't be denied, but it's the relationship between D and Orcot that forms the true anchor of the book throughout its ten volumes.

The Manga of Matsuri Akino

Matsuri Akino has carved out an interesting niche for herself in the manga community. With three stellar supernatural titles under her belt, she's become known as a master of the episodic manga series. You've already discovered Genju no Seiza. Let's take a look at two of Akino-sensei's other books.

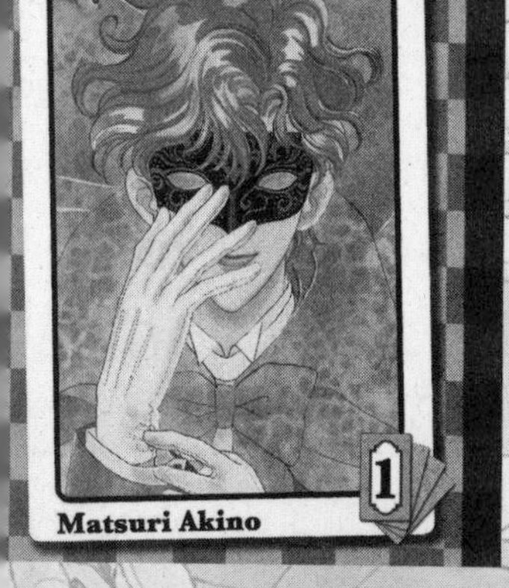

From the creator of Pet Shop of Horrors
KAMEN TANTEI
TOKYOPOP
1
Matsuri Akino

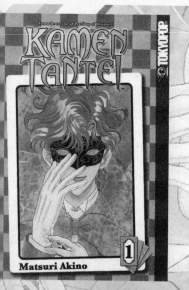

Kamen Tantei

This four-volume mystery manga is now available in English. Exploring the cases of Haruka Akashi and Masato Nishina, the two sole members of Agasa Academy's Mystery Novels Club, Kamen Tantei is lighter in tone than some of Akino-sensei's other work. However, with mysteries involving killer ghosts, feline "cat burglars," and a mysterious masked detective that always shows up in the nick of time, this sure isn't your mother's mystery series!

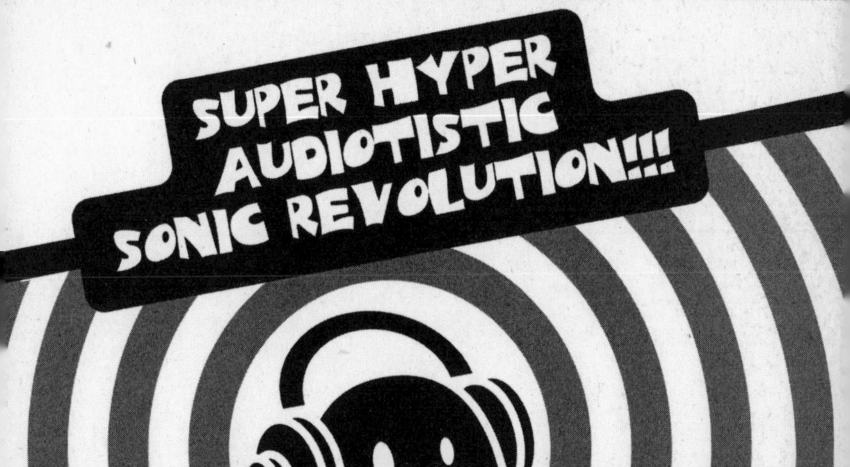
SUPER HYPER
AUDIOTISTIC
SONIC REVOLUTION!!!
www.myspace.com/tokyopop
www.TOKYOPOP.com

TOKYOPOP RECORDS

Available at the iTunes Music Store and everywhere music downloads are available. Keyword: TOKYOPOP

New releases every month! Check out these great albums AVAILABLE NOW!!!

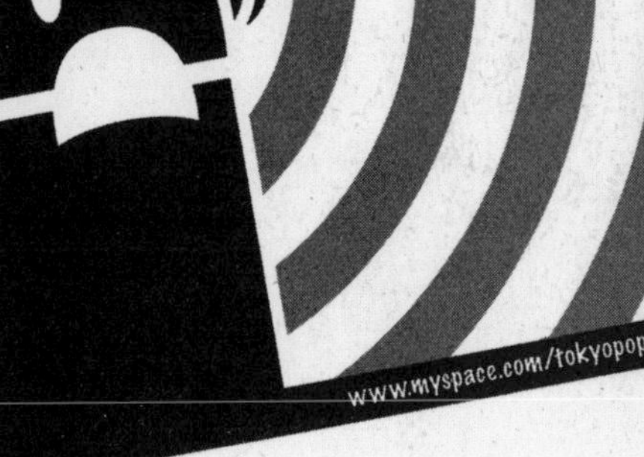
A MIDNIGHT OPERA
ANIME TRAX
DRIFT 2 DIE

FOR MORE INFORMATION VISIT: WWW.TOKYOPOP.COM

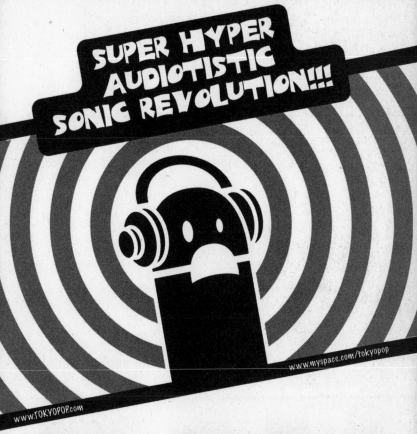

STOP!

This is the back of the book.
You wouldn't want to spoil a great ending!

This book is printed "manga-style," in the authentic Japanese right-to-left format. Since none of the artwork has been flipped or altered, readers get to experience the story just as the creator intended. You've been asking for it, so TOKYOPOP® delivered: authentic, hot-off-the-press, and far more fun!

DIRECTIONS

1
2
3
4
5
6
7
8
9
10

If this is your first time reading manga-style, here's a quick guide to help you understand how it works.

It's easy... just start in the top right panel and follow the numbers. Have fun, and look for more 100% authentic manga from TOKYOPOP®!

THE MANGA REVOLUTION · LEADING · 漫画革命

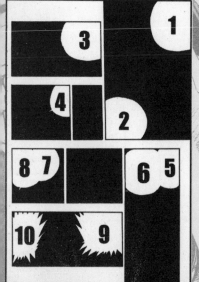

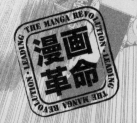